Readings in Indigenous Religions

Readings in Indigenous Religions

Edited by
Graham Harvey

continuum
LONDON • NEW YORK

Continuum

The Tower Building, 11 York Road, London, SE1 7NX

370 Lexington Avenue, New York, NY 10017-6503

First published 2002

British Library Cataloguing-in-Publication Data
A catalogue record for this book is available from the British Library.

ISBN 0-8264-5100-4 (hardback)
    0-8264-5101-2 (paperback)

Library of Congress Cataloging-in-Publication Data
  Readings in indigenous religions / edited by Graham Harvey.
      p. cm.
  Includes bibliographical references and index.
  ISBN 0-8264-5100-4—ISBN 0-8264-5101-2 (pbk.)
  1. Indigenous peoples—Religion. I. Harvey, Graham.

  BL380 .R43 2002
  299—dc21   200107406

Typeset by YHT Ltd, London
Printed and bound in Great Britain by MPGBooksLtd, Bodmin, Cornwall

Contents

Acknowledgements

I am grateful to the various authors and publishers who have given permission to reprint material in this book. This gratitude is not merely formal but genuine and deep: academia at its best is a conversation or a series of collaborations and good scholarship deserves continuous reconsideration and argument. The fact that these works have already been published once is cause for celebration; that they will be read and re-read is immensely valuable.

Thanks also go to those who have recommended particular works for inclusion, and those whose websites and syllabi I have checked to see what is used often and what deserves further attention.

Janet Joyce and others at Continuum are to be thanked for valuable advice and encouraging enthusiasm. It has been a pleasure to work with Susan Dunsmore on both this and a previous volume.

This volume is another expression of love to my love.

Part I: Ontology

A. Irving Hallowell, 'Ojibwa ontology, behavior, and world view' from *Culture in History*, ed. Stanley Diamond. © 1960 Columbia University Press. Reprinted by permission of the publisher.

Marilyn Strathern, 'Partners and consumers: Making relations visible' © 1997 from *The Logic of the Gift: Toward an Ethic of Generosity*, ed. Alan Schrift. Reproduced by permission of Routledge, Inc., part of the Taylor & Francis Group.

Nurit Bird-David, ' "Animism" revisited: Personhood, environment, and relational epistemology' from *Current Anthropology* 40, pp. 67-91, 1999. Reprinted by permission of the University of Chicago Press.

Kenneth Morrison, 'Sharing the flower: A non-supernaturalistic theory of grace' from *Religion* 22, pp. 208-20, 1992, by permission of the publisher, Academic Press.

Part II: Performance

Margaret Thompson Drewal, 'The ontological journey' from *Yoruba Ritual: Performers, Play, Agency*, Margaret T. Drewal, Indiana University Press, 1992. Reprinted by permission of Indiana University Press.

Edith Turner, 'A visible spirit form in Zambia' from *Being Changed: The*

Anthropology of Extraordinary Experience, eds David E. Young and Jean-Guy Goulet, Broadview Press, 1994. Reprinted by permission of Broadview Press.

Dale Stover, 'Postcolonial Sun Dancing at Wakpamni Lake' from *Journal of the American Academy of Religion* 69(4), 2001. Reprinted by permission of Oxford University Press.

Laurel Kendall, 'Divine connections: The *mansin* and her clients' from *Shamans, Housewives and Other Restless Spirits: Women in Korean Ritual Life*, © 1985 University of Hawai'i Press. Reprinted by permission of University of Hawai'i Press.

Berel Dov Lerner, 'Understanding a (secular) primitive society' from *Religious Studies* 31, 1995. © Cambridge University Press. Reprinted by permission of Cambridge University Press and the author.

Part III: Knowledge

T. P. Tawhai, 'Maori religion' from *The Study of Religion, Traditional and New Religions*, eds Peter Clarke and Stewart Sutherland, Routledge, 1988. Reprinted by permission of the Taylor & Francis Group.

Emma Webber-Dreadon, 'He Taonga Tuku Iho, Hei Ara: A gift handed down as a pathway' from *Te Komako: Social Work Review*, New Zealand Association of Social Workers, 1997. Reprinted by permission of Aotearoa New Zealand Association of Social Workers.

Patricia Grace, extract from *The Sky People* by Patricia Grace, published in Great Britain by The Women's Press Ltd, 1995, 34 Great Sutton Street, London EC1V 0LQ. Reprinted by permission of The Women's Press Ltd and Penguin Books (N.Z.) Limited. Extract from *Potiki* by Patricia Grace, published in Great Britain by The Women's Press Ltd, 1995, 34 Great Sutton Street, London EC1V 0LQ. Reprinted by permission of The Women's Press Ltd and Penguin Books (N.Z.) Limited.

Ward Churchill, 'I am indigenist: Notes on the ideology of the Fourth World' from *The Z Papers*, Vol. 1, No. 3. Reprinted by permission of the author.

Gordon Bennett, 'Australian icons: Notes on perception' from *Double Vision: Art Histories and Colonial Histories in the Pacific*, eds Nicholas Thomas and Diane Losche, Cambridge University Press, 1999. Reprinted by permission of Cambridge University Press and the author.

Part IV: Land

Deborah Bird Rose, 'Sacred site, ancestral clearing, and environmental ethics' from *Emplaced Myth: Space, Narrative, and Knowledge in Aboriginal Australia and Papua New Guinea*, eds Alan Rumsey and James F. Weiner, University of Hawai'i Press. Reprinted by permission of the author.

R. K. Nelson, 'The watchful world', from *Make Prayers to the Raven*, 1983. Reprinted by permission of the University of Chicago Press.

For Molly

Introduction

Graham Harvey

One story is never enough. We do not gain full understanding, let alone wisdom, the first time we hear or do something – however powerful it or our engagement might be. We might not even remember something we are told or observe only once. Certainly we are unlikely to appreciate all the nuances of one telling or performing. Even performing in a play or telling a story might not alert us to all the possibilities and potentialities that ripple outwards, subtly or dramatically affecting other hearers or performers or tellers of tales. In one sense, this book is a sequel to a collection of articles by gifted scholars which I was privileged to edit (Harvey 2000). In another sense this is a companion volume, chapters here engaging in potent dialogue with chapters in the previous book. Yet again, parts of this book are foundational – sometimes even ancestral – to the other, as for example where they inspired or authorized chapters in the other work.

This collection of *Readings* includes some 'classic' texts in the study of indigenous religions. It also contains more recent scholarly works that not only inform about indigenous religions but, more importantly – and more interestingly – elucidate ways of knowing and researching. These *Readings* are intended to widen and deepen debates initiated or developed in *Indigenous Religions: A Companion*, and important in the study of indigenous and other religions. Such debates are not only concerned with descriptive detail, but also with improving methodologies by which the meanings and implications of such descriptions might be better understood and discussed. These *Readings* exemplify recent developments and suggest further possibilities. The study of indigenous religions is no longer the preserve of one academic discipline, nor is it undertaken by one methodology. Thus, not all the scholarly writing here arises within the study of religions, but all of it is of value in that discipline.

Meanwhile, recent methodological developments intersect with the increasing availability of significant indigenous writings which enrich engagement, for example, by providing narratives more like 'traditional' modes of discourse or performance. Religion, like music, seduces those who would stand back and observe at a distance, tempts them to tap their feet and hum along. Some get drawn in and find themselves dancing to the rhythm, responding with body, mind, and soul. Others withdraw only to find themselves whistling a refrain later. This is how it should be, how it always should have been. Religious activities, like music, expect vigorous and passionate involvement, and make disengagement equivalent to misunderstanding. Just as a previous project (Ralls MacLeod and Harvey 2001) included a CD as an attempt to provoke a somewhat more sensitive and sensual engagement, so this book includes two excerpts from indigenous creative fiction.

There are, of course, plenty of other texts that might have been included or that might be vital to the study of indigenous religions. Many of these are referred to in chapters or the editorial notes that preface them.

Structure and themes

Indigenous Religions: A Companion was divided into three parts entitled Persons, Powers and Gifts. These relate to the outworking of 'existential postulates' or principles that inform many (if not all) indigenous worldviews, and 'highlight the vitality of human expressiveness' (Morrison 1992: 202-3). Those generative principles (Person, Power, Gift) have been of varying significance for, and the subject of varying degrees of attention by, academics. The fact that they are integral to one another in the formation of particular lifeways made it difficult to decide where to place each chapter in the previous volume. It also requires readers to make connections across the (as always) permeable boundaries implied by the structure. The present volume of *Readings* adds a further layer of complexity by encouraging readers to see the connections between material in two volumes. Further notes on how that might be done are offered below.

While some of the chapters here reflect on the concepts Person, Power, Gift in relation to particular indigenous worldviews and lifeways, a new set of themes arises from them to structure this book. Chapters are divided into four parts labelled Ontology, Performance, Knowledge, Land. Clearly these are only signposts to one matter that is central to the chapters within each section. For example, since persons are required to perform ceremonies in particular places, known in particular ways, so it should be obvious that chapters discussing the construction of persons might discuss not only Ontology but also Performance, Knowledge and/or Land. Similarly, to perform is to engage in relationship and to know one's place in the scheme of things. And so on. It is difficult to know, after the fact, whether any particular chapter was included because it focuses on a particular theme or whether the themes became clear only as the chapters were placed side by side. This difficulty reinforces the arbitrary nature of the boundaries suggested by the division of the book into four parts. However, just so long as readers recognize these facts, we can proceed by considering matters to which the signposts point. (More detailed introductions to the significance of each chapter are provided in linked introductory notes.)

Part I includes four chapters under the general heading 'Ontology'. These provide four different perspectives – neither *necessarily* opposing nor agreeing with one another – on the construction of persons, communities, and/or cosmos in particular indigenous societies. In doing so they are also vital to the reconsideration of the ontology or meaning of 'religion' as an academic concept and as lived reality. Does 'religion' refer to a discrete aspect of life in which people internalize ideas (as 'beliefs' or 'knowledge') relevant to some putative otherworldly realm? Does the discourse of religion require use of words like 'supernatural' or 'spiritual' to refer to a realm essentially separate from the 'mundane' realm of everyday life? Or is religion a facet of the continuously ongoing construction of persons and personal (whether individual or dividual) identity? Of course, these are not absolute alternatives: even for those religionists for whom the 'natural' is of less religious significance than the 'supernatural', religion is still about the construction of relationships and relational persons. However, it is certainly true that the academic study of religions has been skewed by the centrality of theological discourse about belief, spirituality, and the divine origins of grace (or Gift). In various ways these four chapters ground attention to indigenous worldviews in the relational nexus of particular lifeways and their daily lived realities.

Part II pays greater attention to religious activities under the heading of Performance. In a broad sense everything we do is performance. The identification of religious performance as a special category – ritual – has generated considerable debate, but little of it has been as exciting as recent moves to reconnect such activities with other forms of performance. The first chapter bridges the divide between this and the previous part. The balance between description, reflection, and theorizing varies in and between the five chapters (and might be further energized by reference to other works or chapters by the authors). The performances with which these chapters engage include divination, healing, world- and kinship-renewal (perhaps the same thing), shamanry, and magic. These bald labels cannot do justice to the richness of the debate, or to the careful critical

3

reflection on terms that might be either misleadingly alien or valuable in scholarly but not local communities. Clearly there is much to debate here.

Part III concerns indigenous knowledges. Partly in order to demonstrate the diversity of modes in which knowledges are relevant (although, even so, only a small sample of the possibilities are evident here), four of the six chapters relate to Maori knowledge. Traditional knowledge informs contemporary oratory, relationships (including attempts to heal them), literature, and legislation. The latter is represented by copies of the Treaty upon which present-day political, economic, and social relationships are enabled and constrained in New Zealand. However, it is prefaced by the previous attempted Declaration of Independence to demonstrate that indigenous knowledge demands sovereign expressions of self-presentation and self-worth. The theme is continued by the inclusion of a programmatic elaboration of a contemporary indigenous vision or ideology. The section concludes with another kind of vision, not only because it relates to Aboriginal (and Euro-) Australia, but also because it pays further attention to the expression and construction of indigenous knowledge in art.

Part IV may be brief, containing only two chapters, but it is of considerable importance. Discussions of land – variously construed as ecology, environment, subsistence, sovereignty, cosmology, geomentality, and others – have generated a vast literature. The very language of 'indigeneity' demands attentive consideration of land. In no way is it implied that the chapters included here are sufficient or even representative of all that might be said. They certainly raise some important issues, and they point beyond themselves not only to the important books from which they are extracted, but also to other important books that they cite. And there is more.

Both chapters pay attention to the relationships of power inherent in any discourse about land. Even when neighbouring indigenous peoples meet, the sovereignty and ecology of living in places can be contentious. But, far and above such fraught dynamics, the world is now thoroughly colonized following European expansion. It is further permeated by 'globalization'. In recent years, academia has faced up to the polemics inherent in its ancestral assertions of 'objectivity'. Realizing that this too is a construction of relationship – and one that has been central to colonization – has inspired a wealth of debate about more respectful and more engaged means of research and discourse. In many ways, it is these new moves in academia that are of most importance in the various chapters included in this book. While each chapter can be read for what it says about facets of indigenous religiosity, a central motive for inclusion has been their various contributions to the de- and re-construction of academia.

Methodology and relationships

Academia has struggled to find ways of achieving and maintaining objectivity. It has attempted to engage with people and phenomena in ways that permit clear understanding and communication to those (students, readers, listeners) who were not present. However, these attempts have often been damaged by the simultaneous participation of academics in the construction of an ideology in which rationality and knowledge have been constructed *against* other ways of knowing and being. Field work and participant observation were certainly attempts to understand what indigenous (and other) people were doing – and what they thought they were doing. Scholars attempted to put aside preconceptions and to unfetter curiosity from the constraints of prior dogma or expectation. That these attempts were often flawed is clear from the regularity with which academics denigrate 'going native' or belittle insiders' claims. Researchers needed training and engaged in writing or lecturing as a form of debriefing that re-established their identity as academics of a particular (partisan?) discipline. Things have changed. Or, if that is too wishful, they are changing. Western rationality is not as secure as it once seemed. Even in its most elaborate form, 'science', it is now revealed as one more way of participating in the world. (Note: not 'just' one more way – this participation is, after all, something to celebrate.)

This selection of *Readings* is intended to enhance the more recent tendency of academia towards a fuller mode of participation. Engaged and dialogical forms of research are becoming more commonplace, alongside awareness and even celebration of indigenous or insider's sovereignty (the right to self-determination and self-expression). Academics who 'go native' – for example, to the degree, at least, that they 'see the spirits' – can now say that they have had this experience. The dissemination of research can now celebrate the fact that 'I was there'. Perhaps more importantly, scholars and scholarship can now be constructed as participation. For example, indigenous scholars can now participate in both scholarly and insiderly communities without rejecting the authority of traditional knowledges, and while employing traditional modes of discourse. Other-than-indigenous scholars can participate as performers in ceremonies of healing and kinship-renewal, and so on. Indeed, to observe is to participate in a mode that changes the nature of a performance unobserved by 'researchers'. None of this is entirely straightforward, of course. Academia engages in continuous debate rather than the codification of dogmatic or final metanarratives. At least, this is true of academia as an ideal type; there are plenty of examples of unreconstructed authoritarians who think they have spoken the last word or written the last book on a subject.

Little of the above is particularly radical. It might be simply a matter of academia coming to its senses about the limits and particularity of its (or the West's) form of rationality. It should also be clear that what I have said so far continues to operate within a Western dualistic framework: there are insiders and outsiders, academics and the public, indigenous people and the West, experiencers and describers. However, the study of indigenous religions is far more exciting than this. It goes far beyond the possibly dangerous access of insiders into the academy (threatening, for example, to reassert theological methods and discourse into otherwise broadly phenomenological disciplines). It has begun to respond to a different rhythm and has at least begun to hum along to a different song. Boundaries are, in fact, permeable. Academics (indigenous or Western) who engage in ceremonies are changed. They discover, for example, that there are other ways to find things out, other ways to learn and teach, research and disseminate ideas. There are relationships beyond insider and outsider. It is possible to engage with others as guests, friends, even family – these relationships producing quite different results to the aggressive approach evident in much of the colonizing work of 'traditional' academia. (It should be noted, however, that 'aggressor' is also a relationship, albeit one of power that distances researcher from researched.)

All of this is to say that academia has proceeded, by a variety of means, to construct both itself and its object, in this case 'indigenous religions'. Not all these means are equally just or equally valuable. None is beyond debate. The selection of readings in this volume has been chosen to reflect modes of encounter which recognize and attempt to communicate indigenous ways of knowing and being. Most, but not all, address a 'Western' audience, given that many indigenous people are now part of the 'West' (although some continue to suffer subordinate status within First and New World societies). That is, this book contains writings addressed to a book-buying, journal-reading or web-surfing audience. 'Audience' suggests hearing and thereby reveals a limitation of this and all other written, visual texts: it is difficult to replicate aural/oral modes of communication. In fact, all the writings that follow contain transcriptions, evocations, elaborations or explanations of spoken/heard events. There are conversations, discussions, ceremonies, incantations, and so on. Even sound recordings would not fully redress the overstress on words here. Touch, smell, and taste are implicated in the subject matter of this book alongside sight and sound. But so too are senses of place, time, belonging, and mood, as well as states of awareness and statuses of relationship. Words are significant in stating and constructing these senses, states, and statuses, but experience is richer. In short, the construction of academic and indigenous knowledge (especially in dialogue) encourages participation

6

and a high degree of presence (of body as well as of mind).

It is worth pausing here to consider curiosity and secrecy. The West's rationality insistently expresses boundless curiosity. Consider modernity's inability to understand those offended by 'blasphemy'. Or consider the otherwise inexplicable contradiction that is 'eco-tourism' (a coalition of polluting transportation, unsupportable alien populations, and disruptive lifeways invading damaged or fragile environments). Or consider the proliferation of cell-phones, webcams and bureaucratic audits. Spy technology challenges any attempt to hide particular local knowledges, say, of the existence or position of missile silos. Privacy, the poor cousin of secrecy, is endangered by continuous surveillance and barely protected by laws which can only operate by further intruding into infringed domains. More positively, consider the growth of learning systems and their availability throughout life – from pre-school 'language nests' or swimming lessons for toddlers, to seminars on mortality and immortality for the terminally ill or advanced elders. Western knowledge is predicated on the absence of secrecy. Meanwhile, indigenous religions frequently require some central moment of secrecy or even its permanent enforcement and regular policing. The construction of adult humans in rites of passage typically requires the erection of barriers to curiosity. Further, the socializing of some adults (for example, 'women', 'men', 'clan x' or 'clan y') requires that they internalize forms of disinterest, ignorance, and absence from particular ceremonies or places. The curiosity that scholars are trained by modernity and academia to direct on (against?) subjects/objects of interest is in conflict with this secrecy maintenance. Some scholars have breached secrecy in favour of curiosity, for example in photographing ceremonies against the objections of participants. Others honour the boundaries and say only what they have been permitted to say, such as that there is another ceremony or story. The irony is, of course, that most 'secret' ceremonies are only provisionally barred – at least some 'outsiders' are potential initiates – and secrecy is educative, as a means by which people and societies are constructed and in which difference may be celebrated and maintained. This book contains no secrets that cannot be told without violence to the traditional knowers. It also celebrates the kind of curiosity which seeks knowledge through conversation. This acknowledges the wisdom enshrined in Alice Walker's characters' conversation:

I think it is ridiculous and ultimately insulting to study people, said Irene. I think you would only need to study other human beings if you were worried you were not human yourself.

Susannah laughed. I've often thought what a European trait studying other people is. Other folk who meet strange people want to dance and eat with them,

7

go swimming and talk about what colorful or peculiar wildlife there is about. They prefer to sit around smoke ganja or the peace pipe, listen to music and just kick back.

That's because they haven't come to steal everything, said Irene. (Walker 1998, p. 187)

What makes this all the more remarkable is the politeness with which many indigenous communities have hosted academics. All along, researchers have been integrated in various, locally significant ways into communities – as 'guests' for example. Instead of celebrating and reflecting on these relationships, academics have gone to amazing lengths to reassert their distance and absence.

The chapters in this book foreground, reinforce, and inspire very different approaches. In doing so, they demonstrate the immense value of relational, dialogical, experiential, participative, and present methodologies. By way of example, chapters by Hallowell, Turner, Stover, Tawhai, and Rose demonstrate just a few of the dynamics important here.

Irving Hallowell's importance to later scholars is in his attempt to understand and communicate the cultural realities experienced and constructed by his Ojibwe hosts. His dialogical approach is entirely congruent with his subject matter: the relationships in which identities are constructed, contested, and negotiated. His rejection of the dichotomy implicit in the language of 'spirits', demonstrated in his evocative phrase 'other-than-human person', offers a powerful challenge to Western cosmology and academic practice.

Edith Turner's participant-observation took a major step forward not principally when she shared her host's experience of the reality of intrusive alien spirits (her word), but even more so when she accepts and insists that it is data for reflection and discussion. Academia does need to deal with the reality of such experiences – and also, perhaps, the reality of that of which they seem to be experiences. Turner's work has been inspirational for many other researchers/writers, even though its force is partially contested by the title of the book in which it was first published. Are these ordinary (if unwanted) experiences or 'extraordinary experiences'?

Dale Stover confronts the colonial nature of academia face-to-face. Without claiming to have finally distanced himself from the power dynamics inherent in his (academic and cultural) position, he engages in a dialogue that reaches forward towards postcolonial understandings. His argument that the ceremonial complex that he discusses is itself essentially and experientially postcolonial is of vital importance to relationships and understanding.

T. P. Tawhai's chapter establishes the importance of speaking from a position (in this case, from within his people's tradition and contemporary life). He elaborates their 'religion' by utilizing traditional knowledges which were not intended to be used in this way. His warning about the dangers inherent in this process might be emblematic for all the partial (engaged and unfinished) discussions in this book and in the study of indigenous and other religions.

Deborah Rose not only provides and discusses the meaning of case studies, but demonstrates one way in which scholarship participates in political, social, economic, and religious debates. That this cannot be easy is made clear in her refusal to treat 'the politics of sacred sites' in isolation from enormously important and urgent questions of responsibility for the continuity of life. The seemingly benign term 'development' seems as iconic for scholarly discourse as it is for international policy-making and financial dealings. Thus, once again, academics' integral role in the construction of modernity cannot but demand a fuller, more just and relational participation.

Similar notes could be offered in relation to each of the other chapters. However, this would only reiterate points already made. It remains now to offer some suggestions about further reading. First, some ways in which this volume might be read alongside *Indigenous Religions: A Companion* will be suggested. This is followed by some pointers to other significant works in the emergent study of indigenous religions.

Using *Readings* alongside the *Companion*

No one-to-one relationship exists between chapters in this set of *Readings* and those in *Indigenous Religions: A Companion*. Without wishing to limit the creative use or possibilities of either book, those studying indigenous (and other) religions may value some hints about the cross-fertilization of material.

There are some obvious links. The two books share some common themes; for example, rituals of various kinds are important in the 'Performance' chapters here, and in 'Gifts' there. Shamanism, magic, and land are discussed in both books. A number of particular indigenous peoples or nations are referred to, some more than others. Similarly, a couple of authors have chapters in both books. There is no implication that the previous works were inadequate, far from it. However, academia would only be diminished by the assertion of the finality of any writing. New implications might be found in classic texts. New relevance in material well known in other contexts.

Another kind of link exists between some of the *Companion* chapters and those here. For example, the importance of Irving Hallowell's chapter is considerable. This is most evident in Kenneth Morrison's discussion of 'The cosmos as intersubjective: Native American other-than-human persons' (Harvey 2000: 23–36), but is true elsewhere too. That still more can be said is demonstrated by Nurit Bird-David's citation of Hallowell in her excellent revisitation of the term 'animism'. Similarly, Margaret Drewal and T. P. Tawhai are cited as authorities in the *Companion* and included here.

Such obvious links are evident from even a cursory examination of the contents and index pages. More possibilities unfurl with careful attention to what the chapters themselves might say about the state of academic interest in indigenous religions.

First, there is a confluence between the *Companion*'s discussion of Person, Power, and Gift – elaborated with reference to particular exemplars of persons, powers, and gifts – and these *Readings'* interest in Ontology, Performance, Knowledge, and Land. The ontology of persons is constructed in gift exchange and performed in ceremonies that engage with and are bounded by powers, the knowledge of which is locally meaningful. Or we might begin the other way around: engagement and presence in lands require knowledge of powers that constrain performance but also require the exchange of gifts in ceremonies that construct persons in the mediation of ontological realities. And so on. Basically, almost any chapter might be read alongside any other and prove abundantly fruitful.

Second, the two volumes might be read in concert for what they say about academic approaches, disciplines, and methodologies. The study of religions has always been inherently interdisciplinary, drawing methods from and finding foci of attention in kindred disciplines. These volumes have drawn not only on religious studies scholars and scholarship, but also on ethnography, anthropology, environmentalist, and other discourse. They have included fiction that speaks the truth more forcefully that non-fiction, and indigenous position papers and nation-building statements. In these and other ways, the volumes are intended to contribute to the reassessment of academic approaches to the study of indigenous and other religions.

It might also be true that both books share certain limitations. Most obviously, more attention is paid to Native North Americans and Maori in both books than to indigenous peoples from (or in) other continents. However, it would be foolish to attempt to say something about every indigenous religion in a single book (however long). In fact, even a total of six chapters devoted to various aspects of Maori spirituality does not and cannot exhaust all that might be said. My intention has been to include expert and important works which require and reward further reflection. This could certainly and valuably take place with reference to other indigenous peoples and/or other themes. For example, further consideration of the contested academic terms 'myth' and 'ritual' might well begin with chapters included here, but it cannot end there. Hopefully these volumes will be received as a further provocation to do more and do better!

Further significant writing

Most of the chapters included here are extracted from other books of considerable importance, or were written by authors of equal stature. (The only exceptions are, of course, the Declaration and Treaty that are in themselves of incalculable significance.) Second, each chapter and its introductory note cite material that either underlies or furthers particular debates. Readers are strongly recommended to read more widely in what these authors and their colleagues have written.

There are some invaluable introductions to indigenous religions, in particular continents and large geographical areas. A sample of these includes the following list.

Australia, Melanesia, Micronesia, and Polynesia: Swain and Trompf 1995.

Native North America, Alaska and Hawaii: Weaver 1998; Champagne 1999; and Sullivan 2000.

South and Central America: Gossen and León-Portilla 1997.

Africa: Olupona 1991; Platvoet, Cox, and Olupona 1996; and Clarke 1998.

There are, of course, gaps here – Asia, Europe, the Arctic are absent. There are plenty of more focused, more localized, discussions. This sample is only meant to draw attention to a few of the books that are available. While there is a tension between broad introductions and tightly focused ethnographies, both have value and limits. The perception, for example, that only dense ethnographies of particular peoples can provide adequate treatments of the 'whole complex that is their culture' is countered by the probability that such constructions of 'culture' are fictions alien to lived reality.

As the study of indigenous religions is increasingly making a contribution to the whole discipline of the study of religions, it is worth cross-referencing material here with, for example, chapters in Braun and McCutcheon (2000) and Taylor (1998). Anthropology too has recently been provided with excellent introductions and spurs to further work (see

11

Bowie 2000, and Rapport and Overing 2000). Brian Morris's earlier (1987) introduction to *Anthropological Studies of Religion* remains valuable. It is to be expected that similar introductions and critical interventions will soon be available or more widely known for the various disciplines of indigenous studies (Native American studies, Maori studies, Zulu studies, and so on).

The temptation to present any more elaborate suggestions as to quality works about particular themes (gender, place, vitalization movements, and so on), or about particular peoples, would never result in completion and is already far too extensive for an introductory chapter. (And this is to discount the disappointingly heavy weight of less valuable books and articles.) However, it is vitally important to note that the study of indigenous religions does require interaction with a range of literatures and other modes of discourse beyond academic writing. There are increasingly valuable autobiographies and biographies of indigenous people (especially leaders, e.g. Yellowtail 1991). There are collections of previously oral/aural literatures (e.g. Lang 1994). There is fiction that engages far more senses than most academic writing, and therefore touches the heart of things more closely (e.g. Silko 1977). These few examples, drawn entirely from Native American writing, could be replicated with reference to many indigenous peoples, and – in some cases at least – multiplied many times for each. (See Irwin 1998 for a fuller introduction to some of the 'Native voices in the study of Native American religions'.)

Conclusion

Religions are ways of being human in which the world/cosmos is both found to be and constructed as meaningful. Particular ways of relating, knowing, acting, considering, communicating, discovering, and sharing are themselves enacted and communicated within larger or smaller groups. Some of these identities, knowledges, and actions are considered 'ultimate', but most humans pay at least as much attention to immediate as to ultimate concerns and, if asked, would consider both as important. Scholars have obsessively viewed and constructed religion as 'ultimate concern' orientated (due perhaps to the historical dominance of one religious lifeway and worldview) towards a 'transcendent' deity. They have thereby participated in constructing their own agency (as being, knowing, and relating persons) as outsiders seeking objective knowledge. They have not noticed that all along they have been participants in relationships grounded in significant everyday experiences. Or when they have noticed, they have feared 'going native' and taken immediate evasive action – or been reprimanded by more orthodox colleagues.

The study of indigenous religions is at the forefront of developments in academia in which scholarly participation in and celebration of relational identities entail a similar celebration of relational knowledges and, therefore, result in a strengthening of relational methods of research. If this sounds like another dualism (bad modernity versus good indigeneity) it is important to reflect on the common indigenous perceptions that difference can be good (e.g. Deloria 1999), and that a part of one always exists in its seeming opposite (e.g. Turner 2001). The distance created by attempts at objectivity are, in fact, relational – albeit in aggressive, distancing, and alienating relationships. If this is so, then all human cultures offer particular means to relate with people who were previously strangers. If people will not relate as friends, neighbours, or kin, perhaps they insist on relating as enemies. Having stood back and tried not to be moved or involved, the study of religions (and other academic pursuits) is beginning to find out how guests and friends relate. The old choices between objective distance and 'going native', or between insider, outsider, and researcher, now seem tired. In the light of the material in this volume, it should be evident that there are more appropriate and more valuable ways of engaging with those with whom we share the world and the future.

Quite what this means for academia (and its publishers) remains to be seen. What are the implications of finding knowledge not principally *within* heads or books (as individually known ideas or beliefs) but as played out in shared, communal, and relational lifestyle and performance?

It is to be hoped that consideration of the following chapters will contribute to the realisation of a truly postcolonial engagement between practitioners of academic and religious lifeways.

References

Bowie, Fiona. 2000. *The Anthropology of Religion*. Oxford: Blackwell.

Braun, Willi, and Russell T. McCutcheon (eds). 2000. *Guide to the Study of Religion*. London: Cassell.

Champagne, Duane. 1999. *Contemporary Native American Cultural Issues*. Walnut Creek, CA: Altamira.

Clarke, Peter B. (ed.). 1998. *New Trends and Developments in African Religions*. Westport, CT: Greenwood Press.

Deloria, Vine. 1999. *For This Land: Writings on Religion in America*. London: Routledge.

Gossen, Gary H., and Miguel León-Portilla (eds). 1997. *South and Meso-American Native Spirituality*. New York: Crossroad.

Harvey, Graham (ed.). 2000. *Indigenous Religions: A Companion*. London and New York: Cassell.

Irwin, Lee. 1998. 'Native Voices in the Study of Native American Religions', *Critical Review of Books in Religion 1998*. Atlanta: Scholars Press. pp. 97-147.

Lang, Julian. 1994. *Ararapíkva: Creation Stories of the People: Traditional Karuk Indian Literature from Northwestern California*. Berkeley: Heyday Books.

Morris, Brian. 1987. *Anthropological Studies of Religion*. Cambridge: Cambridge University Press.

Morrison, Kenneth. 1992. 'Beyond the Supernatural: Language and Religious Action', *Religion* 22: 201-5.

Olupona, Jacob. 1991. *African Traditional Religions in Contemporary Society*. St. Paul: Paragon House.

Platvoet, Jan G., James Cox, and Jacob Olupona (eds). 1996. *The Study of Religion in Africa: Past, Present and Prospects*. Cambridge: Roots and Branches.

Ralls MacLeod, Karen, and Graham Harvey (eds). 2001. *Indigenous Religious Musics*. Aldershot: Ashgate.

Rapport, Nigel, and Joanna Overing. 2000. *Social and Cultural Anthropology*. London: Routledge.

Silko, Leslie M. 1977. *Ceremony*. New York: Viking.

Sullivan, Lawrence E. (ed.). 2000. *Native Religions and Cultures of North America*. New York: Continuum.

Swain, Tony, and Gary Trompf. 1995. *The Religions of Oceania*. London: Routledge.

Taylor, Mark (ed.). 1998. *Critical Terms for Religious Studies*. Chicago: University of Chicago Press.

Turner, David. 2001. 'From Here into Eternity: Power and Transcendence in Australian Aboriginal Music'. In Karen Ralls MacLeod and Graham Harvey (eds), *Indigenous Religious Musics*. Aldershot: Ashgate, pp. 35-55.

Walker, Alice. 1998. *By the Light of My Father's Smile*. London: Women's Press.

Weaver, Jace. (ed.). 1998. *Native American Religious Identity: Unforgotten Gods*. Maryknoll: Orbis.

Yellowtail, Thomas. 1991. *Yellowtail, Crow Medicine Man and Sun Dance Chief: An Autobiography as Told to Michael Oren Fitzgerald*. Norman: University of Oklahoma Press.

Part I
Ontology

1. Ojibwa ontology, behavior, and world view

A. Irving Hallowell

Editor's introduction

Hallowell's own summary of this article says,

> In this paper I have assembled evidence, chiefly from my own field work on a branch of the Northern Ojibwa, which supports the inference that in the metaphysics of being found among these Indians, the action of persons provides the major key to their world view.

It is hard to overestimate the importance of this article. It is exemplary in paying careful attention to the worldviews and knowledges of the researcher's hosts. It led the way in challenging the stress on the 'supernatural' character of Native American (and all other) religions.[1] Hallowell's coining of the term 'other-than-human persons' has not only been central to both previous points, but also enriched discussion of indigenous environmentalism, and of notions of respect, sacrality, and power. It is important to the work of, among others, Kenneth Morrison (1992 and 2000) and Terri Smith (1995). Again, these writers stress the Western (largely Christian) reference of words like 'spirit', and note that a study of religion rooted in this language-world will be misdirected. In fact, of course, much of the study of religions has continued to operate with the assumption that beliefs are central to, or definitive of, religion – particularly beliefs about transcendent (non- or super-

---

[1] A similar point is powerfully made by Saler (1977) and extended in most articles in a special issue of *Religion* edited by Kenneth Morrison: 22 (1992), pp. 201-69.

Reprinted from *Culture in History*, ed. Stanley Diamond. © 1960 Columbia University Press. By permission of the publisher. The courtesy of the Stanford University Press is acknowledged for permission to use portions of a paper by the author which appeared in *Person Perception*, ed. R. Tagiuri and L. Peteullo.

human) beings. A more recent trend has arisen in the study of ritual and reinstated what should have been obvious all along: religions are complexes of actions in which people engage. Some powerful examples of this kind are included later in this volume (e.g. Turner and Drewal).

Hallowell also provides important material for a reconsideration of the term 'animism'. This is taken up by Nurit Bird-David (reprinted in this volume) and discussed there more fully.

Rather than extract shorter portions of Hallowell's work that make points relevant to these issues, I have chosen to include his entire article so that readers can appreciate the way issues are raised and discussed. In fact, there are plenty of connections to be made between Hallowell's work and other material in this volume.

References

Morrison, Kenneth M. 1992. 'Beyond the Supernatural: Language and Religious Action', *Religion* 22: 201-5.

Morrison, Kenneth M. 2000. 'The Cosmos as Intersubjective: Native American Other-than-Human Persons', in Graham Harvey (ed.), *Indigenous Religions: A Companion*. London and New York: Cassell, pp. 23-36.

Saler, Benson. 1977. 'Supernatural as a Western Category', *Ethnos* 5: 31-53.

Smith, Theresa S. 1995. *The Island of the Anishinaabeg: Thunderers and Water Monsters in the Traditional Ojibwe Life-World*. Moscow: University of Idaho Press.

৵৽৻

It is, I believe, a fact that future investigations will thoroughly confirm, that the Indian does not make the separation into personal as contrasted with impersonal, corporeal with impersonal, in our sense at all. What he seems to be interested in is the question of existence, of reality; and everything that is perceived by the sense, thought of, felt and dreamt of, exists.

Paul Radin

Introduction

It has become increasingly apparent in recent years that the potential significance of the data collected by cultural anthropologists far transcends in interest the level of simple, objective, ethnographic description of the

peoples they have studied. New perspectives have arisen; fresh interpretations of old data have been offered; investigation and analysis have
been pointed in novel directions. The study of culture and personality,
national character and the special attention now being paid to values are
illustrations that come to mind. Robert Redfield's concept of world view,
'that outlook upon the universe that is characteristic of a people,' which
emphasizes a perspective that is not equivalent to the study of religion in
the conventional sense, is a further example.

> '*World* view' [he says] differs from culture, ethos, mode of thought, and national
> character. It is the picture the members of a society have of the properties and
> characters upon their stage of action. While 'national character' refers to the
> way these people look to the outsider looking in on them, 'world view' refers to
> the way the world looks to that people looking out. Of all that is connoted by
> 'culture,' 'world view' attends especially to the way a man, in a particular
> society, sees himself in relation to all else. It is the properties of existence as
> distinguished from and related to the self. It is, in short, a man's idea of the
> universe. It is that organization of ideas which answers to a man the questions:
> Where am I? Among what do I move? What are my relations to these things? ...
> Self is the axis of 'world view.'[1]

In an essay entitled 'The Self and Its Behavioral Environment,' I have
pointed out that self-identification and culturally constituted notions of the
nature of the self are essential to the operation of all human societies and
that a functional corollary is the cognitive orientation of the self to a world
of objects other than self. Since the nature of these objects is likewise
culturally constituted, a unified phenomenal field of thought, values, and
action which is integral with the kind of world view that characterizes a
society is provided for its members. The behavioral environment of the self
thus becomes structured in terms of a diversified world of objects other
than self, 'discriminated, classified, and conceptualized with respect to
attributes which are culturally constituted and symbolically mediated
through language. Object orientation likewise provides the ground for an
intelligible interpretation of events in the behavioral environment on the
basis of traditional assumptions regarding the nature and attributes of the
objects involved and implicit or explicit dogmas regarding the "causes" of
events.'[2] Human beings in whatever culture are provided with cognitive
orientation in a cosmos; there is 'order' and 'reason' rather than chaos.

---

[1] Redfield 1952, p. 30; cf. *African Worlds*.
[2] Hallowell 1955, p. 91. For a more extended discussion of the culturally constituted behavioral
     environment of man see ibid., pp. 86-9 and note 33. The term 'self' is not used as a synonym
     for ego in the psychoanalytic sense. See ibid., p. 80.

There are basic premises and principles implied, even if these do not happen to be consciously formulated and articulated by the people themselves. We are confronted with the philosophical implications of their thought, the nature of the world of being as they conceive it. If we pursue the problem deeply enough we soon come face to face with a relatively unexplored territory – ethno-metaphysics. Can we penetrate this realm in other cultures? What kind of evidence is at our disposal? The forms of speech as Benjamin Whorf and the neo-Humboldtians have thought?[3] The manifest content of myth? Observed behavior and attitudes? And what order of reliability can our inferences have? The problem is a complex and difficult one, but this should not preclude its exploration.

In this paper I have assembled evidence, chiefly from my own field work on a branch of the Northern Ojibwa,[4] which supports the inference that in the metaphysics of being found among these Indians, the action of persons provides the major key to their world view.

While in all cultures 'persons' comprise one of the major classes of objects to which the self must become oriented, this category of being is by no means limited to *human* beings. In Western culture, as in others, 'supernatural' beings are recognized as 'persons,' although belonging, at the same time, to an other than human category.[5] But in the social sciences and psychology, 'persons' and human beings are categorically identified. This identification is inherent in the concept of 'society' and 'social relations.' In Warren's *Dictionary of Psychology* 'person' is defined as 'a human organism regarded as having distinctive characteristics and social relations.' The same identification is implicit in the conceptualization and investigation of social organization by anthropologists. Yet this obviously involves a radical abstraction if, from the standpoint of the people being studied, the concept of 'person' is not, in fact, synonymous with human being but transcends it. The significance of the abstraction only becomes apparent when we stop to consider the perspective adopted. The study of

---

[3] See Basilius 1952; Carroll in Whorf 1956; Hoijer 1954; Feuer 1953.

[4] Hallowell 1955, chap. 5.

[5] Bruno de Jésus-Marie 1952, p. xvii: 'The studies which make up this book fall into two main groups, of which the first deals with the theological Satan. Here the analysis of exegesis, of philosophy, of theology, treat of the devil under his aspect of a personal being whose history – his fall, his desire for vengeance – can be written as such.' One of the most startling characteristics of the devil ' ... is his agelessness' (p. 4). He is immune to 'injury, to pain, to sickness, to death ... Like God, and unlike man, he has no body. There are in him, then no parts to be dismembered, no possibilities of corruption and decay, no threat of a separation of parts that will result in death. He is incorruptible, immune to the vagaries, the pains, the limitations of the flesh, immortal' (p. 5). 'Angels have no bodies, yet they have appeared to men in physical form, have talked with them, journeyed the roads with them fulfilling all the pleasant tasks of companionship' (p. 6).

20

social organization, defined as human relations of a certain kind, is perfectly intelligible as an objective approach to the study of this subject in any culture. But if, in the world view of a people, 'persons' as a class include entities other than human beings, then our objective approach is not adequate for presenting an accurate description of 'the way a man, in a particular society, sees himself in relation to all else.' A different perspective is required for this purpose. It may be argued, in fact, that a thoroughgoing 'objective' approach to the study of cultures cannot be achieved solely by projecting upon those cultures categorical abstractions derived from Western thought. For, in a broad sense, the latter are a reflection of *our* cultural subjectivity. A higher order of objectivity may be sought by adopting a perspective which includes an analysis of the outlook of the people themselves as a complementary procedure. It is in a world view perspective, too, that we can likewise obtain the best insight into how cultures function as wholes.

The significance of these differences in perspective may be illustrated in the case of the Ojibwa by the manner in which the kinship term 'grandfather' is used. It is not only applied to human persons but to spiritual beings who are persons of a category other than human. In fact, when the collective plural 'our grandfathers' is used, the reference is primarily to persons of this latter class. Thus if we study Ojibwa social organization in the usual manner, we take account of only one set of 'grandfathers.' When we study their religion we discover other 'grandfathers.' But if we adopt a world view perspective no dichotomization appears. In this perspective 'grandfather' is a term applicable to certain 'person objects,' without any distinction between human persons and those of an other-than-human class. Furthermore, both sets of grandfathers can be said to be functionally as well as terminologically equivalent in certain respects. The other-than-human grandfathers are sources of power to human beings through the 'blessings' they bestow, i.e., a sharing of their power which enhances the 'power' of human beings. A child is always given a name by an old man, i.e., a terminological grandfather. It is a matter of indifference whether he is a blood relative or not. This name carries with it a special blessing because it has reference to a dream of the human grandfather in which he obtained power from one or more of the other-than-human grandfathers. In other words, the relation between a human child and a human grandfather is functionally patterned in the same way as the relation between human beings and grandfathers of an other-than-human class. And, just as the latter type of grandfather may impose personal taboos as a condition of a blessing, in the same way a human grandfather may impose a taboo on a 'grandchild' he has named.

Another direct linguistic clue to the inclusiveness of the 'person' category

21

in Ojibwa thinking is the term *windīgo*. Baraga defines it in his *Dictionary* as 'fabulous giant that lives on human flesh; a man that eats human flesh, cannibal.' From the Ojibwa standpoint all *windīgowak* are conceptually unified as terrifying, anthropomorphic beings who, since they threaten one's very existence, must be killed. The central theme of a rich body of anecdotal material shows how this threat was met in particular instances. It ranges from cases in which it was necessary to kill the closest of kin because it was thought an individual was becoming a *windīgo*, through accounts of heroic fights between human beings and these fabulous giant monsters, to a first-hand report of a personal encounter with one of them.[6]

The more deeply we penetrate the world view of the Ojibwa the more apparent it is that 'social relations' between human beings (*änícinábek*) and other-than-human 'persons' are of cardinal significance. These relations are correlative with their more comprehensive categorization of 'persons.' Recognition must be given to the culturally constituted meaning of 'social' and 'social relations' if we are to understand the nature of the Ojibwa world and the living entities in it.[7]

Linguistic categories and cognitive orientation

Any discussion of 'persons' in the world view of the Ojibwa must take cognizance of the well known fact that the grammatical structure of the language of these people, like all their Algonkian relatives, formally expresses a distinction between 'animate' and 'inanimate' nouns. These particular labels, of course, were imposed upon Algonkian languages by Europeans;[8] it appeared to outsiders that the Algonkian differentiation of objects approximated the animate–inanimate dichotomy of Western thought. Superficially this seems to be the case. Yet a closer examination indicates that, as in the gender categories of other languages, the distinction in some cases appears to be arbitrary, if not extremely puzzling, from the standpoint of common sense or in a naturalistic frame of reference. Thus substantives for some, but not all – trees, sun-moon (*gīzis*), thunder, stones, and objects of material culture like kettle and pipe – are classified as 'animate.'

If we wish to understand the cognitive orientation of the Ojibwa, there is

---

[6] Hallowell 1934b, pp. 7-9; 1936, pp. 1308-9; 1951, pp. 182-3; 1955, pp. 256-8.

[7] Kelsen 1943, chapter 2, discusses the 'social' or 'personalistic interpretation of nature' which he considers the nucleus of what has been called animism.

[8] In a prefatory note to *Ojibwa Texts*, Part I, Jones (1919) says (p. xiii) that "Being" or "creature" would be a general rendering of the animate while "thing" would express the inanimate.' Cf. Schoolcraft's (1834) pioneer analysis of the animate and inanimate categories in Ojibwa speech, pp. 171-2.

an ethno-linguistic problem to be considered: What is the meaning of animate in Ojibwa thinking? Are such generic properties of objects as responsiveness to outer stimulation – sentience, mobility, self-movement, or even reproduction – primary characteristics attributed to all objects of the animate class irrespective of their categories as physical objects in our thinking? Is there evidence to substantiate such properties of objects independent of their formal linguistic classification? It must not be forgotten that no Ojibwa is consciously aware of, or can abstractly articulate the animate–inanimate category of his language, despite the fact that this dichotomy is implicit in his speech. Consequently, the grammatical distinction as such does not emerge as a subject for reflective thought or bear the kind of relation to individual thinking that would be present if there were some formulated dogma about the generic properties of these two classes of objects.

Commenting on the analogous grammatical categories of the Central Algonkian languages with reference to linguistic and nonlinguistic orders of meaning, Greenberg writes: 'Since all persons and animals are in Class I (animate), we have at least one ethnoseme, but most of the other meanings can be defined only by a linguiseme.' In Greenberg's opinion, 'unless the actual behavior of Algonquian speakers shows some mode of conduct common to all these instances such that, given this information, we could predict the membership of Class I, we must resort to purely linguistic characterization.'[9]

In the case of the Ojibwa, I believe that when evidence from beliefs, attitudes, conduct, and linguistic characterization are all considered together the psychological basis for their unified cognitive outlook can be appreciated, even when there is a radical departure from the framework of our thinking. In certain instances, behavioral predictions can be made. Behavior, however, is a function of a complex set of factors – including actual experience. More important than the linguistic classification of objects is the kind of vital functions attributed to them in the belief system and the conditions under which these functions are observed or tested in experience. This accounts, I think, for the fact that what we view as material, inanimate objects – such as shells and stones – are placed in an 'animate' category along with 'persons' which have no physical existence in our world view. The shells, for example, called *mígis* on account of the manner in which they function in the Midewiwin, could not be linguistically categorized as 'inanimate.' 'Thunder,' as we shall see, is not only reified as an 'animate' entity, but has the attributes of a 'person' and may be referred to as such. An 'inanimate' categorization would be unthinkable

---

[9]   Greenberg 1954, pp. 15-16.

from the Ojibwa point of view. When Greenberg refers to 'persons' as clearly members of the animate grammatical category he is, by implication, identifying person and human being. Since in the Ojibwa universe there are many kinds of reified person-objects which are other than human but have the same ontological status, these, of course, fall into the same ethnoseme as human beings and into the 'animate' linguistic class.

Since stones are grammatically animate, I once asked an old man: Are *all* the stones we see about us here alive? He reflected a long while and then replied, 'No! But *some* are.' This qualified answer made a lasting impression on me. And it is thoroughly consistent with other data that indicate that the Ojibwa are not animists in the sense that they dogmatically attribute living souls to inanimate objects such as stones. The hypothesis which suggests itself to me is that the allocation of stones to an animate grammatical category is part of a culturally constituted cognitive 'set.' It does not involve a consciously formulated theory about the nature of stones. It leaves a door open that our orientation on dogmatic grounds keeps shut tight. Whereas we should never expect a stone to manifest animate properties of any kind under any circumstances, the Ojibwa recognize, *a priori*, potentialities for animation in certain classes of objects under certain circumstances.[10] The Ojibwa do not perceive stones, in general, as animate, any more than we do. The crucial test is experience. Is there any personal testimony available? In answer to this question we can say that it is asserted by informants that stones have been seen to move, that some stones manifest other animate properties, and, as we shall see, Flint is represented as a living personage in their mythology.

The old man to whom I addressed the general question about the animate character of stones was the same informant who told me that during a Midewiwin ceremony, when his father was the leader of it, he had seen a 'big round stone move.' He said his father got up and walked around the path once or twice. Coming back to his place he began to sing. The stone began to move 'following the trail of the old man around the tent, rolling

---

[10] I believe that Jenness (1935) grossly overgeneralizes when he says (p. 21): 'To the Ojibwa ... all objects have life ... ' If this were true, their *inanimate* grammatical category would indeed be puzzling.

Within the more sophisticated framework of modern biological thought, the Ojibwa attitude is not altogether naïve. N.W. Pine (1937) points out (pp. 184-5) that the words 'life' and 'living' have been borrowed by science from lay usage and are no longer serviceable. 'Life is not a thing, a philosophical entity: it is an attitude of mind towards what is being observed.'

over and over, I saw it happen several times and others saw it also.'[11] The animate behavior of a stone under these circumstances was considered to be a demonstration of magic power on the part of the Midé. It was not a voluntary act initiated by the stone considered as a living entity. Associated with the Midewiwin in the past there were other types of large boulders with animate properties. My friend Chief Berens had one of these, but it no longer possessed these attributes. It had contours that suggested eyes and mouth. When Yellow Legs, Chief Berens's great-grandfather, was a leader of the Midewiwin he used to tap this stone with a new knife. It would then open its mouth, Yellow Legs would insert his fingers and take out a small leather sack with medicine in it. Mixing some of this medicine with water, he would pass the decoction around. A small sip was taken by those present.[12]

If, then, stones are not only grammatically animate, but, in particular cases, have been observed to manifest animate properties, such as movement in space and opening of a mouth, why should they not on occasion be conceived as possessing animate properties of a 'higher' order? The actualization of this possibility is illustrated by the following anecdote:

A white trader, digging in his potato patch, unearthed a large stone similar to the one just referred to. He sent for John Duck, an Indian who was the leader of the *wábano*, a contemporary ceremony that is held in a structure something like that used for the Midewiwin. The trader called his attention to the stone, saying that it must belong to his pavilion. John Duck did not seem pleased at this. He bent down and spoke to the boulder in a low voice, inquiring whether it had ever been in his pavilion. According to John, the stone replied in the negative.

It is obvious that John Duck spontaneously structured the situation in terms that are intelligible within the context of Ojibwa language and culture. Speaking to a stone dramatizes the depth of the categorical

---

[11] Field notes. From this same Indian I obtained a smoothly rounded pebble, about two inches long and one and a half inches broad, which his father had given him. He told me that I had better keep it enclosed in a tin box or it might 'go.' Another man, Ketegas, gave me an account of the circumstances under which he obtained a stone with animate properties and of great medicinal value. This stone was egg shaped. It had some dark amorphous markings on it which he interpreted as representing his three children and himself. 'You may not think this stone is alive,' he said, 'but it is. I can make it move.' (He did not demonstrate this to me.) He went on to say that on two occasions he had loaned the stone to sick people to keep during the night. Both times he found it in his pocket in the morning. Ketegas kept it in a little leather case he had made for it.

[12] Yellow Legs had obtained information about this remarkable stone in a dream. Its precise location was revealed to him. He sent two other Indians to get it. These men, following directions, found the stone on Birch Island, located in the middle of Lake Winnipeg, some thirty miles south of the mouth of the Berens River.

difference in cognitive orientation between the Ojibwa and ourselves. I regret that my field notes contain no information about the use of direct verbal address in the other cases mentioned. But it may well have taken place. In the anecdote describing John Duck's behavior, however, his use of speech as a mode of communication raises the animate status of the boulder to the level of social interaction common to human beings. Simply as a matter of observation we can say that the stone was treated *as if* it were a 'person,' not a 'thing,' without inferring that objects of this class are, for the Ojibwa, necessarily conceptualized as persons.

Further exploration might be made of the relations between Ojibwa thinking, observation, and behavior and their grammatical classification of objects but enough has been said, I hope, to indicate that not only animate properties but even 'person' attributes may be projected upon objects which to us clearly belong to a physical inanimate category.

The 'persons' of Ojibwa mythology

The Ojibwa distinguish two general types of traditional oral narratives. 1. 'News or tidings' (*täbätcamowin*), i.e., anecdotes, or stories, referring to events in the lives of human beings (*änícinábek*). In content, narratives of this class range from everyday occurrences, through more exceptional experiences, to those which verge on the legendary. (The anecdotes already referred to, although informal, may be said to belong to this general class.) 2. Myths (*ätíso'kanak*),[13] i.e., sacred stories, which are not only traditional and formalized; their narration is seasonally restricted and is somewhat ritualized. The significant thing about these stories is that the characters in them are regarded as living entities who have existed from time immemorial. While there is genesis through birth and temporary or permanent form-shifting through transformation, there is no outright creation. Whether human or animal in form or name, the major characters in the myths behave like people, though many of their activities are depicted in a spatio-temporal framework of cosmic, rather than mundane, dimensions. There is 'social interaction' among them and between them and *änícinábek*.

A striking fact furnishes a direct linguistic cue to the attitude of the Ojibwa towards these personages. When they use the term *ätíso'kanak*, they are not referring to what I have called a 'body of narratives.' The term refers to what we would call the characters in these stories; to the Ojibwa

---

[13] Cognate forms are found in Chamberlain's (1906) compilation of Cree and Ojibwa 'literary' terms.

they are living 'persons' of an other-than-human class. As William Jones said many years ago, 'Myths are thought of as conscious beings, with powers of thought and action.'[14] A synonym for this class of persons is 'our grandfathers.'

The *ätíso'kanak*, or 'our grandfathers,' are never 'talked about' casually by the Ojibwa. But when the myths are narrated on long winter nights, the occasion is a kind of invocation: 'Our grandfathers' like it and often come to listen to what is being said. In ancient times one of these entities (*Wísekedjak*) is reputed to have said to the others: 'We'll try to make everything to suit the *änícinábek* as long as any of them exist, so that they will never forget us and will always talk about us.'

It is clear, therefore, that to the Ojibwa, their 'talk' about these entities, although expressed in formal narrative, is not about fictitious characters. On the contrary, what we call myth is accepted by them as a true account of events in the past lives of living 'persons.'[15] It is for this reason that narratives of this class are significant for an understanding of the manner in which their phenomenal field is culturally structured and cognitively apprehended. As David Bidney has pointed out, 'The concept of "myth" is relative to one's accepted beliefs and convictions, so that what is gospel truth for the believer is sheer "myth" and "fiction" for the non-believer or skeptic ... Myths and magical tales and practices are accepted precisely because pre-scientific folk do not consider them as merely "myths" or "magic", since once the distinction between myth and science is consciously accepted, the acquired critical insight precludes the belief in and acceptance of magic and myth.'[16] When taken at their face value, myths provide a reliable source of prime value for making inferences about Ojibwa world outlook. They offer basic data about unarticulated, unformalized, and unanalyzed concepts regarding which informants cannot be expected to generalize. From this point of view, myths are broadly analogous to the concrete material of the texts on which the linguist depends for his derivation, by analysis and abstraction, of the grammatical categories and principles of a language.

In formal definitions of myth (e.g., *Concise Oxford Dictionary* and Warren's *Dictionary of Psychology*) the subject matter of such narrative

---

[14] Jones, 1919, Part II, p. 574n.

[15] The attitude manifested is by no means peculiar to the Ojibwa. Almost half a century ago Swanton (1910) remarked that 'one of the most widespread errors, and one of those most unfortunate for folk-lore and comparative mythology, is the off-hand classification of myth with fiction. ...' On the contrary, as he says, 'It is safe to say that most of the myths found spread over considerable areas were regarded by the tribes among which they were collected as narratives of real occurrences.'

[16] Bidney 1953, p. 166.

often has been said to involve not only fictitious characters but 'super-natural persons.' This latter appellation, if applied to the Ojibwa char-acters, is completely misleading, if for no other reason than the fact that the concept of 'supernatural' presupposes a concept of the 'natural.' The latter is not present in Ojibwa thought. It is unfortunate that the natural–supernatural dichotomy has been so persistently invoked by many anthropologists in describing the outlook of peoples in cultures other than our own. Linguists learned long ago that it was impossible to write grammars of the languages of nonliterate peoples by using as a framework Indo-European speech forms. Lovejoy has pointed out that 'The sacred word "nature" is probably the most equivocal in the vocabulary of the European peoples ... '[17] and the natural–supernatural antithesis has had its own complex history in Western thought.[18]

To the Ojibwa, for example, *gízis* (day luminary, the sun) is not a nat-ural object in our sense at all. Not only does their conception differ; the sun is a 'person' of the other-than-human class. But more important still is the absence of the notion of the ordered regularity in movement that is inherent in our scientific outlook. The Ojibwa entertain no reasonable certainty that, in accordance with natural law, the sun will 'rise' day after day. In fact, *Tcakábec*, a mythical personage, once set a snare in the trail of the sun and caught it. Darkness continued until a mouse was sent by human beings to release the sun and provide daylight again. And in another story (not a myth) it is recounted how two old men at dawn vied with each other in influencing the sun's movements.

> The first old man said to his companion: 'It is about sunrise now and there is a clear sky. You tell the sun to rise at once.' So the other old man said to the sun: 'My grandfather, come up quickly.' As soon as he had said this the sun came up into the sky like a shot. 'Now you try something,' he said to his companion. 'See if you can send it down.' So the other man said to the sun: 'My grandfather, put your face down again.' When he said this the sun went down again. 'I have more power than you,' he said to the other old man, 'The sun never goes down once it comes up.'

We may infer that, to the Ojibwa, any regularity in the movements of the sun is of the same order as the habitual activities of human beings. There are certain expectations, of course, but, on occasion, there may be tem-porary deviations in behavior 'caused' by other persons. Above all, any

---

[17] Lovejoy and Boas 1935, p. 12; Lovejoy 1948, p. 69.
[18] See, e.g., Collingwood 1945, also the remarks in Randall 1944, pp. 355-6. With respect to the applicability of the natural–supernatural dichotomy to primitive cultures see Van Der Leeuw 1938, pp. 544-5; Kelsen 1943, p. 44; Bidney 1953, p. 166.

concept of *impersonal* 'natural' forces is totally foreign to Ojibwa thought.

Since their cognitive orientation is culturally constituted and thus given a psychological 'set,' we cannot assume that objects, like the sun, are perceived as natural objects in our sense. If this were so, the anecdote about the old men could not be accepted as an actual event involving a case of 'social interaction' between human beings and an other-than-human person. Consequently, it would be an error to say that the Ojibwa 'personify' natural objects. This would imply that, at some point, the sun was first perceived as an inanimate, material thing. There is, of course, no evidence for this. The same conclusion applies over the whole area of their cognitive orientation towards the objects of their world.

The Four Winds and Flint, for instance, are quintuplets. They were born of a mother (unnamed) who, while given human characteristics, lived in the very distant past. As will be more apparent later, this character, like others in the myths, may have anthropomorphic characteristics without being conceived as a human being. In the context she, like the others, is an *ätíso'kan*. The Winds were born first, then Flint 'jumped out,' tearing her to pieces. This, of course, is a direct allusion to his inanimate, stony properties. Later he was penalized for his hurried exit. He fought with *Misábos* (Great Hare) and pieces were chipped off his body and his size reduced. 'Those pieces broken from your body may be of some use to human beings some day,' *Misábos* said to him. 'But you will not be any larger so long as the earth shall last. You'll never harm anyone again.'

Against the background of this 'historic' event, it would be strange indeed if flint were allocated to an inanimate grammatical category. There is a special term for each of the four winds that are differentiated, but no plural for 'winds.' They are all animate beings, whose 'homes' define the four directions.

The conceptual reification of Flint, the Winds and the Sun as other-than-human persons exemplifies a world view in which a natural–supernatural dichotomy has no place. And the representation of these beings as characters in 'true' stories reinforces their reality by means of a cultural device which at the same time depicts their vital roles in interaction with other persons as integral forces in the functioning of a unified cosmos.

Anthropomorphic traits and other-than-human persons

In action and motivations the characters in the myths are indistinguishable from human persons. In this respect, human and other-than-human persons may be set off, in life as well as in myth, from animate beings such as ordinary animals (*awésiak*, pl.) and objects belonging to the inanimate grammatical category. But, at the same time, it must be noted that 'persons' of the other-than-human class do not always present a human appearance in the myths. Consequently, we may ask: What constant attributes do unify the concept of 'person'?, What is the essential meaningful core of the concept of person in Ojibwa thinking? It can be stated at once that anthropomorphic traits in outward appearance are not the crucial attributes.

It is true that some extremely prominent characters in the myths are given explicit human form. *Wísekedjak* and *Tcakábec* are examples. Besides this they have distinctive characteristics of their own. The former has an exceptionally long penis and the latter is very small in size, yet extremely powerful. There are no equivalent female figures. By comparison, Flint and the Winds have human attributes by implication; they were born of a 'woman' as human beings are born; they speak, and so on. On the other hand, the High God of the Ojibwa, a very remote figure who does not appear in the mythology at all, but is spoken of as a 'person,' is not even given sexual characteristics. This is possible because there is no sex gender in Ojibwa speech. Consequently an animate being of the person category may function in their thinking without having explicitly sexual or other anthropomorphic characteristics. Entities 'seen' in dreams (*pawáganak*) are 'persons'; whether they have anthropomorphic attributes or not is incidental. Other entities of the person category, whose anthropomorphic character is undefined or ambiguous, are what have been called the 'masters' or 'owners' of animals or plant species. Besides these, certain curing procedures and conjuring are said to have other-than-human personal entities as patrons.

If we now examine the cognitive orientation of the Ojibwa towards the Thunder Birds it will become apparent why anthropomorphism is not a constant feature of the Ojibwa concept of 'person.' These beings likewise demonstrate the autonomous nature of Ojibwa reification. For we find here a creative synthesis of objective 'naturalistic' observation integrated with the subjectivity of dream experiences and traditional mythical narrative which, assuming the character of a living image, is neither the personification of a natural phenomenon nor an altogether animal-like or human-like being. Yet it is impossible to deny that, in the universe of the Ojibwa, Thunder Birds are 'persons.'

My Ojibwa friends, I discovered, were as puzzled by the white man's conception of thunder and lightning as natural phenomena as they were by the idea that the earth is round and not flat. I was pressed on more than one occasion to explain thunder and lightning, but I doubt whether my somewhat feeble efforts made much sense to them. Of one thing I am sure: My explanations left their own beliefs completely unshaken. This is not strange when we consider that, even in our naturalistic frame of reference, thunder and lightning as perceived do not exhibit the lifeless properties of inanimate objects. On the contrary, it has been said that thunder and lightning are among the natural phenomena which exhibit some of the properties of 'person objects.'[19] Underlying the Ojibwa view there may be a level of naïve perceptual experience that should be taken into account. But their actual construct departs from this level in a most explicit direction: Why is an avian image central in their conception of a being whose manifestations are thunder and lightning? Among the Ojibwa with whom I worked, the linguistic stem for bird is the same as that for Thunder Bird (*pinési*; pl. *pinésiwak*). Besides this, the avian characteristics of Thunder Birds are still more explicit. Conceptually they are grouped with the hawks, of which there are several natural species in their habitat.

What is particularly interesting is that the avian nature of the Thunder Birds does not rest solely on an arbitrary image. Phenomenally, thunder does exhibit 'behavioral' characteristics that are analogous to avian phenomena in this region.[20] According to meteorological observations, the average number of days with thunder begins with one in April, increases to a total of five in midsummer (July) and then declines to one in October. And if a bird calendar is consulted, the facts show that species wintering in the south begin to appear in April and disappear for the most part not later than October, being, of course, a familiar sight during the summer months. The avian character of the Thunder Birds can be rationalized to some degree with reference to natural facts and their observation.

But the evidence for the existence of Thunder Birds does not rest only on the association of the occurrence of thunder with the migration of the summer birds projected into an avian image. When I visited the Ojibwa an Indian was living who, when a boy of twelve or so, saw *pinési* with his own eyes. During a severe thunderstorm he ran out of his tent and there on the rocks lay a strange bird. He ran back to call his parents, but when they arrived the bird had disappeared. He was sure it was a Thunder Bird, but his elders were skeptical because it is almost unheard of to see *pinési* in such a fashion. But the matter was clinched and the boy's account accepted when a man who had *dreamed* of *pinési* verified the boy's description. It will be apparent later why a dream experience was decisive. It should be added at this point, however, that many Indians say they have seen the nests of the Thunder Birds; these are usually described as collections of

---

[19] Krech and Crutchfield 1948 write (p. 10): 'clouds and storms and winds are excellent examples of objects in the psychological field that carry the perceived properties of mobility, capriciousness, causation, power of threat and reward.'

[20] Cf. Hallowell 1934a.

large stones in the form of shallow bowls located in high and inaccessible parts of the country.

If we now turn to the myths, we find that one of them deals in considerable detail with Thunder Birds. Ten unmarried brothers live together. The oldest is called *Mätcíkiwis*. A mysterious housekeeper cuts wood and builds a fire for them which they find burning when they return from a long day's hunt, but she never appears in person. One day the youngest brother discovers and marries her. *Mätcíkiwis* is jealous and kills her. She would have revived if her husband had not broken a taboo she imposed. It turns out, however, that she is not actually a human being but a Thunder Bird and, thus, one of the *ätíso'kanak* and immortal. She flies away to the land above this earth inhabited by the Thunder Birds. Her husband, after many difficulties, follows her there. He finds himself brother-in-law to beings who are the 'masters' of the duck hawks, sparrow hawks, and other species of this category of birds he has known on earth. He cannot relish the food eaten, since what the Thunder Birds call 'beaver' are to him like the frogs and snakes on this earth (a genuinely naturalistic touch since the sparrow hawk, for example, feeds on batrachians and reptiles). He goes hunting gigantic snakes with his male Thunder Bird relatives. Snakes of this class also exist on this earth, and the Thunder Birds are their inveterate enemies. (When there is lightning and thunder this is the prey the Thunder Birds are after.) One day the great Thunder Bird says to his son-in-law, 'I know you are getting lonely; you must want to see your people. I'll let you go back to earth now. You have nine brothers at home and I have nine girls left. You can take them with you as wives for your brothers. I'll be related to the people on earth now and I'll be merciful towards them. I'll not hurt any of them if I can possibly help it.' So he tells his daughters to get ready. There is a big dance that night and the next morning the whole party starts off. When they come to the edge of Thunder Bird land the lad's wife said to him, 'Sit on my back. Hang on tight to my neck and keep your eyes shut.' Then the thunder crashes and the young man knows that they are off through the air. Having reached this earth they make their way to the brothers' camp. The Thunder Bird women, who have become transformed into human form, are enthusiastically received. There is another celebration and the nine brothers marry the nine sisters of their youngest brother's wife.

This is the end of the myth but a few comments are necessary. It is obvious that the Thunder Birds are conceived to act like human beings. They hunt and talk and dance. But the analogy can be pressed further. Their social organization and kinship terminology are precisely the same as the Ojibwa. The marriage of a series of female siblings (classificatory or otherwise) to a series of male siblings often occurs among the Ojibwa themselves. This is, in fact, considered a kind of ideal pattern. In one case that I know of six blood brothers were married to a sorority of six sisters. There is a conceptual continuity, therefore, between the social life of human beings and that of the Thunder Birds which is independent of the avian form given to the latter. But we must infer from the myth that this avian form is not constant. Appearance cannot then be taken as a permanent and distinguishable trait of the Thunder Birds. They are capable of metamorphosis, hence, the human attributes with which they are endowed transcend a human outward form. Their conceptualization as 'persons' is not associated with a permanent human form any more than it is associated with a birdlike form. And the fact that they belong to the category of *ätíso'kanak* is no barrier to their descending to earth and mating with human beings. I was told of a woman who claimed that North Wind was the father of one of her children. My informant said he did not believe this; nevertheless, he thought it would have been accepted as a possibility in the past.[21] We can only infer that in the universe of the Ojibwa the conception of 'person' as a living, functioning social being is not only one which transcends the notion of person in the naturalistic sense; it likewise transcends a human appearance as a constant attribute of this category of being.

The relevance of such a concept to actual behavior may be illustrated by one simple anecdote. An informant told me that many years before he was sitting in a tent one summer afternoon during a storm together with an old man and his wife. There was one clap of thunder after another. Suddenly the old man turned to his wife and asked, 'Did you hear what was said?' 'No,' she replied, 'I didn't catch it.' My informant, an acculturated Indian, told me he did not at first know what the old man and his wife referred to. It was, of course, the thunder. The old man thought that one of the Thunder Birds had said something to him. He was reacting to this sound in the same way as he would respond to a human being, whose words he did not understand. The casualness of the remark and even the trivial character of the anecdote demonstrate the psychological depth of the 'social relations' with other-than-human beings that becomes explicit in the behavior of the Ojibwa as a consequence of the cognitive 'set' induced by their culture.

---

[21] Actually, this was probably a rationalization of mother–son incest. But the woman never was punished by sickness, nor did she confess. Since the violation of the incest prohibition is reputed to be followed by dire consequences, the absence of both may have operated to support the possibility of her claim when considered in the context of the Ojibwa world view.

Metamorphosis as an attribute of persons

The conceptualization in myth and belief of Thunder Birds as animate beings who, while maintaining their identity, may change their outward appearance and exhibit either an avian or a human form exemplifies an attribute of 'persons' which, although unarticulated abstractly, is basic in the cognitive orientation of the Ojibwa.

Metamorphosis occurs with considerable frequency in the myths where other-than-human persons change their form. *Wísekedjak*, whose primary characteristics are anthropomorphic, becomes transformed and flies with the geese in one story, assumes the form of a snake in another, and once turns himself into a stump. Men marry 'animal' wives who are not 'really' animals. And *Míkīnäk*, the Great Turtle, marries a human being. It is only by breaking a taboo that his wife discovers she is married to a being who is able to assume the form of a handsome young man.

The senselessness and ambiguities which may puzzle the outsider when reading these myths are resolved when it is understood that, to the Ojibwa, 'persons' of this class are capable of metamorphosis by their very nature. Outward appearance is only an incidental attribute of being. And the names by which some of these entities are commonly known, even if they identify the character as an 'animal,' do not imply unchangeableness in form.

Stith Thompson has pointed out that the possibility of transformation is a 'commonplace assumption in folk tales everywhere. Many of such motifs are frankly fictitious, but a large number represent persistent beliefs and living tradition.'[22] The case of the Ojibwa is in the latter category. The world of myth is not categorically distinct from the world as experienced by human beings in everyday life. In the latter, as well as the former, no sharp lines can be drawn dividing living beings of the animate class because metamorphosis is possible. In outward manifestation neither animal nor human characteristics define categorical differences in the core of being. And, even aside from metamorphosis, we find that in everyday life inter-action with nonhuman entities of the animate class are only intelligible on the assumption that they possess some of the attributes of 'persons.'

So far as animals are concerned, when bears were sought out in their dens in the spring they were addressed, asked to come out so that they could be killed, and an apology was offered to them.[23] The following encounter with a bear, related to me by a pagan Ojibwa named Birchstick, shows what happened in this case when an animal was treated as a person:

[22] Thompson 1946, p. 258.
[23] Hallowell 1926.

One spring when I was out hunting I went up a little creek where I knew suckers were spawning. Before I came to the rapids I saw fresh bear tracks. I walked along the edge of the creek and when I reached the rapids I saw a bear coming towards me, along the same trail I was following. I stepped behind a tree and when the animal was about thirty yards from me I fired. I missed and before I could reload the bear made straight for me. He seemed mad, so I never moved. I just waited there by the tree. As soon as he came close to me and rose up on his hind feet, I put the butt end of my gun against his heart and held him there. I remembered what my father used to tell me when I was a boy. He said that a bear always understands what you tell him. The bear began to bite the stock of the gun. He even put his paws upon it something like a man would do if he were going to shoot. Still holding him off as well as I could I said to the bear, 'If you want to live, go away,' and he let go the gun and walked off. I didn't bother the bear anymore.[24]

These instances suffice to demonstrate that, at the level of individual behavior, the interaction of the Ojibwa with certain kinds of plants and animals in everyday life is so structured culturally that individuals act as if they were dealing with 'persons' who both understand what is being said to them and have volitional capacities as well. From the standpoint of perceptual experience if we only take account of autochthonous factors in Birchstick's encounter with the bear his behavior appears idiosyncratic and is not fully explained. On the other hand, if we invoke Ojibwa concepts of the nature of animate beings, his behavior becomes intelligible to us. We can understand the determining factors in his definition of the situation, and the functional relations between perception and conduct are meaningful. This Indian was not confronted with an animal with 'objective' ursine properties, but rather with an animate being who had ursine attributes and *also* 'person attributes.' These, we may infer, were perceived as an integral whole. I am sure, however, that in narrating this episode to another Indian, he would not have referred to what his father had told him about bears. That was for my benefit!

Since bears, then, are assumed to possess 'person attributes,' it is not surprising to find that there is a very old, widespread, and persistent belief that sorcerers may become transformed into bears in order better to pursue their nefarious work.[25] Consequently some of the best documentation of the metamorphosis of human beings into animals comes from anecdotal

---

[24] Hallowell 1934a, p. 397.

[25] Sorcerers may assume the form of other animals as well. Peter Jones, a converted Ojibwa, who became famous as a preacher and author says that 'they can turn themselves into bears, wolves, foxes, owls, bats, and snakes ... Several of our people have informed me that they have seen and heard witches in the shape of these animals, especially the bear and the fox. They say that

material referring to cases of this sort. Even contemporary, acculturated Ojibwa have a term for this. They all know what a 'bearwalk' is, and Dorson's recent collection of folk traditions, including those of the Indian populations of the Upper Peninsula of Michigan, bears the title *Bloodstoppers and Bearwalkers*. One of Dorson's informants gave him this account of what he had seen:

> When I was a kid, 'bout seventeen, before they build the highway, there was just an old tote road from Bark River to Harris. There was three of us, one a couple years older, coming back from Bark River at nighttime. We saw a flash coming from behind us. The older fellow said, 'It's a bearwalk, let's get it. I'll stand on the other side of the road (it was just a wagon rut) and you stand on this side.' We stood there and waited. I saw it 'bout fifty feet away from us – close as your car is now. It looked like a bear, but every time he breathe you could see a fire gust. My chum he fall over in a faint. That brave feller on the other side, he faint. When the bear walk, all the ground wave, like when you walk on soft mud or on moss. He was goin' where he was goin'.[26]

It is clear from this example, and others that might be added, that the Indian and his companions did not perceive an ordinary bear. But in another anecdote given by Dorson, which is not told in the first person, it is said that an Indian 'grabbed hold of the bear and it wasn't there – it was the old woman. She had buckskin bags all over her, tied on to her body, and she had a bearskin hide on.'[27] I also have been told that the 'bearwalk' is dressed up in a bearskin. All such statements, of course, imply a skeptical attitude towards metamorphosis. They are rationalizations advanced by individuals who are attempting to reconcile Ojibwa beliefs and observation with the disbelief encountered in their relations with the whites.

An old-fashioned informant of mine told me how he had once fallen sick, and, although he took various kinds of medicine these did him no good. Because of this, and for other reasons, he believed he had been bewitched by a certain man. Then he noticed that a bear kept coming to his camp almost every night after dark. This is most unusual because wild animals do not ordinarily come anywhere near a human habitation. Once

continued
> when a witch in the shape of a bear is being chased all at once she will run around a tree or hill, so as to be lost sight of for a time by her pursuers, and then, instead of seeing a bear they behold an old woman walking quietly along or digging up roots, and looking as innocent as a lamb' (Jones 1861, pp. 145-6).

[26] Dorson 1952, p. 30.

[27] Ibid., p. 29. This rationalization dates back over a century. John Tanner, an Indianized white man who was captured as a boy in the late eighteenth century and lived with the Ottawa and Ojibwa many years, refers to it. So does Peter Jones.

the bear would have entered his wigwam if he had not been warned in a dream. His anxiety increased because he knew, of course, that sorcerers often transformed themselves into bears. So when the bear appeared one night he got up, went outdoors, and shouted to the animal that he knew what it was trying to do. He threatened retaliation in kind if the bear ever returned. The animal ran off and never came back.

In this case there are psychological parallels to Birchstick's encounter with a bear. In both cases the bear is directly addressed as a person might be, and it is only through a knowledge of the cultural background that it is possible fully to understand the behavior of the individuals involved. In the present case, however, we can definitely say, that the 'animal' was perceived as a human being in the form of a bear; the Indian was threatening a human person with retaliation, not an animal. A question that I have discussed in *Culture and Experience* in connection with another 'bearwalk' anecdote, also arises in this case.[28] Briefly, the Ojibwa believe that a human being consists of a vital part, or *soul*, which, under certain circumstances may become detached from the body, so that it is not necessary to assume that the body part, in all cases, literally undergoes transformation into an animal form. The body of the sorcerer may remain in his wigwam while his soul journeys elsewhere and appears to another person in the form of an animal.

This interpretation is supported by an account which an informant gave me of a visit his deceased grandchild had paid him. One day he was traveling in a canoe across a lake. He had put up an improvised mast and used a blanket for a sail. A little bird alighted on the mast. This was a most unusual thing for a bird to do. He was convinced that it was not a bird but his dead grandchild. The child, of course, had left her body behind in a grave, nevertheless she visited him in animal form.

Thus, both living and dead human beings may assume the form of animals. So far as appearance is concerned, there is no hard and fast line that can be drawn between an animal form and a human form because metamorphosis is possible. In perceptual experience what looks like a bear may sometimes *be* an animal and, on other occasions, a human being. What persists and gives continuity to being is the vital part, or soul. Dorson goes to the heart of the matter when he stresses the fact that the whole socialization process in Ojibwa culture 'impresses the young with the concepts of transformation and of power', malign or benevolent, human or demonic. These concepts underlie the entire Indian mythology, and make sensible the otherwise childish stories of culture heroes, animal husbands, friendly thunders, and malicious serpents. The bearwalk idea fits

---

[28] Hallowell 1955, pp. 176-7.

at once into this dream world – literally a dream world, for Ojibwa go to school in dreams.'[29]

We must conclude, I believe, that the capacity for metamorphosis is one of the features which links human beings with the other-than-human persons in their behavioral environment. It is one of the generic properties manifested by beings of the person class. But is it a ubiquitous capacity of all members of this class equally? I do not think so. Metamorphosis to the Ojibwa mind is an earmark of 'power.' Within the category of persons there is a graduation of power. Other-than-human persons occupy the top rank in the power hierarchy of animate being. Human beings do not differ from them in kind, but in power. Hence, it is taken for granted that all the ätíso'kanak can assume a variety of forms. In the case of human beings, while the potentiality for metamorphosis exists and may even be experienced, any outward manifestation is inextricably associated with unusual power, for good or evil. And power of this degree can only be acquired by human beings through the help of other-than-human persons. Sorcerers can transform themselves only because they have acquired a high order of power from this source.

Powerful men, in the Ojibwa sense, are also those who can make inanimate objects behave as if they were animate. The *Midé* who made a stone roll over and over has been mentioned earlier. Other examples, such as the animation of a string of wooden beads, or animal skins, could be cited.[30] Such individuals also have been observed to transform one object into another, such as charcoal into bullets and ashes into gunpowder, or a handful of goose feathers into birds or insects.[31] In these manifestations, too, they are elevated to the same level of power as that displayed by other-than-human persons. We can, in fact, find comparable episodes in the myths.

The notion of animate being itself does not presume a capacity for manifesting the highest level of power any more than it implies person-attributes in every case. Power manifestations vary within the animate class of being as does the possession of person-attributes. A human being may possess little, if any, more power than a mole. No one would have been more surprised than Birchstick if the bear he faced had suddenly become human in form. On the other hand, the spiritual 'masters' of the various species of animals are inherently powerful and, quite generally, they possess the power of metamorphosis. These entities, like the ätíso'kanak, are among the sources from which human beings may seek to

---

[29] Dorson 1952, p. 31.
[30] Hoffman 1891, pp. 205-6.
[31] Unpublished field notes.

enhance their own power. My Ojibwa friends often cautioned me against judging by appearances. A poor forlorn Indian dressed in rags might have great power; a smiling, amiable woman, or a pleasant old man, might be a sorcerer.[32] You never can tell until a situation arises in which their power for good or ill becomes manifest. I have since concluded that the advice given me in a common sense fashion provides one of the major clues to a generalized attitude towards the objects of their behavioral environment – particularly people. It makes them cautious and suspicious in interpersonal relations of all kinds. The possibility of metamorphosis must be one of the determining factors in this attitude; it is a concrete manifestation of the deceptiveness of appearances. What looks like an animal, without great power, may be a transformed person with evil intent. Even in dream experiences, where a human being comes into direct contact with other-than-human persons, it is possible to be deceived. Caution is necessary in 'social' relations with all classes of persons.

Dreams, metamorphosis, and the self

The Ojibwa are a dream-conscious people. For an understanding of their cognitive orientation it is as necessary to appreciate their attitude towards dreams as it is to understand their attitude towards the characters in the myths. For them, there is an inner connection which is as integral to their outlook as it is foreign to ours.

The basic assumption which links the *ätíso'kanak* with dreams is this: Self-related experience of the most personal and vital kind includes what is seen, heard, and felt in dreams. Although there is no lack of discrimination between the experiences of the self when awake and when dreaming, both sets of experiences are equally self-related. Dream experiences function integrally with other recalled memory images in so far as these, too, enter the field of self-awareness. When we think autobiographically we only include events that happened to us when awake; the Ojibwa include remembered events that have occurred in dreams. And, far from being of subordinate importance, such experiences are for them often of more vital importance than the events of daily waking life. Why is this so? Because it is in dreams that the individual comes into direct communication with the *ätíso'kanak*, the powerful 'persons' of the other-than-human class.

In the long winter evenings, as I have said, the *ätíso'kanak* are talked about; the past events in their lives are recalled again and again by *änícinábek*. When a conjuring performance occurs, the voices of some of

---

[32] See Hallowell 1955, chapter 15.

the same beings are heard issuing from within the conjuring lodge. Here is actual perceptual experience of the 'grandfathers' during a waking state. In dreams, the same other-than-human persons are both 'seen' and 'heard.' They address human beings as 'grand-child.' These 'dream visitors' (i.e., *pawáganak*) interact with the dreamer much as human persons do. But, on account of the nature of these beings there are differences, too. It is in the context of this face-to-face personal interaction of the self with the 'grandfathers' (i.e., synonymously *átíso'kanak, pawáganak*) that human beings receive important revelations that are the source of assistance to them in the daily round of life, and, besides this, of 'blessings' that enable them to exercise exceptional powers of various kinds.

But dream experiences are not ordinarily recounted save under special circumstances. There is a taboo against this, just as there is a taboo against myth narration except in the proper seasonal context. The consequence is that we know relatively little about the manifest content of dreams. All our data come from acculturated Ojibwa. We do know enough to say, however, that the Ojibwa recognize quite as much as we do that dream experiences are often qualitatively different from our waking experiences. This fact, moreover, is turned to positive account. Since their dream visitors are other-than-human 'persons' possessing great power, it is to be expected that the experiences of the self in interaction with them will differ from those with human beings in daily life. Besides this, another assumption must be taken into account: When a human being is asleep and dreaming his *òtcatcákwin* (vital part, soul), which is the core of the self, may become detached from the body (*mïyó*). Viewed by another human being, a person's body may be easily located and observed in space. But his vital part may be somewhere else. Thus, the self has greater mobility in space and even in time while sleeping. This is another illustration of the deceptiveness of appearances. The body of a sorcerer may be within sight in a wigwam, while 'he' may be bearwalking. Yet the space in which the self is mobile is continuous with the earthly and cosmic space of waking life. A dream of one of my informants documents this specifically. After having a dream in which he met some (mythical) anthropomorphic beings (*mémengwécïwak*) who live in rocky escarpments and are famous for their medicine, he told me that he had later identified precisely the rocky place he had visited and entered in his dream. Thus the behavioral environment of the self is all of a piece. This is why experiences undergone when awake or asleep can be interpreted as experiences of self. Memory images, as recalled, become integrated with a sense of self-continuity in time and space.

Metamorphosis may be *experienced* by the self in dreams. One example will suffice to illustrate this. The dreamer in this case had been paddled out to an island by his father to undergo his puberty fast. For several nights he dreamed of an anthropomorphic figure. Finally, this being said, 'Grandchild, I think you are strong enough now to go with me.' Then the *pawágan* began dancing and as he danced he turned into what looked like a golden eagle. (This being must be understood as the 'master' of this species.) Glancing down at his own body as he sat there on a rock, the boy noticed it was covered with feathers. The 'eagle' spread its wings and flew off to the south. The boy then spread his wings and followed.

Here we find the instability of outward form in both human and other-than-human persons succinctly dramatized. Individuals of both categories undergo metamorphosis. In later life the boy will recall how he first saw the 'master' of the golden eagles in his anthropomorphic guise, followed by his transformation into avian form; at the same time he will recall his own metamorphosis into a bird. But this experience, considered in context, does not imply that subsequently the boy can transform himself into a golden eagle at will. He might or might not be sufficiently 'blessed.' The dream itself does not inform us about this.

This example, besides showing how dream experiences may reinforce the belief in metamorphosis, illustrates an additional point: the *pawáganak*, whenever 'seen,' are always experienced as appearing in specific form. They have a 'bodily' aspect, whether human-like, animal-like, or ambiguous. But this is not their most persistent, during and vital attribute any more than in the case of human beings. We must conclude that all animate beings of the person class are unified conceptually in Ojibwa thinking because they have a similar structure – an inner vital part that is enduring and an outward form which can change. Vital personal attributes such as sentience, volition, memory, speech are not dependent upon outward appearance but upon the inner vital essence of being. If this be true, human beings and other-than-human persons are alike in another way. The human self does not die; it continues its existence in another place, after the body is buried in the grave. In this way *änícinábek* are as immortal as *ätíso'kanak*. This may be why we find human beings associated with the latter in the myths where it is sometimes difficult for an outsider to distinguish between them.

Thus the world of personal relations in which the Ojibwa live is a world in which vital social relations transcend those which are maintained with human beings. Their culturally constituted cognitive orientation prepares the individual for life in this world and for a life after death. The self-image that he acquires makes intelligible the nature of other selves. Speaking as an Ojibwa, one might say: all other 'persons' – human or other than human – are structured the same as I am. There is a vital part which is enduring and an outward appearance that may be transformed under certain conditions. All other 'persons,' too, have such attributes as self-awareness and understanding. I can talk with them. Like myself, they have personal identity, autonomy, and volition. I cannot always predict exactly how they will act, although most of the time their behavior meets my expectations. In relation to myself, other 'persons' vary in power. Many of them have more power than I have, but some have less. They may be friendly and help me when I need them but, at the same time, I have to be prepared for hostile acts, too. I must be cautious in my relations with other 'persons' because appearances may be deceptive.

The psychological unity of the Ojibwa world

Although not formally abstracted and articulated philosophically, the nature of 'persons' is the focal point of Ojibwa ontology and the key to the psychological unity and dynamics of their world outlook. This aspect of their metaphysics of being permeates the content of their cognitive processes: perceiving, remembering, imagining, conceiving, judging, and reasoning. Nor can the motivation of much of their conduct be thoroughly understood without taking into account the relation of their central values and goals to the awareness they have of the existence of other-than-human, as well as human, persons in their world. 'Persons,' in fact, are so inextricably associated with notions of causality that, in order to understand their appraisal of events and the kind of behavior demanded in situations as they define them, we are confronted over and over again with the rolls of 'persons' as *loci* of causality in the dynamics of their universe. For the Ojibwa make no cardinal use of any concept of impersonal forces as major determinants of events. In the context of my exposition the meaning of the term *manitu*, which has become so generally known, may be considered as a synonym for a person of the other-than-human class ('grandfather,' *ätíso'kan, pawágan*). Among the Ojibwa I worked with it is now quite generally confined to the God of Christianity, when combined with an augmentative prefix (*k'tci manītu*). There is no evidence to suggest, however, that the term ever did connote an impersonal, magical, or supernatural force.[33]

---

[33] Cf. Skinner 1915, p. 261. Cooper (1933, p. 75) writes: 'The Manitu was clearly personal in the minds of my informants, and not identified with impersonal supernatural force. In fact, nowhere among the Albany River Otchipwe, among the Eastern Cree, or among the Montagnais have I been able thus far to find the word Manitu used to denote such force in connection with the Supreme Being belief, with conjuring, or with any other phase of magico-religious culture. *Manitu*, so far as I can discover, always denotes a supernatural personal being ... The word *Manitu* is, my informants say, not used to denote magical or conjuring power among the coastal Cree, nor so I was told in 1927, among the Fort Hops Otchipwe of the upper Albany River.'

In an essay on the 'Religion of the North American Indians' published over forty years ago, Radin asserted 'that from an examination of the data customarily relied upon as proof and from individual data obtained, there is nothing to justify the postulation of a belief in a universal force in North America. Magical power as an "essence" existing apart and separate from a definite spirit, is, we believe, an unjustified assumption, an abstraction created by investigators.'[34] This opinion, at the time, was advanced in opposition to the one expressed by those who, stimulated by the writings of R. R. Marett in particular, interpreted the term *manitu* among the Algonkians (W. Jones), *orenda* among the Iroquois (Hewitt) and *wakanda* among the Siouan peoples (Fletcher) as having reference to a belief in a magical force of some kind. But Radin pointed out that in his own field work among both the Winnebago and the Ojibwa the terms in question 'always referred to definite spirits, not necessarily definite in shape. If at a vapor-bath the steam is regarded as *wakanda* or *manitu*, it is because it is a spirit transformed into steam for the time being; if an arrow is possessed of specific virtues, it is because a spirit has either transformed himself into the arrow or because he is temporarily dwelling in it; and finally, if tobacco is offered to a peculiarly-shaped object it is because either this object belongs to a spirit, or a spirit is residing in it.' *Manitu*, he said, in addition to its substantive usage may have such connotations as 'sacred,' 'strange,' 'remarkable' or 'powerful' without 'having the slightest suggestion of "inherent power", but having the ordinary sense of these adjectives.'[35]

With respect to the Ojibwa conception of causality, all my own observations suggest that a culturally constituted psychological set operates which inevitably directs the reasoning of individuals towards an explanation of events in personalistic terms. *Who* did it, *who* is responsible, is always the crucial question to be answered. Personalistic explanation of past events is found in the myths. It was *Wísekedjak* who, through the exercise of his personal power, expanded the tiny bit of mud retrieved by Muskrat from the depths of the inundating waters of the great deluge into the inhabitable island-earth of Ojibwa cosmography. Personalistic explanation is central in theories of disease causation. Illness may be due to sorcery; the victim, in turn, may be 'responsible' because he has offended the sorcerer – even unwittingly. Besides this, I may be responsible for my own illness, even without the intervention of a sorcerer. I may have committed some wrongful act in the past, which is the 'cause' of my sickness. My child's illness, too, may be the consequence of my past

---

[34] Radin 1914a, p. 350.
[35] Ibid., pp. 349-50.

transgressions or those of my wife.[36] The personalistic theory of causation even emerges today among acculturated Ojibwa. In 1940, when a severe forest fire broke out at the mouth of the Berens River, no Indian would believe that lightning or any impersonal or accidental determinants were involved. *Somebody* must have been responsible. The German spy theory soon became popular. 'Evidence' began to accumulate; strangers had been seen in the bush, and so on. The personalistic type of explanation satisfies the Ojibwa because it is rooted in a basic metaphysical assumption; its terms are ultimate and incapable of further analysis within the framework of their cognitive orientation and experience.

Since the dynamics of events in the Ojibwa universe find their most ready explanation in a personalistic theory of causation, the qualitative aspects of interpersonal relations become affectively charged with a characteristic sensitivity.[37] The psychological importance of the range and depth of this sensitive area may be overlooked if the inclusiveness of the concept of 'person' and 'social relations' that is inherent in their outlook is not borne in mind. The reason for this becomes apparent when we consider the pragmatic relations between behavior, values, and the role of 'persons' in their world view.

The central goal of life for the Ojibwa is expressed by the term *pīmädäzīwin*, life in the fullest sense, life in the sense of longevity, health and freedom from misfortune. This goal cannot be achieved without the effective help and cooperation of *both* human and other-than-human 'persons,' as well as by one's own personal efforts. The help of other-than-human 'grandfathers' is particularly important for men. This is why all Ojibwa boys, in aboriginal days, were motivated to undergo the so-called 'puberty fast' or 'dreaming' experience. This was the means by which it was possible to enter into direct 'social interaction' with 'persons' of the other-than-human class for the first time. It was the opportunity of a lifetime. Every special aptitude, all a man's subsequent successes and the explanation of many of his failures, hinged upon the help of the 'guardian spirits' he obtained at this time, rather than upon his own native endowments or the help of his fellow *änícinábek*. If a boy received 'blessings' during his puberty fast and, as a man, could call upon the help of other-than-human persons when he needed them he was well prepared for meeting the vicissitudes of life. Among other things, he could defend himself against the hostile actions of human persons which might threaten

---

[36] 'Because a person does bad things, that is where sickness starts,' is the way one of my informants phrased it. For a fuller discussion of the relations between unsanctioned sexual behavior and disease, see Hallowell 1955, pp. 294-5, 303-4. For case material, see Hallowell 1939.

[37] Cf. Hallowell 1955, p. 305.

him and thus interfere with the achievement of *pīmä́däzīwin*. The grandfather of one of my informants said to him: 'you will have a long and good life if you dream well.' The help of human beings, however, was also vital, especially the services of those who had acquired the kind of power which permitted them to exercise effective curative functions in cases of illness. At the same time there were moral responsibilities which had to be assumed by an individual if he strove for *pīmä́däzīwin*. It was as essential to maintain approved standards of personal and social conduct as it was to obtain power from the 'grandfathers' because, in the nature of things, one's own conduct, as well as that of other 'persons,' was always a potential threat to the achievement of *pīmä́däzīwin*. Thus we find that the same values are implied throughout the entire range of 'social interaction' that characterizes the Ojibwa world; the same standards which apply to mutual obligations between human beings are likewise implied in the reciprocal relations between human and other-than-human 'persons.' In his relations with 'the grandfathers' the individual does not expect to receive a 'blessing' for nothing. It is not a free gift; on his part there are obligations to be met. There is a principle of reciprocity implied. There is a general taboo imposed upon the human being which forbids him to recount his dream experiences in full detail, except under certain circumstances. Specific taboos may likewise be imposed upon the suppliant. If these taboos are violated he will lose his power, can no longer count on the help of his 'grandfathers.'

The same principle of mutual obligations applies in other spheres of life. The Ojibwa are hunters and food gatherers. Since the various species of animals on which they depend for a living are believed to be under the control of 'masters' or 'owners' who belong to the category of other-than-human persons, the hunter must always be careful to treat the animals he kills for food or fur in the proper manner. It may be necessary, for example, to throw their bones in the water or to perform a ritual in the case of bears. Otherwise, he will offend the 'masters' and be threatened with starvation because no animals will be made available to him. Cruelty to animals is likewise an offense that will provoke the same kind of retaliation. And, according to one anecdote, a man suffered illness because he tortured a fabulous *wíndīgo* after killing him. A moral distinction is drawn between the kind of conduct demanded by the primary necessities of securing a livelihood, or defending oneself against aggression, and unnecessary acts of cruelty. The moral values implied document the consistency of the principle of mutual obligations which is inherent in all interactions with 'persons' throughout the Ojibwa world.

One of the prime values of Ojibwa culture is exemplified by the great stress laid upon sharing what one has with others. A balance, a sense of

45

proportion must be maintained in all interpersonal relations and activities. Hoarding, or any manifestation of greed, is discountenanced. The central importance of this moral value in their world outlook is illustrated by the fact that other-than-human persons share their power with human beings. This is only a particular instance of the obligations which human beings feel towards one another. A man's catch of fish or meat is distributed among his kin. Human grandfathers share the power acquired in their dreams from other-than-human persons with their classificatory grandchildren. An informant whose wife had borrowed his pipe for the morning asked to borrow one of mine while we worked together. When my friend Chief Berens once fell ill he could not explain it. Then he recalled that he had overlooked one man when he had passed around a bottle of whiskey. He believed this man was offended and had bewitched him. Since there was no objective evidence of this, it illustrates the extreme sensitivity of an individual to the principle of sharing, operating through feelings of guilt. I was once told about the puberty fast of a boy who was not satisfied with his initial 'blessing.' He demanded that he dream of all the leaves of all the trees in the world so that absolutely nothing would be hidden from him. This was considered greedy and, while the *pawágan* who appeared in his dream granted his desire, the boy was told that 'as soon as the leaves start to fall you'll get sick and when all the leaves drop to the ground that is the end of your life.' And this is what happened.[38] 'Overfasting' is as greedy as hoarding. It violates a basic moral value and is subject to a punitive sanction. The unity of the Ojibwa outlook is likewise apparent here.

The entire psychological field in which they live and act is not only unified through their conception of the nature and role of 'persons' in their universe, but by the sanctioned moral values which guide the relations of 'persons.' It is within this web of 'social relations' that the individual strives for *pīmädäzīwin*.

---

[38] Radin (1927, p. 177), points out that 'throughout the area inhabited by the woodland tribes of Canada and the United States, overfasting entails death.' Jones (Part II, pp. 307-11) gives two cases of overfasting. In one of them the bones of the boy were later found by his father.

References

African Worlds: Studies in the Cosmological Ideas and Social Values of African Peoples. 1954. Published for the International African Institute. London: Oxford University Press.

Baraga, R. R. Bishop. 1878. *A Theoretical and Practical Grammar of the Otchipive Language.* Montreal: Beauchemin and Valois.

Baraga, R. R. Bishop. 1880. *A Dictionary of the Otchipive Language Explained in English.* Montreal: Beauchemin and Valois.

Basilius, H. 1952. 'Neo-Humboldtian Ethnolinguistics', *Word* 8.

Bidney, David. 1953. *Theoretical Anthropology.* New York: Columbia University Press.

Bruno de Jésus-Marie, Père (ed.). 1952. *Satan.* New York: Sheed & Ward.

Chamberlain, A. F. 1906. 'Cree and Ojibwa Literary Terms', *Journal of American Folklore* 19: 346-7.

Collingwood, R. G. 1945. *The Idea of Nature.* Oxford: Clarendon Press.

Cooper, John M. 1933. 'The Northern Algonquian Supreme Being', *Primitive Man* 6: 41-112.

Dorson, Richard M. 1952. *Bloodstoppers and Bearwalkers: Folk Traditions of the Upper Peninsula.* Cambridge, MA: Harvard University Press.

Feuer, Lewis S. 1953. 'Sociological Aspects of the Relation between Language and Philosophy', *Philosophy of Science* 20: 85-100.

Fletcher, Alice C. 1910. 'Wakonda', in *Handbook of American Indians.* Washington, DC: Bureau of American Ethnology, Bull. 30.

Greenberg, Joseph H. 1954. 'Concerning Inferences from Linguistic to Non-linguistic Data', in *Language in Culture*, ed. Harry Hoijer. Chicago University Comparative Studies in Cultures and Civilizations. Chicago: University of Chicago Press.

Hallowell, A. Irving. 1926. 'Bear Ceremonialism in the Northern Hemisphere', *American Anthropologist* 28: 1-175.

Hallowell, A. Irving. 1934a. 'Some Empirical Aspects of Northern Saulteaux Religion', *American Anthropologist* 36: 389-404.

Hallowell, A. Irving. 1934b. 'Culture and Mental Disorder', *Journal of Abnormal and Social Psychology* 29: 1-9.

Hallowell, A. Irving. 1936. 'Psychic Stresses and Culture Patterns', *American Journal of Psychiatry* 92: 1291-310.

Hallowell, A. Irving. 1939. 'Sin, Sex and Sickness in Saulteaux Belief', *British Journal of Medical Psychology* 18: 191-7.

Hallowell, A. Irving. 1951. 'Cultural Factors in the Structuralization of Perception', in John H. Rohver and Muzafer Sherif, *Social Psychology at the Crossroads.* New York: Harper.

Hallowell, A. Irving. 1955. *Culture and Experience.* Philadelphia: University of Pennsylvania Press.

Hewitt, J. N. B. 1902. 'Orenda and a Definition of Religion', *American Anthropologist*, 4: 33-46.

A. IRVING HALLOWELL

Hoffman W. J. 1891. *The Mide'wiwin or 'Grand Medicine Society' of the Ojibwa*. Washington, DC: Bureau of American Ethnology, 7th Annual Report.

Hoijer, Harry (ed.). 1954. *Language in Culture*. Memoir 79. American Anthropological Association.

Jenness, Diamond. 1935. *The Ojibwa Indians of Parry Island: Their Social and Religious Life*. Ottawa: Canada Department of Mines, National Museum of Canada Bull. 78, Anthropological Series 12.

Jones, Peter. 1861. *History of the Ojibway Indians*. London.

Jones, William. 1905. 'The Algonkin Manitu', *Journal of American Folklore*, 18: 183-90.

Jones, William. 1919. *Ojibwa Texts*. Publications of the American Ethnological Society, vol. 7, parts I and II. Leyden, 1917; New York, 1919.

Kelsen, Hans. 1943. *Society and Nature: A Sociological Inquiry*. Chicago: University of Chicago Press.

Krech, David, and Richard S. Crutchfield. 1948. *Theory and Problems of Social Psychology*. New York: McGraw-Hill.

Lovejoy, Arthur O. 1948. *Essays in the History of Ideas*. Baltimore: Johns Hopkins University Press.

Lovejoy, Arthur O., and George Boas. 1935. *Primitivism and Related Ideas in Antiquity*. Baltimore: Johns Hopkins University Press. Vol. 1 of *A Documentary History of Primitivism and Related Ideas*.

Pine, N. W. 1937. 'The Meaninglessness of the Terms "Life" and "Living"', in *Perspectives in Biochemistry*, ed. J. Needham and D. Green. New York: Macmillan.

Radin, Paul. 1914a. 'Religion of the North American Indians', *Journal of American Folklore* 27: 335-73.

Radin, Paul. 1914b. *Some Aspects of Puberty Fasting among the Ojibwa*. Geological Survey of Canada, Department of Mines, Museum Bull. No. 2, Anthropological Series, No. 2, pp. 1-10.

Radin, Paul. 1927. *Primitive Man as Philosopher*. New York: D. Appleton & Co.

Randall, John Herman, Jr. 1944. 'The Nature of Naturalism', in *Naturalism and the Human Spirit*, ed. H. Krikorian. New York: Columbia University Press.

Redfield, Robert. 1952. 'The Primitive World View', *Proceedings of the American Philosophical Society* 96: 30-6.

Schoolcraft, Henry R. 1834. *Narrative of an Expedition through the Upper Mississippi to Itasca Lake, the Actual Source of the River ...* New York: Harper.

Skinner, Alanson. 1915. 'The Menomini Word "Häwätûk"', *Journal of American Folklore* 28: 258-61.

Swanton, John R. 1910. 'Some Practical Aspects of the Study of Myths', *Journal of American Folklore* 23: 1-7.

Tanner, John. 1830. *Narrative of the Captivity and Adventures of John Tanner*, ed. E. James.

Thompson, Stith. 1946. *The Folktale*. New York: Dryden Press.

Van Der Leeuw, G. 1938. *Religion in Essence and Manifestation*. London: Allen Unwin.

Whorf, Benjamin Lee. 1956. *Language Thought and Reality: Selected Writings of Benjamin L. Whorf*, ed. with Introduction by J. B. Carroll; Foreword by Stuart Chase. New York: Wiley.

2. Partners and consumers: Making relations visible

Marilyn Strathern

Editor's introduction

Marilyn Strathern's chapter shares, in some respects, similar territory to that of Hallowell: both are concerned with relationships that constitute persons. She writes, 'For the anthropological expert, "person" is an analytic construct whose utility is evinced through cross-cultural comparison.'

Both articles are also concerned with ways of knowing and disseminating knowledge. How does the researcher, for example, find out what is known to their hosts? How can a worldview, or central dynamics within one, be communicated to those whose horizons are (or seem) entirely different?

In this article Strathern compares discourses and actions that construct and constitute Melanesian and Euro-American persons. To do so she employs the concept of 'gift' as a lens through which to see that which may be so self-evident as to be unremarkable within those cultures. At the same time the explication and analysis of comparative material are intended to permit (or provoke) appreciation by those whose own taken-for-granted world stands in the way of seeing what the other sees.

'Gift' has been particularly associated with the work of Marcel Mauss (1990).

© 1997 Marilyn Strathern. Reprinted from *The Logic of the Gift: Toward an Ethic of Generosity*, ed. Alan Schrift. By permission of Routledge, Inc., part of the Taylor & Francis Group. This was initially presented to the conference on *The Gift and Its Transformations*, organized by Natalie Davis, Rena Lederman, and Ronald Sharp, National Humanities Center, N.C., November 1990. I am most grateful for comments from the participants. I should add that I have retained the original mode of address, since the paper was written for a multidisciplinary audience. [The paper was first published in *New Literary History*, 1991.]

Strathern links it with other theorists and observers too, and the publication of her work in a collection on *The Logic of the Gift* (Schrift 1997) is more than suggestive of the relational constitution of academics. Similarly, the division of *Indigenous Religions: A Companion* (Harvey 2000) into three sections labelled 'Persons', 'Powers', and 'Gifts', deliberately played with what Morrison (1992, drawing on Blackburn 1975) calls 'existential principles' or 'postulates', i.e. 'Person', Power' and 'Gift'. This was a move similar to that made here by Strathern, who writes,

> the concept of gift seemed readily applicable to self-evident and concrete 'gifts.' The term trailed a reassuring visualism. One could 'see' gift exchange because one could see the gifts, the things that people exchanged with one another. It also trailed a concern, as Panoff, Parry, and others have noted, with individual autonomy (voluntarism) and interpersonal relations measured by degrees of interestedness (altruism).[1]

The gifts that reveal 'Gift' among Euro-Americans and Melanesians reveal different kinds of persons as well as different kinds of gifting.

In the process of this exciting discussion, Strathern touches a host of issues that are germane to the way that religions have been, are being, and might be studied.

References

Blackburn, Thomas C. 1975. *December's Child: A Book of Chumash Oral Narratives*. Berkeley: University of California Press.
Harvey, Graham (ed.). 2000. *Indigenous Religions: A Companion*. London: Cassell.
Mauss, Marcel. 1990. *The Gift: The Form and Reason for Exchange in Archaic Societies*, trans. W. D. Halls. New York: Norton.
Morrison, Kenneth M. 1992. 'Beyond the Supernatural: Language and Religious Action', *Religion* 22: 201-5.
Panoff, Michel. 1970. 'Marcel Mauss's *The Gift* Revisited', *Man,* n.s. 5: 60-70.
Parry, Jonathan. 1986. '*The Gift*, the Indian Gift and the "Indian Gift"', *Man* n.s. 21: 453-73.
Schrift, Alan D. 1997. *The Logic of the Gift: Toward an Ethic of Generosity*. London: Routledge.

At the 1990 meetings for the British Association for the Advancement of Science, an experimental embryologist expounded an expert's view to a lay

---

[1] Citing Panoff 1970, and Parry 1986.

audience.[1] Martin Johnson was concerned to demonstrate the continuity of biological process. A person's birth begins with primitive gametes laid down when one's parents were embryos in the grandparental womb. Subsequent development depends not only on genetic coding but on extragenetic influences that operate on chromosomes from the start; these include stimulation from material enveloping the egg,[2] as well as nutritive and other effects derived from placenta and uterus.

It was a powerful origin story,[3] especially in the context of current legislative decisions with respect to the Human Fertilization and Embryology Act (1990). Here, however, the problem has been to formulate discontinuities between developmental phases. The House of Commons decided that research on human embryos is permissible up to fourteen days, by which time, among other things, the pre-embryonic material is now discernably divided into those cells that will form the future embryo-fetus and those that will form the placenta. The Secretary for Health was reported as saying that status as an individual could begin only at the stage where cells could be differentiated.[4] Yet while biology appeared to provide an index,[5] the further problem of personhood raised the same notion of continuous process. Another member of the Commons pointed out. 'It is a very difficult matter to say at what stage do you have a citizen, a human being. At various stages fresh rights are acquired.'[6] Rights can only be acquired of course, in this view, if there is an individual person to bear them.[7]

Here are experts informing lay persons (the BAAS talk), experts informing experts (the Secretary for Health is briefed on what the fourteen-

[1] See also Martin Johnson, 'Did I Begin?', *New Scientist*, 9 December 1989, pp. 39-42. The BAAS meetings are intended to present scientific investigations and discoveries to the public. The debate, *Human Embryo Research: What are the Issues?*, was organized by the Ciba Foundation.

[2] The early conceptus is dependent on the developmental history of the egg in the mother, which provides 'a mature physical and biochemical entity within which the whole complex process' of early development operates (Johnson, 'Did I Begin?', p. 40), an interaction quite distinct from the egg's genetic contribution to the conceptus.

[3] See Sarah Franklin, 'Making Sense of Missed Conceptions: Anthropological Perspectives on Unexplained Fertility,' a paper presented to the 152nd Annual Meeting of the British Association for the Advancement of Science (Swansea, 1990).

[4] See Martin Linton and Nikki Knewstub, 'MPs Give Overwhelming Backing to Medical Research on Embryos,' *The Guardian*, 24 April 1990, p. 6.

[5] To the lay person. To the embryologist, 'Biology does not tell us that a line should or should not be drawn' (Johnson, 'Did I Begin?', p. 41). It is the job of legislation to draw the lines.

[6] Linton and Knewstub, 'MPs', p. 6.

[7] See Gordon Dunstan, 'The Moral Status of the Human Embryo,' in *Philosophical Ethics in Reproductive Medicine*, eds David R. Bromham, Maureen E. Dalton, and Jennifer C. Jackson (Manchester: Manchester University Press, 1990), p. 6.

day stage means), and lay persons (Members of Parliament) turning expert in making legislative decisions. An anthropologist might wish to bracket all of them lay insofar as they promote a common view of the person that, in his/her eyes, must have the status of a folk model. For the anthropological expert, 'person' is an analytic construct whose utility is evinced through cross-cultural comparison. One draws, as always, from one's culture of origin, but to be an expert in anthropology is to demonstrate simultaneously the cultural origins of one's analytic constructs and their cross-cultural applicability.

A person cannot in this sense be seen without the mediation of analysis. Yet those who discuss the potential personhood of the embryo implicitly contest such an appropriation of the concept. Visual representations of first the division of cells and then the human form as it takes shape regularly accompany not just talks designed to popularize the findings of science but attempts to make vivid the political issues at stake.[8] Indeed, a flurry of fascination/repulsion was created by the Society for the Protection of Unborn Children which in April (while the Act was still in debate) sent all 650 MPs a life-sized model of a twenty-week-old fetus. This parody of the ubiquitous free gift was intended to mobilize a parallel concern over the limit for legal abortions. The plastic fetus lifted out from a sectional womb,[9] and its message was clear. One can 'see' a (potential) person, and a person is known by its individuality. Individuality in turn means a naturally entire and free-standing entity: the claim was that at twenty weeks a fetus is a viable whole.

Between the anthropologist as expert and the layperson with his or her folk model lies more than an epistemological issue over what is usefully designated a 'person'; there is an ontological issue over the nature of the category. The anthropologist is dealing with a category that refers to certain analytical constructions. The laity may argue over what they see and what they call it but take for granted that the category refers to persons existing as visible and substantial entities. So while it may be hard to tell when a person begins, and while the law may have to define the stages at which rights accrue, it seems self-evident that the subject of these debates is a concrete human being. The anthropologist is not, of course,

---

[8] See Rosaline Pollack Petchesky, 'Foetal Images: The Power of Visual Culture in the Politics of Reproduction,' in *Reproductive Technologies: Gender, Motherhood and Medicine,* ed. Michelle Stanworth (Cambridge: Polity Press, 1987), pp. 57-80.

[9] The fetus was entire (a homunculus), but its cord was severed, and the womb was in half-section with the placenta visibly sectioned as well. The severed cord was painted in such a way as to invite horror at the tearing away of the fetus; but the womb itself was 'severed' for no other purpose it would seem than to have it provide a convenient cup for the model of the fetus. A simulated horror.

untouched by this cultural certitude.

Now for 'person' one could write 'gift.' That concept was drawn into anthropology from various domains of Western or Euro-American discourse (economy, theology, and so forth) though its most notable proponents made out of the indigenous connotation of presentations voluntarily made an analytical category that also included the social fact of obligation. The point is that the concept of gift seemed readily applicable to self-evident and concrete 'gifts.' The term trailed a reassuring visualism. One could 'see' gift exchange because one could see the gifts, the things that people exchanged with one another. It also trailed a concern, as Panoff, Parry, and others have noted, with individual autonomy (voluntarism) and interpersonal relations measured by degrees of interestedness (altruism).[10]

As an anthropologist I am crippled, so to speak, by expertise – by the desire to appropriate the category 'gift' in a special way, insofar as those negotiations of relationships known as gift exchange in Melanesia have a character whose uniqueness I would be reluctant to relinquish. I say crippled to the extent that this position appears to set up barriers. Blind: I do not believe the evidence of my eyes, that one will recognize a gift when one sees it. Constricted: I cannot stride across the world map looking for gifts at all times and places. The wrong color: monochrome rather than polychrome, for exhilarating as the company of other disciplines can be, I lose appropriative capability, feel very lay in the presence of other expertise. Other knowledge does not necessarily repair deficiencies in one's own. Not something that concerns Melanesians, one should add for they borrow from foreigners all the time, including the most intimate powers of reproduction.

Melanesians borrow origin stories, wealth, and – as in the area I know best (Mount Hagen) – the expertise by which to organize their religion and their future. One clan takes from another its means of life. Indeed, exchanges surrounding the transfer of reproductive potential are intrinsic to the constitution of identity. From a clan's point of view, foreign wives are drawn to them by virtue of bridewealth, and such items of wealth are themselves considered to have reproductive potential. Pigs create pigs and money creates money, as shell valuables also reproduce themselves, an idea given visible form in the iconography that developed with the influx of pearlshells into the Hagen area at the time of contact. Shells for circulation in gift exchange were mounted on resin boards vividly colored with red ochre. The whole appeared a free-standing entity. But it was not an image

---

[10] See Michel Panoff, 'Marcel Mauss's *The Gift* Revisited,' *Man* n.s. 5 (1970), pp. 60-70; and Jonathan Parry, '*The Gift*, the Indian Gift and the "Indian Gift,"' *Man* n.s. 21 (1986), pp. 453-73.

of one. Rather than plastic molding a visible homunculus, the child/embryo in its netbag/womb was indicated in the abstract by the curvature of the shell crescent, and the resin molded a container around it.[11]

Personalized commodities?

In taking off from some of the expert discourse of Melanesian anthropology, I confine myself to certain issues in the understanding of gifts, namely those concerned with reproduction and the life cycle. It is arguable that all Melanesian gift exchanges are 'reproductive,' but I make a more restricted point. The reason is to provide an approximation of the indigenous Euro-American understanding of gifts as 'transactions within a moral economy, which [make] possible the extended reproduction of social relations.'[12] This account ignores those aspects of the Melanesian gift that have seemed most strange to the twentieth-century Westerner (competition and the political striving for prestige), in order to focus on the apparently familiar (the celebration of kinship).

From the perspective of the Papua New Guinea Highlands, of the kind that Lederman has described for Mendi,[13] I thus appear to privilege one nexus of gifting (kinship-based) over another (clan-based). Or, more accurately, to evoke one type of sociality, for it is also arguable that each set of relations transforms the moral base of the other. But my interest is not in the relative moralities of exchanges.[14] It is in whether Melanesian gifting can illuminate the very idea of there being part-societies ('moral economies') that 'typically consist of small worlds of personal relationships that are the emotional core of every individual's social experiences' (*GE* 15).

Whatever parallels might be useful for earlier European materials,[15] in the late twentieth century any understandings of such part-societies must in turn be put into their specific Euro-American context: consumer culture. Cheal himself goes on to give a consumerist definition of sociality. Everywhere (he says) people live out their lives in small worlds; the primitive (he says) because the societies were small, the modern because

---

[11] The shell is both procreative and procreated. The point is stimulated by two unpublished papers in which Jeffrey Clark has analyzed the remarkable iconography of Wiru pearlshells.

[12] David Cheal, *The Gift Economy* (London: Routledge, 1988), p. 19; hereafter cited in text as *GE*.

[13] See Rena Lederman, *What Gifts Engender: Social Relations and Politics in Mendi, Highland Papua New Guinea* (Cambridge: Cambridge University Press, 1986).

[14] See Jonathan Parry and Maurice Bloch, *Money and the Morality of Exchange* (Cambridge: Cambridge University Press, 1989).

[15] See, e.g., Mario Biagioli, 'Galileo's System of Patronage,' *History of Science*, 28 (1990), pp. 1-62.

people 'prefer to inhabit intimate life worlds' (*GE* 15) [!].[16] Now recent anthropological discussion of the gift has turned, among other things, on the analytic advantage of distinguishing gift-based economies from commodity-based ones. Gregory has been notable here,[17] and while his arguments explicated the contrast between gifts and commodities in terms of production, they have also opened up the question of consumption. In the formula he adopts, it is through consumption that things are drawn into the reproduction of persons, and reproduction can be understood as a process of personification. But consumption as a universal analytic is one thing. I take my own cue from the further fact that we live in a self-advertised 'consumer' culture.

A consumer culture is a culture, one might say, of personalization. And to Euro-Americans, gift-giving seems a highly personalized form of transaction. After all, it was the person in the gift that attracted anthropological attention to the concept in the first place. But whether useful parallels can be drawn between the personalizations of consumerism and the personifications of Melanesian gift exchange remains to be seen.

Free-standing entities

The notorious individualism of Western culture has always seemed an abstraction of the state or of the market economy that lies athwart those concrete persons we recognize in interactions with others. No one is really an isolate. This was a point the embryologist wanted to get across, and for which he offered biological reasoning.

Johnson was concerned to demonstrate the influence of the environment in all stages of fetal development. Its significance for him lies in its contribution to the identity of the emergent individual: personal identity is the outcome not just of a unique genetic combination but of a unique history of continuous development which affects the way genetic factors themselves take effect. The organism is a finite and discrete entity; the process is continuous. Thus, he opined, an individual is always in interaction with its environment. This provoked a comment from the gynecologist Modell who observed that, as far

---

[16] In the 1990s, life-world-style worlds are already passé, if one is to believe upmarket consumer experts. I refer to the concept of the personalized market here. 'If the modern world is based on the notion of an endless repetition of a few products, then its successor is based on the idea of short-runs and the targeting of many, different, products' (Charles Jencks and Maggie Keswick, *What Is Post-Modernism?*, 2nd edn (London: Academy Editions, 1987), pp. 48-9) though, as Jencks observes, individual tastes are not as variable as the potential production of variety.

[17] See C. A. Gregory, *Gifts and Commodities* (London: Academic Press, 1982).

as the embryo is concerned, the environment is immediately the mother and the mother is *another person*. Among other things, the embryo undergoes the effects of the parent's changing perceptions of it.

The point slid by without much comment. What I see in that interchange is more than a dispute among experts, for it barely registered as a dispute. It epitomized the simultaneous delineation of a hegemonic model (of personhood) and the possibility of contesting it, somewhat parallel to the manner in which anthropologists have extricated the idea of gift from hegemonic understandings in Western culture in order to contest either the application of these understandings to non-Western cultures or the dominance of the model in people's lives.[18] Modell's mild intervention sounded, in fact, almost like a version of critiques well rehearsed through the contested notion of rights in abortion debates. The right of the mother against the right of the child presents a contest of alternatives.[19] However, I wish to make a different kind of contest appear.

Johnson's idea of the individual person doubly defined by genetic programming and by environmental factors seems a solution to the old nature/ nurture debate: we have, so to speak, put the individual back into its environment, in much the same way as social scientists are perpetually putting individuals back into 'society.' This is an individualism that gives full recognition to the context in which persons flourish, and we may read off from the image of the embryo an image of the individual person in a responsive, interactive, and creative mode with the external world. Indeed, it is colloquial English to speak of an individual's 'relationship' to its environment as we do of an individual's 'relationship' to society.

But what a bizarre coupling! The whole person is held to be a substantial and visible entity. The environment, on the other hand, like society, is regularly construed as existing in the abstract, for it cannot be seen as a whole.[20] We may concretize the environment through examples of its parts, as uterus or as trees and mountains, as we may concretize society through referring to groups and institutions. But there was more to Johnson's purpose. He wished

---

[18] See Lisette Josephides, *The Production of Inequality: Gender and Exchange among the Kewa* (London: Tavistock Publications, 1985).

[19] See Faye Ginsburg, 'Procreation Stories: Reproduction, Nurturance and Procreation in Life Narratives of Abortion Activists,' *American Ethnologist* 14 (1987), pp. 623-36.

[20] I read this off from Johnson's presentation of the epigenetic factors. These were indicated in highly generalized terms by contrast with the specific representation of the fetus/person. No doubt his professional view is more sophisticated than the image I have derived from his talk (an organism as a free-standing entity within an environment to which it 'adapts'), but for a critique of similar perceptions as they have informed the concept of culture in anthropology, see Tim Ingold, 'Culture and the Perception of the Environment' (n.d.); for EIDOS workshop on *Cultural Understandings of the Environment* (London, 1989).

to convey how it is potentially *everything* beyond the individual person that may influence that unique person and help make it what it is. The forces that continuously shape us are always, as he comments elsewhere, both genetic and epigenetic, and 'epigenetic' is the biologist's catchall 'for everything else besides the genes.'[21] I would add that this makes the latter of a different order from the former precisely insofar as they are imagined, hypothetically and thus abstractly, as infinite. 'Myriad' is his word; the environment consists in this view of the sum of all the factors that might have an effect.

The view against which Johnson argues would hold that the whole and finite individual is determined largely by its genetic programming. But rather than contest, perhaps we should see analogy between the conceptualizations here. Suppose the concept of the genetic program were analogous to that of the individual, then the concept of epigenetic forces would appear analogous to that of environment/society. In turn, the relationship between genetic and epigenetic forces that Johnson postulates would be seen to miniaturize or replicate commonsense understandings of that between individual organism and enveloping world. And the interest of Modell's remark would be in the way it cut across the analogies. For she displaced the image of a (finite, concrete) person contextualized by an (infinite, abstract) society/environment with another image: the exterior world imagined as another (finite, concrete) person.

She thus gave voice to a capability that also rests in English: of imagining a world that does not imagine such abstractions for itself, where sociality impinges in the presence of other persons. English speakers readily enough personify the agency of 'society' or even 'environment,' though they would be hard put to think of these entities as persons. Yet that is exactly the way in which they might imagine that Melanesians imagine the world beyond themselves.[22] What contains the child is indeed 'another person,' whether that other person is the mother, or the clan that nurtures its progeny, or the land that nurtures the clan and receives a fertilizing counterpart in the burial of the placenta. This other person may be regarded as the cause or origin of the effective agency of those it contains.[23]

When Euro-Americans think of more than one person, they are faced with the disjunction of unique individuals and overcome this in the notion

[21] Johnson, 'Did I Begin?', p. 39.

[22] See, e.g., Maurice Leenhardt, *Do Kamo. Person and Myth in the Melanesian World,* trans. Basia Miller Gulati (1947; rpt. Chicago: University of Chicago Press, 1979). For non-Melanesian depictions of the world imagined as a plurality of bodies and of the body containing a plurality of worlds, see the chapter by Malamoud and Levi in Michel Feher *et al., Fragments for a History of the Human Body,* 3 vols. (New York: Zone Books, 1989).

[23] See, e.g., Roy Wagner, *Asiwinarong: Ethos, Image, and Social Power among the Usen Barok of New Ireland* (Princeton: Princeton University Press, 1986).

that individuals 'relate' to one another. What lies between them are relationships, so that society may be thought of as the totality of made relationships. That relationships are made further supposes that what are linked are persons as individual subjects or agents who engage in their making: '[i]nterpersonal dependence is everywhere [!] the result of socially constructed ties between human agents' (GE 11). The idea of persons in the plural evokes, then, the image of the interactions between them, in turn the immediate social environment for any one of them.

It is because society is likened to an environment that it is possible for Euro-Americans to think of individual persons as relating not to other persons but to society as such, and to think of relations as after the fact of the individual's personhood rather than integral to it. Or so the folk model goes. Anthropologists, for their part, have captured the category of person to stand for subjects understood analytically in the context of social relations with others. In the particular way she/he looks to making 'society' visible,[24] the anthropologist would be scandalized at the idea of a non-relation definition of persons.

The analytical necessity appears to have been given by just such societies as are found in Melanesia. Indeed, the anthropological experience may be that in such societies everything is relational. Certainly Melanesians constantly refer to the acts and thoughts of other persons. But if they seemingly situate themselves in a world full of what we call 'social' relationships,' such relationships do not link individuals. Rather, the fact of relating forms a background sociality to people's existence, out of which people work to make specific relationships appear.[25] Relations are thus integral to the person or, in Wagner's formulation,[26] persons may be understood fractally: their dimensionality cannot be expressed in whole numbers. The fractal person is an entity with relationships integrally implied. Any scale of social activity mobilizes the same dimensionality of person/relation.

There is no axiomatic evaluation of intimacy or closeness here. On the contrary, people work to create divisions between themselves. For in the activation of relations people make explicit what differentiates them.[27]

[24] See Daniel Miller, Material Culture and Mass Consumption (Oxford: Blackwell, 1987), p. 14.

[25] See James F. Weiner, The Heart of the Pearlshell: The Mythological Dimension of Foi Sociality (Los Angeles: University of California Press, 1988).

[26] See Roy Wagner, 'The Fractal Person,' in Big Men and Great Men: Personifications of Power in Melanesia, eds Maurice Godelier and Marilyn Strathern (Cambridge: Cambridge University Press, 1991).

[27] See James F. Weiner, 'Diseases of the Soul: Sickness, Agency and the Men's Cult among the Foi of New Guinea,' in Dealing with Inequality, Analysing Gender Relations in Melanesia and Beyond, ed. Marilyn Strathern (Cambridge: Cambridge University Press, 1987), pp. 255-77.

One may put it that it is the relationship between them that separates donor from recipient or mother from child. Persons are detached, not as individuals from the background of society or environment, but from other persons. However, detachment is never final, and the process is constantly recreated in people's dealings with one another. To thus be in a state of division with respect to others renders the Melanesian person dividual.

Persons are not conceptualized, therefore, as free-standing. A Hagen clan is composed of its agnates and those foreigners detached from other clans who will give birth to its children; a woman contains the child that grows through the acts of a man; shells are mounted on the breast. One person may 'carry' another, as the origin or cause of its existence and acts. An implicate field of persons is thus imagined in the division or dispersal of bodies or body parts.[28] From their viewpoint, Western Euro-Americans cannot readily think of bodies and body parts as the substance of people's interactions. They can imagine objects flowing between persons 'as though' they 'symbolized' body parts, but for them to discover that a shell is like a fetus in a womb is simply to uncover an image, a metaphorical statement about (say) fertility. So let me return to the embryologist's address and to a moment when he seemed at a loss for a metaphor.

During his presentation, Johnson flashed on the screen a picture of twin babies with their common placenta between them. The three were genetically identical, he briefly observed. Three what? One may fill in the silence, that of course they were not three persons, for only the twins, not the placenta, would grow into autonomous subjects. The placenta is regarded as a source of support, at once part of the fetus and part of the fetus's environment, yet only through detachment from it is the individual person made;[29] the picture included the cut cords and the scissors that cut them. Not at all how the Melanesian 'Are'Are of Malaita in the Solomon Islands would see it. There the placenta both remains part of the person and, in becoming detached at birth, is treated as another person. Detachment is conceptualized as a separation of (dividual) persons from one another.

De Coppet describes how the placenta is buried in ancestral land, linking the living person to a network of ancestral funeral sites and returning to

---

[28] See Gillian Gillison, 'The Flute Myth and the Law of Equivalence: Origins of a Principle of Exchange,' in *Big Men and Great Men*; and Jadran Mimica, *Intimations of Infinity: The Cultural Meanings of Iqwaye Counting System and Number* (Oxford: Berg, 1988).

[29] See Lynn M. Morgan, 'When Does Life Begin? A Cross-Cultural Perspective on the Personhood of Fetuses and Young Children,' in *Abortion Rights and Fetal 'Personhood'*, eds Edd Doerr and James W. Prescott (Long Beach: Centerline Press, 1989). Morgan observes that in the United States it is generally thought that the neonate becomes a person with the cutting of the umbilical cord.

source two vital parts of personal substance.[30] It is planted like a dead taro that has lost its living stem (the baby); taro denotes 'body.' The 'Are'Are placenta is also referred to as the baby's pig, an allusion to animate 'breath.' (What the placenta lacks is a third part, the ancestral 'image' that adults assume when they die naturally, that is, are killed by their own ancestors; the unimaged placenta is buried somewhat after the manner of an unimaged murder victim.) Pig and taro assure the vitality of the living child; it is also expected that scavenging pigs will eat the buried placenta and that taro will grow there. The land that nourishes the food that nourishes the child is also constituted of what constitutes the living person and is a cause of its life. 'Are'Are personify the land, territorialize the person. When one understands how the land owns people, de Coppet was told,[31] one can understand how people own land.

This relationship to the land is not quite the same as the English-speaking conceptualization of a (concrete) person's relationship to the (abstract) environment/society. For the 'Are'Are person (land) thereby *enters into an exchange* with the land (person). If your placenta has been buried, 'it proves that, in return for your life, through the land, you have given back the share of "body" and "breath" which must rejoin the universal circulation.'[32]

It is for such a world as this, where persons' actions always seem to be caused by or elicited by other 'persons,' that the borrowed concept of the gift captures what a Westerner would sense as a pervasive sociality. It seems just the formula to emphasize the personal nature of interpersonal relations. Perhaps that is because gifts in turn typify a sector of Western culture which seemingly parallels the pervasive sociality of Melanesian life: the close interpersonal relations of kinship and friendship. Here one gives and takes on an intimate basis. Yet the appearance of similarity is, inevitably, misleading. Euro-American intimacy is signaled by two constructs peculiar to it, altruism and voluntarism.

---

[30] See Daniel de Coppet, '. . . Land Owns People,' in *Contexts and Levels: Anthropological Essays on Hierarchy,* eds R. H. Barnes, Daniel de Coppet, and R. J. Parkin (Oxford: JASO, 1985), pp. 78-90.

[31] My interpretation of the sequence of statements made to de Coppet by the paramount chief Eerehau.

[32] De Coppet, 'Land Owns People,' p. 87.

Altruism: donors and partners

Advances in reproductive medicine that have highlighted artificial mechanisms to assist procreation have also heightened certain Western perceptions of the interaction between procreating partners. Thus in the context of discussing artificial insemination by donor Sissa recalls the assumption 'that semen is donated, the uterus only loaned.'[33] That paternity should in addition be thought a matter of opinion, maternity a matter of fact, turns not on the certainty about donation but on certainty about social identity. It is because semen has the appearance of a (visible) detachable bodily substance that it seems alienable. Because it is alienable, its source may be in doubt. Both the substantial nature of semen and the asymmetry of the relationship between semen and uterus (individual and environment) present an inverse of the supposition found in Aristotle, that semen provided form and maternal blood the substance of the child. The potency of semen in this ancient view was that it was efficacious in the way a craftsman's activities were efficacious; it had an activating force on female blood but did not contribute particles of matter to the embryo. The movement of the male body, the act of donation, constituted the male part in procreation.[34]

Sissa draws the inevitable parallel with the Trobriands, between the multiple fathering made possible by insemination by donor and the fact (as she puts it) that the Trobriand child has two fathers, one whose semen molds somatic identity and one (the mother's brother) who defines the kin group to which the child belongs. Yet the parallel is a poor one, since the social identity of the Trobriand father is integral to his somatic role, whereas in the case of DI knowing the father's identity is both optional and after the fact of the donation. Donation linking a person to a source of genetic endowment does not necessarily link the person to another person. Indeed, twentieth-century people who talk of semen 'donation' treat it as a substance that will fertilize the maternal egg *whether or not* its identity is

---

[33] Giulia Sissa, 'Subtle Bodies,' in *Fragments for a History of the Human Body*, Part 3, p. 133. See Verena Stolcke, 'New Reproductive Technologies – Same Old Fatherhood,' *Critique of Anthropology* 6 (1986), pp. 5-31. The term *semen* may be used either for the vehicle that carries sperm or as an alternative for sperm itself. It is sperm donation that is strictly at issue here.

[34] Rather in the way that gifts of money in 'Are'Are (see below) encompass, transcend, and differentiate the three components of the person (body, breath, and image) (Daniel de Coppet, 'The Life-Giving Death,' in *Mortality and Immortality: The Anthropology and Archaeology of Death*, eds S. C. Humphreys and Helen King (London: Academic Press, 1981), and 'Land Owns People'), so Aristotelian semen is the vehicle for the three 'principles,' soul, form, and movement (Sissa, 'Subtle Bodies,' p. 136).

known. This is the crux. Semen is potentially alienable (from the body), I suggest, because of the possibility of its being produced without being elicited by another person. This is, in turn, a general conceptual possibility, regardless of whether or not DI is at issue, captured in its visual representation as a detachable substance.[35] DI adds the further conceptual possibility that conception need not be accompanied by bodily movement; movement is only required to produce the semen. Sissa points out that Aristotle's emphasis on the transcendent and nonsubstantial aspect of the semen led him to assert it could never be frozen, whereas twentieth-century people keep frozen specimens in banks for future use.

Nonetheless, the new reproductive technologies have repaired some of the asymmetry, for it would seem that 'egg donation' has passed into the lay imagination as a process analogous to semen donation.[36] Anonymity may or may not be preserved. In the case of maternal surrogacy, however, a partnership of a kind has to be set up between the commissioning couple and the surrogate mother. People talk crudely of womb-renting, or more delicately of the gift of life.[37]

Donation is here conceptualized in two ways. On the one hand it may simply involve an act of bodily emission intended for an anonymous recipient; on the other hand it may involve a relationship between donors and recipients as partners in a single enterprise. This corresponds to the double conceptualization of sociality in consumer culture, as much a matter of an individual's relationship to society in the abstract as of interaction between concrete persons.

The terminology of donation and gift is seemingly encouraged by clinical and other experts by virtue of this double evocatory power. It evokes the charitable altruism of blood and organ donors; it also evokes the intimate altruism of transactions that typify personal relations outside the market. (1) Organ donors can give anonymously because human organs are regarded as anonymous: kidneys differ in physical condition rather than

---

[35] However, its alienability is a contested point. A recent study by Jeanette Edwards (personal communication) points to diverse views on men's part about the extent to which semen is or is not felt to be disposable in the way body organs potentially are.

[36] The relative complexities of the techniques render the physical operations quite different. See Frances Price, 'Establishing Guidelines: Regulation and the Clinical Management of Infertility,' in *Birthrights: Laws and Ethics at the Beginnings of Life,* eds Robert Lee and Derek Morgan (London: Routledge, 1989), pp. 46-7. While artificial semen donation is a two-hundred-year-old practice, scientific papers about pregnancies from donated oocytes did not appear in professional journals until 1983-4 (Frances Price, personal communication).

[37] A phrase applied to interventionist medicine in general. In a world of punning acronyms, it is no accident that GIFT should occur, though for a process (gamete intra-fallopian transfer) that need involve no 'donation' from outside sources.

social identity.[38] Such organs or materials as can be excised or secreted from the body become freestanding entities. So although semen carries formative genetic material that will contribute to a person's identity, it is also possible to think of contributing one's part to a general supply. Donation here carries connotations of the charitable gesture, the personal sacrifice for the public good, a gift to society. (2) Alternatively, sometimes in the case of egg donation and certainly of willingness to carry a child, altruism may be embedded in specific relations. A partnership is created between donor and recipient. An egg donated from a close relative can thus be regarded as belonging to a relationship that already exists, an expression of love. The carrying mother, related or not, is regarded as sacrificing comfort and ease in order to enable others to have children; because of the nature of her labor and the attempt to protect such acts from commercial exploitation, as in the case of charity the language of gift-giving becomes the language of altruism.

But do these gestures and does this language constitute a gift economy?

Cheal has argued exactly this in examining the nexus of present-giving among friends and relatives, as at Christmas and birthdays, in suburban Canada (see *GE*). Gifts indicate community membership (the reproduction of social status) as well as relations of intimacy. In either case, they symbolize the central values of a 'love culture,' he argues, whether the love is generally or specifically directed. We encounter here the same double: gifts for society and gifts for persons. Cheal introduces a further distinction between the immediate society of the moral economy (his 'small world,' the real community) and the further society of the political economy. Gifts make gestures of altruism within, it would seem, the near society, whereas the far society is seen as a realm of commerce. It is in their immediate circles that persons 'make' relationships as they 'make' love, and community-giving is a diffuse, impersonal version of intimacy-giving.

While I would dispute neither the evocation of emotions and (society-near) relational behavior among friends and relatives nor the way this mobilizes conventions distinct from those that regulate other (society-far) areas of life, I add one comment: *the circulation of gifts does not create distinct kinds of persons.* 'Gifts' (presents) are free-standing entities just like commodities, alienable, as Cheal says. Indeed the person who purchases a present to give to a friend simply puts in reverse the same process

---

[38] However, see Ray Abrahams, 'Plus ça change, plus c'est la même chose?' For Festschrift for J. A. Barnes (n.d.). Ties are occasionally established between the relatives of organ donors and the recipients. Abrahams, drawing on analogies with gift-giving, explores what is both new and old in the identities set up by organ transplant; 'racial' origin remains an uninvited guest at the debate. I am grateful for permission to cite the paper.

which makes it possible for him/her to donate body substance to a blood bank, cadaver to science. An anonymously-produced object becomes part of a store on which others draw. Preserving the social anonymity of market goods is of course fundamental to the supposition that goods are available for all. That such goods can be appropriated by the consumer and fashioned to the ends of personal identity[39] – the wrapped present, the exhibited taste – is part of the cultural interpretation of consumption as consumerism.[40]

While they may express personal identity, *goods do not have to be made into gifts* in order to do so. Gifts between persons can make statements about relationships, yet a relationship is not necessary to the creation of identity. The analogy with reproductive process is evident: genetic identity does not imply a social relationship.

As I understand it, what Euro-Americans call gifts in late twentieth-century consumer culture, whether body substance or merchandise, are regarded as extensions of the self insofar as they carry the expression of sentiments. Sentiments are commonly expressed toward other persons, but they may equally well be directed to abstract entities such as 'society.' For sentiments emanate outwards from the person, *whether or not they are 'received' by specific others*. They thus appear as the person would like to appear, autonomous, charitable. Sentiment is supposed to have positive connotations in the same way as near relations are supposed to be benign, and presents carry positive overtones of sociability and affection. Hence Cheal's closeted language of community and intimacy.

Indeed, the kinds of presents Cheal describes are like the 'goods' of classical economy: objects of desire. It is individuals, he observes, who give and receive goods and who reproduce their relations with others, though they do so, I would add, from their own vantage point (of desire). Cheal himself offers a comparison (*GE* 10); he takes the free disposition of items as distinguishing the gift in the moral economy of suburban Canada from those reciprocities allegedly described by Gregory that put people into a state of (his term not Gregory's) bondage.[41] It is the alienability of the former that confers freedom. The sentiment such items express springs

---

[39] See Miller, *Material Culture and Mass Consumption;* and Daniel Miller, 'Appropriating the State on the Council Estate,' *Man* n.s. 23 (1988), pp. 353-72.

[40] For nonconsumerist appropriations, I cite two examples. One is Pnina Werbner's remarkable account of 'capital, gifts and offerings among British Pakistanis' (*The Migration Process: Capital, Gifts and Offerings among British Pakistanis* (Oxford: Berg, 1990)); the other Mayfair Mei-Hui Yang's critique of 'second-economy' arguments in relation to gifts and the state redistributive economy in contemporary China ('The Gift Economy and State Power in China,' *Comparative Studies in Society and History* 31 (1989), pp. 25-54).

[41] See Gregory, *Gifts and Commodities.*

from within the individual person, and it is the flow of sentiment (the ideology of love) that makes relationships. As a consequence Euro-American gift-giving really only works as a sign of personal commitment if it is also a sign of benign feeling. Benign feeling in turn is presented as an attribute of the small-scale, with its dialectic of intimacy and community. This confident equation of the small-scale with the interpersonal is, to say the least, an interesting cultural comment on the dimensions of persons.

Where the cycling of gifts among kin effects the procreation and regeneration of relationships, this can comprise activity of a cosmic order. Consider the Melanesian Sabarl on the eastern tip of the Massim archipelago.[42] Not only is this tiny dialect group of fewer than a thousand people able to account for the beginning of time, their gift exchanges are of universal dimensions. No part-societies here; the entire system of production, distribution, and consumption is a process of personification 'that converts food and objects and people into other people.'[43] And society does not exist apart from other people; rather, persons are of global dimensions, sociality integral to them. This is made evident by their parentage. A person is forever a dependant with respect to his or her father's clan, with whom he/she is involved in a lifetime of exchanges. Dependency is conceptualized in terms of specific relations: a member of the father's clan acts as a designated 'father' to the eternal 'child' whom he 'feeds,' an activity that lasts from conception till burial when it must be stopped.[44] In this matrilineal society, paternal kin are keepers of mortality and the father's donations have effect (only) for as long as the child lives. This is no more nor less 'bondage' than one might say one is a slave to life or, in Aristotle's terms, a victim of paternal motility.

The partner in such exchanges is always another and specific person. Gifts are never free-standing: they have value because they are attached to one social source ('father') in being destined for another ('child') and, whether they originate in labor or in other transactions, carry identity. Yet when all such encounters are interpersonal encounters, they convey no special connotations of intimacy. Nor of altruism as a source of benign feeling.

The Western notion of persons being contained by their environment/ society is indeed significant here, though not quite for Johnson's reasons. It enables Euro-Americans to think of the gift as altruistic by the conceivable

[42] See Debbora Battaglia, *On the Bones of the Serpent: Person, Memory and Mortality in Sabarl Island Society* (Chicago: University of Chicago Press, 1990).

[43] Ibid., p. 191, emphasis omitted.

[44] See Debbora Battaglia, ' "We Feed Our Father": Paternal Nurture among the Sabarl of Papua New Guinea,' *American Ethnologist* 12 (1985), pp. 427-41.

analogy of a gesture toward exactly such abstract entities.[45] Altruistic gestures toward other persons are invariably tempered by the after-effect of realizing that one's own self-interest must be bound up somewhere, if only in maintaining one's (social) environment. Conversely, it is possible to think of gifts as voluntarily given despite social pressure and obligation precisely because they conventionally typify those relations that are made through the spontaneous emission of emotions.

Voluntarism: recipients and consumers

Consumer culture, it would seem, springs from the perpetual emanations of desire held to radiate from each individual person. This wellspring is like the bottomless pit of need that Euro-Americans are also supposed to suffer, such as the celebrated biological need for women to have children – a 'drive to reproduce.'[46] In meeting need and desire, the individual person expresses the essential self. A rhetoric of accumulation is thus bound to the voluntarism of individual effort. One might remark that the constant necessity for the individual to implement his or her subjectivity has its own coercive force.

If there is a similarity between the coercions of gift-giving in Melanesia and late-twentieth-century consumerism, then we may indeed find its echo in the desire/drive/need for the individual to act as a free agent. With two differences. One, that on the Melanesian side the need is located not in the agent but in those 'other persons' who cause the agent to act. Two, that Melanesian accumulation is tempered by the fact that acts, like relations, work to substitutive effect. Relations are not perpetually 'made.' Rather, relations are either made to appear or appear in their making; every new relationship displaces a former one. Each gift is a substitution for a previous gift. One extracts from another what one has had extracted from oneself. Thus de Coppet points to the chain of transformations that constitute the common task on which 'Are'Are society is based. An endless process of perpetual dissolution by which 'objects, animals, persons, or elements of persons' change continuous decay into life.[47]

---

[45] Parry arguing on this point also reinstates Mauss's purpose in *The Gift* as demonstrating just how we ever came to contrast interested and disinterested gifts. 'So while Mauss is generally represented as telling us how in fact the gift is never free, what I think he is really telling us is how we have acquired a theory that it should be' (Parry, 'The Gift,' p. 458, emphasis omitted). I merely point here to the further coercions of choice in the consumer world of compulsory subjectivity.

[46] Quoted in Stanworth, *Reproductive Technologies*, p. 15.

[47] De Coppet, 'The Life-Giving Death,' p. 201.

As elsewhere in Austronesian-speaking Melanesia,[48] a death divides survivors into mourners (feast givers) and workers (who bury the deceased and are feasted). In 'Are'Are each side makes a pile of food, topped with money, which reconstitutes the dead person. Not only do both piles incorporate food items from the other, the two piles are then exchanged. They replace the deceased with a composition both of the relations once integral to him or her, and of his or her basic elements, 'body' (taro and coconut), 'breath' (pork), and 'image' (money). These replacements enable the deceased's body/breath to be consumed, later themselves replaced by a further display composed entirely of money. First the workers take charge of it, then reassemble it for the mourners (the deceased's family) to dispose of; the latter return all the wealth received in the course of the funeral and thereby complete the final element, the ancestor's image.[49] The new ancestor is now accessible to his living descendants.

De Coppet refers to 'replacement' rather than substitution,[50] which for him carries too many resonances of displacing one individual object by another. Yet, as we have seen, what are also replaced are not just the elements that compose an individual but the relationships of which the person is composed. A relationship is 'replaced' through the substitution of a counterpart. The point is explicit in Battaglia's account of Sabarl mortuary ritual, where the actions of mourning and burial mobilize the respective maternal and paternal kin of the deceased. That person is visibly reconstituted in the assembling of funeral foods (sago pudding) and wealth (axe blades), simultaneously semen and bones being returned by maternal kin to the paternal.

These are gifts of life. Life is given in the necessity to consume the deceased as a physical presence and thus release the future – the ancestor to future descendants – from present relationships. As a consequence, the relations that composed and supported the deceased must be made finally visible. Most importantly, in the course of the funeral feasts, relations between maternal and paternal kin appear in the division between donors and recipients. The 'father' makes a final presentation of axe blades; maternal kin then substitute for these blades of their own and hand back the items with increment. But more than this. Food and valuables are composed into an image of the deceased before being given to the paternal kin. The Sabarl deceased is thus rendered into a form at once visible (in the abstract) and dissoluble (in its substance): its components can be consumed

---

[48] See *Death Rituals and Life in the Societies of the Kula Ring,* eds Frederick Damon and Roy Wagner (DeKalb, IL: Northern Illinois University Press, 1989).

[49] See de Coppet, 'The Life-Giving Death,' p. 188.

[50] See ibid., p. 202, n. 17.

or dissipated. '[P]eople consume other people.'[51] The dead die because the link between persons out of which the person was born is dissolved.

Insofar as one might imagine elements of this exchange sequence as involving the transfer of gifts, the obligation to receive cannot be reduced to the enactment of any one particular exchange. For the person to die, relationships must be undone. And once the person has died, paternal kin on Sabarl can no more avoid being the recipients of funeral gifts than the maternal body in Western discourse can avoid bearing a child.

Sabarl recipients are also consumers: that is, they turn these things (food, valuables) into their own bodies (to be eaten, distributed). Similarly de Coppet suggests that 'Are'Are life is dominated by the fact that it is one's own kin who have the ultimate right to consume one, body and breath being thereby absorbed back into body and breath to be available for future generations. The capacity to consume is thus the capacity to sub-stitute future relations for past ones. It depends on a double receptivity – to reabsorb parts of oneself and to be open to the (body) parts of others. The difference between death and life is the absence or presence of such rela-tionships with 'other' persons.

The Melanesian recipient of a gift who puts wealth into the recesses of a house, as a clan contains the external sources of its fertility within, is literally 'consuming' the gift. But the vitalizing power of the gift lies in the fact that it derives from an exogenous source. One attaches and contains the parts of specific others, for the process of attachment and detachment is the motility that signals life. Actions are registered (fractally) in the actions of other persons, each person's acts being thereby replaced, reconstituted, in new and even foreign persons/forms. Thus is the living person per-sonified.

By contrast, the latter-day Euro-American consumer draws from an impersonal domain, such as the market, goods that, in being turned into expressions of self-identity, become personalized. The exercise of choice is crucial; choice creates consumption as a subjective act. To evince sub-jectivity is to evince life. One may even appear to exercise 'more' sub-jectivity in some situations/relationships than in others. This rather bizarre notion – that ideally one ought always to act as a subject but cannot always do so – is symbolized in the special domain of interpersonal relations.

The Euro-American person is presented, then, as a potentially free-standing and whole entity (an individual subject or agent) contained within an abstract impersonal matrix which may include other persons but also includes other things as its context (environment/society). And this is the image of the consumer. Consumer choice is thinkable, I would suggest,

---

[51] Battaglia, *On the Bones of the Serpent*, p. 190.

precisely insofar as 'everything else' is held to lie beyond the fetus/embryo/ person: *anything consumed by that person comes from the outside,* whether or not the source is other persons. For generative power lies in the individual person's own desire for experience. Desire and experience: the principal dimensions of the consumer's relationship with his/her environment. And the field is infinite; it consists of the sum of all the possibilities that may be sampled. Satisfied from without, the impetus is held to spring from within.[52] While individual desires may be stimulated by the outside world – advertising, marketing, and so forth – that in turn is supposed to be oriented to the consumer's wants.

Whereas the Melanesian capacity to receive has to be nurtured in and elicited from a partner, sometimes to the point of coercion, the twentieth-century consumer is depicted as having infinite appetite. Above all, the consumer is a consumer of experience and thus of him/her self. Perhaps it is against the compulsion of appetite, the coercion of having to choose, the prescriptiveness of subjective self-reference, that the possibility of unbidden goods and unanticipated experiences presents itself as exotic. The 'free gift.'

My assertions have no doubt resisted certain commonsense formulations (one cannot see a gift) only to substitute others (we know what a consumer is). And to suggest that the issues which the concept of the gift trails through anthropological accounts – a relational view of the person, altruism, voluntarism – have to be understood in terms of its culture of origin is hardly original. But perhaps the particular substitution I mention here has interest. Given the part that so-called gift exchange plays in the reproduction of persons in Melanesia, it was not inapposite to consider the new language of gifting that accompanies the propagation of late-twentieth-century reproductive technologies. There we discover the Euro-American person as a free-standing entity interacting with its environment, a figure missing from the twentieth-century Melanesian pantheon. The first question to ask, then, is what kind of person the Melanesian gift reproduces.

The double orientation of gifts in consumer culture presupposes two kinds of relationships: an individual person's interpersonal relations with others and an individual person's relations with society. Melanesian gifts on the other hand presuppose two kinds of persons, partners divided by their transaction: paternal from maternal kin, fetus from placenta, clans-

---

[52] I am compressing several arguments and contested positions here, and do not specify where the view is held. It alludes but does not do justice to Miller's reading of consumption as symbolic labor (the consumer recontextualizes the commodity and objectifies it afresh as a source of inalienable value). See Miller, *Material Culture and Mass Consumption.*

men from the ground they cultivate, descendants from ancestors. Gifts may come from an outside source, but that source is hardly imagined as beyond persons in the way the talents and the riches of the world seemingly come from God in Davis's sixteenth-century France.[53] For even where the other person is imagined as a deity or spirit or as the very land itself, the Melanesian act of giving that divides recipient from donor presupposes a partnering of finite identities. By contrast, the gift capable of extending a personalized self into a potentially infinite universe turns the person into a potential recipient of everything.

Late twentieth-century and Euro-American, the embryo visualized as a homunculus is a consumer in the making. For the consumer actualizes his or her relationship with society/the environment in its own body process. This prompts a second question: whether gift-giving in a consumer culture contests the coercive nature of this relationship or is another example of it.

---

[53] See Natalie Zemon Davis, 'Gifts, Markets and Communities in Sixteenth-Century France,' a paper presented to the conference *The Gift and Its Transformations*, National Humanities Center (1990). For a Melanesian Christian counterpart, see C. A. Gregory, 'Gifts to Men and Gifts to God: Gift Exchange and Capital Accumulation in Contemporary Papua,' *Man* n.s. 15, pp. 626-52.

71

3. 'Animism' revisited: Personhood, environment, and relational epistemology

Nurit Bird-David

Editor's introduction

Nurit Bird-David's re-visitation of the term 'animism' in anthropology and ethnography identifies Irving Hallowell's article as a 'provocative starting point'. Her rich analysis contributes to the reclamation of a contested term most associated with Edward Tylor's *Primitive Culture* (1871). The original abstract of her article noted that

> 'Animism' is projected in the literature as simple religion and a failed epistemology, to a large extent because it has hitherto been viewed from modernist perspectives. In this paper previous theories, from classical to recent, are critiqued. An ethnographic example of a hunter-gatherer people is given to explore how animistic ideas operate within the context of social practices, with attention to local constructions of a relational personhood and to its relationship with ecological perceptions of the environment. A reformulation of their animism as a relational epistemology is offered.

In short, 'animism' is redefined not as a primitive category error (that delayed the evolution of real science by proffering childish religion) but as a complex relational epistemology and engagement with particular environments.

Reprinted from *Current Anthropology* 40, pp. 67-79, 1999. By permission of the University of Chicago Press. I am indebted to Ingrid Jordt for her penetrating insights and commentary. I thank Tim Ingold for instructive comments, some of which will await follow-up work. I acknowledge with pleasure comments on earlier drafts generously offered by Kalman Applbaum, Debbi Bernstein, Eva Illouz, Steve Kaplan, Yoram Carmeli, Nira Reiss, and Zvi Sobel.

Hallowell is praised for circumventing modernist dichotomies such as spirit/body and natural/supernatural that have arisen from and reinforced Western theorising about the 'supernatural' and 'spirit' as central to a social domain called 'religion'. It is also important that he showed that it is possible to discuss indigenous world-views without presuming that they are erroneous because they (might) conflict with objectivist dogma. However, Hallowell 'does not explain how the beliefs are engendered and perpetuated'. This is what she aims to do with reference to 'ethnographic material largely drawn from my work with Nayaka, a hunter-gatherer community of the forested Gir Valley in the Nilgiri region of South India'. In the process Bird-David draws on various other ethnographies and theorists.

The original article was followed by a series of 'comments' (critical and supportive) and the author's response (pp. S79-91). These significantly further the debate and will repay close consideration, but are not reprinted here.

The article is included in this collection because it contributes to a number of significant debates in the study of indigenous religions. Animism itself has been a leitmotif of such study, constructing and deconstructing indigeneity in its own right and in relation to modernity. Questions about human engagement with their environments (perhaps 'nature') are equally important and pervasive. In this regard, Bird-David's work develops not only that of Hallowell, but also that of Marilyn Strathern with reference to the giving of gifts in the construction of identity. The article is also immensely useful in the consideration of appropriate methods for research and communication, and of the representation of informants' and researcher's position, voices and reflections.

Reference

Tylor, Edward B. 1871. *Primitive Culture*. vol. 1: *Religion in Primitive Culture*. Reprinted in 1958, New York: Harper & Row.

᷈ᷠᷤ

Wherever there are Nayaka, there are also devaru, for Nayaka want to have them and always find them.

(Karriyen)

The concept of animism, which E. B. Tylor developed in his 1871 masterwork *Primitive Culture*, is one of anthropology's earliest concepts, if not the first.[1] The intellectual genealogy of central debates in the field goes back to it. Anthropology textbooks continue to introduce it as a basic notion, for example, as 'the belief that inside ordinary visible, tangible bodies there is normally invisible, normally intangible being: the soul ... each culture [having] its own distinctive animistic beings and its own specific elaboration of the soul concept' (Harris 1983: 186). Encyclopedias of anthropology commonly present it, for instance, as 'religious beliefs involving the attribution of life or divinity to such natural phenomena as trees, thunder, or celestial bodies' (Hunter and Whitten 1976: 12). The notion is widely employed within the general language of ethnology (e.g., Sahlins 1972: 166, 180; Gudeman 1986: 44; Descola 1996: 88) and has become important in other academic disciplines as well, especially in studies of religion (as belief in spirit-beings) and in developmental psychology (referring to children's tendency to consider things as living and conscious). Moreover, the word has become a part of the general English vocabulary and is used in everyday conversations and in the popular media. It appears in many dictionaries, including such elementary ones as the compact school and office edition of *Webster's New World Dictionary* (1989), which defines it as 'the belief that all life is produced by a spiritual force, or that all natural phenomena have souls.' It is found in mainstream compendia such as the *Dictionary of the Social Sciences* (Gould and Kolb 1965), which sums it up as 'the belief in the existence of a separable soul-entity, potentially distinct and apart from any concrete embodiment in a living individual or material organism.' The term is presented in dictionaries of the occult: the *Encyclopedia of Ghosts and Spirits* (Guilei 1992), for example, defines it as 'the system of beliefs about souls and spirits typically found in tribal societies,' and the *Dictionary of Mysticism and the Occult* (Drury 1985) defines it as 'the belief, common among many pre-literate societies, that trees, mountains, rivers and other natural formations possess an animating power or spirit.'

Amazingly, the century-old Tylorian concept appears in all these diverse sources (popular and academic, general and specific) revised little if at all. Animism, a 19th-century representation of an ethnographically researchable practice particularly conspicuous among indigenous peoples but by no means limited to them, is depicted by them all as an 'object' in-the-world. The survival of the Tylorian representation is enigmatic because the logic underlying it is today questionable. Tylor was not as rigid a positivist as he is often made out to be (see Ingold 1986: 94-6; Leopold 1980). However, he developed this representation within a positivistic spiritual/materialist

---

[1]   *Primitive Culture* led Tylor to an appointment as Reader in Anthropology in Oxford University, the first such position in the academic world (Preus 1987: 131).

dichotomy of 19th-century design in direct opposition to materialist science, in the belief (and as part of an effort to prove this belief) that only science yielded 'true' knowledge of the world. Furthermore, the moral implications of this representation are unacceptable now. Tylor posited that 'animists' understood the world childishly and erroneously, and under the influence of 19th-century evolutionism he read into this cognitive underdevelopment. Yet the concept still pervasively persists.

Equally surprisingly, the ethnographic referent – the researchable cultural practices which Tylor denoted by the signifier/signified of 'animism' – has remained a puzzle[2] despite the great interest which the subject has attracted. Ethnographers continue to cast fresh ethnographic material far richer than Tylor had (or could have imagined possible) into one or more of the Tylorian categories 'religion,' 'spirits,' and 'supernatural beings' (e.g., Endicott 1979; Howell 1984; Morris 1981; Bird-David 1990; Gardner 1991; Feit 1994; Povinelli 1993; Riches 1994). At the same time, they have commonly avoided the issue of animism and even the term itself rather than revisit this prevalent notion in light of their new and rich ethnographies.[3]

A twofold vicious cycle has ensued. The more the term is used in its old Tylorian sense, without benefit of critical revision, the more Tylor's historically situated perspective is taken as 'real,' as the phenomenon which it only glosses, and as a 'symbol that stands for itself' (Wagner 1981). In turn, anthropology's success in universalizing the use of the term itself reinforces derogatory images of indigenous people whose rehabilitation from them is one of its popular roles.

This paper attempts a solution generally drawing on a synthesis of current environment theory (insisting that the environment does not necessarily consist dichotomously of a physical world and humans) and current personhood theory (asserting that personhood does not necessarily consist dualistically of body and spirit). These dualistic conceptions are historical constructs of a specific culture which, for want of a better term, will henceforth be referred to by the circumlocution 'modernist.' ('Modernist' signals neither the dichotomous opposite of 'primitive' nor the equivalent of 'scientific' but ideas and practices that dominated the Euro-American cultural landscape from the 17th to the 20th century. Furthermore, 'modernist self-concepts' will be used as an objectification of what is often only a fragment of peoples' composite identity, a part of their

---

[2] It is regarded 'one of the oldest anthropological puzzles' by Descola (1996: 82).

[3] An exception coming close to revisiting the notion is Hallowell (1960); a liminal exception is Guthrie's recent revisit (1993); Descola (1992; 1996) contrasts 'totemic systems' and 'animic systems' but does not look deeply into animism as such.

consciousness, while 'local person-concepts' will be used as an objectification of fragments of today's complex indigenous identities and, in partial ways, of parts of Western identities, too.) The argument will develop through three subsequent sections to its twofold conclusion: a fresh visit to the animism concept and to the indigenous phenomena themselves. It will posit a plurality of epistemologies by refiguring so-called primitive animism as a relational epistemology. The perspective to be employed is presented not as more valid than any other but as one now needed in studies of the complex phenomena which Tylor denoted as 'animism.'

The first part offers a critical perspective on the 'textual conversation' (to use Gudeman and Rivera's (1990) term) relevant to animism to date, singling out for close attention the theories of Tylor (1958 (1871), Durkheim (1960 [1914]; 1915), Lévi-Strauss (1962; 1966 [1962]), and Guthrie (1993). It is argued that positivistic ideas about the meaning of 'nature,' 'life,' and 'personhood' misdirected these previous attempts to understand the local concepts. Classical theoreticians (it is argued) attributed their own modernist ideas of self to 'primitive peoples' while asserting that the 'primitive peoples' read their idea of self into others! This led the theoreticians to prejudge the attribution of 'personhood' to natural objects as empirically unfounded and consequently to direct analytical effort to explaining why people did it and why and how (against all appearances) their 'belief' was not a part of their practical knowledge but at best a part of their symbolic representations or a mistaken strategic guess.

The second part of the paper offers an ethnographic analysis of the phenomenon which Tylor termed 'animism' largely drawn from my work with hunter-gatherer Nayaka in South India.[4] A case is developed through the ethnographic material, starting from Hallowell's remarkable 1960 'Ojibwa Ontology, Behavior, and World View' and circumventing the 'spirit/body' and 'natural/supernatural' modernist dichotomies that have often landed other ethnographers in 'spirit,' 'supernatural,' and 'religion' descriptions. Nayaka *devaru* (superpersons) are tackled as a concept and a phenomenon, both composite and complex, in a threefold manner. First, using Strathern's (1988) notion of the 'dividual' (a person constitutive of relationships), after Marriott's (1976) 'dividual' (a person constitutive of transferable particles that form his or her personal substance), I argue that devaru are dividual persons. They are constitutive of sharing relationships

---

[4] Fieldwork was conducted in 1978-9 and was followed by a revisit in 1989. Research was supported by a Smutz Visiting Fellowship, an Anthony Wilkin Studentship, an H. M. Chadwick Studentship, and funds from the Jerusalem Foundation for Anthropological Studies and the Horovitz Institute for Research of Developing Countries. For ethnographic background see Bird-David (1989; 1996).

reproduced by Nayaka with aspects of their environment. The devaru are objectifications of these relationships and make them known. Second, drawing on Gibson (1979) and Ingold (1992), I posit that in another sense devaru are a constitutive part of Nayaka's environment, born of the 'affordances' of events in-the-world. Nayaka's 'attention' ecologically perceives mutually responsive changes in things in-the-world and at the same time in themselves. These relatednesses are devaru in-the-world, met by Nayaka as they act in, rather than think about, the world. Lastly, I argue that devaru performances – in which performers in trance 'bring to life' devaru characters, with whom the participants socialize (talking, joking, arguing, singing, sharing or just demand-sharing, and asking for advice and help) – are social experiences which are nested within (not dichotomized from) social-economic practice. These performances are pivotal in both 'educating the attention' to devaru in-the-world (Gibson 1979) and reproducing devaru as dividual persons.

The third part of the paper theorizes animism as animisms, arguing that hunter-gatherer animism constitutes a relational (not a failed) epistemology. This epistemology is about knowing the world by focusing primarily on relatednesses, from a related point of view, within the shifting horizons of the related viewer. The knowing grows from and *is* the knower's skills of maintaining relatedness with the known. This epistemology is regarded by Nayaka (and probably other indigenous peoples we call hunter-gatherers) as authoritative against other ways of knowing the world. It functions in other contexts (including Western) with, against, and sometimes despite other local authoritative epistemologies. Diversifying along with person-concepts and environmental praxis, animisms are engendered neither by confusion nor by wrong guesses but by the employment of human socially biased cognitive skills.

Animism in the modernist mirror

Sir Edward Burnett Tylor (1831-1917), the founding father of anthropology, took his notion of animism from the 17th-century alchemist Stahl, who had himself revived the term from classical theory (Tylor 1958 [1871]: 9). Drawing on secondhand accounts of 'primitive' peoples (to use the period's term), Tylor observed that many of them attributed life and personality to animal, vegetable, and mineral alike. He developed a theory of this phenomenon in a series of papers written between 1866 and 1870 that culminated in *Primitive Culture*. Tylor offered a situated perspective, limited by the time's ethnography and theory, and it should be studied in its context.

As he developed his theory of animism, Tylor took an interest in the modern spiritualist movement, fashionable at the time. He even went to London from Somerset for a month to investigate spiritualist séances (Stocking 1971). In 1869 he argued that 'modern spiritualism is a survival and a revival of savage thought' (quoted in Stocking 1971: 90). This argument probably influenced his view of 'savage thought,' which he had acquired only from reading. In an odd reversal, he constructed the origin of 'savage thought' from his first-hand knowledge of what he presumed was its remnant – modern spiritualism. He even considered using the term 'spiritualism' rather than 'animism' but decided against it because it had 'become the designation of a particular modern sect' (1958 [1871]: 10). Under the probable influence of his knowledge of modern spiritualism, Tylor argued that in the savage view every man had, in addition to his body, a 'ghost-soul,' a 'thin unsubstantial human image,' the 'cause of life or thought in the individual it animates,' capable 'of leaving the body far behind' and 'continuing to exist and appear to men after the death of that body' (quoted in Stocking 1987: 192). Being 'a confirmed scientific rationalist' (p. 191), Tylor suggested that this view was a delusion, in the same way that he regarded the spiritual séances of his time as a delusion.

Tylor's work was probably also influenced by observations of children (see Stocking 1971: 90). He argued that the 'savages' were doubly mistaken, believing in their own 'ghost-souls' but like children attributing the same to things around them. Durkheim (1915: 53) neatly made the point as follows:

> For Tylor, this extension of animism was due to the particular mentality of the primitive, who, like an infant, cannot distinguish the animate and the inanimate. Since the first beings of which the child commences to have an idea are men, that is, himself and those around him, it is upon this model of human nature that he tends to think of everything. ... Now the primitive thinks like a child. Consequently, he also is inclined to endow all things, even inanimate ones, with a nature analogous to his own.

Tylor's view conformed with the contemporaneous identification of early people with the child state of society (animating society!) and with the identification of contemporaneous 'primitives' with early people and so with the child state too. However, while arguing that in thinking like a child the primitive 'endow[s] all things, even inanimate ones, with a nature analogous to his own,' Tylor read into the primitive view the modernist spiritualist understanding of 'one's own nature,' not the primitive's or the child's sense of 'his own nature.'

At issue at the time was how religion had evolved and how it ought to be related to science. This evolutionary question engaged Tylor, who suggested that modern religion had evolved in stages from animistic beliefs. By them early peoples had tried to explain the world to themselves, and these beliefs had 'survived' into the present and (re)appeared universally among children and 'primitive' people and in certain modern cults. In Tylor's view, as one of his commentators put it, 'it was as though primitive man, in an attempt to create science, had accidentally created religion instead, and mankind had spent the rest of evolutionary time trying to rectify the error' (Stocking 1987: 192).

In Tylor's view, animism and science (in a 'long-waged contest' (1886), quoted by Stocking 1987: 192) were fundamentally antithetical. Consequently, animistic beliefs featured as 'wrong' ideas according to Tylor, who clinched the case by explaining in evolutionary terms (as was the custom at the time) how the primitive came to have this spiritualist sense of his 'own nature.' Tylor suggested that dreams of dead relatives and of the primitive himself in distant places had led him to form this self idea. The thesis projected the primitive as delirious as well as perceiving the world like a child.

Tylor's theory has had deep and lasting influence on anthropological theory. It was pivotal in its time, and subsequent theories developed in dialectical relations with it in turn became themselves influential theories in dialectical relations with which further theories were formulated. I point to one critical theoretical trend pertinent to my study by means of several examples (selected for temporal diversity, not necessarily centrality in the field) from classic theories to recent ones. My examples chronologically advance from Emile Durkheim's work on religion (1960 [1914]; 1915) through Claude Lévi-Strauss's work on totemism and the 'savage mind' (1962; 1966 [1962]) to a recent work on anthropomorphism by Stewart Guthrie (1993).

Durkheim rescued the primitive from the Tylorian image of a delirious human, but in doing so he embroiled himself further in the modernist self model(s). In an article significantly entitled 'The Dualism of Human Nature and Its Social Conditions' (1960 [1914]), he argued that the primitive self model is 'not a vain mythological concept that is without foundations in reality' (p. 329) – that 'in every age' man had had a dualistic model originating from a basic and universal social experience, the simultaneous sense of bodily sensations and being part of society. The primitive self model, in his view, was a specific case of this (modernist) universal model. He argued that the primitive makes abstract society tangible to himself by a totem and so views his own self as dualistically consisting of body/totemic parts (rather than body/mind in the modernist view). Durkheim restored credence in the primitive self model but remained critical, along with Tylor, of its attribution to other than human entities. He still cast this attribution (again, with Tylor) as the erroneous mental operation of a child.

Durkheim also read his own modernist (biologistic) kinship into accounts suggesting that 'primitive peoples' regarded as kin and friends some entities that were animated by them. Drawing on richer ethnographic sources than Tylor's, he noted that 'primitives' believed that the bonds between them and these natural entities were 'like those which unite the members of a single family' (1915: 139): bonds of friendship, inter-dependence, and shared characteristics and fortunes (pp. 158-60).[5] To explain this, he argued that they mistook the spiritual unity of the totemic force, which 'really' existed, for a bodily unity of flesh, which did not. He himself obviously mistook their kinship for his modernist construction of it as shared biological matter (flesh, blood, DNA, or whatever other finer biological connection will be discovered by scientists (Schneider 1968; 1984)).

Claude Lévi-Strauss addressed the anthropological category 'totemism,' which encompasses aspects of the phenomenon which Tylor termed 'ani-mism.' His work provided the first modern explanation that accepted indigenous knowledge of the world. However, the explanation rested on dissociating that knowledge from totemic notions, reducing the latter to symbolic representations. Lévi-Strauss did not question the authority of the Western objectivist view of reality, which accepted a priori the nature/society dualism. To rehabilitate the Durkheimian primitives he argued that indigenous peoples perceived the world in this way, too. They perceived the discontinuity between nature and society and viewed nature itself as a world of discrete objects; then they used nature as 'something good to think with' about societal divisions. They drew analogies between things in nature and groups in society (1962). They concerned themselves with the same representations of things in the world as Westerners did, but their 'totemic thought' fancifully intermingled these representations with mys-tical tales, like the *bricoleur,* whereas our 'scientific thought' logically sorted them out, like the engineer (1966 [1962]). The indigenous accounts of kinship relationships with natural entities, Lévi-Strauss argued, only evinced the analogical and totemic nature of their thought – neither an erroneous epistemology nor an adequate alternative to our own. He cri-ticized earlier theory for placing indigenous peoples on the 'nature' side of the dualistic nature/culture split. However, while he correctively placed them on the 'culture' side, he placed the dualistic split itself inside their

---

5 Durkheim distinguished between natural entities, or 'individual totems,' regarded as friends and kin, and 'group totems,' the artifactual representations of natural entities, worshipped in celebrations.

'savage mind' (1966 [1962]). He did not explain animism but explained it away. Animists by his theory did not perceive the natural world differently from others.

A recent attempt at a solution to the century-old problem why people animate what we regard as inanimate objects is that of Stewart Guthrie (1993), who defines animating things in these words: 'Scanning the world for what most concerns us – living things and especially humans – we find many apparent cases. Some of these prove illusory. When they do, we are animating (attributing life to the nonliving) or anthropomorphizing (attributing human characteristics to the nonhuman)' (1993: 62). The expression 'attributing life to the nonliving' at a stroke relegates animistic beliefs to the category of 'mistake,' regressing from the earlier advance made by Lévi-Strauss. Guthrie regards modernist meanings of such notions as 'life,' 'nonliving,' and 'human' as naturally given.[6]

Guthrie reduces what Tylor offered as a universal cultural category (Preus 1987) to a universal biological one. He views animistic thinking as a natural 'perceptual strategy' for the survival of any animal (pp. 38, 41, 47, 54, 61):

> We not infrequently are in doubt as to whether something is alive. When we are in doubt, the best strategy is to assume that it is ... risking over-interpretation by betting on the most significant possibility ... because if we are wrong we lose little and if we are right we gain much ... Animism, then, results from a simple form of game theory employed by animals ranging at least from frogs to people ... [it] is an inevitable result of normal perceptual uncertainty and of good perceptual strategy ... The mistake embodied in animism – a mistake we can discover only after the fact – is the price of our need to discover living organisms. It is a cost occasionally incurred by any animal that perceives.

This cognitive evolutionist explanation of animism seems ingeniously simple. Assuming, with Tylor, that animistic interpretations are erroneous, Guthrie argues that the *making* of animistic interpretations itself is part of 'a good perceptual strategy.' Animistic interpretations are 'reasonable' errors that 'we can discover only after the fact.'

---

[6] Guthrie perceptively discusses the boundaries 'life'/'nonliving' and 'human'/ 'animal' as they are diversely drawn across cultures (e.g., 1993: 86-9, 112-13), but he makes this observation in support of his argument that it is difficult to differentiate between these entities.

81

But Guthrie's thesis is weak in its own terms.[7] We lapse into animistic expressions under uncertainty, but we use such expressions more, and more consistently, when we regularly and closely engage with things we are not doubtful about: plants we grow, cars we love, computers we use. (Guthrie himself mentions these examples.) Even professional ethologists, who are trained to regard their study animals as objects, regard them as persons the more they interact with them (see Kennedy 1992: 27). The theory in any case does not resolve the classic enigma of so-called primitive people's maintenance of animistic beliefs. At best, the question remains why (if they retrospectively recognize their animistic interpretations as mistakes) they culturally endorse and elaborate these 'mistakes.' At worst, the theory further downgrades indigenous cognitive ability, for now they cannot do even what frogs can do, namely, 'after the fact' recognize their 'mistakes.' In this case, the theory even regresses from the advances made by Tylor.

Local senses of devaru

Personhood concepts and ecological perception are two fruitful areas from which to reevaluate our theories of animist practices and beliefs. Irving Hallowell's ethnography of the Ojibwa (from fieldwork conducted in the Lake Winnipeg area of northern Canada during the 1930s) and especially his paper 'Ojibwa Ontology, Behavior, and World View' (1960) are provocative starting points for our reassessment of theories of animism. Hallowell observed that the Ojibwa sense of personhood, which they attribute to some natural entities, animals, winds, stones, etc., is fundamentally different from the modernist one. The latter takes the axiomatic split between 'human' and 'nonhuman' as essential, with 'person' being a subcategory of 'human.' The Ojibwa conceives of 'person' as an overarching category within which 'human person,' 'animal person,' 'wind person,' etc., are subcategories. Echoing Evans-Pritchard's account of Azande magic (1937), Hallowell furthermore argues that, contrary to received wisdom and in the absence of objectivist dogma, experience itself does not rule out Ojibwa animistic ideas. On the contrary, he argues (a

---

[7] Guthrie focuses on what he calls 'the West' because 'animism is usually attributed to simple societies.' His examples, taken out of their contexts, range from French and Spanish cave art through Greek, Roman, and medieval philosophy and the arts to modern science, social science, literature and advertisement, and 'daily life in the contemporary United States.' His scant references to 'simple societies' draw not on the richer new ethnography but on outdated secondary sources such as Thompson (1955) and Ehnmark (1939).

point reiterated by later ethnographers (see Scott 1989; Feit 1994)), experience is consistent with their reading of things, given an animistic dogma.

Hallowell's contribution is to free the study of animistic beliefs and practices first from modernist person-concepts and second from the presumption that these notions and practices are erroneous. However, the case needs to be further pursued. He states that the Ojibwa sense of personhood is different without exploring its sense far enough, perhaps because, although the concept goes back to Marcel Mauss's work of 1938,[8] before the 1960s research into the 'person' as a cross-cultural category hardly existed. He argues that Ojibwa engagement in the world does not rebuff their animistic views but does not explain how the beliefs are engendered and perpetuated. I shall pursue his insight through ethnographic material largely drawn from my work with Nayaka, a hunter-gatherer community of the forested Gir Valley in the Nilgiri region of South India.[9] My objective will be to understand the senses of what they call devaru, a concept which is not just a foreign word requiring translation but enigmatic to positivistic thought. Neither 'spirits' (deriving from the spirit/body dualism of the modernist person-concept) nor 'supernatural beings' (mirroring the Western idea of nature)[10] is an appropriate English equivalent, though these are the common translations of corresponding notions in other studies.[11] Hallowell's alternative 'other-than-human persons' escapes these biased notions but still conserves the primary objectivist concern with classes (human and other-than-human). I use 'superpersons' (persons with extra powers) as a general reference and let the local composite meanings grow from the context.

Devaru as objectifications of sharing relationships

In her critically oriented comparison of the Melanesian and the Euro-American 'person,' Strathern (1988) argues that the irreducibility of the individual is a peculiarly modernist notion.[12] It is not everywhere that the individual is regarded as 'a single entity,' 'bounded and integrated, and set

---

[8] Mauss's work was first translated into English only in 1979 (and see 1985). For some recent works on the 'self' see Morris (1994); Carrithers, Collins, and Lukes (1985); and Shweder and LeVine (1984).

[9] The Gir Valley is a fictive name for one of the Nilgiri-Wynaad's valleys.

[10] See Durkheim (1915); Lovejoy (1948); Saler (1977); Descola (1996).

[11] See Endicott (1979); Howell (1984); Morris (1981); Bird-David (1990); Gardner (1991); Feit (1994); Povinelli (1993); and, for a comparison, Mageo and Howard (1996).

[12] See also Dumont (1966).

contrastingly against other such wholes and against a natural and social backgrounds' (Clifford Geertz, quoted in Strathern 1988: 57). The Melanesian 'person' is a composite of relationships, a microcosm homologous to society at large (1988: 13, 131). This person objectifies relationships and makes them known. She calls it a 'dividual,' in contrast with the (Euro-American) '*in*dividual.'[13] This is a notion well known in South Asian scholarship from the work of McKim Marriott and Ronald Inden (Marriott 1976; Marriott and Inden 1977; see Daniel 1984; Raheja 1988a; 1988b; and Barnett 1976 for ethnographic explorations), who agree with Dumont (1966) that 'the Indian is misrepresented if depicted as an individual, but less because the person has a holistic-collectivist identity than because, according to Indian ways of thinking and explaining, each person is a composite of transferable particles that form his or her personal substance' (Mines 1994: 6).

I derive from Strathern's 'dividual' (a person constitutive of relationships) the verb 'to dividuate,' which is crucial to my analysis. When I individuate a human being I am conscious of her 'in herself' (as a single separate entity); when I dividuate her I am conscious of how she relates with me. This is not to say that I am conscious of the relationship with her 'in itself,' as a thing. Rather, I am conscious of the *relatedness with* my interlocutor *as I engage with her,* attentive to what she does in relation to what I do, to how she talks and listens to me as I talk and listen to her, to what happens simultaneously and mutually to me, to her, to *us.*

Nayaka, I argue, lived in a social environment which facilitated and was reproduced by dividuating fellow Nayaka.[14] Numbering in 1978-79 fewer than 70 persons, they occupied five sites at a distance of 2-10 km from each other. The largest was made up of five dwellings, the others of between one and three. The dwellings (thatched huts with walls made of interwoven strips of bamboo) stood close to each other, though the terrain would have allowed their dispersal. They contained one, two, or sometimes even three living spaces, barely separated from each other, each occupied by a nuclear family. Weather permitting, families rested, ate, and slept in the open beside outdoor fireplaces only a few meters apart. They led their domestic lives together, sharing space, things, and actions. They experienced simultaneously what happened to them and to their fellow Nayaka. This

---

[13] Ingold (personal communication) points out that Strathern's use of the concept 'dividual' is unsatisfactory. She argues for a relational personhood, but the concept assumes that the person is some kind of substantive entity, divisible or indivisible. Perhaps another term is called for.

[14] Elsewhere I have examined other aspects of this social environment, calling it an 'immediate social environment' (Bird-David 1994), absorbing Schutz and Luckmann's (1973) sense of 'immediacy' and the earlier use of the word in hunter-gatherer scholarship (esp. Meillassoux 1973 and Woodburn 1980; 1982).

was the case with respect to most Nayaka in the Gir area, not just the residents of one's own place, because there was much movement between sites and people stayed at each other's places for days, weeks, and even months at a time.

The idea that one shared space, things, and actions with others was central to the Nayaka view of social life. A Nayaka was normatively expected to share with everybody *as and when present,* especially (but not only) large game, irrespective of preexisting social ties, criteria, and entitlement. Sharing with anyone present was as important as if not more important than effecting a distribution of things among people. A Nayaka was, furthermore, expected to give others what they asked for, whatever this might be, to preempt refusals and hence challenges to the felt sense that 'all of us here share with each other.' The idea and practice of sharing constituted a habitus within which agentive negotiation, manipulation, and nonconformity took place (see Bird-David 1990). For example, normally people shared things requested of them, but when exceptionally they did not want to part with something, rather than disrupt the ongoing sense of sharing – the rhythm of everyday social life – they hid that thing or avoided people. This way, they preempted chances of sharing requests and refusals. Equally, people excessively requested things from people they wanted to embarrass or manipulate into persistent giving.

As I understand it, this common experience of sharing space, things, and actions contextualized Nayaka's knowledge of each other: they dividuated each other. They gradually got to know not how each talked but how each *talked with* fellows, not how each worked but how each *worked with* fellows, not how each shared but how each *shared with* fellows, etc. They got to know not other Nayaka in themselves but Nayaka *as they interrelated with* each other, Nayaka-in-relatedness with fellow Nayaka. Through cumulative experiences, they sensed each other as dividuated personalities, each with a relatively persisting way of engaging with others against the relative change involved in their mutual engagement. Nayaka speakers, for example, commonly described fellow Nayaka by the way they behaved vis-à-vis themselves, for instance, as 'Mathen who laughs a lot,' 'Mathen who listens attentively,' and so on (Mathen being one of a few personal names in circulation) (see Bird-David 1983).

Nayaka commonly objectified each other not as the Maussian 'character' – 'the locus (in everyday life) of different rights, duties, titles and kinship names within the clan' (Carrithers, Collins, and Lukes 1985: vii) – but as kin, relatives, 'ones related with.' In everyday social interaction they normally referred to and addressed each other by kinship terms ('my big-uncle,' 'my brother', 'my sister-in-law,' etc.). Anyone they persistently shared with (even a non-Nayaka person like the anthropologist) they regarded as kin.[15] They reckoned relationally which kinship term was appropriate at each moment (for example, calling 'my paternal uncle' the relative 'my father' called 'my brother' (see Bird-David 1994: 591-3)). They generally referred to people with whom they shared place, things, and actions as *sonta* ('relatives,' a term usually used with the prefix *nama*, 'our'), a notion that corresponds with other hunter-gatherer notions such as Pintupi *walytja* and Inuit *ila* (see Myers 1986; Guemple 1988). Their kinship was primarily made and remade by recurring social actions of sharing and relating with, not by blood or by descent, not by biology or by myth or genealogy.

Transcending idiosyncratic, processual, and multiple flows of meanings, the Nayaka sense of the person appears generally to engage not the modernist subject/object split or the objectivist concern with substances but the above-mentioned sense of kinship. The person is sensed as 'one whom we share with.' It is sensed as a relative and is normally objectified as kin, using a kinship term. The phrase *nama sonta* is used in the generalizing sense of the proverbial phrase 'we, the people.'[16] Its use extends beyond the Nayaka group (family, kindred, neighbors) to the aggregate of local people (Nayaka and others) with whom Nayaka closely engage. To return to Strathern's dividual (a person which objectifies relationships and makes them known), in the Nayaka context the dividual objectifies relationships of a certain kind, local kinship relationships which are objectifications of mutual sharing of space, things, and actions. Analytically referring to these relationships as 'sharing relationships' (because the term 'kinship relationships' inevitably invokes associations of biologistic or rights-and-duties kinship), we can say that the Nayaka dividual objectifies sharing relationships and makes them known. This dividual is *emergent,* constituted by relationships which in Fred Myers's words 'are not totally "given" [but] must be worked out in a variety of social processes' (1986: 159).

We cannot say – as Tylor did – that Nayaka 'think with' this idea of personhood about their environment, to arrive by projection at the idea of devaru. The idea of 'person' as a 'mental representation' applied to the world in pursuit of knowledge is modernist. I argue that Nayaka do not individuate but, in the sense specified above, dividuate other beings in their environment. They are attentive to, and work towards making, relatednesses. As they move and generally act in the environment, they are attentive to mutual behaviors and events. Periodically, they invite local

---

[15] This is a common phenomenon among hunter-gatherers, who have what Alan Barnard called 'a universal kinship system' (1981); Woodburn (1979) described this system as one in which everybody within the political community is regarded as kin.

[16] The name Nayaka is mostly used and was probably introduced by surrounding people.

devaru to visit them and share with them. Their composite personhood is constitutive of sharing relationships not only with fellow Nayaka but with members of other species in the vicinity. They *make* their personhood by producing and reproducing sharing relationships with surrounding beings, humans and others. They do not dichotomize other beings vis-à-vis themselves (see Bird-David 1992a) but regard them, while differentiated, as nested within each other. They recognize that the other beings have their different 'affordances' and are of diverse sorts, which is indicated among other things by the different words by which they refer to them (hills, elephants, etc.). However, Nayaka also appreciate that they share the local environment with some of these beings, which overrides these differences and absorbs their sorts into one 'we-ness.' Beings who are absorbed into this 'we-ness' are devaru, and while differentiated from *avaru* (people), they and avaru, in some contexts, are absorbed into one 'we-ness,' which Nayaka also call *nama sonta*. The devaru are often objectified by kinship terms, especially *ette* and *etta(n)* (grandmother and grandfather) and occasionally *dodawa* and *dodappa* ('big' mother and father). The use of kinship terms for superpersons, especially 'grandparents,' is common also among other hunter-gatherers (e.g., see Hallowell 1960: 27).

Maintaining relationships with fellow Nayaka but also with other local beings is critical to maintaining Nayaka identity because it is critical to maintaining personhood. They retain immediate engagement with the natural environment and hold devaru performances even when they make a living by different means such as casual labor. This is common among many other hunter-gatherers, even those well integrated into their respective states who live by such diverse means as state benefits or jobs in the state bureaucracy (see, e.g., Tanner 1979; Povinelli 1993; Bird-David 1992b). By maintaining relationships with other local beings to reproduce their personhood, Nayaka reproduce the devaru-ness of the other beings with whom they share. The other beings are drawn into interrelating and sharing with Nayaka and so into Nayaka kinship relationships. These relationships constitute the particular beings as devaru.

To summarize this point of the argument, the devaru objectify sharing relationships between Nayaka and other beings. A hill devaru, say, objectifies Nayaka relationships with the hill; it makes known the relationships between Nayaka and that hill. Nayaka maintain social relationships with other beings not because, as Tylor holds, they a priori consider them persons. *As and when* and *because* they engage in and maintain relationships with other beings, they constitute them as kinds of person: they make them 'relatives' by sharing with them and thus make them persons. They do not regard them as persons and subsequently some of them as relatives, as Durkheim maintains. In one basic sense of this

87

complex notion, devaru are relatives in the literal sense of being 'that or whom one interrelates with' (not in the reduced modern English sense of '*humans* connected with others by blood or affinity').[17] They are super-relatives who both need and can help Nayaka in extraordinary ways.

Devaru in-the-world

Devaru *exist* in the world, according to Nayaka, and this view is comprehensible in terms of Gibson's (1979) ecological approach to visual perception (introduced and popularized among anthropologists by Ingold (e.g., 1992, 1996; see Croll and Parkin 1992)). Gibson concerns himself with 'ambient vision,' 'obtained as the observer is turning his head and looking around,' the vision by which people (like other animals) perceive their environment in everyday life. He reconceptualizes the environment in ecological terms. It is permanent in some respects and changing in others; 'the "permanent objects" of the world are actually only objects that persist for a very long time' (p. 13). It consists of 'places, attached objects, objects and substances ... together with events, which are changes of these things' (p. 240). People perceive these things by registering their 'relative persistence' (or persistence-under-change, or 'in-variances') and 'relative change' (or change-above-persistence, or 'variances'). Things are perceived in terms of what they *afford the actor-perceiver because of what they are for him* (p. 138).[18] Their 'affordance,' as Gibson calls it, 'cuts across the dichotomy of subjective–objective ... It is equally a fact of the environment as a fact of behavior. It is both physical and psychical, yet neither. An affordance points both ways, to the environment and to the observer' (p. 123).

'Meaning' is not 'imposed' on things – it is not pre-given in consciousness – but 'discovered' in the course of action; it is also 'both physical and psychical, yet neither.' There is endless 'information' in the environment, by which Gibson means 'the specification of the observer's environment, not ... of the observer's receptors or sense organs' (p. 242). People continuously 'pick up' information in acting within the environment, by means of 'attention.' Gibsonian 'attention' is 'a skill that can be educated' (p. 246) to pick up information that is more and more subtle, elaborate, and precise

---

[17] The *Shorter Oxford English Dictionary: on historical principles* (1973, emphasis added). Interestingly, in premodern English 'relative' meant 'a thing (or person) standing in some relation to another.'

[18] Gibson often lapses into essentializing language – as in this case, where he refers to 'what things are' rather than to 'what things are for the actor-perceiver.' I have added the latter qualification.

(p. 245). Knowing is developing this skill; knowing is continuous with perceiving, of which it is an extension.

According to Gibson, attention is 'educated' through practice and also by means of 'aids to perceiving' such as stories and models of things, words and pictures. These are 'not in themselves knowledge, as we are tempted to think. All they can do is facilitate knowing' (p. 258). They can never 'copy' or 'represent' reality, but they preserve some 'information' (pictures more than words, motion pictures more than pictures). They 'put the viewer into the scene' (p. 282) by inducing 'not an illusion of reality but an awareness of being in the world' (p. 284). They 'transmit to the next generation the tricks of the human trade. The labors of the first perceivers are spared their descendants. The extracting and abstracting of the invariants that specify the environment are made vastly easier with these aids to comprehension' (p. 284).

Events are ecologically perceivable as 'any change of a substance, place, or object, chemical, mechanical, or biophysical. The change may be slower or fast, reversible or nonreversible, repeating or nonrepeating. Events include what happens to objects in general, plus what the animate objects *make* happen. Events are nested within superordinate events ... Events of different sorts are perceived as such ... ' (p. 242). While Gibson's analysis explicitly focuses on things (evincing Western biases), his thesis is concerned with things *and* events, and using his language my argument is that Nayaka focus on events. Their attention is educated to dwell on events. They are attentive to the changes of things in the world in relation to changes in themselves. As they move and act in the forest, they pick up information about the relative variances in the flux of the interrelatedness between themselves and other things against relative invariances. When they pick up a relatively changing thing with their relatively changing selves – and, all the more, when it happens in a relatively unusual manner – they regard as devaru *this* particular thing within *this* particular situation. This is another sense of the complex notion of devaru, and it arises from the stories which Nayaka tell.[19]

For example, one Nayaka woman, Devi (age 40), pointed to a particular stone – standing next to several other similar stones on a small mud platform among the huts – and said that she had been digging deep down for roots in the forest when suddenly '*this* devaru came towards her.' Another man, Atti-Mathen (age 70) pointed to a stone standing next to the aforementioned one and said that his sister-in-law had been sitting under a

---

[19] See Pandya (1993) for a fascinating study of Andamanese focus on movements. Hunter-gatherers are generally known to be concerned not with taxonomies but with behavior (see, e.g., Blurton Jones and Konner 1976).

tree, resting during a foray, when suddenly '*this* devaru jumped onto her lap.' The two women had brought the stone devaru back to their places 'to live' with them. The *particular* stones were devaru *as they* 'came towards' and 'jumped on' Nayaka. The many other stones in the area were not devaru but simply stones. Ojibwa approach stones in a similar way: Hallowell recounts how he once asked an old Ojibwa man whether 'all the stones we see about us here are alive.' Though stones are grammatically animate in Ojibwa, the man (Hallowell recalls) 'reflected a long while and then replied, "No! But *some* are"' (1960: 24). From the stories which Hallowell provides, 'alive' stones appear to be ones which 'move' and 'open a mouth' towards Ojibwa (p. 25).

The same underlying narrative recurs as Nayaka relate to animal devaru in-the-world. The following four anecdotes on elephants provide us with a clearer understanding of the complexity of Nayaka perceptions of devaru in-the-world. One man, Chathen (age 50), whose home stood next to the one in which I lived, said one morning that during the night he had seen an elephant devaru 'walking harmlessly' between our homes, and this is how he knew, he explained, that it was a devaru, not just an elephant. Another man, Chellan (age 35), similarly related, by way of giving another example, how once an elephant devaru which passed by him as he was walking in the forest searching for honey 'looked straight into his eyes.' Like the stones, these particular elephants were devaru *as they* 'walked harmlessly' and 'looked straight into the eyes,' that is, as and when they responsively related to Nayaka. In contrast, Kungan (age 50) once took me along on a gathering expedition, and on hearing an elephant and knowing by its sounds that it was alone and dangerous, he turned away and avoided it. He did not engage with this elephant and referred to it not as 'elephant devaru' but simply as 'elephant.' The lack of mutual engagement prevented the kind of relatedness which would have constituted *this* elephant (at *this* moment) as devaru while it might be perceived as devaru on other occasions.

A more complex situation is exemplified in an account by Atti-Mathen of how an elephant trampled two huts in a neighboring Nayaka place, luckily not injuring Nayaka, who happened to be away that night. Atti-Mathen referred to the offending elephant simply as 'elephant.' Several months later, during a devaru performance, he asked the devaru involved if they had 'had something to do' with the event in question. The devaru replied that they had 'done it' in response to a Nayaka *aaita* (a fault, deviation from the customary). The devaru did not specify the nature of the fault on this occasion – though sometimes they did, mentioning, for instance, that Nayaka had offered less food during the last devaru performance than in previous times or had started the performance later. This particular elephant (in this particular situation) was neither avoided nor shared with. It was perceived as an instrument, an object, which devaru used in the course of interrelating with Nayaka. In this case, illustrating the Nayaka view at its limits, Nayaka still frame what happened in terms of mutually responsive events, but they are connected narratively in a more complex way.

These four stories show how elephants (as one example among others) may be regarded as persons or as objects, depending on what happens between them and Nayaka, which itself depends on the 'affordances' of events involving elephants and people. An important feature of devaru in-the-world emerges. Devaru are not limited to certain *classes* of things. They are certain things-in-situations of whatever class or, better, certain situations. They are events involving mutual responsiveness and engagement between things, events, moreover, which prototypically involve the actor-perceiver. Discriminating devaru is contingent on 'affordances' of environmental events and things and (as I shall next argue) on enhanced attention to them through particular traditions of practice.

Devaru as performance characters

Devaru performances are pivotal in developing attention to devaru in-the-world and reproducing concepts of devaru as objectifications of relationships. These performances are complex affairs which, in the modernist sense, involve 'spirit-possession' by devaru but also a great deal more, including a communal social gathering, healing, an altered state of consciousness, communication with predecessors, secondary burial for people who have died since the previous event, and music and dancing. Each affair spans two days and the intervening night. Nayaka hold them every year or so in each village, one place after the other, each attended by people from the whole area who participate in several events of this sort every year. Nayaka do not seem to refer to this event by any single name or mark it off from everyday experience. 'Pandalu,' the word I apply to the affair, is sometimes used for the purpose, referring to the hut which is specially built for the event as accommodation for the visiting devaru.[20]

In examining one pandalu event, limiting myself to devaru alone, I adopt a performance-centered approach influenced by, among others Tambiah (1970; 1985 [1979]). Unlike the Geertzian tradition, this approach focuses on what the pandalu does rather than what it means. It focuses on the pandalu as an event in-the-world itself, not a 'text.' It is

---

[20] 'Pandalu' means 'temple' to neighboring Hindu people.

concerned with the extent to which such events, instead of referring to or talking about, *do something* in-the-world. I go farther, as I cast the pandalu (following Nayaka) *right away* as an experience, a performance, a social event in-the-world, which is continuous and coherent with and even nested within other Nayaka experiences. (I do not cast it as 'ritual,' as opposed to 'practice,' and then correctively adopt a performance-centered approach to it.) The examination fills a lacuna in the work of Ingold (e.g., 1996), who, like Gibson, pays inadequate attention to interhuman 'action' in-the-world in favor of 'action' towards other species;[21] clearly, action towards fellow humans constitutes an important part of one's 'environment.'

June 9, 1979, Kungan's place[22] *(where I lived at the time with his family)*: People arrive casually during the day, each family at its own time. They engage with the local residents in everyday activities, chatting, sharing food, going to the river, fetching firewood, etc. Late in the afternoon, amidst the action, Kungan (age 50) stands in front of the devaru hut and bows in four directions, inviting the area's devaru to come. A few people shift the devaru stones – originally brought from the forest – from their regular place on a mud platform among the houses to the area in front of the hut. They put next to them various other devaru things (including knives, bells, bracelets, cups, and elephant- and human-shaped figurines of Hindu origin), taking these things out of a box in which they are kept for safety between these events. Food and betel-nuts are laid in front of all these devaru, as well as Hindu puja items purchased with money collected in advance from the participants.[23]

As night falls, several men start going on and off into trances, usually one at a time, which they will continue doing throughout the night and the following day. Each one wraps himself with a special cloth, lifts branches and waves them in the air in four directions, bows in four directions inviting devaru to come, and shakes himself into a trance. Intermittently, rhythmic drumming, flute-and-drum music, and dances help set the mood. As the performers fall into trance, they 'bring to life' a variety of devaru.[24] The performers are evaluated in terms of how skillfully they 'bring' the devaru 'to life' at the same time as attendant people *engage with* the devaru which the performers evoke.

---

[21] Ingold (1997) questions the autonomy of social relations.
[22] Nayaka have no fixed names for places and refer to them by mentioning a prominent landmark or the name of a central person living there.
[23] See Bird-David (1996) for a detailed examination of how Nayaka incorporate Hindu influences into their pandalu tradition.
[24] They also 'bring to life' predecessors, who for lack of space are not discussed here.

Devaru of all sorts can 'come to life' during the devaru performance. Nayaka extend them an open invitation by the recurring bows in the four directions. Nayaka *engage* with the devaru characters who appear, who are devaru *as they* appear and engage with Nayaka. Nayaka identify each visiting devaru by its dividuated personality: by how it idiosyncratically interrelates with Nayaka (how it laughs with, talks with, gets angry at, responds to Nayaka, etc.). Sometimes, various devaru come together in a gang, evoked by the same performer, who then switches gestures, speech styles, dialects, and even languages (Nayaka, Malayalam, and Tamil) from one sentence to the next.[25] Some devaru are vivified by the performers with great finesse, and they are recognized by most or all Nayaka. Other devaru are so crudely specified that they are barely distinguishable, and they are identified by few Nayaka, and sometimes differently. The devaru are objectified by kinship terms; occasionally by names; sometimes only by their dividuated characters (as 'the one who always requests wild fowl for food' or 'waves a knife,' etc.) and sometimes just as devaru in general. The most vivid and generally known devaru are hill devaru, whose existence appears to go far back into the past. (Among neighboring hunter-gatherer Pandaram and Paliyan, hill chavu and hill devi are also singled out (Morris 1981; Gardner 1991).) Other vivid devaru are elephant devaru, minor Hindu deities worshiped locally, and a deity of the Kurumba people who lived in the locality several decades before. Generally, the more devaru appear year after year and are related with, the more vividly they are invoked, the more they are known, the more, in a sense, they 'exist.' Hardly anything is said *about* devaru in myth or other oral tradition either within the performance or outside it (Morris reports the same for Hill Pandaram (1981: 208)).

The devaru evoked often improvise on the same repetitive phrases. The saying, the voicing, the gesturing are important. These principal aspects of their behavior are, in Bateson's term (1979), meta-communication, namely, communicating that devaru are communicating, because the devaru are present *as* they move, talk, make gestures, etc. They are present *as* they communicate and socially interact with Nayaka. At peak times,

[25] Similarly, Brightman (1993: 172) describes the Rock Cree's 'shaking lodge ritual' as follows: '[It] features a recurring stock of characters, variable to some degree among different operators and different performances by the same operator. Many characters possess individuating speech characteristics, familiar to the audience from hearsay and from other performances ... Today, most spirits speak in Cree, and others use English, French, Saulteaux, and Chipewyan, or unknown human languages' (p. 172). 'During the course of the performance, they [the spirits] conversed among themselves, with the operator, and with members of the audience outside, responding to questions either in known languages or in unintelligible speech requiring translation by other spirits or by the operator' (p. 171).

everyone gathers around the visiting devaru, taking an active part in the conversation or just closely listening to it. At other times, only a few people do this while the others busy themselves with their own domestic affairs. The conversation has to be kept going at all times. When it slackens, the devaru complain and urge more people to join in. At the extreme, at dull moments in the heat of the day and deep in the night, this or that Nayaka grudgingly comes forward and engages the devaru in conversation. (I became helpful at various points in this event, letting Nayaka go about their business as I recorded and listened to the devaru by myself.) Keeping the conversation going is important because it keeps the Nayaka–devaru interaction and in a sense the devaru themselves 'alive.'

Conversation with the devaru is highly personal, informal, and friendly, including joking, teasing, bargaining, etc. In its idiomatic structure it resembles the demand-sharing discourse which is characteristic of Nayaka and hunter-gatherers generally (see Bird-David 1990). With numerous repetitions or minor variations on a theme, Nayaka and devaru nag and tease, praise and flatter, blame and cajole each other, expressing and demanding care and concern. For example, Nayaka stress that they are taking proper care of the devaru (or apologizing for not giving more or moaning about not being able to give more, etc.) and complain that the devaru, in turn, do not take care of them (or not enough or not as in previous years, etc.). The devaru stress how much they care for Nayaka and request better hospitality (more offerings, an earlier start for the event, more dancing, etc.). The Nayaka request cures from illnesses.

The ordinary round of everyday affairs continues during the two days of the pandalu. Domestic chores are not marginalized on account of the occasion but constitute a significant part of its structure. Throughout the two days, Nayaka families go on with their domestic activities, frequently sharing with each other and, in some ways, with their devaru visitors, too. The devaru hut resembles ordinary Nayaka dwellings. Some men occasionally take naps there, sharing the hut with the devaru. In the morning, when people go to wash in the river and bring back water, they bow in the four directions, inviting local devaru to join them. Women on their way back sprinkle water from their vessels in the four directions, sharing the water with devaru around. In the course of conversation devaru request betel-nuts from their Nayaka interlocutor. One elderly Nayaka woman falls into a trance. She does not utter coherent words; in her frenzy she only sweeps the ground around the devaru hut and starts to undress (which bystanders stop her from doing). A joint meal of rice, cooked by Kungan's daughter and her husband, brings the event to a close. The food is shared equally among those present, and some food is spread in the four directions.

The pandalu makes known the Nayaka–devaru relatednesses and at the same time reproduces them. Objectified as kinship relationships, the relatednesses reconstitute all the participants as *sonta* and each of them as a person (Nayaka person, hill person, stone person, etc.). Furthermore, the pandalu constitutes (in the Gibsonian sense) 'aids to perceiving' that 'put the viewer into the scene' (Gibson 1979: 282, cited above). It 'educates the attention' to perceive and specify the environment (while engaging with it) in a relational way. The pandalu 'preserves information' (as effectively as books and even motion pictures); moreover, it encourages the learner to engage interactively with this information and so to experience it socially. The engagement with devaru characters 'educates the attention' to notice devaru *as they interact with* oneself. It improves the skill of picking up information about the engagement itself, within its confines, from an engaged viewpoint.

If Nayaka only *subsisted* by hunting and gathering in their environment, they might perceive only its utilitarian affordances: an animal as something edible; a stone as something throwable; a rock as something one can shelter under. Within the practice of engaging with devaru characters in the pandalu they are educated to perceive that animals, stones, rocks, etc., are things one can relate with – that they have relational affordances, that is, what happens to them (or how they change) can affect and be affected by what happens to people (or how they change): an animal-avoiding-me in relation to me-upsetting-the-animal, a stone-coming-towards-me in relation to me-reaching-for-the-stone, a rock-securing-me in relation to me-seeking-a-shelter. Participants learn from conversing and sharing with devaru characters to discriminate mutually responsive changes in themselves and things they relate with; they become increasingly aware of the webs of relatedness between themselves and what is around them. From the bargaining and demand-sharing with devaru characters they learn to pursue individual interests within the confines of a relatedness – to negotiate for what they need while simultaneously taking care to reproduce the framing relatedness within which they do so. From year upon year of conversations, which in part repeat themselves and in part change, participants are increasingly sensitized to pick up information on the emergent, processive, historical, and reciprocal qualities of relatednesses. In sum, we can say that the pandalu involves '*making* [devaru] alive,' that is, raising people's awareness of their existence in-the-world and, dialectically, producing and being produced by this, socializing with them.

Animism as relational epistemology

Within the objectivist paradigm informing previous attempts to resolve the 'animism' problem, it is hard to make sense of people's 'talking with' things, or singing, dancing, or socializing in other ways for which 'talking' is used here as shorthand. According to this paradigm, learning involves acquiring knowledge *of* things through the separation of knower and known and often, furthermore, by breaking the known down into its parts in order to know it. To study, say, the tropical forest – the kind of forest in which Nayaka live and with which they 'talk' – botanists of this persuasion cut down a strip of trees with machetes, sort out the fallen vegetation into kinds, place characteristic bits and pieces of each kind in small bags, and take them out of the forest to a herbarium for botanical classification (see Richards 1952). Compared with their method, 'talking with' trees seems a ritual with no possible connection to the serious business of acquiring knowledge of trees.

If 'cutting trees into parts' epitomizes the modernist epistemology, 'talking with trees,' I argue, epitomizes Nayaka animistic epistemology. 'Talking' is shorthand for a two-way responsive relatedness with a tree – rather than 'speaking' one-way to it, as if it could listen and understand. 'Talking with' stands for attentiveness to variances and invariances in behavior and response of things in states of relatedness and for getting to know such things as they change through the vicissitudes over time of the engagement with them. To 'talk with a tree' – rather than 'cut it down' – is to perceive what *it* does as one acts towards it, being aware concurrently of changes in oneself and the tree. It is expecting response and responding, growing into mutual responsiveness and, furthermore, possibly into mutual responsibility.

If the object of modernist epistemology is a totalizing scheme of separated essences, approached ideally from a separated viewpoint, the object of this animistic knowledge is understanding relatedness from a related point of view within the shifting horizons of the related viewer. Knowledge in the first case is having, acquiring, applying, and improving representations of things in-the-world (see Rorty 1980). Knowledge in the second case is developing the skills of being in-the-world with other things, making one's awareness of one's environment and one's self finer, broader, deeper, richer, etc. Knowing, in the second case, grows from and *is* maintaining relatedness with neighboring others. It involves dividuating the environment rather than dichotomizing it and turning attention to 'we-ness,' which absorbs differences, rather than to 'otherness,' which highlights differences and eclipses commonalities. Against 'I think, therefore I am' stand 'I relate, therefore I am' and 'I know as I relate.' Against materialistic framing of the environment as discrete things stands relationally framing the environment as nested relatednesses. Both ways are real and valid. Each has its limits and its strengths.

Framing the environment relationally does not constitute Nayaka's only way of knowing their environment, though in my understanding they regard it as authoritative among their other ways. Nor is it unique to Nayaka. I would hypothesize that relational epistemologies of this kind enjoy authoritative status in cultures of peoples we call hunter-gatherers. These peoples normalize sharing with fellow persons. They engage intimately with their environment (if only periodically while on a break from other economic pursuits (Bird-David 1992b)). They celebrate animistic performances. Their performance traditions – for example, the Cree 'shaking tent ritual' (e.g., Hallowell 1960; Feit 1994; Brightman 1993), the !Kung 'medicine dance' (e.g., Marshall 1962; Katz 1982), the Hadza 'sacred *epeme* dance' (see Woodburn 1982), the Batek 'fruit-season's singing session' (see Endicott 1979), and Pahyan and Pandaram 'spirit possession' (see Gardner 1991; Morris 1981) – are functionally similar to the Nayaka pandalu. These performances involve the visiting of superpersons who appear through trance and dance or make their voices heard.[26] The people regard these superpersons as friends and relatives and often address and refer to them by kinship terms. They approach them in a personal, friendly, and immediate way. These events are the central communal affairs of these communities and often the main celebrational means by which they sustain their senses of identity.[27] Each event constitutes a 'participation frame' (Lave and Wenger 1991) which, together with the participation frame of hunting-gathering practice itself, nurtures a complex articulation of skills, a double-bind engagement which co-privileges utilizing *and* respecting animated 'things,' self-interest *and* the cooperation within which that self-interest can be achieved.[28]

---

[26] In some cases devaru are additionally invoked by objects, with which one talks, eats, sings, dances, etc. This is less common than their invocation by performance but of considerable theoretical importance.

[27] At their respective times of study, these events were frequently held, for example, weekly among !Kung, monthly among Hadza, and 'whenever need arises' among Pandaram. They spanned a significant stretch of time, for example, 'the whole night' among !Kung, 'two to three nights in succession' among Hadza, and 'from evening into the night' among Paliyan. The events involved the entire community as active spectators and a considerable proportion as performers, for example, 'one-third of the men' among !Kung, 'one-eighth of the men' among Pandaram, and '28% of the adults' among Paliyan. In the case of Nayaka, about one-fifth of the men acted as performers.

[28] Compare Briggs (1982) and Guemple (1988) on the teaching of Inuit children to relate with other people in a double-binding way and Myers's study (1986) of tenuous articulation of personal autonomy and relatedness among the Australian Pintupi.

Furthermore, relational epistemologies function in diverse contexts where other epistemologies enjoy authority, including Western contexts (to a much greater extent than the authoritative status of science permits). When (going back to Guthrie's examples) we animate the computers we use, the plants we grow, and the cars we drive, we relationally frame them. We learn what they do in relation to what we do, how they respond to our behavior, how they act towards us, what their situational and emergent behavior (rather than their constitutive matter) is. As Nayaka get to know animated aspects of their environment, so we get to know these animated things by focusing on our relatedness with them within the confines of that relatedness from a relational viewpoint. This sort of relational framing is articulated with other epistemologies in complex, variable, and shifting ways that deserve study. (The example of ethologists mentioned earlier is a case in point: in regarding as persons the study animals with which they live, they frame them relationally in addition to making them the objects of their scientific study.)

As a hypothesis, furthermore, I am willing to agree with Tylor, not least because Guthrie goes some way towards substantiating the point, that the tendency to animate things is shared by humans. However, this common tendency, I suggest, is engendered by human socially biased cognitive skills, not by 'survival' of mental confusion (Tylor) or by wrong perceptual guesses (Guthrie). Recent work relates the evolution of human cognition to social interaction with fellow humans. Its underlying argument is that interpersonal dealings, requiring strategic planning and anticipation of action–response–reaction, are more demanding and challenging than problems of physical survival (Humphrey 1976). Cognitive skills have accordingly evolved within and for a social kind of engagement and are 'socially biased' (Goody 1995). We spontaneously employ these skills in situations when we cannot control or totally predict our interlocutor's behavior, when its behavior is not predetermined but in 'conversation' with our own. We employ these skills in these situations, irrespective of whether they involve humans or other beings (the respective classification of which is sometimes part of reflective knowing, following rather than preceding the engagement situation). We do not first personify other entities and then socialize with them but personify them *as, when,* and *because* we socialize with them. Recognizing a 'conversation' with a counter-being – which amounts to accepting it into fellowship rather than recognizing a common essence – makes that being a self in relation with ourselves.

Finally, the common human disposition to frame things relationally in these situations is culturally mediated and contextualized in historically specific ways (not least in relation with cultural concepts of the person). A diversity of animisms exists, each animistic project with its local status, history, and structure (in Sahlins's (1985) sense). There follow intriguing questions deserving study, for example: How does hunter-gatherer animism compare with the current radical environmental discourses (e.g., Kovel 1988; Leahy 1991; Regan 1983; Tester 1991) that some scholars have described as the 'new animism' (Bouissac 1989; see also Kennedy's 'new anthropomorphism' (1992))? What other forms of animism are there?[29] How do they articulate in each case with other cosmologies and epistemologies?[30] How do animistic projects relate to fetish practices? Surely, however, the most intriguing question is why and how the modernist project estranged itself from the tendency to animate things, if it is indeed universal. How and why did it stigmatize 'animistic language' as a child's practice, against massive evidence (see Guthrie 1993) to the contrary? How did it succeed in delegitimating animism as a valid means to knowledge, constantly fending off the impulse to deploy it and regarding it as an 'incurable disease' (see Kennedy 1992 and Masson and McCarthy 1995)? The answers are bound to be complex. Ernest Gellner (1988) argued that nothing less than 'a near-miraculous concatenation of circumstances' can explain the cognitive shift that occurred in Western Europe around the 17th century. Ironically, history has it that Descartes – a reclusive man – was once accidentally locked in a steam room, where under hallucination he had the dualist vision on which the modern project is founded (see Morris 1991: 6). Can it be that a Tylorian kind of 'dream thesis' helps explain not the emergence of primitive animism but, to the contrary, the modernist break from it?

Conclusions

How we get to know things is nested within culture and practice and takes multiple forms. Nayaka relationally frame what they are concerned about as their authoritative (but not only) way of getting to know things. They seek to understand relatednesses from a related point of view within the shifting horizons of the related viewer. Their relational epistemology, their study of how things-in-situations relate to the actor-perceiver and, from the actor-perceiver's point of view, to each other, is embodied in the practices which Tylor christened 'primitive animism,' articulated with a

---

[29] For example, compare hunter-gatherer animism with premodern Western 'animism' as described in Merchant (1980) and Burke (1972).

[30] I owe the formulation of this question to Ingrid Jordt's forthcoming work on the articulation of Buddhist and animist epistemologies in Burma.

relational personhood concept and a relational perception of the environment. Previous theories of animism, taking modernist personhood concepts and perceptions of the environment as universal, have grossly misunderstood animism as simple religion and a failed epistemology.

References

Barnard, A. 1981. 'Universal Categorization in Four Bushmen Societies', *L'Uomo* 5: 219-37.

Barnett, S. A. 1976. 'Coconuts and Gold: Relational Identity in a South Indian Caste', *Contributions to Indian Sociology* n.s. 10: 133-56.

Bateson, G. 1979. *Steps to an Ecology of Mind.* New York: Ballantine Books.

Bird-David, N. 1983. "Inside" and "Outside" in Kinship Usage: The Hunter-Gatherer Naiken of South India', *Cambridge Anthropology* 7(1): 47-57.

Bird-David, N. 1989. 'The People and the Ethnographic Myth: An Introduction to the Study of the Nayaka', in *Blue Mountains: The Ethnography and Biogeography of a South Indian Region.* Edited by P. Hockings. New Delhi: Oxford University Press.

Bird-David, N. 1990. 'The Giving Environment: Another Perspective on the Economic System of Gatherer-Hunters', *Current Anthropology* 31: 183-96.

Bird-David, N. 1992a. 'Beyond "The Original Affluent Society": A Culturalist Reformulation', *Current Anthropology* 33: 25-47.

Bird-David, N. 1992b. 'Beyond "The Hunting and Gathering Mode of Subsistence": Observations on Nayaka and Other Modem Hunter-Gatherers', *Man* 27: 19-44.

Bird-David, N. 1994. 'Sociality and Immediacy, or, Past and Present Conversations on Bands', *Man* 29: 583-603.

Bird-David, N. 1996. 'Puja, or Sharing with the Gods? On Ritualized Possession among Nayaka of South India', *Eastern Anthropologist.* 49(3-4): 259-75.

Blurton Jones, N., and M. J. Konner. 1976. '!Kung Knowledge of Animal Behavior (or, The Proper Study of Mankind is Animals)', in *Kalahari Hunter-Gatherers: Studies of the !Kung San and Their Neighbors.* eds R. B. Lee and I. De Vore. Cambridge, MA: Harvard University Press.

Bouissac, P. 1989. 'What Is a Human? Ecological Semiotics and the New Animism', *Semiotica* 77: 497-516.

Briggs, I. L. 1982. 'Living Dangerously: The Contradictory Foundations of Value in Canadian Inuit Society', in *Politics and History in Band Societies.* eds E. Leacock and R. Lee. Cambridge: Cambridge University Press/Paris: Editions de la Maison des Sciences de l'Homme.

Brightman. R. 1993. *Grateful Prey: Rock Cree Human–Animal Relationships.* Los Angeles: University of California Press.

Burke, P. 1972. *Culture and Society in Renaissance Italy 1420-1540.* London: Batsford.

Carrithers, M., S. Collins, and S. Lukes. 1985. *The Category of the Person:*

Anthropology, Philosophy, History. Cambridge: Cambridge University Press.

Croll, E., and D. Parkin. 1992. *Bush Base – Forest Farm: Culture, Environment, and Development*. London: Routledge.

Daniel, E. V. 1984. *Fluid Signs: Being a Person the Tamil Way*. Berkeley: University of California Press.

Descola, P. 1992. 'Societies of Nature and the Nature of Society', in *Conceptualizing Society*, ed. A. Kuper. London and New York: Routledge.

Descola, P. 1996. 'Constructing Natures: Symbolic Ecology and Social Practice', in *Nature and Society: Anthropological Perspectives*, ed. P. Descola and G. Pálsson. London and New York: Routledge.

Descola, P., and G. Pálsson (eds). 1996. *Nature and Society: Anthropological Perspectives*. London and New York: Routledge.

Dewey, I., and A. Bentley. 1949. *Knowing and the Known*. Westport, CT: Greenwood Press.

Drury, N. 1985. *Dictionary of Mysticism and the Occult*. New York: Harper & Row.

Dumont, L. 1966. *Homo Hierarchicus: The Caste System and Its Implications*. Chicago: University of Chicago Press.

Durkheim, E. 1960 (1914). 'The Dualism of Human Nature and Its Social Conditions', in *Essays on Sociology and Philosophy*. ed. K. H. Wolff. New York: Harper & Row.

Durkheim, E. 1915. *The Elementary Forms of Religious Life*. New York: Free Press.

Ehnmark, E. 1939. *Anthropomorphism and Miracle*. Uppsala: Amquist & Wiksells.

Endicott, K. 1979. *Batek Negrito Religion: The World View and Rituals of a Hunting and Gathering People of Peninsular Malaysia*. Oxford: Clarendon Press.

Evans-Pritchard, E. E. 1937. *Witchcraft, Oracles, and Magic among the Azande*. Oxford: Clarendon Press.

Feit, H. 1994. 'Dreaming of Animals: The Waswamipi Cree Shaking Tent Ceremony in Relation to Environment, Hunting, and Missionization', in *Circumpolar Religion and Ecology: An Anthropology of the North*, ed. I. Takashi and T. Yamada. Tokyo: University of Tokyo Press, pp. 289-316.

Fortes, M. 1987. *Religion, Morality, and the Person*. Cambridge: Cambridge University Press.

Friedman, M. S. 1955. *Martin Buber: The Life of Dialogue*. London: Routledge & Kegan Paul.

Gardner, P. 1991. 'Pragmatic Meanings of Possessions in Paliyan Shamanism,' *Anthropos* 86: 367-84.

Gellner, E. 1988. *Plough, Sword, and Book: The Structure of Human History*. London: Paladin.

Gibson, J. J. 1979. *The Ecological Approach to Visual Perception*. Boston: Houghton Mifflin.

Goody, E. N. 1995. 'Introduction,' in *Social Intelligence and Interaction*:

Explorations and Implications of the Social Bias in Human Intelligence. ed. E. Goody. Cambridge: Cambridge University Press.

Gould, Julius, and William L. Kolb (eds). 1965. *Dictionary of the Social Sciences.* New York: Free Press.

Gudeman, S. 1986. *Economics as Cultures: Models and Metaphors of Livelihood.* London: Routledge & Kegan Paul.

Gudeman, S., and A. Rivera. 1990. *Conversations in Colombia: The Domestic Economy in Life and Text.* Cambridge: Cambridge University Press.

Guemple, L. 1988. 'Teaching Social Relations to Inuit Children', in *Hunters and Gatherers: Property, Power, and Ideology*, ed. T. Ingold, D. Riches, and J. Woodburn. Oxford: Berg.

Guilei, R. E. (ed.). 1992. *Encyclopedia of Ghosts and Spirits.* New York and Oxford: Facts on File.

Guthrie, S. 1993. *Faces in the Clouds: A New Theory of Religion.* Oxford: Oxford University Press.

Hallowell, A. I. 1960. 'Ojibwa Ontology, Behavior, and World View,' in *Culture in History: Essays in Honor of Paul Radin.* New York: Octagon Books.

Harris, M. 1983. *Cultural Anthropology.* New York: Harper & Row.

Howell, S. 1984. *Society and Cosmos: Chewong of Peninsular Malaysia.* Oxford: Oxford University Press.

Humphrey, N. K. 1976. 'The Social Function of Intellect', in *Growing Points in Ethology*, eds P. P. G. Bateson and R. A. Hinde. Cambridge: Cambridge University Press.

Hunter, D. E., and P. Whitten (eds). 1976. *Encyclopedia of Anthropology.* New York: Harper & Row.

Ingold, T. 1986. *Evolution and Social Life.* Cambridge: Cambridge University Press.

Ingold, T. (ed.). 1988. *What Is an Animal?* London: Unwin Hyman.

Ingold, T. 1992. 'Culture and the Perception of the Environment', in *Bush Base – Forest Farm: Culture, Environment, and Development,* eds E. Croll and D. Parkin. London: Routledge.

Ingold, T. 1996. 'Hunting and Gathering as Ways of Perceiving the Environment', in *Redefining Nature: Ecology, Culture, and Domestication*, eds R. Ellen and K. Fukui. Oxford: Berg.

Ingold, T. 1997. 'Life Beyond the Edge of Nature? or, The Mirage of Society', in *The Mark of the Social*, ed. I. B. Greenwood. Lanham, MD: Rowman & Littlefield, pp. 231-52.

Katz, R. 1982. *Boiling Energy: Community Healing among the Kalahari Kung.* Cambridge, MA: Harvard University Press.

Kennedy, J. S. 1992. *The New Anthropomorphism.* Cambridge: Cambridge University Press.

Kovel, J. 1988. *The Radical Spirit: Essays on Psychoanalysis and Society.* London: Free Association Books.

Lave, J., and E. Wenger. 1991. *Situated Learning: Legitimate Peripheral Participation.* Cambridge: Cambridge University Press.

Leahy, M. P. T. 1991. *Against Liberation: Putting Animals in Perspective*. London: Routledge.

Leopold, J. 1980. *Culture in Comparative and Evolutionary Perspectives: E. Tylor and the Making of Primitive Culture*. Berlin: Dietrich Reimer Verlag.

Lévi-Strauss, C. 1962. *Totemism*. Boston: Beacon Press.

Lévi-Strauss, C. 1966 (1962). *The Savage Mind*. London: Weidenfeld & Nicolson.

Lovejoy, A. O. 1948. *Essays in the History of Ideas*. Baltimore: Johns Hopkins University Press.

MacCormack, C., and M. Strathern. 1980. *Nature, Culture, and Gender*. Cambridge: Cambridge University Press.

Mageo, J. M., and A. Howard (eds). 1996. *Spirits in Culture, History, and Mind*. New York and London: Routledge.

Marriott, M. 1976. 'Hindu Transactions: Diversity without Dualism', in *Transaction and Meaning: Directions in the Anthropology of Exchange and Symbolic Behavior*, ed. B. Kapferer. Philadelphia: Institute for the Study of Human Issues.

Marriott, M., and R. Inden. 1977. 'Towards an Ethno-sociology of South Asian Caste Systems', in *The New Wind: Changing Identities in South Asia*, ed. D. Ken. The Hague: Mouton.

Marshall, L. 1962. 'Kung Bushmen Religious Belief', *Africa* 32: 221-5.

Masson, J. M., and S. McCarthy. 1995. *When Elephants Weep: The Emotional Lives of Animals*. New York: Delta.

Mauss, M. 1985 (1938). 'A Category of the Human Mind: The Notion of Person, the Notion of Self', in *The Category of the Person: Anthropology, Philosophy, History*, ed. M. Carrithers, S. Collins, and S. Lukes. Cambridge: Cambridge University Press.

Meillassoux, C. 1973. 'On the Mode of Production of the Hunting Band', in *French Perspectives in Africanist Studies*, ed. P. Alexandre. London: Oxford University Press for the International African Institute.

Merchant. C. 1980. *The Death of Nature: Women, Ecology, and the Scientific Revolution*. San Francisco: Harper & Row.

Mines, M. 1994. *Public Faces, Private Voices: Community and Individuality in South India*. Berkeley: University of California Press.

Morris, S. 1981. 'Hill Gods and Ecstatic Cults: Notes on the Religion of a Hunting and Gathering People', *Man in India* 61: 203-36.

Morris, S. 1991. *Western Conceptions of the Individual*. New York: Berg.

Morris, S. 1994. *Anthropology of the Self: The Individual in Cultural Perspective*. London: Pluto Press.

Myers, F. 1986. *Pintupi Country, Pintupi Self: Sentiment, Place, and Politics among Western Desert Aborigines*. Washington, D.C., and Canberra: Smithsonian Institution Press and Australian Institute of Aboriginal Studies.

Pandya, V. 1993. *Above the Forest: A Study of Andamanese Ethnoanemology, Cosmology, and the Power of Ritual*. Delhi: Oxford University Press.

Povinelli, E. 1993. *Labor's Lot: The Power, History, and Culture of Aboriginal Action*. Chicago: University of Chicago Press.

Preus, J. S. 1987. *Explaining Religion: Criticism and Theory from Bodin to Freud*.

New Haven: Yale University Press.

Raheja, G. I. 1988a. 'India: Caste, Kingship, and Dominance Reconsidered'. *Annual Review of Anthropology* 17: 497-522.

Raheja, G. I. 1988b. *The Poison in the Gift: Ritual, Prestation, and the Dominant Caste in a North Indian Village*. Chicago: University of Chicago Press.

Regan, T. 1983. *The Case for Animal Rights*. Berkeley: University of California Press.

Richards, P. W. 1952. *The Tropical Rain Forest: An Ecological Study*. Cambridge: Cambridge University Press.

Riches, D. 1994. 'Shamanism: The Key to Religion', *Man* 29: 381-405.

Rorty, R. 1980. *Philosophy and the Mirror of Nature*. Princeton: Princeton University Press.

Sahlins, M. 1972. 'The Original Affluent Society', in *Stone Age Economics*. London: Tavistock.

Sahlins, M. 1985. *Islands of History*. Chicago: University of Chicago Press.

Saler, B. 1977. 'Supernatural as a Western Category', *Ethos* 5: 31-53.

Schneider, D. M. 1968. *American Kinship: A Cultural Account*. Englewood Cliffs: Prentice-Hall.

Schneider, D. M. 1984. *American Kinship: A Critique of the Study of Kinship*. Ann Arbor: University of Michigan Press.

Schutz, A., and T. Luckmann. 1973. *The Structure of the Life-World*, trans. R. M. Zaner and H. T. Engelhart. Ann Arbor: University of Michigan Press.

Scott, C. 1989. 'Knowledge Construction among Cree Hunters: Metaphors and Literal Understanding', *Journal de la Société des Americanistes* 75: 193-208.

Shweder, R., and R. Le Vine (eds). 1984. *Culture Theory: Essays on Mind, Self, and Emotions*. Cambridge: Cambridge University Press.

Stocking, C. W. 1971. 'Animism in Theory and Practice: E. B. Tylor's Unpublished "Notes on spiritualism"', *Man* 6: 88-104.

Stocking, C. W. 1987. *Victorian Anthropology*. New York: Free Press.

Strathern, M. 1988. *The Gender of the Gift: Problems with Women and Problems with Society in Melanesia*. Berkeley: University of California Press.

Tambiah, S. 1970. *Buddhism and the Spirit Cults in North-East Thailand*. Cambridge: Cambridge University Press.

Tambiah, S. 1985 (1979). 'The Cosmological and Performative Significance of a Thai Cult of Healing through Meditation', in *Culture, Thought, and Social Action: An Anthropological Perspective*. Cambridge, MA: Harvard University Press.

Tanner, A. 1979. *Bringing Home Animals: Religious Ideology and Mode of Production of the Mistassini Cree Hunters*. London: E. Hurst.

Tester, K. 1991. *Animals and Society: The Humanity of Animal Rights*. London: Routledge.

Thompson, Stith. 1955. *Motif-Indexes of Folk-Literature*. Revised and enlarged edition. Bloomington: Indiana University Press.

Tylor, E. B. 1958 (1871). *Primitive Culture*, Vol. 1: *Religion in Primitive Culture*. New York: Harper & Row.

Wagner, R. 1981 (1975). *The Invention of Culture*. Revised and expanded edition. Chicago and London: University of Chicago Press.

Woodburn, J. 1979. 'Minimal Politics: The Political Organization of the Hadza of North Tanzania', *Politics in Leadership: A Comparative Perspective*, eds P. Cohen and W. Shacks. Oxford: Clarendon Press.

Woodburn, J. 1980. 'Hunters and Gatherers Today and Reconstruction of the Past', in *Soviet and Western Anthropology*, ed. E. Gellner. London: Duckworth.

Woodburn, J. 1982. 'Egalitarian Societies', *Man* 17: 431-51.

4. Sharing the flower: A non-supernaturalistic theory of grace

Kenneth M. Morrison

Editor's introduction

Morrison concludes this article by noting that

> This phrase – which Painter [1986] notes is implicit in all ceremonial forms – 'Come, share the flower' – captures the sense of ritual work. Sharing the flower unites the Christian great others, the Yaqui church groups, and the traditional singers and dancers in an empowering system of co-operative, mutual acts of giving witness. And, it is this non-supernaturalistic character of Yaqui ritual work that is not understood either in Muncie, Indiana, or in the academic study of religion.

In the previous three chapters little explicit discussion has been devoted to the question of what 'religion' might be. Hallowell certainly feels the need to challenge 'conventional' understandings of religion in which it is separated from everyday, mundane, secular, or ordinary life. Imposition of this dichotomy on to Ojibwe experience and epistemology would lead to the mystification and spiritualization of relationships that are, in Ojibwe terms, ontologically the same. For example, 'grandfathers' is a relational honorific applicable to all who act and are acted towards in particular ways – regardless of their species. In one telling reference, Strathern notes that 'Melanesians borrow origin stories, wealth, and – as in the area I know best (Mount Hagen) – the expertise by which to organize their religion and

Reprinted from *Religion* 22, pp. 208-20, 1992. By permission of the publisher, Academic Press, London.

their future'. But her elaboration of this point says little about religion as 'conventionally' understood. Bird-David only refers to 'religion' in challenging earlier mistakes in academic understanding of indigenous and other 'animisms'. These small points are, in fact, enormously important clues towards the rethinking of religion. The study of religions, as an academic discipline, might be said to have arisen in the context of rethinking such categories. It has become axiomatic in the discipline that a focus on 'belief' has misdirected attention to interiority and privacy, at the same time as it colluded with hierarchical definitions of religions 'as they should be'. More adequate explorations and theorizing have been concerned with experience and performance (religion as action). Certainly religion must be considered as inseparable from other aspects of life.

Ken Morrison's article pays particular attention to contemporary Yaqui religion, especially manifest in a particular ceremonial complex. He notes that a 'performance approach [exemplified by Gill 1987] to the study of religion is more productive than one that emphasizes belief'. Later chapters in this book (especially Drewal and Stover), along with those in *Indigenous Religions: A Companion* (especially in the 'Gifts' section) reinforce the importance of this point.

As if this were insufficient reason for including Morrison's article, it is also important for its clarity about what some label 'syncretism'. This term has generated widespread debate (e.g. Clarke 1998; Greenfield and Droogers 2001) but still seems to be used most frequently with little real engagement with the dynamics at issue. The study of indigenous religions certainly requires the kind of clarity Morrison provides – especially if it is to respond adequately to contemporary assertions of indigenous self-determination.

References

Clarke, Peter B. (ed.). 1998. *New Trends and Developments in African Religions*. Westport, CT: Greenwood Press.

Evers, Lawrence, and Felipe S. Molina, 1987. *Yaqui Deer Songs/Maso Bwikam*. Tucson: Sun Tracks and University of Arizona Press.

Gill, Sam D. 1987. *Native American Religious Action: A Performance Approach to Religion*. Columbia: University of South Carolina Press.

Greenfield, Sidney M. and André Droogers (eds). 2001. *Reinventing Religions: Syncretism and Transformation in Africa and the Americas*. Lanham, MD: Rowman & Littlefield.

Painter, Muriel. 1986. *With Good Heart: Yaqui Beliefs and Ceremonies in Pascua Village*. Tucson: University of Arizona Press.

107

❧❧

Åke Hultkrantz's 1983 essay, 'The concept of the supernatural in primal religions' has set the stage for a re-examination of both the ethnography and the history of Native American religions. Hultkrantz insists that the supernatural has one outstanding characteristic: it enjoys a vertical superiority over everyday reality. Wittingly, or not, Hultkrantz thus aligns himself with the Christian worldview in which not only does grace come from on high, but the cosmos is hierarchically constituted in a great chain of being from God's perfection to a natural world tainted by human sin. This essay examines one Native American group which has, despite several centuries' engagement with Catholicism, no idea of a privileged supernatural.[1]

The need to rethink the assumed supernaturalistic cast of Yaqui religion can be seen in the work of anthropologist Edward H. Spicer. Between 1940 and 1980, Spicer struggled to make sense of the syncretistic cast of Yaqui Catholicism, a Catholicism which differed, he observed, from that practiced in Muncie, Indiana.[2] Two elements of Yaqui Catholicism troubled Spicer. The first had to do with the way in which Yaqui religion diverged from contemporary Catholicism. For Spicer, that difference lay in the 'medieval' character of Yaqui religion, particularly its appropriation of the Passion Play in what is now called the Easter Ceremony. The second element had to do with the ritual practices of the *Pascola* clowns and the Deer dancer. In 1940 and 1950, Spicer contended that, although these figures derived from traditional transcendent realms, they were not religious. They were, in fact, profane, and were being historically displaced.[3] By 1980, Spicer gave the Deer and Pascolas more importance, although he still contended that they were partly secularized.

In retrospect, it is possible to see that Spicer struggled to make sense of Yaqui religion because of the supernaturalistic assumptions that he made about the nature of religion. In his 1980 overview of Yaqui cultural history, Spicer's view of the Pascolas and the Deer wavered. He characterized

---

[1]   Åke Hultkrantz, 'The concept of the supernatural in primal religion', *History of Religions* 22 (February 1983), pp. 231-53. It will become clear from the argument that follows that the Yaqui data suggests that a performance approach to the study of religion is more productive than one that emphasizes belief. See Sam D. Gill, *Native American Religious Action: A Performance Approach to Religion*, Columbia, SC, University of South Carolina Press, 1987.

[2]   Edward H. Spicer, *Pascua: A Yaqui Village in Arizona*, Chicago, IL, University of Chicago Press 1940 (reprinted Tucson, AZ, University of Arizona Press 1984); Edward H. Spicer, 'Potam: A Yaqui village in Sonora', *American Anthropologist* 56 (August 1954), pp. 1-220, observation at p. 114.

[3]   Spicer, *Pascua*, pp. 173, 175-6, 184, 202, 228, 282, 295, 298; Spicer, 'Potam', pp. 159-60, 182-3, 205, 207.

them as the opposite of the sacred which he associated with the Catholic 'supernatural'. He contended, on the one hand, that the Pascola dance was 'merely an adjunct activity', and, on the other, stated that the Pascolas were 'an essential feature' of Yaqui fiestas. Elsewhere, he described the Deer and Pascola side of the dance ramada as profane, even though he also noted that the ramada was made sacred by being danced over. Spicer also said that 'the Church gives sacred sanction to the Pascolas' profane jokes ... '.[4] In effect, Spicer failed to see not only that the Deer and the Pascolas articulated an indigenous theory of ritual, and also explained the Yaquis' understanding of the relationship to Catholic 'supernaturals'.

As early as 1950, however, Spicer noted that the symbol *sewa*, flower, needed special analysis, and his 1980 book came close to understanding that flower was the key to appreciating all forms of Yaqui ritual.[5] To gain such an understanding, then, it is necessary to explore the place of the Deer and Pascolas in relation to Yaqui Catholicism, to reconstruct the symbolic character of Yaqui rituals, and to contrast the Yaquis' view of ritual efficacy to the Christian theory of divine grace.

To anticipate the conclusion, Yaqui Catholicism now appears to have added Christian cosmology and great persons to those of the traditional system. In other words, Spicer was correct in saying that the Yaqui had juxtaposed, in what he calls an 'oppositional integration', old and new cosmologies. But, he did not realize that they have also applied the ancient symbol of Flower associated with the Deer to the similar sacrificial acts of Jesus.[6] In this way, the Yaqui explain Christianity and their own ritual responsibilities in terms of an indigenous theory of ritual power. Although much of the apparently Catholic system has non-Christian characteristics, the Deer and the Pascolas remain relatively untouched by Catholicism. There has been an ongoing tendency to rationalize traditions associated with the Deer and Pascolas in Catholic terms, as Spicer documented as occurring at Pascua in the 1930s,[7] but traditional meanings have not been eliminated.

Deer and Pascolas have remained independent actors in the Yaquis' religious system, and their powers derive from the non-Christian side of the post-contact cosmology. By extension, the deer's symbol, flower, has

---

4 Edward H. Spicer, *The Yaquis: A Cultural History*, Tucson, AZ, University of Arizona Press 1980, pp. 94, 102, 103, 105, 193, 274, 314, 326-7. For a discussion that suggests that the concept of the supernatural is closely related to the orientational metaphor 'Up Is Good', see George Lakoff and Mark Johnson, *Metaphors We Live By*, Chicago, University of Chicago Press 1980, especially pp. 14-24.

5 Spicer, 'Potam', p. 196; *The Yaquis*, pp. 86-7.

6 Spicer, *The Yaquis*, p. 70.

7 Spicer, *Pascua*, p. 198.

become a master symbol of all the ways in which the Yaqui work toward fulfilling their responsibilities in the overall, cosmic scheme of things. Thus, even though the dominant religious rituals appear to be Christian, and ethnic solidarity seems to be grounded in Christian ritual practice, Deer and Pascolas embody the core religious insight. Despite tremendous changes in subsistence strategies, and particularly in what Spicer calls the secularization of the natural world, Deer and Pascolas survive because they embody and articulate traditional core values which have come to inform Yaqui Catholicism as well.

Seataka as grace: traditions of power

By 1980, Edward Spicer had discovered a number of factors which make it possible to rethink his earlier view that the Deer Dancer and Pascolas had been marginalized in Pascuan culture. In the first place, he carefully developed an argument that the Yaquis only partially accepted the Jesuit missionaries' teaching about Christian cosmology. Spicer shows that the Yaquis came to accept the great others of Catholicism as well as their distinctive location in heaven, or glory. At the same time, however, the Yaquis neither rejected their traditional cosmological system, nor accepted the Jesuits' distinction between a perfect heaven and a tainted worldly existence.[8]

In effect, Spicer argues persuasively that the Yaquis' religious syncretism consisted of creating a world system that accounted for, and juxtaposed, both Christian and traditional cosmologies. In the process, the Yaquis' understanding of their traditional system apparently evolved and what had once been a unitary world, the *Huya Ania* or the Forest of Desert World, became differentiated into what is now called the *Sea Ania*, or Flower World, and the *Yo Ania*, the ancient and honorable realm. Both the Sea Ania and the Yo Ania appear in the desert world the Yaquis call the Huya Ania. In accepting the prophecies of the Singing Tree that missionaries would help them build a new world order, the people who accepted Christian baptism entered a new dimension, the Pueblo, which intersects cosmological domains characteristic of Christianity: Heaven, Hell, and Purgatory. In all of this, Spicer demonstrates, the Yaquis continued to attend to the impinging ancient realms appearing in the Huya Ania and refused the world-rejection which typified Jesuit Catholicism.

Two recent works on the Yaqui, Muriel Painter's *With Good Heart* (1986), and Lawrence Evers and Felipe S. Molina's *Yaqui Deer Songs* (1987), have brought together a great deal more ethnographic information

[8]   Spicer, *The Yaquis*, pp. 62-70.

on Yaqui religion. Significantly, they agree with Spicer's view that the Deer Dancer derives from pre-contact Yaqui tradition.[9] The richness of their data makes it possible to see that Yaqui acceptance of Catholicism hardly amounts to conversion in its usual sense of turning away from the truths of tradition to the truths of another.[10] Instead, the Yaqui extended the religious insights of tradition to make sense of their relationship with the great others of Christianity. Unlike Spicer, then, Evers and Molina, and, to a lesser degree, Painter locate the 'sacred' characteristics of Yaqui religion, its understanding of traditional and Christian power, in the pre-contact tradition.

Those insights derive from the primordial world of myth, and particularly from the Sea Ania, the Flower World, the dimension from which comes the Deer Dancer. The Yaqui understand the Sea Ania as a plenum – a perfect fullness – that spills over into an everyday existence which is less integral than its source.[11] Painter describes the Sea Ania in terms which suggest the cosmic and ethical ideal of sharing: 'Perhaps more than the huya it implies the beneficient and fruitful aspects of nature, such as rivers, streams, lakes, clouds, and rain'.[12] Thus, the Deer embodies the Yaqui cosmological ideal as well as the normative actualities of day to day existence.

The Deer expresses the selfless innocence that characterizes the Flower world and the Yaqui think of him affectionately as a younger brother. They say that he is the most loved of the animals and is the most closely related to human beings. The Deer also embodies the selflessness that is the source of cosmic order in the differentiated cosmology that came into existence as a result of the prophecies of the Singing Tree. In the unitary, pre-contact world, the Yaqui did not yet exist. The people of that realm, the *Surem*, lived without struggle or strife; they were immortal. When the Singing Tree began to speak of the Christian future with its ritual labor and death, an act the Yaqui understand as a pivotal flowering of reality, discord entered the peaceful Surem world. Those who heeded the Tree's invitation accepted baptism and became Yaquis; those who clung to

---

[9] Spicer, *The Yaquis*, p. 67; Muriel Painter, *With Good Heart: Yaqui Beliefs and Ceremonies in Pascua Village*, Tucson, University of Arizona Press, 1986; Lawrence Evers and Felipe S. Molina, *Yaqui Deer Songs/Maso Bwikam*, Tucson, Sun Tracks and the University of Arizona Press, 1987, p. 18.

[10] This understanding of conversion is not, of course, Spicer's view. His work actively deconstructed such a notion: Spicer, *The Yaquis*, pp. 333-62. The crucial point is that there is no evidence that the Yaquis make a distinction between sacred Christian and a profane traditional religious practice. See Evers and Molina, *Yaqui Deer Songs*, pp. 130, 137.

[11] Evers and Molina, *Yaqui Deer Songs*, p. 70.

[12] Painter, *With Good Heart*, p. 18.

tradition withdrew to the Yo Ania, the ancient and honorable realm, and so preserved their immortality.[13]

The ongoing relationship between these transcendent ancient realms can best be seen in a ceremony in which Deer and Pascolas enact the pivotal act of self-sacrifice on which life itself depends.[14] Performed at the end of a first year death anniversary which releases relatives from mourning, the rite called *Maso me'ewa*, 'Running the Deer', plays with the tension between life and death, violence and eating, death and immortality. In the complex interplay between Deer songs describing the hunt from the Deer and the hunters' points of view, the religious nature of violence is celebrated. The rite opens with a life and death struggle between Racoon and agriculturalists for life-giving corn which suggests that struggle is at the center of cosmic process. Other songs allude to coyotes hungrily scouting the edges of a deer kill, vultures who scavenge life from death, and agaves who die in the very act of producing life-giving fruit. The rite culminates in the Deer hunt and the Deer songs about the Deer's flight, loneliness, love of life, and his death:

> Not wanting to die,
>   dodging through the wilderness.
> with my head hanging down toward the ground,
>   as I am walking,
> with foam around my mouth
>   as I am walking.
> Never again I,
> Will I on this world,
>   I, around will I be walking.

In these words, Deer declares that the price of life is life itself, a harsh and unavoidable truth. At the same time, however, the rite declares a heartening mystery. As the Pascolas roast his flesh, throw his internal organs on the ground, and tan his hide, a Deer song proclaims an eternal fact of transformation. In song, the Deer embraces his ultimate fate: 'I become enchanted'. 'I become flower'. The rite expresses the core insight into the character of the Deer's paradigmatic self-sacrifice as the Pascolas dip the Deer's hide in the enchanted water of the Deer singers' drum and then extend the blessing by hitting spectators with it: 'When we do that we are

---

[13] Spicer, *The Yaquis*, p. 67; Painter, *With Good Heart*, pp. 4-11; Evers and Molina, *Yaqui Deer Songs*, pp. 37-51; Kathleen M. Sands, 'The Singing Tree: dynamics of a Yaqui myth', *American Quarterly* 12 (1982), pp. 355-75.

[14] Spicer notes that it was usual to have Pascolas at this death anniversary fiesta in the 1930s but does not mention this ceremony in relationship to it: *Pascua*, pp. 177-8.

blessing the ground',[15] the Yaqui say. This, then, is the ancient recognition of an inexorable and vital reciprocity that exists between all living things, an understanding about sacrificial sharing that in time the Yaqui came to apply to Jesuit teachings about the life and death of Christ and its annual re-enactment in the Easter Ceremony. Significantly, neither Spicer nor Painter thought that this ceremony had religious significance.[16]

In these broad terms, Yaqui mythology and ritual practice share a widespread theme found in many other Native American traditions. Yaqui myth remembers a time when humans and animals shared the same nature, spoke the same language, and lived in an all-encompassing kinship society. It also recalls the onset of linguistic differentiation when an inescapable otherness came into being and relations between humans and animals came to rest on the necessary violence of hunting. This world depended on reciprocities between respectful humans and compassionate animals who graciously give their lives so that others might live. Yaqui myth is distinctive only in that it relates the fact of strife and the need for ritual reciprocity to the historical introduction of Christianity.[17]

In effect, then, Yaqui Catholicism rests on an explanation of cosmic differentiation and on a pivotal understanding of the way in which the various cosmic dimensions continue to intersect. The Yaqui remember a world of violence in which rabbits help the Deer against a figure Evers and Molina call the prototypical deer hunter. In this world, some humans gain power over the Deer. The Deer, nevertheless, expect that hunters acknowledge their gift of life and inflict sickness on the disrespectful.[18] The hunter's ritual acknowledgement empowers the Deer to reincarnate so that death is always defeated and life itself circulates throughout the cosmological system. Yaqui understanding of the empowerment that the Deer contributes to cosmic process derives from two terms: *tekia* and *seataka*, both of which were originally applied only to native dancers, but were later extended to explain the nature of Christian ceremonial labor.[19]

Tekia describes a gift of power from the Yo Ania (and sometimes from God) that makes it possible for ritual performers to work efficaciously. The

---

[15] Evers and Molina, *Yaqui Deer Songs*, pp. 129-81.

[16] Spicer, *Pascua*, p. 298; Painter, *With Good Heart*, p. 345.

[17] See Barbara G. Myerhofl, *Peyote Hunt: The Sacred Journey of the Huichol Indians*, Ithaca, NY, Cornell University Press 1974, p. 58; Stith Thompson, *Tales of the North American Indians*, Bloomington, IN, Indiana University Press 1966 (1929); Åke Hultkrantz, *The Religions of the American Indians*, Berkeley, CA, University of California Press 1979, pp. 29-30; David M. Guss, *The Language of the Birds: Tales, Texts, and Poems of Interspecies Communication*, San Francisco, Northpoint Press 1985.

[18] Evers and Molina, *Yaqui Deer Songs*, pp. 47-54.

[19] Painter, *With Good Heart*, p. 246.

concept particularly describes the sense of duty and obligation that derives from the compassionate empowerment the Yaqui call seataka, which refers to powers deriving from the Sea Ania and the Deer, and from the Yo Ania and the Surem. The term itself is closely associated with sewa, flower, the master symbol uniting all domains of the Yaquis' complex cosmological system. Painter observes that 'all informants knew and believed in seataka which is said to be fundamental to Yaqui thought and total life'. Pascuans think of seataka, Painter continues, 'as the way of life in the yo ania – of life in ancient times', and they see it as particularly embodied in 'kindness and consideration for others'.[20] In this sense, seataka might be thought of as a surviving pre-Christian theory of 'grace' deriving from ancient religious dimensions, given in the womb, accessed in dreams and visions, and expressed in the ritual action of the Deer Dancer and his singers, and the Pascolas and their musicians.[21] Painter notes that seataka is rarely associated with the ritual work of the Catholic church.[22]

Pascuans nevertheless extend flower symbolism to explain their reciprocal relations with the great others of Christianity. Various stories relate that the Virgin Mary became impregnated by a rose so that Jesus could transform 'Himself into a human being to save mankind'. Even though Jesus was God, he required help from others in order to come into existence: 'in order to send His Son', God enlisted the aid of the planets, sun, moon, North Star and Milky Way. What is more, 'Twelve angels were chosen to make the heart of Jesus, and the ingredients for the heart were all taken from the planets'. In this way, the Yaqui applied the ethical logic of the Sea Ania to the nature of Jesus: 'Each one gave, donated, one to make the heart of Jesus', who was 'born an innocent infant in a world of turmoil'.[23]

Jesus' earthly life is closely associated with the Huya Ania where he wandered. As one Yaqui put it: 'the Lord went among the flowers all the time, seven years ... '. Symbolically, then, the association of Jesus with flowers extends the moral virtues that Pascuans associate with the Deer. 'In his earthly manifestation', Painter writes, 'Jesus had qualities with which Pascuans can identify and with which they are comfortable, such as compassion, love, the gifts of healing; also a stern self-discipline during fatigue ... '. Painter also observes that these virtues explain why the Yaqui stress the value of 'generous and compassionate acts'. Dying, Jesus' blood fell to the ground, only to spring up as flowers. Since the lenten season

[20] Painter, *With Good Heart*, pp. 11-12, 15.
[21] Ibid., references too numerous to cite. See index under dreams, ordeal dreams, and vision.
[22] Ibid., p. 13.
[23] Ibid., pp. 73, 78-80.

annually replicates Jesus' death and rebirth, winter is understood to be a time symbolically opposed to flowers.[24]

Flower symbolism is also closely associated with the Virgin Mary, who the Yaqui call *Itom Ae*, 'Our Mother'. Mary's nurturing and healing role in Yaqui life is related to summer, the fructifying season when the Sea Ania blooms in the Huya Ania. Mary plays an essential role in Christian cosmology, assisting Christ to resurrect Himself, and mediating between Jesus and the Yaqui people. As mother, 'Mary seems more accessible than Jesus when favors are entreated'. She has a special relationship with one ceremonial dance group, the Matachinis, who dance throughout the summer and suspend their labor on Mary's behalf during the lenten season.[25]

Because the Christian great others are so closely associated with flowers, it can be said that, in what Spicer calls the juxtapositional integration of traditional and Catholic cosmologies, the seataka of the Deer continues to express the key insight: world order depends fundamentally on acts of self-sacrifice. On Holy Saturday the Deer singers in fact juxtapose Christ's resurrection with the eternal metamorphosis of deer and thus suggest that an ancient mythic logic has come to explain Christianity and its seasonal polarization.[26] Like the Deer, Jesus is a selfless innocent who annually gives his life so that others might live. And just as the violence of hunting must be assuaged by ritual action that empowers the Deer's reincarnation, the dying Christ requires the Yaquis' ritual labor to empower his resurrection. That obligation to Christ the Yaqui describe with the term *tekipanoa*, the service of a person, *el destino*, or what God wants him to do in the service.[27] The term is associated with a God-given talent to do ceremonial labor. It also expresses a reciprocal interdependence between God and humans since it is closely related to the vow in which an individual promises to do ritual work in return for being cured of an illness. Such a vow is at once an act of penance and an exercise of ritual responsibility, and failure to perform ritual duties can result in Jesus' and Mary's retribution: misfortune, sickness, even death.[28]

Sharing the flower

The pivotal terms of Yaqui religion – seataka, tekia, and tekipanoa – all

---

[24] Painter, *With Good Heart*, pp. 71, 75, 504.
[25] Ibid., pp. 80-4.
[26] Evers and Molina, *Yaqui Deer Songs*, p. 54.
[27] Painter, *With Good Heart*, p. 95.
[28] Ibid., pp. 123-33.

derive their meanings from the Sea Ania, the ancient realm that is the home of the Deer. They are all in their respective ways related to the idea that the symbol Flower identifies a religious theory of ritual action in which actors from all the cosmic dimensions join forces to counter disorder. Painter's rich collection of the Yaquis' reflections about their ritual system, and Evers' and Molina's careful interpretation of the creative character of Deer songs make it possible to understand not only that the Deer and Pascolas are inherently religious in their own right, but also that they operate as independent actors in a cosmological system in which Jesus needs their assistance. The Yaqui say that Deer and Pascolas work for Jesus, but they have remained associated with a traditional cosmology whose rules do not conform to a theistic, Christian notion of grace from on high.

In fact, the Yaquis have no word of their own for grace except flower, and Painter specifically notes that they do not recognize the Catholic distinctions between actual and sanctifying grace. Instead, they use the Spanish *gracias*, sometimes meaning tekia, or, 'in Yaqui, with *apo a grasiak* (that is his grace or talent)'. Although tekia is a gift, ability, and obligation deriving from the aboriginal dimensions, gracias is also sometimes associated with the 'holy light' which surrounds God in heaven and which is especially imagined in the resurrection of Jesus. In fact, one Yaqui states that the flowers of the Easter Ceremony 'refers to two things': life in the grace of God on earth and heavenly flower after death. In life, grace refers to the daily bread of the Lord's prayer, and especially to the need to do hard work. 'To earn heavenly glory one must do good deeds on earth, such as praying with faith and devotion, and charity, such as helping other needy persons and helping the sick and making contributions'.[29]

The same person links grace from God with flowers, and with the indulgence that accrues to good works. Another person specifically relates ceremonial work, flowers, and heaven, with the notion of grace as God's gratitude: 'When a man is having a hard time carrying out his duty as a working man, he is encouraged by being told not to worry, for later all that will be flower for him. In other words, a reward for his labor. ... So the symbol of the flower is put in the sermons ... It truly is the heavenly money for the thanks we have received ... Gracia is the reward for work and is often referred to as flower'. Said another Yaqui in agreement: 'It [flower] means you are being thanked'. While these remarks richly reverberate with the flower symbolism of the Deer and the Sea Ania, they suggest little of the Christian view of grace as the free gift of a transcendent God. Instead, the idea of gracias derives from traditional ideas of cosmic interdependence and reciprocity. When the Matachinis finish dancing for Mary, for

---

[29] Ibid., pp. 93, 103, 106.

example, they say to her: 'I place in your hand this holy flower which I earned being in your holy work during the night just gone'.[30]

Not surprisingly, then, flowers show up everywhere in the ceremonial regalia of both Christian and traditional religious actors. The Deer's horns are decorated with flowers, his singers use flower raspers in their music, and the dance ramada is often called the flower patio. The Pascolas tie their hair into a tuft bound with a red string called the 'fiesta flower string'. 'Those who own Our Mother's flowers', the Matachini dancers, wear a headdress that is called flower and they bless the fiesta ground with a flower wand. Flag girls and child angels wear flower crowns. The tassel that hangs from the bottom of the Yaqui rosary is also called flower. Even the Chapayeka masks which embody those beings seeking to kill Christ are called flower. It is evident that Painter is correct when she observes that:

> All groups are wrought into a harmonious whole. The Roman Catholic European tradition dominates, but there is also a covert commitment to the traditions of the yoania. The flower complex draws the whole together into a unity.

That unity is most clearly expressed in the actions of Holy Saturday morning when, having successfully killed Jesus, the triumphant Chapayekas attack his church. In the complex ritual action, the Deer blesses flowers heaped on a flower carpet. In defense of the church, Matachinis dance Mary's flowers, the church group and Pascolas throw flowers, and all the while the Deer dances.[31]

Painter, though clearly aware of the multi-dimensional referential play of the flower symbol, does not appreciate that it expresses an ancient Yaqui ethical logic about power that shapes their relations with the great Catholic others. She also over-interprets the symbol as fundamentally Christian. In effect, Painter makes Jesus the central actor in the Holy Saturday rites: 'The blood of Jesus, transformed into flowers, is, in the end, the victorious weapon against evil'. In actuality, each group of actors in the Easter Ceremony, including Christ, contribute flowers and so mutually empower each other. It is a pivotal reversal of the Christian theory of grace that originates from on high that, at the end of a fiesta, St Michael is called to pick up and carry to heaven the flowers (good deeds) which result from ceremonial action.[32] In this way, the Yaqui, whether members of the church groups or traditional singers and dancers, respectively do their part in a scheme of cosmic reciprocity that departs from the vertical superiority the theory of the supernatural associates with the Christian God.

[30] Ibid., pp. 93, 95, 103-6, 172.
[31] Ibid., pp. 103, 115, 146, 148, 159, 166, 169, 243, 284-6, 295, 335.
[32] Ibid., pp. 83-4, 102-3, 412.

Larry Evers and Felipe S. Molina identify linguistic insights about Deer songs which help to explain the Yaquis' flowering theory of ritual, and the way in which the Yaqui play a pivotal role in the cosmic scheme of things. Evers and Molina observe, first, that 'Yaquis have always believed that a close communication exists among *all* the inhabitants of the Sonoran desert world in which they live: plants, animals, birds, fishes, even rocks and springs. All of these come together as a part of one living community ... '. They also note that the Yaquis regard song as the language of this cornmunity, 'a kind of lingua franca of the intelligent universe'. They note that in preserving this language, Deer songs betray few Spanish influences.[33]

In fact, Yaqui ceremony powerfully juxtaposes several languages: Latin, Spanish, English, gestural languages of the various actors, ancient and contemporary forms of the Yaqui language, and the inverted language of the Pascolas. Evers and Molina detail some of this complexity:

> Like other languages, Yaqui may be used in many special ways. Expressed in some of its own terms, for example, the Yaqui language may be used *nooka*, to talk; *lionoka*, to pray (from Dios + noka, God talk); *hinabaka*, to give a sermon; *etehoi*, to tell, especially in the sense of an etehoim, story; and, of course *bwiika*, to sing. There are likewise many special ways to sing in Yaqui tradition. *Suru bwikam*/fly songs, *wo'i bwikam*/coyote songs, and the *maso bwikam*/deer songs ... Each one has its own subject matter, its own style of performance, and its own performance settings.

Even more tellingly, Evers and Molina identify several Yaqui views that reveal the central insight that flowers are the language of ritual. In Deer songs, the Singing Tree who prophesied Christianity is called 'flower stick', and it is said that 'when it talked, it was just like a song'. They also provide evidence, as does Muriel Painter, that the Yaqui equate the transformative power of Deer songs with that of Christian prayers. They relate one tradition to the effect that hunters gained power by eavesdropping on Deer and thus learning their language. In reflecting on a word characteristic of the Deer, Evers and Molina identify the closely related meanings of flower, song, and language:

> *Seyewailo* names, we think, that convergence of time, place, direction, and quality of being that is for Yaquis the essence of what they call the *sea ania*, the flower world, the convergence at which *Wok Vake'o* found the little fawn and the inspiration for the first deer song.

[33] Evers and Molina, *Yaqui Deer Songs*, pp. 18-19.

And, in noting that the Yaqui also associate songs with heaven, Evers and Molina insist that 'the single concept *sewa* provides a place for the notions of the good and the beautiful from both sides of the Talking Tree to come together, a place where the *sea ania* and *teweka* [heaven] can meet'.[34]

That meeting occurs in the Yaquis' ceremonial work which they understand as a flowering act of language. As Painter notes, ' "Flower" is truly the symbol of all righteous and holy acts, devotions, duties – all forms of compassionate and religious expression'. Flower describes 'the actual behavior' of ritual performances. Dancing their special truth shared with Mary, saying *in lutu'uria yi'ine*, 'I will dance my truth', Matachinis invite the participation of others: 'An invitation to participate in a fiesta may contain the phrase "share the truth with me", which is the same as "come and serve God with me".' This sharing explains the Yaquis' sense that they are all kinfolk because even a person without vows (kia pueblo, just pueblo ...) is expected to participate by whatever offerings he is able to make and by the performance of small duties. The Yaquis understand such ritual sharing as their blessing on God: 'the Lord truly received the holy benediction made like this for all baptized people; the contribution they made – truly one candle, or one skyrocket, or even one cent, if contributed with the one holy truth'. Even spectators contribute by giving witness.[35]

That holy truth also embraces the Deer and the Pascolas. The Deer works in close association with the transcendent Deer leader (and deceased Deer dancers) making manifest the flowering, sacrificial truths of the Sea Ania. At the end of fiestas, the Deer blows water from the flower bowl that produces Deer music, and so blesses spectators: 'It is sacred water', one Yaqui declares, 'because it has all the alabanzas [hymns, prayers comparable to those of the church group] of the deer'. The Pascolas protect the rites by warding off witches and the devil. In these ways, the Deer and the Pascolas serve the community, as well as Jesus.[36]

It can thus be seen that an understanding of flower leads to the conclusion that Yaqui Catholicism remains traditional in its theory of ritual action rather than compartmentalized as Edward Spicer thought. In both Spicer's and Muriel Painter's work, there is a strong tendency to interpret contemporary Yaqui religion from the Christian side of the cosmos. The result is that Spicer characterizes Deer and Pascolas as profane and the church groups as sacred. The effect on Painter's interpretation can be seen in the title of her book, *With Good Heart*, as well as in her thinking that Yaqui Christianity is supernaturalistic. The problem is that the phrase

[34] Evers and Molina, *Yaqui Deer Songs*, pp. 28, 33, 36-84; Painter, *With Good Heart*, p. 496.
[35] Painter, *With Good Heart*, pp. 58, 97-8, 100, 106, 358.
[36] Ibid., pp. 17, 242, 297, 329, 343, 496.

suggests a sense of individual sinfulness, guilt, and salvation that is not typical of the Yaquis' collective religious activity. It is true that both successful deer hunting and all forms of ritual activity require the necessary compassionate selflessness and self-discipline that the Yaqui convey in saying that ritual work must be done with good heart. Nevertheless, another phrase more closely captures the ways in which the Yaquis reciprocate with the positive religious others, and counter the evil others, of their complex cosmological and religious system. This phrase – which Painter notes is implicit in all ceremonial forms – 'Come, share the flower' – captures the sense of ritual work. Sharing the flower unites the Christian great others, the Yaqui church groups, and the traditional singers and dancers in an empowering system of co-operative, mutual acts of giving witness. And, it is this non-supernaturalistic character of Yaqui ritual work that is not understood either in Muncie, Indiana, or in the academic study of religion.

Part II
Performance

5. The ontological journey

Margaret Thompson Drewal

Editor's introduction

Ritual studies have passed through a number of overlapping stages. It seems to have taken quite some time to shake off the burden imposed by Enlightenment and Protestant associations between ritual and 'mere' or 'vain' repetition. Jonathan Z. Smith argues that there is, in fact, a useful insight to be gained from considering the emptiness of ritual, but in a rather different sense (see Smith 1987: 96-117). On the other hand, the emptiness of ritual as a category is argued forcefully by Catherine Bell (1992): ritual is something scholars construct by extracting aspects of people's engagement in life.

Much discussion of ritual continues to be interested in the structural forms that appear to describe and define 'ritual', or particular kinds of rituals. For example, Arnold van Gennep's (1960) formulation of the tripartite structure of rites of passage has been widely adopted. Important clarifications have been offered by Victor Turner (1991) and Bruce Lincoln (1981 and significantly furthered in the 1991 edition). It may also be worth noting that there has been debate about the relationship between 'ritual' and 'myth' (again, see Smith 1987, especially 102-3). For a summary of the current state of ritual studies, along with an expert assessment of 'some of [its] more promising directions', see Grimes (2000).

Margaret Drewal's chapter is an excellent exemplar of performance studies approaches to ritual. 'The ontological journey' resonates richly with themes that establish the integration of Drewal's multi-layered book, as well as with other trends in the study of ritual and (or as) performance. She does not neglect the experiential motivations and impact of the agents performing and playing their identities.

Reprinted from *Yoruba Ritual, Performers, Play, Agency*, Margaret T. Drewal, Indiana University Press, 1992. By permission of Indiana University Press.

There is truth in the notion that modernity constructs itself and indigeneity as alterities of one another (e.g. the 'settler' needs 'natives' and 'wilderness' to colonize). Similarly, it seems that modernity's notion of time as linear (an invaluable aid to industrialization) requires continuous reference to an alternative in which time is cyclical. However, Yoruba thought challenges this seemingly neat dichotomy, instead operating in ways that blend and re-configure experiences of stability and flux. This thought, and Drewal's discussion of it, are significant to Taiwo (2000).

References

Bell, Catherine. 1992. *Ritual Theory, Ritual Practice*. Oxford: Oxford University Press.

Gennep, Arnold van. 1960. *The Rites of Passage*. London: Routledge & Kegan Paul.

Grimes, Ronald L. 2000. 'Ritual', in Willi Braun and Russell T. McCutcheon (eds), *Guide to the Study of Religion*. London: Cassell, pp. 259-70.

Lincoln, Bruce. 1981. *Emerging from the Chrysalis: Studies in Rituals of Women's Initiations*. Cambridge, MA: Harvard University Press.

Lincoln, Bruce. 1991. *Emerging from the Chrysalis: Studies in Rituals of Women's Initiations*. Oxford: Oxford University Press.

Smith, Jonathan Z. 1987. *To Take Place: Toward a Theory in Ritual*. Chicago: University of Chicago Press.

Taiwo, Olu. 2000. 'Music, Art and Movement among the Yoruba', in Graham Harvey (ed.), *Indigenous Religions: A Companion*. London and New York: Cassell, pp. 173-89.

Turner, Victor. 1991. *The Ritual Process: Structure and Anti-Structure*. Ithaca: Cornell University Press.

∂∞6

'In a muddy land, a person slips and falls easily. Those who follow behind beware.' These were the words of wisdom spoken to Ọrunmila when he was traveling in a strange land called Ejibọnmẹfọn.

Before he set out, his diviners warned him to perform a sacrifice [*erubo*] so that he could be disgraced only to be later blessed. He sacrificed animals, birds, yams, palm oil, and all sorts of foodstuffs. The diviners put everything in a clay bowl, instructing Ọrunmila to carry it on his journey. He followed their instructions. Thank goodness he made the sacrifice. On the way, he first passed through the market on the outskirts of the town. There, Ẹṣu decided to humiliate him.

Causing it to rain heavily, Ẹṣu made the land slippery, but Ọrunmila persevered. As he reached the marketplace he slipped and fell down. The animals' blood, the palm oil, the food splattered all over his body. It was not pleasant to be so dirty. When the women and children in the market saw what happened, they began to laugh and ridicule him.

Ọrunmila did not know anybody. Ashamed and disgraced, he sat down feeling sorry for himself. That night when the marketwomen and their children went to sleep, Eṣu made them dream of blood spilling over their bodies. They were startled. Some woke up in fright, some became ill, some fell unconscious. Their husbands and fathers worried. Eṣu suddenly appeared inquiring:

What happened?

Husbands: The women woke up frightened and now they are ill.
Eṣu: Oh! You must consult a diviner.
Husbands: But there is no diviner around.
Eṣu: Yes, there is. You don't know? He is in the market.
Husbands: Take me to him.
Eṣu: Well then, bring a ram, a cow, some fish, a he-goat, a she-goat, and plenty of money.

Everybody went, one-by-one, each taking the prescribed animals and cash. Ọrunmila received everybody and helped them. In addition to the wealth he accumulated in that strange land, he also became famous.

Ọrunmila decided to thank the diviners who had advised him on his journey. During his thanksgiving service, he described how his beloved, learned diviners, in interpreting Ifa for him so wisely, had given him the words of wisdom that slippery land slips people up. Those who follow behind take note and be cautious.

But Ọrunmila's diviners said they were not to be thanked, that they themselves had to thank Ifa for giving them their wisdom. Then Ifa interjected that he is with God and God is with him.[1] Thus he too must not be thanked, but he must thank God Almighty.

In celebration, Ọrunmila's diviners summoned *apere* musicians from Ilara, *apesi* musicians and dancers from Ikija, and *iṣerimọle* dancers from Kijikiji, gathering them from different quarters.[2] As they played, Ọrunmila sang:

I fell down and everybody saw me.
They ridiculed me.
Who knew what the result would be?
I fell down and everybody saw me.
They ridiculed me.

---

[1]   Biblical phrasing is contextualised here.
[2]   *Kijikiji* is an ideophonic word meaning 'rowdiness'.

Mo ṣubú, wọ'n rí mi ò.
È lí sì mù'gbè yìn.
È lí sì mù'gbèhìn eti mi o?
Mo ṣubú o, wọ'n rí mi ò.
È lí sì mù'gbè yìn.

(Ọṣitọla #86.75)

Stories such as this often narrate the experiences of ancient diviners or animals on their distant journeys. 'Words of wisdom' begin the verses, framing the story, teaching lessons about life. But these words require interpretation and contemplation. Thus the wisdom of the story above is not to beware of slipping and falling, but has to do with humility, humiliation, and reciprocity. Ọrunmila withstood humiliation only to be blessed with fame and wealth. He thanked his diviners, who thanked Ifa, who in turn thanked God. Who slipped – Ọrunmila or those who ridiculed him? And who gained most from the humiliation? Ọrunmila learned humility through the experience of humiliation, while ones who humiliated him suffered most and in the end paid the greater price. This journey is only one among the many represented in Ifa literature that posit uncountable life situations. Such stories are always told in relation to an individual's personal problem.

Ọṣitọla, my diviner friend who lives in the town of Imodi only a few kilometers outside Ijẹbu-Ode, told me this story in relation to a personal experience of mine, so that I would not feel discouraged. Things had been going amiss; it was one of those kinds of days that is often associated with the workings of Eṣu, the unpredictable trickster/messenger, who in the story was instrumental in transforming Ọrunmila's disgrace into fame and fortune. According to his family history, Ọṣitọla is a seventh-generation diviner as well as a drummer and a member of the Ọṣugbo society, formerly the indigenous judiciary in Yoruba communities (M. Drewal and H. Drewal 1983). He and I have been working together since 1982, tape-recording more than one hundred fifty hours of conversations. Our talks, mostly in English, but interspersed with key concepts and discussions in Yoruba, covered religious and ritual topics.

Trained in the two hundred and fifty-six sets of divination texts (Odu Ifa), each with uncountable verses (*ẹsẹ*), Ọṣitọla has a keen memory.[3] In

---

[3]   The printed literature on Ifa texts and the divination process is enormous, some of it in Yoruba. The most extensive works are by Abimbọla (1968; 1969; 1975; 1976; 1977); Bascom (1969); Beyioku (1971); McClelland (1982); and Epega (1987). They tend to focus on the content of the texts, literary devices, the instruments of divination, and the casting process rather than on the situated context of meaning or the social use of metaphor. For a piece specifically on the training of diviners, see Abimbọla (1983).

1986, he remembered details of our discussions from 1982, sometimes reminding me that I was being redundant. When I responded that I was merely cross-checking, he retorted, 'no, you are double-crossing.' He always looked forward to 'wonderful' questions, that is, ones that made him wonder. They were not always easy for me to produce; Ọṣitọla thinks analytically and by his own account used to pester his father and grand-father quizzing them incessantly on the whys and wherefores of various ritual acts. He learned divination as a young boy simply by accompanying them during ritual, and at recess in primary school he used to divine for classmates on the ground. By the age of ten he was already taking leading ritual roles. From his grandmother, who was a priest of the deity Orisanla, he learned how to prepare shrines and care for the deities.

Nicknamed Abidifa (A-bi-di-Ifa, 'One who teaches the ABC's of Ifa'), Ọṣitọla can go on at great length naming the segments that make up the rituals he performs, describing the action associated with them, and explicating their meanings. In interviews, after exhausting all my questions, he would usually end by telling me what I had failed to ask. This eventually developed into an almost structural feature of our interviews. My most 'wonderful' questions by his standards were the ones for which there were no ready answers, the ones that required thought and some-times left him momentarily blank.

We discovered that the best method of working was simply for him to narrate what he does – step by step – and for me to ask questions for clarification. The Ijẹbu Yoruba term for a discrete ritual segment is *aito*, which is related to the noun *eto*, an order or program, the root word for *letoleto*, implying 'in an orderly fashion one after the other.' The serial form of performance is evoked in the very terms Yoruba use to char-acterize it (M. Drewal and H. Drewal 1987). Therefore, not only are participants' experiences of ritual fragmented, but the form itself is seg-mented.

During our many discussions of various kinds of rituals Ọṣitọla performs, he kept referring to the 'journey' as a way of conveying the experiential impact that ritual has on its participants. Finally I asked him explicitly, 'are all rituals journeys?' He explained,

the whole life span is wonderful. And even the actors are wonderful, I mean, the human beings. They are the main actors. The two are wonderful. One proverb says, when a young child falls, he looks to the front, but if an elder is falling he will always turn to look back in search of what befell him. Nowadays, the elders don't look back to see what has befallen them.

It is a sort of wisdom to reflect on past events to make a good decision on where we should try to go or what should happen. And this makes a journey.

127

But it seems to me as if everybody is contented, everybody is satisfied, everybody has already completed their journeys. No more journeys. Then I get worried. The actors want to end the journey. Or the journey wants to end. But to my knowledge the journey ends not. That is one of the things that makes your question wonderful to me because I know you are one of the actors. And I wondered how you could even ask, are they all journeys.

(Ọṣitọla #86.75)

Ọṣitọla does not use the word 'actors' in the Western sense of 'players of roles.' Rather, he means people of action. I perceived the significance of his use of the metaphor of the journey only after I began to realize just how many Yoruba rituals are actually constructed as journeys.

Journeying in orature and ritual

Divination verses tell of the journeys of ancient diviners and of deities and witches, 'when they were coming from heaven to earth' (*nigba ti wọn n t'ọrun bọ w'aye*). The journey (*irin ajo*, or simply *ajo*) is an important organizing metaphor in Yoruba thought.[4] The verb *rin*, 'to walk,' when compounded means 'to travel' (*rin irin* or *rinrin*). More than simply a movement forward, the act of traveling implies a transformation in the process, a progression.

Rituals in the form of masking displays travel in the sense that trained specialists 'bring them into the world' from their otherworldly domain and send them away again through their performances of spectacle (H. Drewal and M. Drewal 1983: 2-4). The deities journey into the world, too, by mounting the heads of their priests, who go into states of possession trance (M. Drewal 1986; 1988). Elaborated transitional stages mark the deity's arrival and withdrawal.

Wherever Yoruba religion thrives – Brazil, Cuba, the United States – this practice of journeying through possession trance has been maintained. Cast in a myriad of ways – in narratives and in ritual performances – the journey as a metaphor highlights the experiential, reflexive nature of day-to-day living. Nowhere is this more explicit than in the oral tradition and

---

[4] Interestingly, the journey as metaphor in African ritual may be quite widespread. In addition to Ọṣitọla (1988), see Ottenberg (1988); Nevadomsky and Rosen (1988); and H. Drewal on the journey's manifestation in other African ritual practices in *The Drama Review: A Journal of Performance Studies* (1988) on ritual performance in Africa today.

performance of Oṣugbo, the traditional society of elders that historically formed the judiciary in communities throughout southern Yorubaland.[5] Oṣitọla recited the following Ifa verse as the foundation of Oṣugbo (taped discussion #86.83):

A small child works his way off the edge of his sleeping mat.
A bird soars high above it all.
They divined for our elderly people,
When they were preparing to leave heaven to go to the world.
They said, what are we going to do?
They asked themselves, where are we going?
We are going in search of knowledge, truth, and justice.
In accordance with our destiny,
At the peak of the hill
We were delayed.
We are going to meet success.[6]
We will arrive on earth knowledgeable.
We will arrive on earth in beauty.
We are searching for knowledge continuously.
Knowledge has no end.

Ọmọ ilé tí a gbà gbé l'órí ẹní, yí o já bọ́.
Òkè l'ẹyẹ fò wún.
A díá fún àwọn àgbàgbà,
Tí wọ́n ti ìkọ̀lè ọrun bọ̀ wá ilé ayé.
Wọ́n ní kíni wọ́n ńlọ ṣe?
Ènyìn ọ̀rò, níbo lò ńlọ?
À ńlọ wá ìmò, òtító, àti òdodo.
Kádàrá àyànmò,[7]
L'órí òke
Àtì pẹ̀tẹ́lẹ̀.
À ńlọ sí ààfin ọba réré.
A ó dé ilẹ̀ mímọ̀.
A ó sì dé ilẹ̀ tó l'ẹ̀wà.
À ń wá ìmọ̀ síi l'ójo júmó.
Ìmò kò ló'pin.

Oṣitọla's gloss on this verse was as follows:

---

5   This society is also known as Ogboni. On the role of Oṣugbo/Ogboni in Yoruba society, see, among others, Dennett (1916); Bovell-Jones (1943); Bascom (1944); Biobaku (1956); Morton-Williams (1960); Agiri (1972); Atanda (1973); and H. Drewal (1989).

6   Literally, 'we are going to the beneficent king's palace.'

7   *Kadara* is the Hausa word for destiny; *ayanmọ* is Yoruba for the same idea.

'A small child works his way off the edge of his sleeping mat. A bird soars high above it all.' These were the words of wisdom spoken to some wise elders when they were leaving on a journey from heaven to the world. The classic meaning is just that a person should not be elevated unless he is prepared to fly above and search more.

Ifa told the elders to make a sacrifice. He told every one of them to carry along a walking stick for themselves, because their journey was far and they would feel tired. They did, and their path was blessed when they grew old.

These people in youth had the power to do things; in middle age the spreading world still had power;[8] then they moved to the elderly age. Their sacrifice was the staff, their assistant.

The elders thought. They started to search. They felt uncomfortable in their positions. They wanted to know more throughout the world. They decided to search for more, more, more. Because they were getting old, they felt worn out. That is why they were assisted by their staffs. Then their minds struck and asked them, 'you, where are you going?' *Enyin ọrọ, nibo lo nlọ?* It started changing their conscience. Then they remembered what Ifa had told them. On their journey they are searching for truth, wisdom, and knowledge. *A nlọ wa imọ, otito, ati ododo* in obedience to their *kadara ayanmọ,* destiny. In accordance with our destiny, we are searching for true knowledge and the facts. Then their conscience told them to continue with the search.

A person still searches with a staff in his hand after he has labored. Then the elders quickly remembered that their conscience told them that if they search for knowledge and wisdom, it will be through all the rough paths, *ori oke on pẹtẹlẹ.* That means, if they want to fulfill their destiny, they have to walk the path through the land, the hills, the water, the thorns, the troubles. They have to pass all troubles so that they can fulfill their destiny. And if they can afford to do this, they are sure to land at a holy place. *L'ori oke, ati pẹtẹlẹ, a nlọ si aafin ọba rere, a o wa dẹlẹ mimọ, a o si wa a dẹlẹ to lẹwa.* That means, if we can continue to search, to search, the end of our journey will be a cooler place where we have a good head, where it is holy, where it is smooth. This story is in Ifa.

Why I am telling this story is that it is related to Osugbo. That is their guidance or their foundation. When you are a member and you are upgraded to a point, that is your foundation – that Ifa verse relates to the behavior, the belief, the thinking, and the reasoning of the Osugbos. That was why you saw me nodding when we concluded that the journey continues, the search continues.

You know Ogboni means elderly people. You think that you still start, you feel that you still begin. And even at your dying point, you will feel that you will decide you will still continue. You will not be sure whether you have searched enough. And even on your death, after you have found yourself at the resting place, at the cooler place, then you will feel you are leaving the search to be continued with those who will take it from you. They will bid you bye, and say you are expected to continue. That is why you see me so serious that night when

---

[8] 'The spreading world' is a reference to the way people put on weight in middle age.

we are trying to agree that, oh, the search continues.

This story may not be so interesting, but it is a true picture of our discussion, and it is a true picture of Ọṣugbo. It relates to the research of the elders and why elders are still searching. You know nowadays elders get contented, even at [age] forty.

The reason why I am trying to translate or transcribe it or share the view with you to digest is because it is very serious. That is one of the foundations of our family. Their foundation is the search continues. That is one of the motives behind our continued inheritance of Ifa and Ogboni in our family. We want the search to be continued. Even my grandfather wants me to continue; my father wants to continue; I want to continue. Since Ọṣijo [the father seven generations back] we want the search to be continued.

The verse is one of the important things my grandfather gave me. And I have been graduating on it. He didn't elaborate it to such an extent, but when I became a staunch member of Ọṣugbo and I learned more, I found more, I could get what he was really concerned with deeply from my initiation, going through some rituals, and I found out that, oh, the search continues in fact. In my family circle, it is my life.

Ọṣitọla's explanation was an improvised narrative based on a pre-formulated verse. As he commented, his grandfather 'gave' him the verse, but did not elaborate it. Only later – Ọṣitọla claimed – after going through rituals did he come to understand his grandfather's deep concerns. The verse served as a precedent for the narrative and to some extent guided it.[9] He contextualized both the verse and the improvised narrative within our conversations, regarding the latter not only as a 'true picture' of what it means to be a member of Ọṣugbo, but as a 'true picture' of our own conversations. By that time, I had in fact gone through a preliminary initiation into Ọṣugbo at Imodi so that the story was meaningful for me on two levels. The narrative also reflected Ọṣitọla's perception of my work as a researcher, which he correlated with the 'journeying' of Ọṣugbo elders and Ifa priests.

At Ọṣugbo meetings during the annual festival – I attended six in three different society lodges (*iledii*) between October 11 and December 1, 1986 – each of the titled elders danced solos from one end of the enclosed space to the other, giving concrete expression to the idea of the journey. Their

---

[9] The relationship between esoteric verses and improvised narratives comes up again in [Drewal 1992] chapters 4 and 5 on divination rituals. By juxtaposing the verse with the narrative here, I have tried to give the reader a sense of their relationship and the extent to which the narrative elaborates and deviates from the verse. In the following chapters I have provided only the performer's re-tellings of the narrative. For discussions of the social use of metaphor and a distinction between narrative performances and reports of narrative performances and their relative value, see Kirshenblatt-Gimblett (1976).

131

performances were improvised. Each dance was a personal condensation of life's journey (*ajo l'aye*), performed to the drum language of music called *ẹwẹlẹ*, an ideophonic word implying an assortment of rhythms considered good for dancing. As an Oṣugbo drummer, Oṣitọla says he changes the rhythms according to the particular dancer's concentration. By approximating the tonal patterns and rhythm of spoken Yoruba, Oṣitọla weaves into the music praise epithets (*oriki*) particular to each dancing elder. For Akọnọrọn – to take one example – the titled elder who acts as the defense counselor in criminal cases, Oṣitọla sometimes plays:

> Teacher of the art of speaking
> The one who teaches how to state a case
> Pleads for the innocent

> *A kóni ní oro*
> *A kó-ni léjọ́*
> *Àwi jàre*

In and around the praise epithets, Oṣitọla weaves dance instructions – one-liners that are mixed and repeated to form a free rhythm, each alluding to life's journey. One tells the dancing elder in effect to watch where he or she is stepping. It alludes to life's potential pitfalls – 'the thorns, the troubles' and the value of reflecting on the past in order to guide present action:

> Elder, watch the ground

> *Àgbà wolẹ̀*

Improvisationally in step with the *agba* drums, the dancer enacts 'checking up' the ground, visibly watching where she or he places the foot. Or, in another example:

> Carry on [stepping] on the ground

> *Ṅṣó n'lẹ̀*

The *lẹ* in both verses above refers to the ground or earth, *ilẹ*. To the latter rhythm the dancer is supposed to step lively and confidently on the earth. How the rhythm is interpreted spatially and stylistically is left to each dancer's discretion. The latter verse, Oṣitọla explained to me, is an assertion that the elders have authority over the earth; therefore, the drummers direct them to 'carry on' with the business at hand. Their authority is rooted in the precolonial, gerontocratic government of Yorubaland.

It was with his experience of this kind of ritual performance described above that Ọṣitọla said he came to understand his grandfather's deep concerns. On the surface, the verbal content of the drummed messages does not say much. It is only in living, or 'journeying,' that elders begin to read meaning into such esoteric words and actions. My own understanding comes from Ọṣitọla's explanations, and only then after my initiation, which entitled me to enter Ọṣugbo lodges to participate in certain performances.

In many kinds of Yoruba ritual, the performance processes embody all of the characteristics of a journey: 1) travel from one place to another, and a return – sometimes actual, sometimes virtual, 2) new experiences, 3) joys and hardships along the route, 4) material for further contemplation and reflection, and 5) presumed growth or progress as a result of the whole experience. Rites of passage that scholars mark in a tripartite movement from separation and liminality to reaggregation (Turner 1977: 94) are in a very real sense journeys. But transition is not merely social, not simply a collective adjustment to internal changes or an adaptation to the external environment.

Like journeys, rites of passage are fundamentally transformations of experience, a deepening and broadening of each individual's understanding in relation to his or her prior experience and knowledge. If this were not so, how would participants *feel* social transition? Or, from another point of view, why is it that social transition cannot often simply be legislated or ordained? Even in our own society, rituals often attend legislated transitions. Thus what constitutes a marriage legally has little to do with what getting married means performatively. The latter in most cases constitutes the greater part of the experience of transition. Both in rituals and in journeys, participants operate at different levels of understanding and also have different capacities for making meaning.

As Ọṣitọla argued for a ritual he conducts:

All people who go to the sacred bush [*igbodu*] benefit from it. They may be observers; they may be priests; they may be the initiate. Only we concentrate on the initiate most. Yet everybody is involved, particularly the priests, for there is a belief – and it's an agreement between ourselves and Odu [the deity] within the sacred bush – that we are reborning ourselves. Even we priests, we are getting another rebirth. At every ritual, we are becoming new because we have something to reflect upon. We have something to contemplate during the journey, at the journey, after the journey. Our brains become sharper. We become new to the world. We think of everything. We *do* there, and we *see* there. And even more simply we pray for everybody.

(Ọṣitọla #86.134)

With each restoration of behavior, even the ritual specialist is transformed and 'becomes new to the world.' This is also true for me as I experience Yoruba ritual repeatedly. Through a process of observation/participation, conversations with participants, contemplation, and reflection, I too become a ritual traveler in Ọṣitọla's sense, although what I derive from the experience will not necessarily be the same as what anyone else derives from the same experience. This is so not only because of differences in cultural and personal experience, but because of differences in the motives and motivations of the various participants. Most important is the idea that the sojourner may return to the same place physically, but not experientially.

Rituals attend both birth and death and serve as temporal articulation points of ontological transformation analogous to the spatial point of articulation represented by the crossroads. Such rituals are the focus of the remainder of this chapter and [in Drewal 1992] the next. As a member of Oṣugbo, Ọṣitọla narrated to me a detailed outline of funeral ritual from the practitioner's point of view, designating the names of the various stages of performance. Ọṣitọla's outline is an individual's normative account of what he knows from personal experience, not a presentation of dogma. Whether or not a funeral *always* happens just this way is not my concern here, although his descriptions of the public portions do correspond to what I have observed.

My intention is threefold: 1) Ọṣitọla's account illustrates how Yoruba practitioners conceptualize, order, and explicate ritual. Both the doing and the talking about the doing derive from the same stock of performance knowledge (Giddens 1986: 29). 2) His specialist's view is also revealing about the concept of the ontological journey. This is critical at the end of the chapter for a reevaluation of the notion of cyclical time in Mircea Eliade's sense (1959: 77-8).[10] 3) Equally important, Ọṣitọla's conceptual model underscores the centrality of play in Yoruba ritual, a topic I explore throughout the rest of the chapters [of Drewal 1992]. It is apparent throughout that Ọṣitọla is conscious that ritual specialists are engaged in acts of interpretation and representation. Although I have not always quoted him verbatim, I have preserved his language, descriptions, and explanations quite literally, restricting my own comments to footnotes.

---

[10] Cyclical time in this sense is 'a reactualization of the cosmogony,' implying 'starting time over again at its beginning, that is, restoration of the primordial time, the "pure" time, that existed at the moment of Creation.' The phrase as used by Eliade should not be confused with ritual cycle – the periodic recurrence of ritual.

The funeral passage

There are many different kinds of funerals. The circumstances of death, its perceived causes, the age and social as well as religious affiliations of the deceased all are taken into account as a family decides what type of funeral to perform. Here Ọṣitọla narrates the structure and content of the funeral he claims everyone hopes to have – the desired one – except if the deceased is Muslim or Christian.[11] These funerals (*isinku*) are for those who have died of old age. They are not simple matters of burying the corpse; rather, they involve seven days of ritual (*etutu*) performed to convey the spirit of the deceased to its otherworldly realm, where it remains along with other ancestral spirits. Friends of the deceased's family experience a funeral primarily as a time of dancing and feasting in celebration of the elder's long successful life. For the family, however, a funeral demands great effort and an enormous expense to ensure the continued beneficence of the elder's spirit toward those still on earth. A funeral is a critical time when the deceased's spirit lingers in the world, disembodied. There is also the expectation that the spirit will eventually return in newborn children. A funeral in this way marks an ending as well as a new beginning.

The actual interment of the corpse is conceived only as a preliminary event to the funeral process. The performances that follow are more critical for the family. After the interment, family members gather to decide on a date for the performances that complete the *isinku*, the funeral. Since the *isinku* entails great expense, it is incumbent on the family to set a date far enough in the not-too-distant future to give them time to gather sufficient resources. The funeral may therefore occur anywhere from a month to a year, or more, after burial. What follows interment, according to Ọṣitọla, is a seven-day program in which certain days are set aside for celebration: the first, or 'main,' funeral day of ritual (*ọjọ isinku*); the third day, for feasting (*itaoku*); the fourth day, a public celebration or day of play (*irenoku*, literally 'playing on the deceased's behalf'); and a seventh and final celebration day (*ijeku*).[12] Funerals are in this way elaborated with feasting and public performances, part of the sacrifice to the deceased.

Most of the rituals that revolve around interment are exclusive. They are the prerogative of the Ọṣugbo society, whose membership in the past was

---

[11] With the increase in Christianity and Islam, fewer people have such funerals than would have in the past, although certain elements carry over. For comparison, see Peter R. McKenzie's study of Christian burials and his composite account of 'traditional' funerals based on secondary sources (1982: 12-13).

[12] This seven-day period corresponds to two Yoruba four-day weeks in which the last day of the first week is also counted as the first day of the second week.

135

restricted to those whose parents were dead. Prior to the colonial period, Oṣugbo included the senior members of each family in a community. Because of their age, accumulated knowledge, and power, they comprised the segment of the community that was indeed closest to the ancestors by virtue of their proximity to death.

Interment (*Ifẹhin Oku-Tilẹ*)[13]

'Washing the corpse' (*Iweku*): A cosmetologist (*ọnatoniṣe*, 'one skilled in the art of restoration'), who is a member of Oṣugbo, prepares the corpse by first sacrificing a cock or a hen, depending on whether the deceased is male or female. In the case of a female, for example, it is said that the voice of the hen follows the deceased to the otherworld.[14] The sacrificial blood, together with a preparation of water and herbs, is used to wash the corpse.

'Rubbing chalk on the deceased's palms' (*Ikefunlọwọ*) and 'Rubbing camwood on the palms' (*Ikosunlọwo*): After washing the corpse, the eldest living offspring of the deceased rubs chalk (*efun*) and then camwood (*osun*) on the deceased's palms. This means that the child who was nurtured is now nurturing the deceased parent in return. Or, in other words, as a parent brings a child into the world so must the child assist in the parent's passage into the otherworld. As the eldest applies the chalk, the children say to the deceased, 'you put chalk in my hand for me' (*ikefun lọwọ fun mi*).[15]

'Wrapping the corpse of the wise elder' (*Idiku Ọlọgbọn*): Relatives and other supporters of the deceased each bring cloth for the Oṣugbo members to wrap around the corpse. The cloth expresses their gratitude to the deceased for his or her good deeds. The sheer volume of the wrapped corpse is indicative of the social significance of the deceased. The word *ọlọgbọn* literally means 'a wise person.' In this context it refers both to the deceased elder and to a colorful, highly patterned cloth known as *aṣọ ọlọgbọn* – a trademark of elders. The importance of wrapping the deceased in cloth is expressed in the adage 'the corpse of the elder should not be thrown away; it is white cloth that I wore from heaven to the world' (*oku ọlọgbọn ki s'oko; ala mo fi b'ọrun w'aye*). The idea is that the elder should

---

[13] Ọṣitọla's account is an edited transcription of taped discussions #s 86.94, 86.144, and 86.145, Ibẹju-Ode, 1 December 1986.

[14] The voice in this sense represents the living spirit itself.

[15] This practice follows literally what parents do to a newborn baby as an abbreviated initiation into the world.

leave the world in a similar manner as the child is born into it.[16]

The multipatterned cloth represents the accumulation of the deceased's experiences while on earth. Hence – to quote directly:

> We bury them with these kinds of cloth to make them more concerned. You know they have gotten experiences. They have lived in hot weather – all sorts of weather – they have mixed with all sorts of people. They will be settling differences between people when they quarrel. They have been seeing women with good characters, with bad characters, and men with good characters and bad characters. They have moved with the elders, the youths, the ancestors. Now they have combined many experiences. This cloth contains within itself their many experiences with animals, with human beings, up and down the hills, with dangerous creatures, with non-dangerous creatures. Experiences make you more open to life and death.[17]

'Washing the coffin' (*Iwegi*): Later in the evening, a representative from both the father's and the mother's sides of the family join the cosmetologist to sacrifice a goat to the coffin, blessing it for the deceased by putting some of the blood in their hands and a little in the coffin. The three of them then wash the coffin inside and out with herbal water: together they dip balls of cotton wool into the water, the left hand washing inside as the right washes outside. Then reversing the process, they cross their arms and use the right hand on the inside and the left on the outside. After working their way around the coffin in this manner three times, the cosmetologist removes the sacrificial goat, whose meat is part of his remuneration for work.

'Laying the back of the deceased on the earth' (*Ifehinkutile*):[18] This occurs in the evening when it is cool. Starting around eight o'clock, the cosmetologist arranges the body in the coffin in preparation for the next stage of the ritual, when the elders gather and feast with the deceased throughout the night.

'Entertaining with the deceased' (*Ibokuu-yaju*): When an elder dies, her or his contemporaries, normally the Oṣugbo members, celebrate with the deceased after they have wrapped the corpse. The high-ranking elders go with their drums before it is too dark and send the naive people away – the youth, the untrained, and the uninitiated. They lay the deceased out on a

---

[16] The 'white cloth' from heaven refers to the birth caul. Like the birth caul, the cloth of ritual novices is white, while the cloth of elders is multicolored and often highly patterned.

[17] The patterns on the cloth do not express this in any literal way. Rather, the complexity of the designs as they float over sometimes strong horizontal stripes suggests the complexities of life itself and the elder's mastery of them.

[18] This ceremony begins the process of interring the body, from which the entire process derives its name. The corpse is usually buried under the floor of the house.

handwoven mat (ẹni fafa), and all sit down with him or her to feast. This ritual is conceived as a kind of 'send-off party' to bid their comrade farewell. The elders wine, dine, and discuss, reaffirming their camaraderie in the deceased's presence.

As Ọṣitọla put it, 'now that the soul is going to join the ancestors, they must present themselves in the same spirit as the deceased and the other ancestors, who may have gathered to receive him, in order to bear witness that they are still loyal. They still love him. Their mind is still open to him.' Each time they put the wine to their lips, they also open the cloth and put it to the deceased's lips to express their cooperation. The cosmetologists then dance as the drums are beaten.

This ritual segment tests the honesty and sincerity of Oṣugbo members. Thus those among them who do not show up are assumed to be dishonest,

> because he[19] will not be able to lead himself between life and death. Because he cannot live to the death point, it means he is not supposed to be among them. That is a test, and it is a belief among Yorubas in the olden days that somebody who cannot go through *ibokuu-yaju* has in his mind that he has not been behaving openly. Hence he must be sure to eat and dine with the dead because it is they who join the ancestors. And the ancestors' spirits are supposed to be ruling the community and guiding the community right. Somebody who cannot join somebody who is joining the ancestors is not for the good of the community. He is not open. He may be a sort of liability. He is not a good asset because nobody will be able to believe him.

This ritual is the deceased's initiation by the society of elders into the group of the ancestors.

'Sending away the spirit of the deceased' (*Ikanku*): After the lid of the coffin is closed, the eldest child takes the cosmetologist's brass staff and raps it three times near the corpse's head. The knocking dispatches the soul of the deceased. Finally, the cosmetologist sees to it that the coffin is placed in the grave, completing the interment of the corpse.

---

[19] Although 'he' is used throughout, the description applies equally to men and women. Pronouns in the Yoruba language do not specify sex. Thus Yoruba speakers of English often use English pronouns interchangeably without reference to gender. Ọṣitọla also often uses he/she interchangeably.

The main funeral day (Ọjọ Isinku)

'Collecting money for the deceased' (Owoetiweku): During the main day of the funeral, family members first of all collect money from all the relatives to buy gin and arrange for food. Formerly bean cakes were most desirable. The relatives contribute money in proportion to their closeness to the deceased. The more distant the relations, the less they are expected to contribute.[20]

'Playing for the funeral' (Ereisinku): The first public ceremony is a spectacle of playing and dancing in honor of the deceased. Relatives of the deceased hire music groups and accompany them around the town dancing and singing the praises of the family.[21] Family members also try to hire music groups that reflect the stylistic tastes of the deceased. Ọsitọla told me of the funeral of his father, Ọsineye, when his father's junior brother attempted to attract musicians from his senior brother's group so that he could personally provide the deceased's favorite musical style. Any style is appropriate as long as the group is mobile, for it is essential to parade throughout the community.

The social importance of the deceased is measured by the amount of ere, or 'play,' going on throughout the town. Forty-three musical groups paraded around for Ọsitọla's father's funeral. The number of groups became a topic of discussion among townspeople. They asked, 'How many groups played for Ọsineye's funeral?' (Ere meloo ni wọn ṣe l'ojọ ti Ọsineye ku?)

The parades of music and dance independently working their ways through the town are a formal ritual segment (aito) that is meaningful beyond the display for its own sake. As Ọsitọla expressed it,

> they think dancing and enjoying after the death will depict the deceased's achievements on earth, how he or she was able to behave to the community. [. . .] It is not that they are extravagant. They do it for a meaning. If they don't do it, then the deceased who is joining the ancestors will be concerned and unhappy – be wandering – because he has not been remembered. The deceased will have to answer queries [that is, from the ancestors]. 'Why are you not properly initiated, or sent to us? Perhaps you have not performed well, have not achieved well? If you have performed well, why is posterity forgetting you?' The only way for us on earth to judge the deceased is to know how much honor was given to him by his descendants.

[20] Or, to put it another way, the amount by extension constructs the quality of the donor's relationship to the deceased.

[21] The children often dress in clothes of the deceased, and it has recently become the style to hold up a framed photograph of the deceased as a kind of centerpiece of the group.

'Taking the achievements of the deceased' (*Imoran Oku, Imu ọran oku*): The main day ends around eight or nine o'clock at night with a more elaborate ceremony to send the deceased's soul to the ancestors. By 'taking' the achievements of the deceased, the family this time introduces the soul into heaven. The cosmetologists lead a representative of both the father and mother of the deceased to the grave site. They carry with them a piece of white cloth, a *fafa* mat, and some of the deceased's personal possessions. There they call the soul of the deceased and offer a goat to his or her inner head in a ritual segment known as *ikankuolowo*.

'Invoking the soul of the deceased' (*Ikankuolowo*): Holding the mat by the corners and dancing to the outskirts of the town to the major cross-roads (*orita*), the relatives send the soul to join the other spirits. They do so simply by mutual agreement that the soul is happy to be sent away hon-orably. On the road, they chant declaratively that the elaborateness of the ceremonies befits the departed ('it befits him,' *o yẹ o*). By extension, then, he or she is presumed worthy to dwell with the ancestors. The mat, the piece of cloth, and other materials are divided up so that a portion can be used for the next ritual stage. This ends the main funeral day. After per-forming the first two parts of the main funeral day, the family feels that they have contributed to the deceased's successful journey to heaven.

The third day of the funeral (*Itaoku*)

The third day is reserved for feasting; at night there is a sacrifice at the grove of Oro (*igbo Oro*).[22] Children of the deceased and other relatives share their favorite foods with their friends throughout the entire day. During that night the caretaker of the Oro bush sacrifices a ram to the ancestor. Those who hold the title of caretaker (*atejumole*) are among the kingmakers (Agba Oke, or Iwarefa) within the Osugbo society.

'Opening the voice of the deceased' (*Ilakuoun* [*Ila oku oun*]): The new ancestor's voice will be heard for the first time.[23] People say, 'Oro is crying.' The voice of Oro on that night is presumed to be the spirit of the newly buried deceased coming to endorse the funeral performances of his

---

[22] Oro is a society whose membership overlaps that of Osugbo. It is concerned specifically with spirits of ancestors and with death. In this capacity, its members were the executioners of those criminals condemned to death by Osugbo. However, people say Oro, not a human being, takes the lives of criminals.

[23] This is done with bullroarers – rhombs that are swung around in the air, producing a shrill, eerie sound to represent the ancestor's voice. The source of Oro's voice is regarded as a secret even though people have an idea what it is, and there are many Oro rhombs in museums around the world.

140

children and other relatives. After the *atejumole* has opened the deceased's voice, he will ask the deceased to follow the male family members into the town to bless the relatives who have provided an honorable burial. Women must close themselves inside their rooms and lock the doors, for it is strictly forbidden for women to witness Oro. They hear only the sound.

Playing on behalf of the deceased (*Irenoku*)

During this fourth day of the funeral, the children and friends parade through the town and feast once again, this time principally to affirm their own success in providing a proper burial, but also to celebrate their ancestor's endorsement of their efforts.[24] It is the second day devoted strictly to dancing and enjoying, a formal ritual segment of play (*aito ku mere muse*) that is simultaneously a sacrifice performed willingly and very elaborately at the expense of the deceased's descendants. The children arrange for musicians, just as they do on the main funeral day, only more elaborately. 'By dancing around the town, everybody can see from their own places how many plays have been done, how the drummers beat respect, how the children finish the ceremony happily.' Again, they also count the number of groups, or plays, on that date as a sign of the ser-iousness of the descendants. The various groups stop at different places, particularly the compounds of relatives, where it is believed the new ancestor's spirit will stay. 'You know the spirit of the father will be going around his children's houses. And he will stop at the marketplace and at important junctions on the outskirts of the town.'

Seventh funeral day for the deceased (*Ejeoku*)

Four days following the play day, the children offer the new ancestor pounded yam and fish soup at home (*ibo osi*). After the descendants per-form this sacrifice, and another in the Oro grove, the ancestor becomes manifest once more, this time together with Oro music played on *agba* drums, in a ritual segment known as *asipelu*. Thus the deceased comes to receive the sacrifice 'in the Oro mood.'[25] Oro society members as well as male relatives of the deceased follow the ancestor's voice, which thanks and blesses all the family members. Once again women must close

---

[24] The ancestor's endorsement had been in evidence the previous day through the sound of Oro's voice.

[25] That is, through the sound of the Oro rhombs accompanied by drums.

themselves inside their rooms and lock the doors.

This outing of the spirit voice is the final act of transference, the incorporation of the spirit of the deceased into ancestorhood. An incantation affirms, 'the deceased who possesses wisdom will not be deaf' (oku ologbon ki ṣeti), that is, will attend his or her descendants in the world in return for their attention during the funeral. In celebrating the deceased, friends and relatives of the family pay homage to the ancestors broadly as a collective. As the living send off the deceased, so too the deities prepare the deceased's place in the otherworld. When somebody dies, it is said, 'the deities establish the father who sleeps' (oriṣa tẹ ni fun, baba o sun).[26]

In Oṣitọla's account of how funerals should be performed, both play and competition were built into the structure of performance. Not merely a display of wealth for its own sake, the funeral literally constructs the social significance, power, and prestige of the deceased and his or her family at the same time that it constructs for the family and community a representation of the quality of the deceased's existence in the otherworld. The family and the community in this way judge themselves by the spectacle they create, and by extension judge the spirit's acceptance by the ancestors. Strong support for a deceased family member at the same time expresses the power of the corporate group.

Variations on the theme

In the periods designed for play, especially on the main and the fourth days, funerals for the elderly take on other dimensions, in addition to those described by Oṣitọla, when the deceased has other kinds of affiliations. If, for example, an elderly man was a hunter, blacksmith, drummer, or brasscaster, the funeral will typically include a send-off known as iṣipadẹ or ipadẹ, literally, the act of opening the way for the hunter (a nṣi ipa odẹ). This ceremony is reportedly conceived to send the spirit of the deceased to join all the other ancestors who during their lifetimes worked specifically with metal implements requiring strong, direct, powerful action – the killing of animals, the forging of iron, the beating of drums (cf. M. Drewal 1989). They include devotees of Ogun, the deity of iron and war, and of Ọbalufọn, the deity of artists.

The members of the funeral party wear old worn-out clothing. If the deceased was a hunter, for example, they carry guns and knives and create havoc around the town. As the drummers play, the spirit of the deceased

---

[26] An honored ancestor is thought to develop and expand in the otherworld and then return in generations of grandchildren.

mounts and possesses the hunter's comrades. The spirits of those in such professions are necessarily brave, fierce, and, above all, active. The participants thus fire their guns, lash and cut themselves, and tear each other's clothes as they engage in mock combat. In the process their clothes become even more ragged.

After parading around the town three times, they then process to a main crossroads on the outskirts. There they remove their clothes and place them at the junction, hanging some on a stake with a crossbar that is reminiscent of a scarecrow. This accumulation at the crossroads is the trace (*ipa*) of the hunter, from which the *ipade* derives its name; more literally, *ipa* refers to the translucent trail left by a snail as it moves along the ground. In this way the participants create an impression of the deceased standing at the crossroads. The clothes are also evidences of the tremendous physical energy that the deceased's supporters have expended on his behalf. Their actions also dramatize the ethos of hunters and those who work with metal.

Such special performances woven into the fabric of funeral rites serve to distinguish groups and group affiliations. 'You know everybody has his own group in the ancestor world,' I was informed. Different affiliations are marked differently. Special funerals are accorded to diviners, as well as to priests of the deities, whose heads have been ritually prepared for possession trance.[27] Likewise, Egungun masks perform as part of the *isinku* of deceased Egungun society members (see [Drewal 1992] chapter 6), Efe and Gelede masks sing and dance for the *isinku* of deceased Gelede society members (H. Drewal and M. Drewal 1983: 59-61, 156, 193), and Agemo masks come out during the *isinku* of Agemo society members (see [Drewal 1992] chapter 7). These performances are part of the public displays on the days set aside for play. There are many other variations along these same lines, both public and private.

The funerals of kings are also special, because their rites of installation elevate them to a sacred status. Thus, kings are hailed, 'the king with metaphysical power is second only to the gods' (*oba alase, ekeji orisa*). Since Agemo priests are also the headmen of their own communities, their funeral rites combine components of those rites performed for kings, priests of deities, and Agemo society members, including the appearances of Agemo masks.

Multiple affiliations give rise to heterogenous funerals that can incorporate many distinct traditions and styles of performance. In 1978 in a

---

[27] These are extremely secret and involve the removal of active medicines from the deceased's head that were placed there during initiation. This practice persists in the United States among priests of Yoruba deities.

western Yoruba town just outside Ilaro, the funeral of a deceased elder included performances of both the Egungun and Igunnuko masking societies. Igunnuko is an imported tradition, introduced into Yoruba country by Nupe emigrants, who are maintaining their own cultural identities and at the same time being assimilated into Yoruba culture. The deceased's affiliations were multiple, reflecting this heterogeneity.[28] The relationship of one Igunnuko mask to the deceased was explicitly drawn when the mask went to stand on the ancestor's grave just outside the house. The two columns that decorate the foot of the grave depict the mask in miniature, while a Muslim writing board with Arabic script is set in relief on the front. Both reflect the deceased's identity as masked performer and Muslim, or at least they reflect the way the family wanted to remember him. The two masking societies to which he belonged worked it out between themselves so that the Igunnuko masks performed in the afternoon, and the Egungun masks performed overnight that same evening.

The competition among families, and even within families, to put on the largest displays around the town – some say – encourages people in the community to perform better in life with the idea that their funerals will 'befit' them. Since funerals are evaluated, elders fear appearing comparatively insignificant, especially after it is too late to do anything about it. If the dimension of public display seems extravagant, even relentless, it is because it is considered a sacrifice. Approval comes back directly from the deceased spirit's voice through the instrumentality of the elders, whose age, special training, and ritual roles make them living representations of the ancestors. That is the essence of the elders' wining and dining the deceased, as Ọṣitọla expressed it. It is the power of public display to proclaim the enormity of the family's concern throughout the town and even into the otherworld.

Ọṣitọla did not elaborate the play segments of music and dance since they are highly variable. Instead, what he stressed was the quantity of the performing groups. The choice of styles, it was suggested, is based primarily on the perceived music tastes of the deceased, his or her social affiliations with performing groups such as Ifa or Agẹmọ, and the tastes of the sponsors. Such funerals incorporate different styles and traditions of performance.

---

[28] A more detailed treatment of Yoruba concepts of identity and personality is in [Drewal 1992] chapters 4 and 5.

Cyclical time and the other

Ritual journeys have a synecdochic relationship to the greater ontological journey of the human spirit in that they are nested in 'life's journey' (*ajo l'aye*). Not conceived as cyclical in the sense of beginning time over or returning to the world the same each time, journeying is always a progression, a transformation. The idea of transformation is implicit in a divination text given by Wande Abimbọla (1976: 132), which narrates how three men, before leaving heaven to come to earth, chose their heads. When two of them, Oriseeku and Oneemere, compared the success of the third, Afuwape, with their own failures, they remarked:

> I don't know where the lucky ones chose their heads,
> I would have gone there to choose mine.

Afuwape answers, concluding the verse:

> We chose our heads from the same place,
> But our destinies are not identical.

Every time spirits return to the world, they choose different heads or personalities (*ori inu*), different bodies (*ara*), and different destinies (*ayanmọ*).

One of the projects of the functionalist-structuralist approach, according to Johannes Fabian (1983: 41), was to contrast 'Western linear Time and primitive cyclical Time, or . . modern Time-centeredness and archaic timelessness.' Ritual tends to be placed in the latter category, even so-called secular rituals (see Moore and Myerhoff 1977: 8). But does this really reflect Yoruba thought?[29]

If in Yoruba thought life on earth is merely a temporary segment in a human spirit's journey, then all time would have to be classified as cyclical, not just ritual time. What Benjamin Ray (1976: 41) terms 'ordinary linear time' would not exist in Yoruba consciousness, since, conceptually, the human spirit is always coming into the world and returning in one unending cycle. On the other hand, since nothing ever repeats itself, and since from this ontological perspective there is always change and transformation – of body, of personality, of mission, of destiny – then existence in time would be more appropriately conceived in spatial terms as a spiral – neither cyclical, nor linear. There is no time-out-of-time, properly

---

[29] For a fairly recent attempt to grapple with this issue, see J. D. Y. Peel (1984), who concludes that both concepts coexist among the Yoruba.

speaking that is, if I have understood the concept as Ọṣitọla expressed it:

> The whole life span of a man or a woman is a journey. That is our belief. *Ajo l'aye* [literally, 'journey of life']. When you are going to start your life, you go through a journey. Even when you are coming to the life, you go through a journey. And if you want to develop on the life, it is a journey. So it is just journey, journey, journey all the while.

Me: When people go on a journey, what does that mean?

Ọṣitọla: I have told you, the whole life span of a human is a journey. What we are doing now is a journey. All movements are journeys. We are progressing, we are moving. (taped discussion #86.77[1])

References

Abimbọla, Wande. 1968. *Ijinle Ohun Enu Ifa, Apa Kiini*. Glasgow: Collins.

Abimbọla, Wande. 1969. *Ijinle Ohun Enu Ifa, Apa Keji*. Glasgow: Collins.

Abimbọla, Wande. 1975. *Sixteen Great Poems of Ifa*. Nigeria: UNESCO.

Abimbọla, Wande. 1976. *Ifa: An Exposition of Ifa Literary Corpus*. Nigeria: UNESCO.

Abimbọla, Wande. 1977. *Ifa Divination Poetry*. New York: Nok.

Abimbọla, Wande. 1983. 'Ifa as a Body of Knowledge and as an Academic Discipline', *Journal of Cultures and Ideas* 1(1): 1-11.

Agiri, B. A. 1972. 'The Ogboni among the Oyo-Yoruba', *Lagos Notes and Records* 3(2): 50-9.

Atanda, J. A. 1973. 'The Yoruba Ogboni Cult: Did It Exist in Old Oyo?', *Journal of the Historical Society of Nigeria* 6(4): 365-72.

Bascom, William. 1944. 'The Sociological Role of the Yoruba Cult-Group', *Memoirs of the American Anthropological Association* 63: 5-76.

Bascom, William. 1969. *Ifa Divination: Communication between Gods and Men in West Africa*. Bloomington: Indiana University Press.

Beyioku, O. A. 1971. *Ifa, Its Worship and Prayers*. Ebute Metta: Salako Press.

Biobaku, S. O. 1956. 'Ogboni, the Egba Senate', in *Proceedings of the Third International West African Conference, Ibadan, December 12-21, 1949*. Lagos: Nigerian Museum, pp. 257-63.

Bovell-Jones, T. B. 1943. 'Intelligence Report on Ijebu-Ode Town and Villages, May 7 (IJE Prof. 2/122, Confidential File C55/1)', National Archives, Ibadan University.

Dennett, R. E. 1916. 'The Ogboni and Other Secret Societies in Nigeria', *African Affairs* 16: 16-29.

Drewal, Henry John. 1988. 'Performing the Other: Miami Wata Worship in West Africa', *Drama Review: A Journal of Performance Studies 32(2)* T118: 160-85.

Drewal, Henry John. 1989. 'Meaning in Osugbo Art among the Ijebu Yoruba' in B. Engelbrecht and B. Gardi (eds), *Man Does Not Go Naked: Textilien und*

Handwerk aus Afrikanischen und Anderen Ländern. Basle: Basler Beiträge zur Ethnologie, pp. 151-74.

Drewal, Margaret Thompson. 1986. 'Art and Trance among Yoruba Shango Devotees', *African Arts* 20(1): 60-7, 98-9.

Drewal, Margaret Thompson. 1988. 'Ritual Performance in Africa Today', *'The Drama Review: A Journal of Performance Studies* 32(2), T118: 25-30.

Drewal, Margaret Thompson. 1989. 'Dancing for Ogun in Yorubaland and in Brazil', in Sandra T. Barnes (ed.), *Africa's Ogun: Old World and New*, Bloomington: Indiana University Press, pp. 199-234.

Drewal, Margaret Thompson. 1992. *Yoruba Ritual, Performers, Play, Agency*. Bloomington: Indiana University Press.

Drewal, Margaret Thompson, and Henry John Drewal. 1983. 'An Ifa Diviner's Shrine in Ijebuland', *African Arts* 16(2): 60-7, 99-100.

Drewal, Margaret Thompson and Henry John Drewal. 1987. 'Composing Time and Space in Yoruba Art', *Word and Image: A Journal of Verbal Visual Enquiry* 3(3): 225-51.

Eliade, Mircea. 1959. *The Sacred and the Profane: The Nature of Religion*. San Diego: Harcourt Brace Jovanovich

Epega, Afolabi A. 1987. *Ifa: The Ancient Wisdom*. New York: Imole Oluwa Institute.

Fabian, Johannes. 1983. *Time and the Other: How Anthropology Makes Its Object*. New York: Columbia University Press.

Giddens, Anthony. 1986. *The Constitution of Society: Outlines of the Theory of Structuration*. Berkeley: University of California Press.

Kirshenblatt-Gimblett, Barbara. 1976. 'A Parable in Context: A Social Interactional Analysis of Storytelling Performance', in D. Ben-Amos and H. S. Goldstein (eds), *Folklore: Performance and Communication*. The Hague: Mouton.

McClelland, Elizabeth. 1982. *Cult of Ifa among the Yoruba: Folk Practice and the Arts*, 1. London: Ethnographica.

McKenzie, Peter R. 1982. 'Death in Early Nigerian Christianity', *Africana Marburgensia* 15(2): 3-16.

Moore, Sally F., and Barbara G. Myerhoff (eds). 1977. *Secular Ritual*. Assen: van Gorcum.

Morton-Williams, Peter. 1960. 'The Yoruba Ogboni Cult in Oyo', *Africa* 30: 362-74.

Nevadomsky, Joseph, with Norma Rosen. 1988. 'The Initiation of a Priestess: Performance and Imagery in Olukan Ritual', *Drama Review: A Journal of Performance Studies* 32(2) T118: 186-207.

Ọṣitọla, Kọlawọle. 1988. 'On Ritual Performance: A Practitioner's View', *The Drama Review: A Journal of Performance Studies* 32(2) T118: 31-41.

Ottenberg, Simon. 1988. 'The Bride Comes to the Groom: Ritual and Drama in Limba Weddings', *Drama Review: A Journal of Performance Studies* 32(2) T118: 42-64.

Peel, J. D.Y. 1984. 'Making History: The Past in the Ijesha Present', *Man* n.s. 19(1): 111-32.

Ray, Benjamin. 1976. *African Religions: Symbol, Ritual, and Community*, Englewood Cliffs, NJ: Prentice-Hall.

Turner, Victor. 1977. *The Ritual Process: Structure and Anti-Structure*. Ithaca, NY: Cornell.

6. A visible spirit form in Zambia

Edith Turner

Editor's introduction

Edith Turner has greatly enriched studies that pay attention to the performative aspects of indigenous religions. It is hard to overestimate the importance of the following chapter, which is rooted in performative participation and experiential engagement. Not only do readers gain a rich ('experience near') sense of an African healing ceremony (or complex), but they are also challenged to consider the possibility that indigenous interpretations of experiences might be accurate. For Edith Turner this challenge came as she participated more fully than she expected in healing. As she says, 'I saw with my own eyes a giant thing emerging out of the flesh of her back. It was a large gray blob about six inches across, opaque and something between solid and smoke.'

For some academics such experiences are interpreted as 'going native' and understood to prevent the scholar achieving objectivity. Such a goal seems increasingly less desirable these days. If Quantum Physics has demonstrated that the 'act of observation changes things' (like the result of wave or particle experiments), research must be seen as a particular form of participation or relationship. At any rate, few scholars remain entirely convinced by the ideology of modernity.

Reprinted from *Being Changed: The Anthropology of Extraordinary Experience*, ed. David E. Young and Jean-Guy Goulet, Broadview Press, 1994. By permission of Broadview Press. My thanks are due to the Wenner-Gren Foundation for Anthropological Research and to the Carter-Woodson Institute for Afro-American and African Studies at the University of Virginia, for grants-in-aid to make a restudy of the Ndembu. I am particularly grateful to William Blodgett whose unstinting help made the enterprise possible; also to Singleton Kahona and Fideli Benwa and their ancestors who were the true authors of this paper (and to whom this paper is dedicated); and to Benwa Muheiwa, Fideli's father, who was also a wise teacher in matters of ritual; to Cecile Clover, and many others. Finally I acknowledge the intellectual legacy of Victor Turner, which is beyond price.

However, few have been as open in insisting on reporting and reflecting on experiences as Edith Turner. This makes the essays surrounding Turner's in Young and Goulet (1994) that much more exciting and important. The playfulness of the book's subtitle, *The Anthropology of Extraordinary Experience*, is highlighted when Turner notes,

> Thus it is becoming clear that what we are referring to are not unusual experiences, because they occur to so many people. Furthermore, when one reviews tests made on telepaths and such specially gifted persons, the phenomena they handle can hardly be called unexpected because such persons have developed skills to induce them. The development of skills is seen, for example, among Balinese trancers, Brazilian Umbandists, and circum-Pacific shamans, as well as among African doctors. It is time that we recognize the ability to experience different levels of reality as one of the normal human abilities and place it where it belongs, central to the study of ritual.

Whether 'different levels of reality' is the correct interpretation of such experiences is open to debate, but it cannot be doubted that this is a significant development both in academic understanding and in academic methodology and discourse (also see Stoller 1998). It repays reading alongside not only the works she cites (especially those of Victor Turner) but also those on ritual and rites of passage in this volume and in *Indigenous Religions: A Companion*.

References

Stoller, Paul. 1998. 'Rationality', in Mark Taylor (ed.), *Critical Terms for Religious Studies*. Chicago: University of Chicago Press, pp. 239-55.

Young, David E. and Jean-Guy Goulet (eds). 1994. *Being Changed: The Anthropology of Extraordinary Experience*. Peterborough: Broadview Press.

Introduction

Africans are acutely conscious of spirits. Anthropologists have long been interested in what Africans believe about spirits and the ritual events which surround spirit encounters. But it is the Africans' reports of experiences with spirits that are regarded as appropriate anthropological material, not the experiences themselves. It is the same with religious studies. Scholars of religion tend to explain accounts of spirit encounters in terms of metaphor. The issue of whether or not spirits actually exist has not been faced.

When an anthropologist has an unusual experience, this is even more difficult to handle because the essence of anthropology, according to some, lies in its impartial observation and the search for objectivity. An unusual experience may take the form of a hexing, seeing a mysterious light (as with Evans-Pritchard 1976 [1937]: 11, among the Azande), encountering a ghost, and so on. These episodes have a variety of fates. Some are recorded but are mentioned only in passing or become the climax in a book which is published as a novel, such as *Return to Laughter* (Bowen 1964 [1954]). By far the majority go unrecorded. One may hear anecdotes brought up in informal conversation, at parties, in students' kitchens, and in other non-structured contexts. But writers (and publishers) usually feel that this material is not suitable for inclusion in a serious anthropological publication.

Favret-Saada, the author of *Deadly Words* (1980), an account of the central role of witchcraft in Bocage culture, maintains that it is necessary for the ethnographer to undergo the experience he/she is attempting to understand. Favret-Saada experienced being the object of witchcraft and learned how to resist it. She says (1980: 22) that to understand the meaning of 'Unwitching': 'there is no other solution but to practice it oneself, to become one's own informant, to penetrate one's own amnesia, and to try and make explicit what one finds unstateable in oneself.' She produced a good ethnography. Paul Stoller experienced witchcraft among the Songhay of Niger and found himself to be changed as a result. He says (1984: 110), 'all my assumptions about the world were uprooted from their foundation on the plain of Western metaphysics ... my view of Songhay culture could no longer be one of a structuralist, a symbolist, or a Marxist.'

What are the implications of the kinds of statements made by anthropologists such as Favret-Saada and Stoller? This article is an attempt on my part to deal as honestly as possible with my own experience of a spirit form among the Ndembu of Zambia. An experience such as this, as in the case of Carl Jung's mystical experiences, takes one into the realm of existential religion and what Paul Tillich (1959) called matters of ultimate concern. In the face of such experiences, academic anthropology seems to fall away and become of lesser concern.

Nevertheless, the ethnographer's own experience of spirits and witches should be treated as anthropological data. Is it correct for our discipline to close itself off from what is of major concern to its field people? I am afraid there is a realm ahead for some of us – a rather frightening one – into which we must pass if we are to hold up our heads as anthropologists: the realm of spiritual experience.

My unusual experience

I had returned to Zambia in 1985 to do four months' fieldwork in my old field area among the Ndembu, known through the publications of my husband Victor Turner (1957; 1967; 1968; 1975) who died in 1983. The Ndembu are a matrilineal people living in what was once high savanna forest. Their homes are circular clusters of huts, each circle housing an extended family, grouped in larger townships or vicinages. They grow cassava and vegetables, keep a few cattle, and also occasionally hunt for antelope. In our early fieldwork in the 1950s, Vic and I had become very interested in the elaborate ritual system, by means of which a situation of conflict or disease could be turned around in the course of a performance into one of relief and amity. At that time, we looked at ritual from the point of view of culture. We believed that symbolism has the power to change the human heart. The strength and sensory richness of a symbol, when linked to some ideological message (see V. Turner on polarization of a symbol 1967: 54-5), could effect a transfer of energy and heal the patient. Vic's analysis of the curative ritual of Ihamba[1] (1968) was strongly empiricist and psychologically based.

Thus I was not prepared in any way for a spirit experience on my return visit, though through the years Vic and I had become closer to 'the anthropology of experience' (Turner and Bruner 1986). In 1980 Vic argued that lived experience in anthropology is primary; thought is its interpreter. My own anthropological writing has attempted to put the reader wholeheartedly into a specific cultural context. I was anti-ethnocentric, allowing the religions of the field people full place in my respect, very much desiring that they be understood, but with little regard to the possibility of encountering an unusual experience myself. I didn't know what I was in for. It was a small experience, but one which demanded a reorganization of the way I did anthropology.

It was curious to be back in Mukanza Village after thirty-one years. The changes were great. The widespread deforestation made me feel cold as if I were walking into a tragedy. All one could do was not to think about it. The complex and beautiful initiation celebrations had been marred and often obliterated by Christianity. I began to hate my own religion. It was a matter all over again of 'Father, forgive them, for they know not what they do.'

But curative rituals were on the upgrade. Almost at once opportunities

---

[1] I capitalize Ihamba when referring to the ritual, and use it uncapitalized (ihamba) for the object, the tooth, and its spirit appearances. This will help to distinguish the ritual from the afflicting agent in the following account, much as the Africans distinguish them contextually.

for participation came my way. The African doctors were businessmen and there were advantages in having my support. Also, as with business enterprises, the rituals were popular because they worked. I began to perceive that through the decades African curing has been passing through an exploratory, experimental stage, in an environment where it was impossible for official medical authorities to hamper and limit it, simply because there was no economic base for licensing and control, and few funds for 'health education.'

In the field with me was Bill Blodgett, the undergraduate son of a friend, who obtained tape recordings of the rituals and discussions, and also took many photographs. Owing to Bill's social activities, we made acquaintance with a couple of Ihamba doctors, those who treat a sick person by removing from his/her body a dead hunter's tooth (ihamba) which has been wandering around inside, giving the patient severe pain.[2] The ritual of extraction was the subject of an important part of the fieldwork Vic and I had done three decades earlier, so I had in hand our own publication on Ihamba (*The Drums of Affliction* 1968) which proved to be of great interest to the Ihamba doctors Bill and I met – Singleton and Fideli, the latter of whom remembered playing with my son Freddie when both were youngsters. Singleton and Fideli invited us to an Ihamba curing session and appointed me as one of the doctors – something I had not really bargained for. Nevertheless I accepted at once. How, I wondered, would this experiment in the anthropology of experience turn out?

Singleton and Fideli first decided to schedule the ritual on Thursday, November 28, 1985, and began to send out messages to participants. Then the news came through that Princess Anne of England was to visit the Ndembu on that day on behalf of Save the Children Fund (the children were indeed growing up stunted because of lack of food). So the date for the Ihamba was rescheduled earlier, for Wednesday the 27th, thus adding an irregularity which became important to the event itself, as we shall see.

Imagine Kahona, a circular village on rough common ground. Eight thatch-roofed houses with mud brick walls rise under the spreading arms of banana trees. Bill and I were walking up a little path of red dirt leading from the motor road to the village. It was 7:00 a.m. and the sun was not yet up. All was damp with a hint of rain. In the dim light we peered about. Was anything going to happen? At last Vesa, an apprentice, approached, followed by Fideli, and they gave us their courteous greeting, 'Shikenu mwani' ('Welcome, come in'). Vesa initiated the ritual by bringing out the

---

[2]   Hunters actually remove a tooth from a dead comrade and carry it with them on their expeditions in order that it might help them kill animals. How the tooth gets into a victim is a matter that may not be published.

drum, a tall African bongo, on which he placed a flat basket containing various items of equipment: a musical rasp, an ax, and two small bags, one made of mongoose skin. The basket's contact with the drum dedicated it to ritual, for the word *ngoma* (drum) also means ritual. Vesa and Fideli then raised the basket between them high into the air, thereby honoring it.

We left Kahona Village and went off single file to collect Singleton at his hut. He came forth sleepily at our call. He was a tall man with a long, lined face – a face capable of unearthly flashes of irony and mischief. He was a man who said what he thought, an elder. Singleton wore old blue overalls. He carried himself with ease even though he was thin and must have been nearly seventy. Fideli was his nephew. Fideli's face shone with the health of early middle age, an able man, a thinker with a knowledge of science. He carried himself this morning with the buoyant air of one looking forward to a procedure in which he was well-versed. His faith was Baha'i, which is tolerant toward other religions.

With Singleton in the lead, we set off into the low scrub to look for *yitumbu* (medicines) – bits of a special tree and plants. None of the plants, as far as I could ascertain, were mind-altering drugs. But they had power, as will be demonstrated as the story unfolds. We soon reached an area wasted with overcropping. Vesa followed after Singleton, carrying the basket that contained the ritual equipment. Then came Fideli with the ax. I came next, followed by Bill with his long legs and youthful goodness of expression. As we walked, Singleton played rhythmically on the wooden rasp, singing a plaintive phrase in which we all joined:

Mukongu, katu-ka-tu-ye.
Mukongu, katu-ka-tu-ye.
Hunter spirit of the medicine tree, let us go.
Hunter spirit of the medicine tree, let us go.

We sang the second line a note below the first, in falling tones, with Fideli's light bass continually sounding a fourth below. Singleton walked swiftly now, weaving toward a bush he had spotted among the mounds. It was *mufungu*, the African oak, and was called *ishikenu* or 'welcome' or 'first' tree, the greeting tree. *Mufungu* means 'the gathering together of a herd of animals.' Singleton hunkered down before the base of the tree and took his mongoose skin bag from which he drew a lump of red clay which he rubbed in a broad line down the west side of the trunk, then in a line from the foot of the tree to himself, and finally down the east side of the tree. He drew the lines to call ihamba (the tooth spirit) to come soon – to direct ihamba along the lines. Singleton told us, 'Ihamba knows "I am soon going to be out of the patient."' (Singleton saw the tooth-spirit as a conscious

154

being.) Then Singleton took a cup of beer and poured it out at the foot of the tree, on both sides, saying loudly and abruptly,

'Maheza!'

'Maheza!' we shouted back.

'Ngambu!'

'Yafwa!' we returned, with special emphasis on the last word. I remembered this chant from the old days (Turner 1968: 167). It means, 'Friend! Sudden death! It is dead!' Singleton addressed the tree, his tone urgent and harsh: 'This medicine was brought by Kamawu; it came down from him to Koshita, and from him to Sambumba, and from him to Chisanji, then to Muhelewa Benwa. Today it is in my hands. True! This red clay of yours has reached us. It's bad that we have often lacked the tooth-removing ritual. We put this red clay of yours on the western side of the tree. You deserve one cup of honey beer; you will be blessed. Give us the power to cure this woman well. You others who made things hard for us, you who were altogether bad, have a drink of beer on the other side. They really fucked up; besides, they failed to shoot animals' (he used the pejorative word for having sex, *kusunja*).

In this conjuration, Singleton emphasized each name of his ihamba doctor ancestors who had handed down the ritual in a kind of apostolic succession. He was talking to those old healers, even including the bad ones, the *ayikodjikodji* as they used to be called in the old days (Turner 1967: 138). I watched seriously, trying to connect with the spirits, although I was not a member of the family to which the doctors belonged.

Following his appeal to the ancestral line, Singleton was told what to do by the spirit of his father, Sambumba, and the others. Fideli explained that we were not going to take any medicine from this tree because it was the mother tree. 'You don't cut the mother.' We soon came across another mufungu, and this one supplied the necessary bark and leaves which would call a large gathering of people. Singing our song to the gentle rasp of the reed as it swished over the musical bar, we went on to a *musengu* tree (which means 'blowing on the food and blessing it for the ancestors,' from *kusengula*, to bless), from which we took some bark to make drinking medicine. We also picked some leaves for washing the patient's body. Then we continued the search.

We stopped and looked around. We were on a path above a long derelict garden without a bush in it. 'It's all been dug,' said Singleton to Vesa with disgust. 'Search carefully in this area. We may never find the tree I've been telling you about. We're back where we started, at the first mufungu. I think I saw the tree I'm after when we passed before. I don't want to go all the way over to Mindolu Village for it.'

'Look! Over there!' said Vesa.

155

It was a small tree called *mukosu* (soap root, derived from *kukosa*, to wash; when well infused, this medicine becomes a lotion to wash all the bad things out of the body) which needed extra care in the cutting. Singleton took the ax while Fideli held the basket beside the trunk. Singleton very neatly cut grooves in the bark outlining a 4 × 6 inch vertical rectangle, with Fideli squatting beside him to catch the chips in the basket, careful not to touch any. 'If any of them fall to earth you can't have Ihamba,' said Fideli. Singleton then levered off the rectangle of bark with his ax and let it drop safely into the basket. 'Ihamba permits us to catch it without running away – just as the piece of bark is caught in the basket. Ihamba might fly away so we must be careful to make ihamba honest. Mukosu has a strong smell; the piece of bark is used as a lid when the ihamba tooth is brought out of the patient's body and put into a tin can. Ihamba doesn't like the strong smell and will not try to come out of the can and escape.'

Then we took bark and leaf medicine from the *mucha* tree (the coco plum), often used for ancestor rituals because its pit is very durable and resists decay. It resists time. The wood is hard and the fruit is sweet. It too wants people to gather. We went to a *mututambulolu* shrub (the Congo pepper, which expels stomach gas and reduces fever; the name means 'to swarm', as bees do around flowers) where Vesa squatted down and proceeded to tear open the whole root, while Singleton addressed the spirits in a throaty voice, 'You are my elders, those that are underground, really underground.' He was speaking to those old hunters, wild man Chisanji, his father, his hunter uncles. Then he said to Vesa, 'Chop some medicine.' The root was large and plump. He took the entire system, then replanted the top and filled up the hole again afterwards until the dirt was level with the surrounding surface. The root is bright orange inside; when mixed with beer it makes ihamba obey. As Fideli the scientist explained it, 'The medicine passes into the bloodstream, goes throughout the body, and kills the germs troubling the patient.'

We took from the *muhotuhotu* some of its long sensitive leaves. Singleton said muhotuhotu was gathered because its leaves fall all at once; every bad thing will come out of the patient with this medicine, including the ihamba inside her. We also took musesi, a very strong tree with hard wood that could even take away the evils of unmotivated witchcraft.

Now Singleton spotted a *kapepi* sapling. He set himself beside it and with rapid deft strokes of his ax, cut it down and made it into a *chishinga* (forked shrine pole), sharpening the branches into tines exactly as Mundoyi had done in 1951. Kapepi sets your teeth on edge with its bitterness. As a result bad teeth drop out – a major desideratum in the case of the ihamba tooth. Its name derives from *mpepela*, the wind, which is ubiquitous and invisible, a quality desired by all hunters (V. Turner 1967: 290).

Then Singleton circled around a bed of what looked like bracken with broad double leaves which I recognized as the stems of the bright red tuber, *nshindwa*. The above-ground knobs are like fruit, thirst quenching with a very tart lemony flavor. The plant itself (*mutungulu*) is used as a medicine. The rest of the underground system was a fine wandering mass of black roots. Singleton sometimes cured malaria with these roots by running them into cuts on the left shoulder of the patient, or used them infused in cold water as a poultice. I wondered if they contained bitter quinine. Mutungulu has other uses as well. Singleton told us that ihamba may have little children inside the patient's body. The drum ritual may successfully bring out the mother ihamba, but her children may remain inside, as indeed the afterbirth may. However, scraped mutungulu roots, put into a cupping horn with other ingredients – a mixture called *nsomu* – can kill the afterbirth inside the body and make the entire ihamba brood come out. So the doctors took several tangles of the long roots.

Singleton circled around another shrub with fixed attention. 'This is the tree which I didn't think anyone could find. Go easy on the leaves. Take them from the eastern side, not the west. It is *musoli*.' He explained that with musoli the ihamba would appear quickly and would not be able to hide. It was the tree of revelation, from *kusolola*, to reveal, but it was now rare. We took a few of the big leaves and some bark from the east side, the side of the sun's revealing, and went on singing – 'Mukongu, kaatu-ka-tu-ye.'

We continued on our way, now searching for an ironwood tree to provide fuel for the ritual fire. Meanwhile we passed among young trees and found a termitary made by a species which produces small mud towers eight inches or so across and about a foot high.

'We are lucky,' said Vesa. 'Here's a big small anthill.'

'Let me see it,' said Singleton. 'Yes, that's it. We won't find another one like this.'

'We should take it out whole, right from the bottom,' said Fideli.

They lifted it out and Vesa sheared off the domed top. We saw the termites flooding the broken bowl below, each grabbing an egg which was borne off to safety. Vesa carved the stump into a house shape, a cube, and put the cube into the basket, then replaced the dome on the broken termite house. The cube would be placed at the foot of the chishinga shrine pole, becoming a grave for ihamba, that is, for the dead hunter who now existed in the form of ihamba as spirit.

We came to a huge anthill and found a *chikwata* thorn tree upon it, a purgative medicine. Chikwata was added so that it would catch (*kukwata*)

157

the ihamba with its thorns. We picked its branches carefully.

We found a plant called *mutuhu* ('no reason') barely four inches high by the side of the path. We took it all, exposing startlingly black roots which showed a brilliant white interior. Mutuhu used along with mututambololu calls ihamba to come out. The two comprise a potent, dangerous coming-out medicine for inducing abortions.

We went on singing. The doctors were concerned about the ritual fire-wood; it had to be ironwood because this wood was strong, tall, and unbending, and had no stringiness in its texture to tie up huntsmanship. At last, just as we were turning back, we came across a felled ironwood tree. Fideli got astride the bare trunk and hacked patiently at it with his ax, careful to let none of the firewood fall to the ground. When they collected enough they gave the wood to me to carry, which I was glad to do.

'There are medicines for the below and the above and inside – every medicine to make ihamba come out,' said Singleton. 'Let's go back to the road.'

We returned to the house of the sick person, Meru, a middle-aged woman who was a classificatory sister of Singleton's. She was still inside. We found a spot behind her open-air kitchen to establish our shrine, and Fideli laid an antelope skin on the ground so that Vesa could set down the basket. First the shrine pole (the forked pole of bitter wood, sharpened into horns to attract the hunter's spirit) was planted and the spirit house set in front. Then the antelope skin was put in the shade of a tree for Meru to sit on.

Singleton and Vesa prepared the medicines, found a can to receive the tooth when it was taken out, and covered the can with a smelly castor oil leaf and soap bark lid to keep the tooth inside. Singleton lit the ironwood fire with matches instead of using kitchen coals. Everything must be new. Etina, a female assistant, pounded the leaves. Then she took a calabash of water and poured some on the ground to the east of the mortar, to the west, and finally into the mortar to make the leaf tea medicine. The libations were for the useless spirits, the *ayikodjikodji*, who must not be left out.

One pan of cold medicinal tea was set aside while another pan of tea was heating on the fire. Cupping horns lay ready in the medicine basket. We needed drums, so a boy was dispatched to find them. People were beginning to collect.

Now Singleton medicated his doctors. He, Fideli, Vesa, Luka the second apprentice, and I drank some of the tea. For a moment it made my head swim, but soon my senses cleared. Singleton announced to the crowd, 'If there are any pregnant women here, go away.' The concentrated 'coming out' influence of the medicines and ritual objects was so strong that there

158

was real danger of a miscarriage.

Singleton inspected the shrine and said, 'Look, we've made a mistake. We should have things laid out so Meru faces east where the sun comes out of the earth, not west the way we've got it.'

'We did that because of the shade,' said Fideli. 'But no matter, we'll leave it. We shall see.'

A small procession was approaching – Vesa leading Meru, the woman with an ihamba tooth in her body. Vesa seated her on the antelope skin. She made faces at the sight of the medicines around her and the razor blade in the basket. This was a miserable, proud, suffering woman. They washed her with spongy masses of the medicine, squeezing all the pounded leaves onto her body until she was entirely drenched with them. This was to open her from the outside. The doctors used red clay to draw a line down her brow and nose, temples and cheekbones, protecting her head. Then they gave her medicine to drink – to open her from the inside. The power was growing.

The doctors took castor oil leaves, laying them over their fists. Then with a concerted shout – 'Paya!', smacked the leaves with the other palm, and the leaves fell on Meru in blessing.

'Maheza! Maheza!'

'Ngambu!' shouted Singleton.

'Tafwa!' ('My friends, he is dead!'), we all replied.

Then began the drums in an irresistible rhythm heightened by clashing ax heads, while we sang and clapped. Singing, Singleton came close to Meru and shouted, 'Come out!', directing his call into her body.

Then they began divining the ihamba's name. 'If it's you, Nkomba, shake. If not, don't shake.' They were speaking to the inside of Meru's body.

She hardly shook at all, sitting there with her legs straight out on the antelope skin. 'Is it Kadochi? Shake if it is. Quick now!' Singleton danced the antelope mating dance in front of Meru. Already the group had increased to a crowd of about thirty people, at least half of whom were children. A young woman with an armful of school books passed behind them, saw what was happening, gave a sniggering laugh, and continued on her way. The doctors made tiny slits in Meru's back, then sucked on cupping horns and placed them over the slits. 'Come out!' shouted Singleton at the place where the horns adhered.

Meru suddenly said her first words (coming out with 'words,' mazu, helps to make the ihamba come out). 'I don't agree. I have something in my liver, my heart. It's my children; all my children have died. I just want to die because there's no one to look after me.' The people heard her frankness and were pleased. They continued to sing.

But Singleton was not satisfied. 'I haven't seen you shake happily yet. You're stiff with worries.'

'I heard how Meru's own younger sister cheated her,' her brother said. 'When the sister went to sell the beer that Meru brewed, she didn't bring Meru the full price. Her own sister cheated her out of her money.' By speaking for her, the brother helped unblock more of her 'words' – grudges which had to come out. Meru shook violently in corroboration, but she was tired. From the divination they perceived that the spirit inside her was the old hunter Kashinakaji.

More 'words' came out such as 'I don't see Paulos in the crowd. Where is he?' Meru was offended. Paulos was her well-to-do classificatory brother. It was revealed that Paulos had never been told of the change of date for the ritual.

'If you want Paulos to come, shake. If not, don't shake,' Singleton said. She shook hard and they sent a messenger for him.

Worse was to follow. The assistant who was supposed to change the tape recording cassette had reversed it instead, thus erasing one side. Bill was angry. The crowd immediately sensed this and turned in silence, hoping to hear Bill's 'words'.

'Perhaps these foreigners are closing up ihamba,' someone said. 'They ought to come out with their grudges.'

'He can't say words,' said Fideli. 'He doesn't know our language. Besides, Edie is a doctor. Why should she close up ihamba?'

Meru broke in with 'words' spoken in a high oratorical tone, reiterating all her complaints and ending with, 'The way things are, I'll die.'

Singleton was still for a moment, attentive. 'I've seen that it is the ihamba, so he must come out.' He was very happy, addressing Kashinakaji in Meru's body, 'Forgive us, grandfather ihamba, I have to take you from the body of my sister so I can keep you with me.' Then he said, 'The man who has come is your brother; he is coming right now.' He was talking to Meru this time, telling her that Paulos had arrived. Paulos had indeed arrived and he was in very ill humor.

'You told me Ihamba was to be on Thursday,' he said. 'And you go and hold it on Wednesday. Is that good manners?' Everyone tried to explain. Then the drums began once more.

The heat was drawing up black clouds above us. Meru fell shaking in the midst of the singing, and Singleton again tried to draw out the tooth.

Voices broke in, 'Yes, let her fall half-dead like that. Do you want the witchcraft dancing in her? You do.' The doctors wanted the spirit to show itself so they could bring it out. Yet there was a tone of horror in the voices. So many grudges were coming out.

It was a long ritual. The cupping horns were reset; the drumming began

160

anew; and Singleton repeatedly traced a path on her back to direct the trouble that he could feel under the skin.

Meru spoke from her ritual position, 'I feel resentment.'

'We have seen the ihamba,' said Fideli. 'And you have put on your words.'

Others in the crowd also enunciated 'words,' coming out with their own resentments. Now Meru would not even shake.

Meru's pain got to us all. We stood with bitter expressions, gazing at her. Fideli took a leaf poke and dripped medicine on Meru's head. Singleton held his skin bag in front of her face, then brushed her face with it. But Meru would not shake.

Meanwhile our translator, dizzy with gin, turned to me and said nastily, 'Paulos is angry because you never came to see him when you said you would.' I was overcome. I was supposed to have gone on the Saturday before. But old Line died on Saturday and I was at the funeral. One thing after another! I left the translator and went around to the other side of the crowd, mortified. Again the crowd sensed anger and waited for my 'words', but I would not speak. After thinking a minute I came back and explained matters to Paulos about the funeral.

I was very upset. How could I publicly bad-mouth the translator? There I was stiff with worry, and it was stalemate in the Ihamba. I was a participant and participants should not be uptight like this.

At the same moment, Singleton remembered that Meru was facing west. Nothing would 'come out' like that. He shifted the whole ritual scene into its mirror image, and we all moved around until Meru was facing east in the direction of sunrise. This was quite different. I gazed across the crowd at my translator. 'They want my words,' I thought. 'I want to participate so much. But how can I?' I was forced to accept the impossible and in accepting it, tears came into my eyes. My eyes stabbed with pain, and the tears came out.

Just then, through my tears, I could see Meru sway deeply, and everyone leaned forward. I realized along with them that the barriers were breaking. Something that wanted to be born was now going to be born. Then a certain palpable social integument broke and something 'calved' in the whole scene, myself along with it. I felt the spiritual motion. It was a tangible feeling of breakthrough encompassing the entire group.

And then Meru fell!

Amid the bellow of the drums, Singleton swooped rhythmically with his finger horn and skin bag, ready to catch the tooth. Bill beat the side of the drum in time to the rhythm, and as for me, I had just found out how to clap. You simply clap with the drums, and clap *hard*. All the rest falls into place. Your whole body becomes deeply involved in the rhythm, and all reaches a unity. Singleton was at Meru's side and the crowd was on its feet clapping. Singleton pressed Meru's back, guiding and leading out the tooth – Meru's face in a grin of tranced passion, her back quivering rapidly.

Suddenly Meru raised her arm, stretched it in liberation, and I saw with my own eyes a giant thing emerging out of the flesh of her back. It was a large gray blob about six inches across, opaque and something between solid and smoke.[3]

I was amazed, delighted. I still laugh with glee at the realization of having seen it, the ihamba, and so big! Everyone was hooting, and we were all jumping with triumph. The gray thing was actually out there, visible, and you could see Singleton's hands working and scrabbling on the back. And then it was there no more. Singleton had whatever it was in his pouch, pressing it in with his other hand. The receiving can was ready; he transferred whatever it was into it and capped the castor oil leaf and bark lid over it. It was done.

But there was one more thing. Everybody knew that they had to go through one last formality, divining the afterbirth. 'If ihamba has not come out, shake. If it has come out, don't shake,' said Singleton. Meru was quiet. At once there was a huge flash of lightning and a clap of thunder that exploded overhead. Meru sat up panting. The longed-for rain poured down and we all rushed into the kitchen shelter.

'Go to the house you two', said Fideli. Bill and I rushed through the curtain of rain to the house. Bill stumbled before he entered, fell into the mud, and then entered out of breath. Singleton came in with his blue shirt dark with water, carrying the receiving can which he set down on the floor. I wore a big smile.

He held up his hands to us. 'See, I have nothing in them,' he said. He squatted down and dredged for a long time in the bloody mixture. At length he drew out an old tooth, a molar, of natural size with a dark root and one side sheared off as if by an ax. It was the ihamba – a tooth of the old dead hunter, Kashinakaji.

On the evening of December 3, Singleton and Fideli visited our hut to discuss the Ihamba. The first thing that Singleton said was, 'The thing that we saw, we were five.' This was his statement that the doctors too had seen a thing. The doctors were Singleton, Fideli, Vesa, Luka, and myself.[4]

I respectfully described what I had seen, but Singleton made no comment. He did not describe what he had seen. I was in no mood to become analytical so I did not push the matter. When the keystone of the bridge is

---

[3] I believe that if I had tried to touch the gray form, my fingers would have gone through.

[4] Bill saw no spirit form; however, in other matters he received 'second-sight' messages from a different African doctor and was interested.

put into position and everything holds, you tend to just look on with your mouth open. This is what happened to me. If I were to have become analytical I would have had to be a different person from the one who saw the spirit form. My role was to be a participant observer so I could describe the background events and how the medicine was collected and used – in other words to tell the story.

Yet in order to complete this kind of story, there is the question whether I actually helped the healing. It should not be forgotten that I was there very much as an auxiliary. But as such I was part of the process, and it is my sense that Fideli knew what he was doing when he invited me. (Some further background to this is available in E. Turner 1992.) Let us say that although I did not come out with any 'words' like the rest of them, my tears must have been obvious, and they are a kind of language. In previous rituals the wave of release had not included me. This time it did. It was something not coming from me, not coming from them, but happening to all of us together.

The time sense was not that of cause and effect; these things come as wholes. Either I was in the group or I wasn't. Such differences from Western ways of thinking are themselves interesting. I feel that my own experience of tension and its release was probably necessary for me to have partaken in the good outcome, just as Singleton and Fideli had previously come out with their 'words' as well. How it was that the release happened to everyone simultaneously, including the patient, I do not know. That is how it was. I am sure it wasn't me that caused the extraction and cure. But maybe I did help, for I certainly was right in it in that particular way. That this is possible for an articulate outsider, is what is both humbling and intellectually exciting about the event. It has made me thirsty for more.

Having completed the description I feel that the reader knows what is mainly important about the ritual and the spirit form. My wider speculations came later. Because the material is so unusual, I include my speculations in the next section.

That same evening, Singleton told us he had sent a hunter into the bush to bring back an antelope, to be shared among the five doctors. We drank honey beer, listened to the tapes, and sang and laughed a lot. Throughout the visit Fideli kept exclaiming, 'I'm so happy!' praising the Baha'i deity Baha'ullah, talking about his upcoming trip to the Baha'i temple at Haifa in Israel, and trying to get Singleton to say what Ihamba was all about. Singleton was stressing the hunger of the ihamba tooth, its desire for meat; and practical as usual, how to satisfy it – which was finally done as follows.

On December 6 at 6:00 a.m., Singleton fed the ihamba with meat from an antelope. He opened the abdomen of the antelope and cut out a half-inch piece of liver which he trimmed into a disc with a hole in the center.

163

He took the disc and a sac of blood into Meru's house, and we followed him. The winnowing basket lay ready on the dirt floor, with Singleton's mongoose skin pouch on it. There was also a clean Vaseline jar with a lid, now half full of maize meal made from the grain 'which is hard like a tooth.' Singleton added his liver disc and sac of blood to the basket. Then he took some red clay out of the pouch, crushed it with the end of his musengu horn, and smeared some clay over his fingers for protection. He picked up the liver ring and carefully removed the ihamba tooth from his pouch. Choosing a tiny piece of red clay, and holding the tooth and clay together, he inserted them into the hole in the liver ring. He put the ring containing the ihamba into the Vaseline jar, stuffing it in and positioning it with his thumb at the center of the surface of the corn meal. Then he poured over it the blood from the sac, and screwed on the lid. The bottle was now a brilliant red above and white below, a union of blood and meal.

Bill wrote later, 'Subjectively, I felt very strange. Images flashed through my mind ... bread and wine; semen and menstrual blood; solid and liquid; yin and yang; a boulder in the stream and the water; time flowing past; life itself.' Apparently, we both felt as if a kind of resolution had occurred. Even the reader may sense the effect. Singleton said that when ihamba was fed with blood it was satisfied, and so it appeared to be.

Now that the feeding was done, Singleton called Meru into the house. She came running, radiant, with smiles all over her middle-aged face. Singleton took the blood sac and marked her on the shoulders and beside her eyes. She was now cured and protected.

Commentary

The principal issue raised by this description of a visible spirit form in Zambia is not the correct method for symbolic analysis, the meaning of the ritual, nor even the style of the report itself, but the question, 'What is actually going on here?' This raises a second question, 'Have I left the field of anthropology entirely by asking the first question?'

My colleagues warn me that not every anthropologist can have such an experience and that it would make other anthropologists anxious about whether they should try to have such an experience. This implies that I should keep quiet about my experience and perpetuate the myth that such things don't happen. I don't intend to do that. Rather, my intention is to engage in dialogue with other anthropologists who have had such experiences in order to build up a reliable body of data on spirits and similar phenomena. Hopefully, the establishment of regularities and thus a more general understanding can be derived from such a body of data.

If it becomes respectable for anthropologists to admit to such experiences when they occur, it would become possible to speak from within a culture, rather than as an outsider. Ethnography could become an endeavor shared by natives and anthropologists. It would become possible to focus in a meaningful way on those rare events that are central to the life of many traditional societies.

To return to the central issue, what was actually going on in Ihamba? The most parsimonious explanation would be that spirits actually exist. This would account for the importance placed upon the rituals by my consultants and it would also account for my own experience. Following the same line of argument, we could say that somehow medicines do really talk to the ihamba in their own way and say 'Come out!' Singleton did really speak to the spirit of Kashinakaji inside Meru's body. As Victor Turner has demonstrated in his work, the deeds of the Ndembu display a coherence and elegance which invite the most complex analysis. This coherence may be due to the fact that, in Ndembu terms, 'the spirits show them the way.'

But there is a matter which does not seem to make sense – the human tooth that Singleton showed Bill and me in Meru's house after the ritual. The existence of this tooth creates certain dilemmas. Which caused the disease, Kashinakaji in spirit form or the tooth? Did two things come out of Meru? Or did Singleton knowingly use sleight-of-hand, to produce the concrete human tooth? How much does it matter?

In this connection, the reader may be reminded of the renowned essay by Lévi-Strauss, 'The Sorcerer and his Magic' (1977: 446-453). The editor of the book in which this account occurs asks the question, 'Since the sorcerer is aware that he is using sleight-of-hand how does he retain his own faith in the system?' (Landy 1977: 445). Quesalid was originally a cynic who for power reasons obtained 'shamanic' training in the art of hiding a tuft of down in the cheek which the practitioner could pretend was the pathological foreign substance he had sucked out of the body of the patient. Having learned and practiced this procedure, Quesalid found to his surprise that he was actually able to cure his patients. Of course it has been pointed out in recent ethnography (for instance, A. Campbell 1989; Stoller 1984) that traditional peoples do not make the same distinctions between 'real magic' and artifice that we do. Does the truth lie in Lévi-Strauss's claim that the cure demonstrates 'the coherence of the psychic universe, itself a projection of the social universe' (1977: 446)?

Lévi-Strauss (1977: 452) lists the many elements of the total situation in a healing ritual:

in which sorcerer, patient, and audience, as well as representations and

165

procedures, all play their parts. Furthermore, the public must participate ... It is this universe of vital effusions which the patient ... and the sorcerer ... allow the public to glimpse as 'fireworks' from a safe distance. In contrast with scientific explanation, the problem is to articulate ... the states, emotions, or representations into a whole or system. The system is valid precisely to the extent that it allows the coalescence or precipitation of these diffuse states, whose discontinuity also makes them painful. To the conscious mind, this last phenomenon constitutes an original experience which cannot be grasped from without.

Certainly one cannot fully grasp the Ihamba experience 'from without,' but I do know what it was like to experience it from within. I was overjoyed at seeing the spirit form and at Meru's obvious deliverance. It was only later that I tried to understand the experience 'from without.' What I saw come out was not a tooth, so how do we account for the existence of the tooth? There was nothing in our audio tapes, recorded in a variety of circumstances, that hinted of duplicity.

Later in my reading I came across a chapter entitled 'Extracting Harmful Intrusions' in *The Way of the Shaman* by Michael Harner, one of the few descriptions that does not ascribe an extraction to trickery (1980: 115-17):

Illness due to power intrusion is manifested by such symptoms as localized pain or discomfort, often together with an increase in temperature, which (from a shamanic point of view) is connected with the energy from the harmful power intrusion ...

A shaman would say that it is dangerous not to know about shamanism. In ignorance of shamanic principles, people do not know how to shield themselves from hostile energy intrusions through having guardian spirit power [for a similar reason Singleton warned us that we should drink leaf medicine to shield ourselves from the escaping ihamba] ...

The shamanic removal of harmful power intrusions is difficult work, for the shaman sucks them out of a patient physically as well as mentally and emotionally. This technique is widely used in shamanic cultures in such distant areas as Australia, North and South America, and Siberia.

If you ever viewed the film *Sucking Doctor*, which shows the healing work of the famous California Indian shaman Essie Parrish, you saw a shaman pulling out intrusive power. But Western skeptics say that the shaman is just pretending to suck something out of the person, an object that the shaman has already secreted in his mouth. Suck skeptics have apparently not taken up shamanism themselves to discover what is happening.

What is happening goes back to the fact that the shaman is aware of two realities. As among the Jivaro, the shaman is pulling out an intrusive power that (in the Shamanic State of Consciousness) has the appearance of a particular creature, such as a spider, and which he also knows is the hidden nature of a

166

particular plant. When a shaman sucks out that power, he captures its spiritual essence in a portion of the same kind of plant that is its ordinary material home. That plant piece is, in other words, a power object. For example, the shaman may store in his mouth two half-inch-long twigs of the plant that he knows is the material 'home' of the dangerous power being sucked out. He captures the power in one of those pieces, while using the other one to help. The fact that the shaman may then bring out the plant power object from his mouth and show it to a patient and audience as 'Ordinary State of Consciousness' evidence does not negate the nonordinary reality of what is going on for him in the Shamanic State of Consciousness.[5]

In this long passage from Harner, the dual nature of the intrusive object is directly addressed: The shaman is aware of more than one reality. He/she captures the essence of the intrusive object (the spirit of Kashinakaji the hunter) – which in the shamanic state of consciousness among the Jivaro may have the appearance of a spider, but among the Ndembu (or at least in my experience of an Ndembu ritual) has the appearance of a six-inch gray blob – which he/she then gathers into something which is seen as a piece of wood or a tooth (which are also significant in themselves). Such a dual system also appears among the Walbiri of Australia whose doctors found a dingo spirit inside the patient which they extracted in the form of a worm (Cawte 1974: 48).

This sort of explanation differs from that of Lévi-Strauss who argued that Quesalid was an imposter who went on to become a great shaman in whom the radical negativism of the skeptic gave way to more moderate feelings until he eventually lost all sight of 'the fallaciousness of the technique which he had so disparaged at the beginning' (1977: 448).

Both the tooth and the tuft of down become more significant when considered in the light of Harner's explanation. Victor Turner had some insight into the concept of alternate realities when he argued that the tooth is the slaying weapon par excellence, the epitome, the personification of the sudden aggressiveness needed by a carnivore to bring down a fleeing

---

5   Victor Turner's book (1968) showed that the extraction of harmful intrusions is not limited to the Americas, Siberia, or Australia, but is found in Africa as well. The distinction between shaman and spirit-guided healer has created confusion here. Singleton was not the kind of shaman defined as one who lies prone while his shamanic consciousness wanders forth to bring back the helping spirit to the sick person. He was the kind of healer who is endowed with a tutelary spirit who guides him in his craft. Both types of healer are guided by a helping spirit. In Africa, it is the patient who falls in trance, and by lying prone in an altered state of consciousness, her body responds to the medicinal and ritual 'calling out' effects so strongly focused upon her. A similar stage of consciousness radiates all around the ritual core, a fact well-known to the doctors, who medicate those who are closely concerned (as we were medicated) in order to give them power to see the spirit and for protection.

animal. In the following passage about the forked pole shrine of the Ndembu, Turner (1967: 298) implies a good deal when he describes the synthesizing and focusing capacity of ritual symbolism:

> It must be stressed that the *chishing'a* [forked pole shrine] is regarded by Ndembu not as an object of cognition, a mere set of referents to known phenomena, so much as a unitary power, conflating all the powers inherent in the activities, objects, relationships, and ideas it represents. What Ndembu see in a chishing'a made visible for them in its furcate, ambivalent, and awe-inspiring nakedness, is the slaughterous power of *Wubinda* itself [the Ndembu spirit and cult of huntsmanship].

The curious thing about this passage is the belief that shines out of it, the transmutation of symbols into reality. In his sympathy with the Ndembu, Turner thus goes beyond the idea of symbol as abstract referent. Now we see the shrine pole as one of the poles (as if magnetic) of the two realities, the one the material shrine pole and the other the spirit realm, between which the power of Wubinda jumps back and forth, as it were, into recognition and out of it.[6] Victor Turner's own writings constantly show this ambiguity, sometimes espousing the beliefs of the people he studied and sometimes speaking from the standpoint of positivism (for the former see V. Turner 1975 and the latter V. Turner 1968).

It was that unitary power, combined with the medicines, the participation of the five doctors and the crowd, and the doctor's tutelary spirits, that drove into visibility the spirit substance that I actually saw. Thus working backwards, the Ndembu were right to regard symbols not as 'objects of cognition, mere sets of referents' but as 'powers,' using Turner's words (1967: 298). And working backward still further, it might even be said that many of Turner's analyses of symbols enable us to trace not psychological processes but actual spirit ones, the paths of their power toward us. But this Turner was only able to suggest, as in the example of the quotation above.

Anthropology forbade that he overstep its boundaries. Because of this, a shallower idea of symbolism has begun to affect many researchers so that their understanding stops at the surface of symbols – at their social and psychological effects. They themselves cannot see these material forms as objects with actual power, even though their field people do. These

---

6   The ritual also gave exercise to the sense of 'off and on,' in the repeated shift into another level of reality and back into the mundane. This shifting occurs in rituals elsewhere, often in masked rites involving masking and unmasking such as in Tubuan initiations in New Ireland, in trance rites where the difference between the realities is clearly seen, and anything of the 'now-you-see-it-now-you-don't' kind.

anthropologists have shown themselves to be fundamentalist secularists, however much they bend over backwards to empathize with the people they study.

So when I consider the ihamba tooth which was the result, the trophy, the material prize gained from the long morning of ritual, and wonder about its appearance at the end, what then? Was it that the tooth, brought into ritual focus, was employed to pull toward itself, like a magnet, the harmful thing I saw? That is not quite it. Singleton used the same word, ihamba, for the thing that was inside – that is, the one I saw coming out – and the tooth, which in the doctor's view had indeed been inside. The doctors could switch from addressing 'grandfather' to commanding a biting 'thing' to come out. When the ihamba, whatever it was, that had invaded the veins and arteries of the victim was extracted, it took the form of a gray blob which seemed to be absorbed into the tooth. This concept of an entity inside reminds me of a report by Essie Parrish, the Pomo shaman referred to above:

> When that sick man is lying there, I usually see the power. These things seem unbelievable but I, myself, I know, because it is in me ... Way inside of the sick person lying there, there is something. It is just like seeing through something – if you put tissue over something, you could see through it. That is just the way I see it inside. I see what happens there and can feel it with my hand – my middle finger is the one with the power [compare the photograph of an Ihamba doctor holding his middle finger over a divining mortar in Victor Turner's book, *The Drums of Affliction* (1968: 169)]. The pain sitting somewhere inside the person feels like it is pulling your hand towards itself – you can't miss it.
>
> (Harner 1980: 127-8)

Singleton's skill appears to correspond to that of Essie Parrish, an articulate, English-speaking woman, albeit from an entirely different culture area. Fideli told us that you could see the ihamba moving through the veins of the body: 'I am telling you the truth.' He did not use the 'tissue' image, but there are many references in the tapes to seeing and sensing the ihamba. Singleton said, 'I've seen that it is the ihamba, so he must come out of her.' 'We have seen the ihamba,' said Fideli. Fideli also said, 'When an ihamba goes into a horn you feel it vibrating.' All of these sayings were vindicated by the actual sight of the spirit form, gray, quite definite, like a round blob of plasm.[7] It is this object which is central to my account. It was, for me, the afflictor in a different shape.

---

[7]   As for the Ndembu, in William Blodgett's field notes of 1985, page 219, Philip Kabwita refers to the bad ghost musalu. 'Munginju medicine makes musalu visible. You can see musalu, which comes in smoke or mist, when you drink pounded leaf medicine.'

What is important in Ihamba is the moment when Singleton clutched the 'thing' in his skin pouch. This is the moment when the ihamba that was formerly within was translated into a concrete object which is placed in the receiving can. The fact that the doctors allowed the same word, ihamba, to run as it were out of Meru's body, into the receiving can, and later into the Vaseline jar, attests to its processual unity, its unbroken flow of identity. We could put it backwards: 'that ihamba tooth in the Vaseline jar was the ihamba that was in the receiving can, which was the ihamba that Singleton clutched in his mongoose skin bag, which was the ihamba that came out of Meru, which was the ihamba that had been hurting her with all the agony of a tooth.'

When operating in the forward, cause-and-effect mode, Meru's affliction by a human tooth looks impossible; in English the only words for such a process are 'trickery,' 'sleight-of-hand,' and the like. But these terms derive from quite a different world from the scene at Kahona. Looking backwards from the outcome of the Ihamba to Meru's sickness, the picture does not seem so impossible. This is because the past is only verified by the future (Wagner, personal communication[8]) and this ihamba was destined to be fed. Thus its past took shape after the event, as a computer shifts everything that has been written to adjust to new insertions or formatting commands.

What the ihamba itself consists of is the biting inside, that hard spirit which cannot come out without a sudden transformation, effected socially by living people communicating with the spirit, ready for the 'coalescence or precipitation of the diffuse states,' in the words of Lévi-Strauss. It is what it is.

The last question concerns particulars and universals in the sensing of spirits in different cultures. The Ndembu cosmology of course is not everyone's. At the moment we cannot fathom why each culture has its own. There appear to be no universal 'spirits'; only a few of the world's cultures have experienced 'angels,' for instance. Others have knowledge of animal helpers, while Africans know the support of dead kin. At least we have found out, partly with the help of Victor Turner, that ritual and systems of spirits and power objects are intimately concerned with people in the living context of their compeers.

In a paper like this, honesty becomes very important, and what is personal is part of the process. Therefore I include a paragraph from my notes that shows a certain distress:

---

[8] Roy Wagner (personal communication) put it this way: 'The body's construct is one ahead, and perception one step behind the "now".'

Writing this last passage is like wading through glue. Something is trying to stop me. The devil disguised as Christianity is furious that I have found him out. 'We are not ready for your universalisms,' he says. 'It is not time. Quick! Back to your old beliefs. You never saw a spirit.'

How does acceptance of the informant's world view affect anthropology? It leaves a door unlocked. Those who have gone so far, like Alan Campbell (1989), could find this little door and be free to come and go. Let me explain. Campbell wrote an extremely sympathetic book on tolerance for the oddities of Wayapi Indian thought. Yet he confessed that he did not regard shamanic manifestations among the Wayapi 'as entities in the form of animals or people'; he felt he ought to see them 'as conceptual devices ... metaphors through which the living world is expressed' (1989: 90), a theory he derives from 'minuscule points of grammar' (1989: 21). Is this faithful reportage of the people's experience? The people would deny it. The 'metaphor' model is everywhere to be found in anthropology, but it is rarely found in the real world where events of the psyche are regarded as commonplace, where different cultures have for long been exploring the intangible in terms of their everyday experience, where to date in some hospitals in America nurses are trained to understand the near-death experience,[9] where stories of spirits and lights and midnight paralysis and hagriding (Hufford 1982) continually emerge when there is a listener who will not mock them.

Thus it is becoming clear that what we are referring to are not unusual experiences, because they occur to so many people. Furthermore, when one reviews tests made on telepaths and such specially gifted persons, the phenomena they handle can hardly be called unexpected because such persons have developed skills to induce them. The development of skills is seen, for example, among Balinese trancers, Brazilian Umbandists, and circum-Pacific shamans, as well as among African doctors. It is time that we recognize the ability to experience different levels of reality as one of the normal human abilities and place it where it belongs, central to the study of ritual.

References

Bowen, Elenore S. 1964 [1954]. *Return to Laughter*. Garden City: Doubleday.
Campbell, Alan T. 1989. *To Square with Genesis: Causal Statements and Shamanic Ideas in Wayapi*. Iowa City: University of Iowa Press.

9   See Josephine Memorial Hospital Nursing Standards, Crescent City, California.

Cawte, John. 1974. *Medicine Is the Law: Studies in the Psychiatric Anthropology of Australian Tribal Societies*. Honolulu: University of Hawaii Press.

Evans-Pritchard, E. E. 1976 [1937]. *Witchcraft, Oracles and Magic among the Azande*. Oxford: Clarendon.

Favret-Saada, Jeanne. 1980. *Deadly Words: Witchcraft in the Bocage*. Cambridge: Cambridge University Press.

Harner, Michael. 1980. *The Way of the Shaman*. New York: Bantam.

Hufford, David. 1982. *The Terror that Comes in the Night*. Philadelphia: University of Pennsylvania Press.

Landy, David (ed.). 1977. *Culture, Disease, and Healing*. New York: Macmillan.

Lévi-Strauss, Claude. 1977. 'The Sorcerer and His Magic', in David Landy (ed.) *Culture, Disease, and Healing*. New York: Macmillan pp. 446-53.

Stoller, Paul. 1984. 'Eye, Mind, and Word in Anthropology', *L'Homme* 24(3-4): 91-114.

Tillich, Paul. 1959. *Theology of Culture*. London: Oxford University Press.

Turner, E. 1992. *Experiencing Ritual: A New Interpretation of African Healing*. Philadelphia: University of Pennsylvania Press.

Turner, V. 1957. *Schism and Continuity in an African Society: A Study of Ndembu Village Life*. Manchester: Manchester University Press.

Turner, V. 1967. *The Forest of Symbols: Aspects of Ndembu Ritual*. Ithaca: Cornell University Press.

Turner, V. 1968. *The Drums of Affliction: A Study of Ritual Processes among the Ndembu of Zambia*. Oxford: Clarendon.

Turner, V. 1975. *Revelation and Divination in Ndembu Ritual*. Ithaca, NY: Cornell University Press.

Turner, V. and E. Bruner (eds) 1986. *The Anthropology of Experience*. Urbana: University of Illinois Press.

7. Postcolonial Sun Dancing at Wakpamni Lake

Dale Stover

Editor's introduction

Paying further attention to indigenous understandings and discourse of the cere-monies and lived realities of traditional lifeways, Dale Stover engages with Sun Dancing at Wakpamni Lake community on Pine Ridge reservation, South Dakota, USA.

He goes beyond the kind of rich description provided by some scholarly visitors to indigenous communities, and offers an interpretation akin to that arising from the engagement and experiential presence of Drewal and Turner. More than that, Stover further attends to the relationship between researchers and the commu-nities they visit and discuss. All researchers are related to such communities. But not all relationships are welcome, respectful, or appropriate. Perhaps few such relationships empower the indigenous hosts researched 'on' or 'among'. The reason for this is not difficult to see: research is generally done (performed) from a position of power. It is almost certainly disseminated in modes that empower the researcher. In short, the sovereignty of the host community is neither recognized (let alone celebrated) nor further empowered.

In recent years a powerful discourse labelled 'postcolonialism' has arisen. Stover describes it as 'one of the more promising critical attempts to counter the per-vasive influence of colonizing categories of thinking and imaging in modern dis-course'. It does not go unchallenged nor should it be uncritically adopted. But it does demand and reward consideration. Stover utilizes it in 'making apparent the

Reprinted from *Journal of the American Academy of Religion*, 69(4), 2001. By permission of Oxford University Press.

essentialism of "self" and "other" that characterizes Eurocentric colonial discourse'. This is not identical to the move made by some anthropologists by which the study of 'others' teaches 'us' about 'ourselves', i.e. 'we' study 'foreigners' (perhaps indigenes) because 'we' need a lens through which to see 'ourselves' properly.

Instead, to further quote the author's original abstract, Stover proposes

> a North American postcolonial hermeneutic ... which focuses on the oral voice of tradition embodied in the lived experience of an indigenous community. Postcolonial interpretation entails an interpreter entering into ritual relationship with a traditional community so that the hegemonic pattern of dominant-culture discourse is circumvented.

In the context of 'the traditional practices of the Wakpamni Lake community' their Sun Dancing is understood 'as a postcolonial undertaking' identifiable through 'four interrelated features described as four ways of respect', namely, respect for living traditions, respect for the sacredness of place, respect for communally lived meanings and respect for cosmic kinship. Just as the religious praxis of this Sun Dancing is a 'politics of kinship' (contradicting 'the colonizing power relations rooted in European American cultural heritage') so, says Stover, 'this politics of kinship offers the dominant culture a way to intercultural relationship that disarms the entrenched essentialism of "self" and "other."'

This article may aid an exceptional phenomenological and experiential encounter with a particular community's ritual life, but far more importantly (because this is what the community's praxis does) it incites participation 'in the transforming reciprocities of new kinship relations that are not limited to 'an exclusively human field of meanings' but are connected 'in specific and palpable ways to the expressive earth'' [citing Abram 1996: 139].

In so doing, Stover participates (with, e.g., Sarris 1993) in anticipating the radical reconstruction of academia as a truly and widely collaborative exercise. Why else are we alive? What else are we working for?

References

Abram, David. 1996. *The Spell of the Sensuous: Perception and Language in a More-Than-Human World*. New York: Vintage Books.

Sarris, Greg. 1993. *Keeping Slug Woman Alive: A Holistic Approach to American Indian Texts*. Berkeley: University of California Press.

જ∞⌒

Postcolonial theory and the discourse of the 'metropole'

Any scholarly attempt to address the place and function of the Sun Dance in contemporary Lakota experience raises the issue of the prejudicial understanding of European American culture regarding indigenous religious traditions. Since academic thinking and writing have long been situated within the prevailing intellectual norms of European or European-derived cultures and since these norms have long been oriented around the colonizing interests of these cultures, it is necessary to recognize that the heritage of academic discourse includes colonizing patterns of perceiving and describing indigenous realities.

One of the more promising critical attempts to counter the pervasive influence of colonizing categories of thinking and imaging in modern discourse has arisen, mostly among Africans and Asians, in the form of postcolonial theory.[1] It has taken shape among intellectuals representing various colonized peoples whose political sovereignty reverted to an indigenous populace in the post-World War II era. These postcolonial voices have typically been concerned with the recovery of both political and cultural sovereignty. However, they have often been preoccupied with the literary voice of their natal culture expressed in the words of a European language, and they often reside in the 'metropole,' their word for the European homeland of the colonizer and its metropolitan culture which usually retains a complex, and sometimes controlling, relation to the economic and cultural life of the former colony. Consequently, postcolonial theory has been dominated by writers who have largely engaged in such theory to present a counterpoint to the intellectual voices of European and European-derived societies, at times producing more of a reactive stance than a truly alternative cultural discourse. Postcolonial writing has, therefore, not necessarily expressed the oral voice of contemporary indigenous traditions.

Nevertheless, these postcolonial literary voices have unmistakably shown that the discourse of the metropole has routinely and pervasively reflected a differential in power relations between the colonizer and the colonized by structuring its thinking and imaging in a binary opposition between 'self' and 'other.' Moreover, postcolonial theory has exposed the essentialism inherent in this dichotomy which supports the hegemonic

---

[1] Positions on postcolonial theory vary widely; a helpful overview can be found in Childs and Williams (1997).

assignment of one's essential identity according to the distribution of power between the colonizing cultural 'self' and the colonized culture of the 'other' so that in the discourse of the metropole one's essence as a 'self' or an 'other' is determined by the circumstances of geography and descent.

North American postcolonial hermeneutic

Jace Weaver, who is Cherokee and a scholar of indigenous religious traditions of North America, has expressed ambivalence about postcolonial theory. In a recent essay he cites numerous negative assessments of postcolonial theory culled from contemporary theorists. In particular, he seems to charge that the postcolonial is necessarily identified with the postmodern and that, since this latter approach is but the latest fashion in European intellectual discourse, postcolonialism, too, may primarily represent a continuance of 'the philosophical hegemony of the West' (Weaver 1998: 14).

Weaver is right to harbor hermeneutic suspicion regarding postmodernism. Philip Deloria, in his recent book, *Playing Indian*, deftly demonstrates how a postmodern sensibility contributes to 'the continued unraveling of the connections between meanings and social realities' (Deloria 1998: 158). Deloria goes on to point out that when 'meanings become liberated from their social moorings, what began to matter most was the relation between the interpreter and the text being interpreted ....' (p. 166). Text then becomes detachable from context. Furthermore, notes Deloria, as detachable items, all cultural elements in a postmodern era, especially indigenous elements, become available for consumption as commodities by individuals of the dominant society (p. 173).

To assess postmodernism and its possible linkage to postcolonial theory, it is important to recognize that postmodernism represents in some crucial respects the breakup of modernism and that modernism has functioned hegemonically by imposing a single authorized version of moral, political, and cultural truth on the rest of the world.[2] Hegemonic modernism has been the indispensable discourse partner of colonial power. As colonialism has changed from overt political control to covert economic and cultural dominance, thoughtful critics must consider whether postmodernism represents a predictable partner for the new colonialism of corporate and consumer culture, or whether some more complex set of changes are afoot. It is reasonable to be wary of the postmodern as a voice issuing from the

---

[2] Postmodernism has a notoriously complicated relation to modernism; an illuminating survey of its intellectual history can be found in Bertens (1995).

culture of the colonizer; yet, if a postcolonial discourse is going to move beyond reactive response in order to effect a decolonizing of both the colonized 'other' and the colonizing 'self,' the voice of the postmodern 'self' may need to be included in the decolonizing process. Moreover, despite the discourse of the metropole being heavily invested in justifying and maintaining colonizing relationships over indigenous peoples, to characterize the whole of metropolitan discourse as colonial discourse might only extend the error of essentializing.

Weaver, after expressing misgivings about postcolonial theory, surprisingly reverses field and adopts the term for his own purposes, asserting that 'Post-colonial critique provides a useful tool for analyzing Native literatures . . . and for deconstructing the ironic and destructive biblical readings that have been imposed upon us' (Weaver 1998: 15). Weaver claims a postcolonial voice for himself by redefining postcolonial theory for use in North American circumstances. Eventually, Weaver goes so far as to identify his decolonizing thematic of a 'we-hermeneutic' as a 'post-colonial Native hermeneutic' (p. 22).

In co-opting the postcolonial rubric, Weaver lays out the characteristics necessary for an interpretive approach that is 'truly post-colonial' (p. 22). His North American postcolonial hermeneutic includes, by my reading, four thematic characteristics: 1) affirmation of the autonomy and contemporary relevance of indigenous religious traditions, 2) recognition of the integrity of the cultural–spiritual bond between indigenous peoples and their lands, 3) respect for communal processes as the proper location for determining all meanings and commitments, and, 4) a rejection of all 'us' versus 'them' dichotomies and an embrace of kinship with 'the entire created order' (p. 22).

Postcolonial theory and indigenous discourse

While I am in agreement with Weaver regarding the choice of categories he includes in his postcolonial hermeneutic, his statement represents a generalized pan-Indian concern to reclaim cultural and political identity, and its hermeneutic focus is on literary rather than oral discourse. Moreover, since this pan-Indian hermeneutic is framed within the language and categories of the colonizers' discourse, its usefulness may depend on its being functionally related to the discourse of traditional indigenous communities. My own appreciation for postcolonial theory began through listening to the oral discourse of my Lakota friends of the Wakpamni Lake community on Pine Ridge Reservation in South Dakota, and I subsequently noticed that the concept of postcolonial interpretation could be construed as a close fit for what the Wakpamni Lake community had taught me over a decade or more. My experience suggests that it is in the lived experience of a contemporary indigenous community that the theoretical meanings of the postcolonial can be properly grounded, because it is there that the social realities of colonization and of resistance to it converge and become apparent.

In the current era of cultural globalization it may seem questionable whether indigenous discourse any longer functions as a traditional oral culture. David Abram claims otherwise in his recent study in which he insists that

> there remain, on the edges and even in the midst of this ever-expanding monoculture, small-scale local cultures or communities where the traditional oral, indigenous modes of experience still prevail – cultures that have never fully transferred their sensory participation to the written word. They have not yet closed themselves within an exclusively human field of meanings, and so still dwell within a landscape that is alive, aware, and expressive. ... Indeed, the linguistic discourse of such cultures is commonly bound, in specific and palpable ways, to the expressive earth. (Abram 1996: 139)

My experience with the Wakpamni Lake community may not measure up to the pristine register of Abram's description, but his emphasis on the more-than-human field of meanings and on the discourse being bound 'to the expressive earth' rings fully true in the Wakpamni Lake context.

While Abram was able to give expression to a perceptive description of the oral discourse of two contemporary indigenous communities based on his direct acquaintance with the communities,[3] his own concern was to employ this description in generating a generalized theory of human relation to the environing world. With the indigenous instance as his paradigm, he endeavors to construct a grand narrative of how human understanding develops linguistically, and the core focus of his story turns out to be, not indigenous oral discourse, but Hebrew and Greek literacy as understood through twentieth-century phenomenology. This is actually a theoretical enterprise in the arena of Eurocentric discourse, and Abram's skillful incorporation into his formulation of ethnographic literature regarding various indigenous traditions, including the Lakota, runs the risk of functioning as an exercise of the colonizer's privilege to exploit indigenous resources without personal knowledge of, or real engagement with, the actual indigenous communities cited.

---

[3] Abram's description is based on his residence with indigenous communities in Indonesia and Nepal.

178

My own relation to the Wakpamni Lake community differs both from Abram's secondhand use of ethnography and from a standard first-person ethnographic approach, because I initially participated in the ceremonial life of the community without the intention to write about it.[4] Moving into the discourse of an indigenous community from the discourse-world of the dominant culture is problematic in itself, but doubly so when the intentionality of written interpretation is involved. As long as one consciously carries an ethnographic intention, the relation to the community is complicated by the colonizer dynamic ordinarily present in such a culturally constituted intention. Some excellent ethnographic interpretation has recently been done regarding religious traditions of contemporary indigenous communities in which the personal relationships established by the scholar-interpreter contribute to a sensitive, collaborative result.[5] Nevertheless, as valuable as such treatments may be in most respects, they characteristically focus on describing an indigenous worldview, and worldview tends to be presented as an objective thing-in-itself which has its own existence quite apart from the oppressive dynamic of the community's past and present experience with the dominant culture. The result is often the reifying of worldview as an apolitical portrait expressed in the terms of the colonizer's discourse which is taken as a normative, rather than charged, field of discourse.[6]

Positive guidance regarding engagement with the oral discourse of contemporary indigenous persons is provided by Greg Sarris, who describes himself as 'a mixed-blood Indian (Pomo-Miwok) and university scholar' (Sarris 1993: 2). He cites a host of hermeneutical theorists as he relates his efforts to tell about Mabel McKay, a Pomo woman who is the last Bole Maru dreamer and who provided a home for Sarris during some of his childhood.[7] Sarris looks to McKay's hermeneutical practices as the standard for evaluating all the theorists. He describes talking with McKay as a 'speech event' that can 'interrupt and simultaneously expose the interlocutor's presuppositions at any point ... ' (p. 28). Sarris suggests that 'Mabel's talk initiates in the interlocutors a kind of internal dialogue where the interlocutors examine the nature of their own thinking ... ' (p. 30). He describes McKay as fighting 'typification' so that 'she rebukes the attempts of those who wish to see her in an ahistorical light,' and 'her talk interferes

---

[4] I began to consider writing about my experiences with the community after a dream in early 1995.

[5] See Frey (1987) on the Crow (Apsaalooke) and Smith (1995) on the Ojibwe (Anishnaabeg).

[6] John Grim's account of his collaboration with a contemporary Crow (Apsaalooke) community is exceptional in its effort to include the political dimension in his description of traditional life; see Grim (1997).

[7] See especially the first two essays in Sarris (1993).

with any move that would displace history from myth ... ' (p. 32). At the same time, claims Sarris, 'the interlocutor's experience is not displaced either; it is held up, and therefore affirmed, juxtaposed not to show how one experience or world view is better than the other but to expose the tension between them' (p. 32). Sarris acknowledges that McKay 'disrupts the kind of dialogue that has been typical between fieldworkers and informants,' but he claims that such disruption promotes dialogue 'that can open the intermingling of the multiple voices and histories within and between people' (p. 33). Sarris describes this dialogue as collaborative. 'For Mabel McKay and her interlocutors, talk itself initiates and sets the goundwork for collaboration. It is an art generating respect for the unknown while illuminating the borders of the known' (p. 33).

Sarris's understanding of Mabel McKay's hermeneutic of collaborative dialogue corresponds with my own interpretive concern to focus on those features of indigenous discourse that 'interrupt' and 'disrupt' my own cultural discourse. To enter into actual relationship with a traditional community, I suggest, is already to initiate a decolonization process that ultimately subverts the old categories of 'self' and 'other' and that generates a new and mutually respectful discourse. Such a discourse may rightly be called postcolonial discourse since it aims at displacing the historical and hegemonic constructions of power and meaning unilaterally imposed by the dominant culture of the American metropole.

Postcolonial discourse on Sun Dance

For traditional Lakota people the contemporary Sun Dance signifies the continuation of and identification with the traditional ways of ancestral generations, whereas for European American culture it represents the epitome of 'otherness,' the imagined 'primitive' world of indigenous America before European contact. Lakota Sun Dancing carries this double marking because it emphatically represents an embodied spirituality that is, on the one hand, deeply characteristic of indigenous traditions and that is, on the other hand, at profound odds with a Eurocentric modernism that dualistically segregates the religious experience of the subjective self from the objective, embodied realities of the world. European American descriptions of Lakota Sun Dancing typically manifest the predilection of the metropole for assigning to indigenous rituals only those meanings that conform to modernist categories of thought. The need for postcolonial interpretation of Lakota Sun Dancing can be made evident by three examples of dominant-culture interpreters who, with astonishing näiveté, project their own meanings onto this complex ritual with little or no actual experience of the ceremony or the ceremonial community.

Clyde Holler's 1995 book on Lakota Sun Dancing indicates that he visited the Sun Dance at Three Mile Camp near Kyle, South Dakota, in 1983 for the final two days of the ceremony, but he writes only of his own observations and the inferences he makes from them. He does not cite any of the elders, singers, or dancers, nor the spiritual leader of the ceremony regarding their understanding of the Sun Dance. Moreover, his chief interest is in determining which of the contemporary Lakota Sun Dances most authentically represents pre-reservation traditions, as though such a 'pedigree' would certify its spiritual credibility. He rationalizes, strictly on the basis of textual references, that the Sun Dance at Three Mile Camp is the most authentic because of its association with Frank Fools Crow, whose residence adjoined the Sun Dance grounds and because, he hypo- thesizes, Fools Crow represents the Sun Dance traditions passed on by Nicholas Black Elk and recorded by Joseph Epes Brown in *The Sacred Pipe*.[8] The insubstantial character of his chain of reasoning about this Sun Dance having the most authoritative linkage with the 'classical' nineteenth- century version becomes evident in his failure to learn that this Sun Dance at Three Mile Camp had been powerfully shaped over a number of years by the visionary leadership of a Lakota holy man named Dawson Has No Horse, Sr., who had died in 1982, the year preceding Holler's visit.

Julian Rice's 1998 book on 'Sioux' spirituality reports that in the sum- mer of 1984 he came to visit Frank Fools Crow at Three Mile Camp, and they walked together from the house to the adjoining Sun Dance arena where Fools Crow told him a single story. 'Once, long time ago, a buffalo came over *that* hill (just outside the circle). Then it turned into a man and he came down and joined the dancers. He danced for the whole time and went back up on the hill. He turned around and looked back once. Then he turned back into a buffalo and went away' (Rice 1998: 35). Rice does not say whether he returned to Three Mile Camp for the Sun Dance itself three weeks later, and he offers no first-hand account of a Sun Dance in his book, but he does offer a confident interpretation of Fools Crow's remarkable story of the buffalo who turned into a Sun Dancer and then turned back into a buffalo at that very Sun Dance location. Instead of expressing curiosity about the power and mystery of such an event having happened at that place, Rice turns the story into a metaphor about himself as a European American scholar being the buffalo who becomes Lakota for a bit and then returns to his world of scholarship. Rice implicitly imposes his own cultural discourse by assigning a non-cosmological and non- empirical meaning of personal metaphor to the story, and he never once

---

[8] See my critique of Holler's book in Stover (1997).

thinks to ask knowledgeable Lakota persons regarding the meaning of such a story within the frame of Lakota discourse.

Although Holler and perhaps Rice made one on-scene visit to a Lakota Sun Dance, however brief, there is some evidence to suggest that Joseph Epes Brown, who represents an earlier era of interpretation, wrote with presumed authority about the Lakota Sun Dance without ever having witnessed an actual ceremony. He seems to confuse the Lakota rite with the Shoshone/Crow ceremony with which he was familiar. His 1978 article on Sun Dance, first published in *Parabola* (3/2)[9] describes 'the circular ceremonial lodge' (Brown 1987: 101), without acknowledging that the Lakota Sun Dance is not performed in a 'ceremonial lodge' but in an open arena, peripherally surrounded by a shade arbor.[10] Brown baldly claims that 'ethnographic description of the particulars of a Lakota, Arapaho, Gros Ventre, Blackfeet, Cree, Cheyenne, or Crow/Shoshone Sun Dance is neither appropriate nor necessary' (p. 102). Ethnographic particulars can be dismissed as insignificant because Brown assumes that as a scholar he possesses the hermeneutic virtuosity to decode all the ethnographic variations, thus unveiling 'what is essentially a single language of sacred act and vision' (p. 102). For Brown, the religious world of the indigenous 'other' is totally transparent to the European-American interpreter.[11]

Not one of these three scholars expresses any awareness that their own cultural perceptions may be influencing their interpretations of Lakota realities. Moreover, the ease with which they incorporate indigenous cultural themes into the intellectual discourse of the dominant culture creates the impression that the 'self' of the dominant culture actually knows the 'other' of the indigenous culture, thus disguising the terrible realities of the colonizing relationship between the two parties in which both the scholars and the readers of their scholarship are complicit. As long as the indigenous domain of embodied existence with its lived experience of conquest, exploitation, and genocide remains unexamined in the interpretive portrayals of Lakota Sun Dancing, the result will be a parody of indigenous spirituality, purged of political meaning and packaged to suit the dominant culture's view of the 'other.'

If postcolonial discourse intends to avoid the colonial legacy of a

---

[9] Citations from 'Sun Dance: Sacrifice, Renewal, Identity' are from its reprinting in Brown's, *The Spiritual Legacy of the American Indian* (1987).

[10] Brown's confusion is evident in his inclusion of a drawing of a Shoshone/Crow 'medicine lodge' to illustrate Black Elk's description of a Lakota Sun Dance arena (see 1953: 81).

[11] Brown's work is based on broad acquaintance with northern Plains traditions and is widely recognized as being perceptive and nuanced, but his interpretive approach, when seen from a postcolonial angle, bears the clear marks of the hegemonic presumptions characteristic of the dominant-culture scholarship of his era.

scholarship that objectifies and reifies indigenous realities from the distant vantage point of the 'knowing' outsider, it must begin with the acknowledgment that indigenous discourse regarding Sun Dance already exists orally and that it deserves interpretive priority. Honoring traditional Lakota discourse means that an other-than-Lakota scholar will necessarily seek the mentorship of knowledgeable Lakota persons and give respectful attention to the lived experience and oral discourse of a contemporary Lakota community.

Sun Dancing at Wakpamni: the four ways of respect

In July 1986 I made my first journey to the Sun Dance encampment at Three Mile Camp and paid my respects to Frank Fools Crow as he sat under the arbor on the north side of the Sun Dance arena. I had been invited to this Sun Dance by the Has No Horse family, whom I had met in May 1986.[12] I had been introduced to this family by my friend, Lloyd Ware, of Lincoln, Nebraska. Lloyd's acquaintance with the Has No Horse family began in the late 1970s when he brought his young, critically ill son to Wakpamni for a *yuwipi* ceremony. The *yuwipi* man conducting the ceremony was Dawson Has No Horse, Sr., a widely respected Lakota *wicasa wakan* (holy man) who died in January of 1982. The Has No Horse family was clearly fond of Lloyd, and they welcomed me warmly. In the years since, Dawson's widow, Emily, his son, Sidney, and his son-in-law, Robert Two Crow, along with other members of the family,[13] and the community, have been gracious hosts and teachers as I have gained acquaintance with traditional Lakota lifeways.

The Sun Dance at Three Mile Camp had been under the spiritual direction of Dawson Has No Horse, Sr. until his death in 1982. Because of Has No Horse's past leadership, the people of Wakpamni Lake were a core group in this ceremony, but it was a large dance that incorporated dancers from several districts of the reservation as well as from other places. I attended this dance annually, camping with the Wakpamni Lake contingent. In 1992 Sidney Has No Horse, following his own visions, began Sun Dancing on family property at Wakpamni, and this dance soon became a spiritual center for the Wakpamni Lake community. There is no

---

[12] The protocol for Sun Dancing at Wakpamni routinely excludes European Americans from becoming dancers, but all those present are considered ritual participants insofar as they enter into various activities that represent the active praying of the ceremonial community.

[13] In particular, Dawson's daughters, Sharon and Shirley, and his oldest son, Dawson, Jr. were most welcoming.

longer a Sun Dance held at Three Mile Camp, though a Sun Dance is still held at another location near Kyle, South Dakota, that incorporates many of the people from the former dance not from Wakpamni Lake.

My effort toward postcolonial discourse concerning Sun Dance is based on my association with the traditional practices of the Wakpamni Lake community. I attempt to pay respect to the local scale of oral discourse so that this community's own understanding of Sun Dancing comes into play for the reader. I look to Jace Weaver's formulation of a North American postcolonial hermeneutic for interpretive guidance. Acknowledging his pan-Indian statement as an articulate form of resistance to the impositions of dominant-culture scholarship, I shall describe four features of Sun Dancing at Wakpamni that to my thinking bear a rough correspondence to the four thematic characteristics indicated by Weaver. What follows, then, is Stover's Wakpamni-based version of Weaver's postcolonial hermeneutic, whereby Weaver's four postcolonial themes are styled as four ways of respect – (1) respect for live traditions, (2) respect for the sacredness of place, (3) respect for communally lived meanings, and (4) respect for cosmic kinship.

Postcolonial Sun Dancing: respect for live traditions

The first of the four ways of respect is respect for live traditions. Among Lakota people, live traditions imply visions or dreams.[14] I had been told by family members that Dawson Has No Horse, Sr. had become the leader of the Sun Dance at Porcupine, South Dakota, in the 1970s through the guidance provided by his visions, and that he oversaw the moving of this dance to Three Mile Camp near Kyle in the late 1970s. I had heard stories about the spirit who appeared in Has No Horse's visions and who had empowered his healing work in *yuwipi* ceremonies. I had even seen the name of this spirit printed in a book,[15] and I had heard Dawson's son, Sidney, speak of his own visionary experiences with this same spirit. It was clear from these stories that this spirit was linked to the power of the *wakinyan oyate*, the thunder-being nation, and that both Dawson and Sidney had had close encounters with thunderbolts.

Robert Two Crow advised me against using the name of the spirit who had been said to be guiding and empowering Dawson and Sidney, because a visionary relationship of that sort was considered to be a sacred matter and was highly individualized so that it was only appropriate for the

[14] Plains traditions make no distinction between visions and dreams; see Irwin (1994: 18).
[15] See Ross (1989: 105).

visionaries themselves or their immediate family members to speak of this spirit. What could be said, according to Two Crow, is that this was an instance of *wokunze*, a spirit encountered in a vision. *Wokunze* is an other-than-theistic personalization of *wakan*, the dimension of sacred being. The *wokunze* empowers the visionary person and the relationship that is established entails, according to Two Crow, consequences, obligations, and a personal destiny; however, this empowerment and destiny are inevitably directed toward the welfare of the community. While the experience of the *wokunze* ultimately has significance for the community, the *wokunze* remains as the unique experience of the individual person who has the vision, and it is that person who falls under the specific direction of the *wokunze*.

In a predawn hour of the fourth day of the Wakpamni Lake Sun Dance in 1997 a fearsome display of lightning strikes in the vicinity of the encampment reached a climactic moment when a powerful thunderbolt hit near the camp and traveled by an underground watercourse to the Sun Dance circle where it struck Sidney Has No Horse. Under visionary influence, Has No Horse had responded to the approach of the storm by wrapping himself in a never-before-used star quilt and lying face-down by the sacred tree at the center of the Sun Dance circle. When the thunderbolt struck, Has No Horse was uninjured, but the star quilt bore scorch marks. After the opening round of that last day of dancing, Has No Horse described the event to everyone at the Sun Dance circle. What he said made it clear that this was an experience of *wokunze*. To repeat his words, however, might misconstrue the experience by giving the impression that the spirit encountered by Has No Horse could be reified in a way that would make the individual relationship available to others. For the community, it was sufficient to acknowledge the *wokunze* as the personalized presence of a power that validated their spiritual traditions as being fully alive, capable of providing contemporary guidance, and deserving of the utmost respect.

Postcolonial Sun Dancing: respect for the sacredness of place

The second way of respect is respect for the sacredness of place. For people at Wakpamni, sacredness of place applies to the sites of vision quests and *yuwipi* ceremonies, which may be places where an individual experiences *wokunze*. Sacredness of place also refers to the way a Sun Dance circle is perceived as sacred during a ceremony so that the total environment becomes empowered and the sacred tree, the circle of sage, cloud formations, storm pathways, bird flight-patterns, and the contours of surrounding hills and lakes all become a dynamic stage for localized encounters with spirit-relatives from various planes of reality.

I was told that the way a place is made sacred is expressed by the word *hocoka*. On the second day of the 1998 Sun Dance at Wakpamni, Robert Two Crow, who was serving as *eyapaha*, the official announcer for the Sun Dance gathering, warned the people that the real meaning of *hocoka* was different from the English word 'circle.' The word 'circle,' he said, implied a general concept, whereas *hocoka* always belonged to the person whose vision directed the formation of the *hocoka*. In the way Two Crow was speaking of it, *hocoka* meant both the place which had been made into a sacred location for this Sun Dance ceremony and also the particular form of the ceremony itself which was being carried out there. This particular *hocoka* belonged, Two Crow said, to his brother-in-law, Sidney Has No Horse. Furthermore, said Two Crow, since it was Sidney's *hocoka*, carried out according to his dream, it was not appropriate for anyone other than Sidney to make interpretive statements about this *hocoka*. A month after the 1998 Sun Dance I talked with Two Crow about his reference to *hocoka*, and he agreed to have his response videotaped in order for it to function as a 'documented' oral text.

> In the Lakota world *hocoka* is a ceremony, a setting for a ceremony to take place, and these *hocokas* are very personal. They are not identical to each other. Every person who is going to have a *hocoka*, (it) is based on a dream, and they themselves know how this *hocoka* is supposed to be set up. So they will instruct their people who work for them or who are his (their) helpers to set that up, and it should not be compared to another person's *hocoka*. It should not be used as a reference point to examine or study another *hocoka*. *Hocokas* are given to people in dreams to help other people understand themselves in the process of daily living or daily life, and to request assistance in making another person feel good, or if that person is ill to bring him back to good health. Those are what the *hocoka* is for. And a lot of times when a non-Indian comes into a situation or a *hocoka* like that, or when people write about those things, they compare them to other *hocoka*, and that isn't the process that the Lakota understand. More of the younger Lakota people are beginning to use that (comparative) process because of the process of education, how we are taught to use European/Euro-American thought process in studying and learning about different things. So, it's beginning to appear, but the real, main significant concept for *hocoka* is very different from the way they have been writing about it, talking about it. So, when you go to someone's Sun Dance, someone's *yuwipi* ceremony, or any kind of ceremony that is taking place, you should go there with honor and respect for whoever is doing that, or conducting that ceremony because they have been

asked to conduct that and it is very special to the people who are requesting that *hocoka*. So, that's how it's different, that's how the Lakota understand *hocoka*.[16]

Two Crow's explanation of *hocoka* makes clear that in Lakota understanding encounter with the sacred mode of being is a matter of profound relational interaction in a ritually charged locale. This understanding of *hocoka* identifies the sacred always with a specific place which may constrain the scholar's bent to frame local ceremonial engagement with sacred modalities by comparative reference. Comparative scholarship in a postcolonial era will be challenged to modify its usual framing by modernist, Eurocentric norms of subjectifying religious experience so that indigenous discourse regarding the sacredness of place may be more fairly and fully engaged.

Postcolonial Sun Dancing: respect for communally lived meanings

The third way of respect is respect for communally lived meanings. On 28 January 1998, while sitting with Robert Two Crow in his school-district office in Batesland, South Dakota, he explained to me how respect for communally lived meanings is expressed in the phrase *Lakol wicoh'an*, which he said meant 'doing things in a Lakota way.' Lakota people typically do not separate spiritual practices from the whole fabric of traditional life-ways, and Two Crow emphasized that *Lakol wicoh'an* specifically included ceremonial practices as being foundational to communal identity.

Two Crow sees *Lakol wicoh'an* as the process by which a contemporary community, still known by the traditional term *tiyospaye*, transforms communally lived meanings to fit the circumstances of the modern situation, and he sees the growth of interest in Sun Dancing and the changes in the form and function of Sun Dancing as part of that process. However, *Lakol wicoh'an* for Two Crow does not mean modernization in the sense of taking on the discourse style of European American culture. Two Crow speaks about *Lakol wicoh'an* as the working out of communally lived meanings in Lakota language and what he calls 'Lakota thought processes,' so that a distinctive discourse is maintained that resists European American concepts of linear time, individualized identity, and the inordinate authority attributed to written documents, all of which he sees as conveying disrespect for communally lived meanings.

According to Two Crow, Lakota meaning is grounded and nurtured

[16] Robert Two Crow, interview with the author, 8 August 1998.

within the *tiyospaye*, which continues to be the fundamental communal structure, though now it functions more as a residential district than as a nineteenth-century hunting band. The functional social identity of the Wakpamni Lake community is its shared life as a *tiyospaye*. The social codes of a *tiyospaye* are not written down, Two Crow noted, and they are not immediately apparent to an outsider because they are transmitted through the oral discourse that constitutes the community's lived experience. Crucial to the local shaping of this communal discourse, Two Crow noted, were the elders who pass on stories and provide interpretations of events and circumstances, along with the medicine men and medicine women who maintain visionary relations between the *tiospaye* and its spirit-relatives. Two Crow stressed that *Lakol wicoh'an* was not a fixed tradition but a dynamic process. He recalled that the stories he was told over the years by knowledgeable elders and medicine people always carried the message of the resourceful adaptation of *Lakol wicoh'an* to changing circumstances.

Two Crow's understanding of *Lakol wicoh'an* as respect for communally lived meanings establishes communal leaders as the authoritative interpreters of Lakota culture-in-process. From this it follows that the contributions of other-than-Lakota scholars can be legitimated only through a collaborative relationship with the living community, and reifications of *Lakol wicoh'an* are to be discredited.

Postcolonial Sun Dancing: respect for cosmic kinship

The fourth way of respect is respect for cosmic kinship. The Wakpamni Lake Sun Dance includes a tradition of dancing during the night of the full moon. This night of dancing is done between the third and fourth days of the Sun Dance.[17] In order to coordinate the dance with the full moon in July, the Sun Dance at Wakpamni breaks with the modern pattern of scheduling Sun Dances from Thursday through Sunday which maximizes attendance by its weekend orientation. Thus, priority is given at Wakpamni to cosmic rhythms and relationships rather than to the economic rhythms of the commercial work schedule.

At the 1998 Wakpamni Lake Sun Dance the full-moon dancing differed noticeably from previous years. Prior to this, the dancing at night featured the songs and dance patterns of the Sun Dance so that the night dancing

---

[17] Sun Dances of the nineteenth century, before the federal ban of the ceremony in 1883, included night dancing; see Holler (1995: 53). Also, Black Elk's description of Sun Dance tradition as recorded by Joseph Brown in *The Sacred Pipe* (1953: 87) includes night dancing.

mirrored the ceremonial practices of the day dancing. This changed in 1998 when the night ceremony featured the enactment of an individual dream by Cleve Her Many Horses, assisted by his uncle, Sidney Has No Horse. The songs and style of the ceremony, though held in the Sun Dance circle, were suggestive of a *lowanpi* or *yuwipi* ceremony which are held at night, but indoors in complete darkness. In such ceremonies the spirits are experienced as more palpably present than in daylight ceremonies, and the 1998 night dancing seemed to evoke for the participants an intensification of a relation with the *wakinyan oyate*, the thunder-being people. This included a dog sacrifice, in honor of the status of the dog as a messenger of the *wakinyan oyate*, and all participants were offered communion with the *wakinyan oyate* through partaking of sacred dog soup.

When I interviewed Two Crow in August of 1998, I asked him about this relationship:

Stover: Also at the Sun Dance, when you were talking and also when others like Sidney Has No Horse spoke, it was suggested that this particular *hocoka* (Sun Dance ceremony) had to do especially with the relation between the community and the *wakinyan oyate*. Is that the case with every Sun Dance, or just with this particular *hocoka*? What does it mean to be in a relationship with the *wakinyan oyate*?

Two Crow: When I was speaking about the *wakinyan oyate*, I was speaking from my own perception of what I saw and how I understood what was taking place. Some other person who is very competent in looking at these things may agree with me or may not, but what I have seen there was a group of people, who had the same belief and followed the same belief pattern and dream patterns, coming together to send voices, to pray together, to establish a *hocoka*, or honor a *hocoka*, that was similar to what they believed in. So, that belief being the *wakinyan*. Every one of these individuals had in some form a connection to the *wakinyan oyate*. And each one of these connections are different and those are personal and cannot be spoken about. And if you want to know about those individual concepts then you should go talk to people and they will discuss with you their beliefs. That's how I've seen this *hocoka* as it developed for the last seven or eight years.

In a later conversation,[18] Two Crow told me that this relationship with the *wakinyan oyate* can be more fully appreciated in the context of the relation between Lakota people and the world above as represented by the stars. Lakota oral traditions tell of a correspondence between the movement of constellations and the seasonal round of ceremonies in connection with

---

[18] Robert Two Crow, telephone conversation with the author, 1 November 1998.

sacred sites imaged by particular constellations.[19] Two Crow does not offer a narrative that definitively ties together the relationship between the constellations and the *wakinyan oyate*.[20] With typical reserve regarding sacred matters, he says simply that whatever this relationship is remains to be seen as the Wakpamni Lake Sun Dancers continue to work out their relationship with the *wakinyan oyate*. Therefore, the answer does not exist in a book but in the lived experience with cosmic kinfolk.

Postcolonial hermeneutics and the politics of kinship

Sun Dancing at Wakpamni Lake is an empowering ceremonial occasion when the four ways of respect are communally endorsed and expressed in lived experience. By giving hermeneutic priority to these four ways of respect, I have attempted to honor the oral voice and ritual experience of the Wakpamni Lake community. This hermeneutic of respect does have a political dimension because it alters the dominant culture's discourse patterns regarding indigenous traditions and practices. This hermeneutic shift evokes a public awareness of the dissonance between a new discourse of respect and the customary structure of the power relations between the dominant society and the indigenous peoples. A hermeneutic of respect draws attention to the political vision evident in the contemporary practice of Sun Dancing at Wakpamni Lake which honors, affirms, and renews an interrelatedness and reciprocity among all life forms on both a local and planetary or cosmic scale. Sun Dancing at Wakpamni Lake manifests a religious praxis that can be described as a politics of kinship, whereas the 'manifest destiny' of the dominant culture represents a religious praxis that legitimates a colonizing politics of essentialism.[21]

Sun Dancing is intrinsically political by virtue of its embodiment of a kinship-oriented worldview antithetical to the politics of essentialism that legitimates dominance of the 'self' over the 'other,' thus denying the possibility of kinship between the two. Differing cosmologies underlie these

[19] Goodman writes, 'The constellations were the visible "scriptures" of the People at night; and the related land forms mirrored those stellar scriptures during the day' (1992: 9).

[20] Anthropologist Marla Powers (1986: 98) cites Lakota tradition about the healing power of plants being controlled by the *wakinyan*. A comparativist scholar may be tempted to speculate about the medial role of *wakinyan* between the sky (star world) and the earth (plant world), but this may impose an alien hermeneutic upon Lakota discourse.

[21] This notion of a 'religious praxis' related to a 'politics of kinship' is similarly worked out in relation to the Lakota holy man, Black Elk, in a postcolonial interpretation that 'considers the voice of Black Elk as a political voice' and claims that his story 'finds its voice as a telling about kinship' in Stover (2000: 145).

two opposed discourses and their respective political practices. The politics of essentialism divides not only the 'self' from the 'other' but also the political from the religious so that the ceremonial life of traditional Lakota people is hermeneutically separated from contemporary political realities and reified as archaic ritual; thus, the Sun Dance is commonly portrayed by dominant-culture scholarship as a fixed form and demythologized as a cultural marker denoting a pre-modern sensibility.

The hermeneutic dilemma facing a scholar-interpreter of indigenous religion is that the discourse of scholarship in religion has been in covert or unconscious league with the politics of essentialism. A postcolonial hermeneutic does not entail some form of 'going native' whereby the scholar plays the role of an adventuring 'self,' nor should it aim at a romanticized reversal to recast the indigenous 'other' as a spiritual guide for postmodern times. What it does entail is some measure of decolonizing the scholar's identity as an essentialized 'self,' and my experience suggests that such decolonizing is most straightforwardly undertaken by actual and open engagement with a local indigenous community that practices the politics of kinship. Once engaged by the modicum of kinship extended even to a scholar-outsider, one can begin to see that the discourse and politics of essentialism routinely conceal the truth that a relation between power and discourse is always present in human relationships, that this relation is not essentialist and fixed but variable and nuanced, and that, like kinship itself, this relation between power and discourse is susceptible to the reconfiguring dynamic of reciprocity.

The politics of kinship requires a scholar to give up both the subterfuge of being a mere individual and the sham of treating as simply normative what is actually European American discourse. By acknowledging his or her communal identification and the cultural and religious accent of his or her discourse, a scholar will no longer pretend to slip into the field of discourse anonymously as though he or she were an apolitical individual without a 'community' or a 'tradition.'[22] When cultural identity is acknowledged by a scholar, she or he will be in a better position to identify the relations of power embedded in the politics of discourse as well as to enter into relations of reciprocity with an indigenous community. It is this experience of relatedness that fosters decolonizing of knowledge since relatedness rather than knowledge becomes privileged; consequently, knowledge is no longer a matter of power relations between 'self' and 'other' but of kinship relations in which knowledge of each other extends freely in both cultural directions as a process of relational reciprocity. This

---

[22] Emily Has No Horse, who died 12 November 1999, referred to me and those others who respectfully participated in indigenous ceremonies as 'traditional white people.'

191

need not imply erasure of cultural difference; it can evoke appreciation for, and even keen-sighted jokes about, each other's distinctiveness.

What Wakpamni Lake Sun Dancing offers to the European American culture shaped by the praxis of colonization is a politics of kinship being lived out in this particular time and place. The four ways of respect embodied in Sun Dancing at Wakpamni Lake represent a ceremonial intention to renew and to celebrate all kinship relations, and the ritual scope of this intention embraces even the terrible alienation stemming from the dichotomy between colonizer and colonized. In this way, a post-colonial meaning 'interrupts' and 'disrupts'[23] the hegemonic interpretation practiced by the colonial mind so that indigenous identity is no longer seen as the questionable 'other' in need of civilizing redemption and the erst-while colonizer is invited by the ceremonial logic of Wakpamni Lake Sun Dancing to participate in the transforming reciprocities of new kinship relations that are not limited to 'an exclusively human field of meanings' but are connected 'in specific and palpable ways to the expressive earth.'[24] Once this begins to happen, the whole edifice of scholarly discourse that was once taken as normative will necessarily require a postcolonial reconstruction that disarms and displaces the former distinction between 'self' and 'other' and that moves toward establishing what Greg Sarris described as collaborative discourse.

References

Abram, David. 1996. *The Spell of the Sensuous: Perception and Language in a More-Than-Human World*. New York: Vintage Books.

Bertens, Hans. 1995. *The Idea of the Postmodern: A History*. London: Routledge.

Brown, Joseph Epes. 1953. *The Sacred Pipe: Black Elk's Account of the Seven Rites of the Oglala Sioux*. Norman: University of Oklahoma Press.

Brown, Joseph Epes. 1987. *The Spiritual Legacy of the American Indian*. New York: Crossroad.

Childs, Peter, and Patrick Williams. 1997. *An Introduction to Post-Colonial Theory*. New York: Prentice-Hall.

Deloria, Philip J. 1998. *Playing Indian*. New Haven: Yale University Press.

Frey, Ronald. 1987. *The World of the Crow Indians: As Driftwood Lodges*. Norman: University of Oklahoma Press.

Goodman, Ronald. 1992. *Lakota Star Knowledge: Studies in Lakota Stellar Theology*. Rosebud, SD: Sinte Gleska University.

---

[23] See Sarris (1993: 33), regarding indigenous discourse that 'interrupts' and 'disrupts' the impositions of dominant-culture discourse.

[24] See Abram (1996: 139).

Grim, John. 1997. 'Cultural Identity, Authenticity, and Community Survival: The Politics of Recognition in the Study of Native American Religions', *American Indian Quarterly* 20(3-4): 353-76.

Holler, Clyde. 1995. *Black Elk's Religion: The Sun Dance and Lakota Catholicism*. Syracuse: Syracuse University Press.

Irwin, Lee. 1994. *The Dream Seekers: Native American Visionary Traditions of the Great Plains*. Norman: University of Oklahoma Press.

Powers, Marla N. 1986. *Oglala Women: Myth, Ritual, and Reality*. Chicago: University of Chicago Press.

Rice, Julian. 1998. *Before the Great Spirit: The Many Faces of Sioux Spirituality*. Albuquerque: University of New Mexico Press.

Ross, A. C. 1989. *Mitakuye Oyasin*. Fort Yates, ND: BEAR.

Sarris, Greg. 1993. *Keeping Slug Woman Alive: A Holistic Approach to American Indian Texts*. Berkeley: University of California Press.

Smith, Theresa S. 1995. *The Island of the Anishnaabeg: Thunderers and Water Monsters in the Traditional Ojibwe Life-World*. Moscow: University of Idaho Press.

Stover, Dale. 1997. 'Eurocentrism and Native Americans', *Cross Currents* 47(3): 390-7.

Stover, Dale. 2000. 'A Postcolonial Reading of Black Elk', in *The Black Elk Reader*, ed. Clyde Holler. Syracuse, NY: Syracuse University Press, pp. 127-44.

Weaver, Jace. 1998. 'From I-Hermeneutics to We-Hermeneutics: Native Americans and the Post-Colonial', in Jace Weaver (ed.), *Native American Religious Identity: Unforgotten Gods*. New York: Orbis Books, pp. 1-25.

8. Divine connections: The *mansin* and her clients

Laurel Kendall

Editor's introduction

Previous chapters have considered relationships between human and other-than-human persons, experiences of this-worldly, otherworldly and cosmic religious significance, and the performative and political dimensions of religious engagements. Such themes are further elaborated in Laurel Kendall's discussion of Korean 'Shamans, housewives and other restless spirits'. Her focus in this extract from her book is on those who visit the house of the *mansin* (shaman): particularly clients, but also divinities, spirits, a wider audience of less regular or committed visitors and researcher. She pays attention to the nature or geography of the *mansin*'s house, the processes by which women are initiated, and conterminously the processes by which 'the gods descend'. She also elaborates upon the diverse relationships between a *mansin*, other women, and participants in other religions, Buddhism and Christianity in particular (also see Samuel 1993). Initiation, training, and being possessed are discussed with reference to both performance and relationships. For example, gods, *mansin*, and clients can all be demanding upon one another. The strain put on relationships is worked out in rituals and more everyday encounters between people embedded in the given-ness of etiquette systems. This is all the more dramatic given that clients visit the *mansin* (and the *mansin* is visited by gods) as persons engaged in difficult relationships. The particularities of relationship meet the generalities of etiquette in the context of women's homes and daily lives. This is exemplified in the following quotation regarding 'household traditions and women's work':

When clients leave after making offerings in the shrine or sponsoring a *kut* there, they give no farewell salutation. The *mansin* carefully reminds new clients of this necessary breach of etiquette, and tells the women to go straight home. A woman brings blessings from the shrine directly to her own house lest they be lost along the way. The woman leaves the shrine without a farewell and enters her own home without a greeting. Salutations mark boundaries and transitions; they are inappropriate here.

Any woman, old or young, married or single, can visit the *mansin*'s house and receive a divination, but the *tan'gol* who make seasonal offerings in the shrine and sponsor *kut* are female householders, the senior women in their households. Commensurate with their temporal responsibilities, they come to the shrine on behalf of husbands, children, and retired parents-in-law.

Such close attention has rarely been paid by academia to the gendering of shamanry, nor has the integration of shamanry with other lifeways and worldviews often been so clearly appreciated.

The importance of Kendall's work is enhanced by the fact that, despite the richness of the study of Korean shamanism (see Kendall's references, also see Howard 2001 and works cited there), studies of shamanism still regularly assume that it is a phenomenon of rural, small-scale, hunter-gatherer societies. In part this may be rooted in the continuing power of the 'myth of primitive piety', or the lure of the archaic (evident in Eliade's (1964) formulation). Kendall's chapter thus complements other important works such as Vitebsky (1995; 2000) and Taussig (1997).

References

Eliade, M. 1964. *Shamanism: Archaic Techniques of Ecstasy*. New York: Pantheon.

Howard, Keith. 2001. 'Sacred and Profane: Music in Korean Shaman Rituals' in Karen Ralls-MacLeod and Graham Harvey (eds), *Indigenous Religious Musics*. Aldershot: Ashgate, pp. 56-83.

Samuel, Geoffrey. 1993. *Civilized Shamans: Buddhism in Tibetan Society*. London and Washington: Smithsonian Institution Press.

Taussig, Michael. 1997. *Shamanism, Colonialism, and the Wild Man: A Study in Terror and Healing*. Chicago: University of Chicago Press.

Vitebsky, Piers. 1995. *The Shaman*. London: Macmillan.

Vitebsky, Piers. 2000. 'Shamanism', in Graham Harvey (ed.). *Indigenous Religions: A Companion*. London: Cassell.

ᘒᓭ

This order is recruited from among hysterical and silly girls as well as from women who go into it for a livelihood or for baser reasons.

H. N. Allen, *Some Korean Customs*

The magistrate said, 'Alas! I thought *mutangs* were a brood of liars, but now I know that there are true *mutangs* as well as false.' He gave her rich rewards, sent her away in safety, recalled his order against witches, and refrained from any matters pertaining to them for ever after.

Im Bang, from 'The Honest Witch'

The *mansin*'s house is much like any other country residence. She hangs no sign outside. Women seek out the *mansin*'s house by word of mouth or on the recommendation of kinswomen or neighbors. Once inside, a client makes herself comfortable, sitting on the heated floor. She should feel at home in the *mansin*'s inner room, for the place resembles her own. The room where Yongsu's Mother divines could be the main room of any prosperous village home, crammed with the stuff of everyday life. Here are cabinets full of clothes and dishes, a dressing table with a neatly arranged collection of bottled cosmetics, an electric rice warmer, and a television set decorated with an assortment of rubber dolls and pink furry puppies.

The gods and their shrine

Yongsu's Mother's shrine, tucked away behind the sliding doors of the one spare room, resembles a rural temple. Gilt-plaster Buddha statues sit on the front altar. Bright printed portraits of Yongsu's Mother's gods hang on the walls. Incense burners, brass candleholders, aluminum fruit plates, water bowls, and stemmed offering vessels clutter the main and side altars. Each utensil and the three brass bells above the altar all bear the engraved phrase 'Grant the wish of,' followed by the name of the client. These are clients' gifts. The *mansin* advises a client to secure a particular god's good offices with appropriate tribute. One incense burner and water bowl bear my name. Yongsu's Mother told me, with some embarrassment, that the Buddhist Sage and the Mountain God requested gifts since I was doing my research through their will. She told a soldier's wife worried about her husband's fidelity and a young wife worried about her husband's job prospects to dedicate brass bells. She told another young wife to dedicate a water bowl because the Mountain God has helped her husband. Other

196

clients gave the *mansin* her drum and battle trident, her cymbals and knives, her robes and hats, all the equipment she uses to perform *kut*. She stores this equipment out of sight under the altar. Like the shrine fittings, each of these accoutrements bears a client's name. A shrine littered with bells, water vessels, and incense pots advertises a successful *mansin*. In the early morning the *mansin* burns incense, lights candles, and offers cold water inside the shrine. Clients leave incense and candles, and the *mansin* echoes their requests in her own prayers.

A *mansin*'s shrine is called a god hall (*sindang*) or hall of the law (*pŏptang*), a Buddhist term. In casual conversation Yongsu's Mother calls her shrine the grandfathers' room *(harabŏjiŭi pang)*. When I first visited her, I mistook the unmarked plural and thought she was renting a spare room to an older man. 'Grandmother' and 'grandfather' are honorific, but not excessively formal, terms. In Korea all old men and all old women, by virtue of the status white hair confers, are politely addressed as grandfather and grandmother. Gods also carry a faint connotation of kinship. Although both power and position set gods (*sillyŏng*) above ancestors (*chosang*), some gods, like the Chŏns' Great Spirit Grandmother, are also known ancestors. They are grandfathers and grandmothers writ large. Whether venerable distant kin or generalized venerable elders, Yongsu's Mother owes her gods respect and good treatment. Her gods are not distant, awesome beings; with a common term of address, she brings them close. She dreads their anger and anticipates their will, but she also expects them to help her, as a Korean child looks to a grandparent for small indulgences.

Standing before the gods in her shrine, Yongsu's Mother assumes the self-consciously comic pose of a young child, head slightly bowed, eyes wide with pleading. Speaking in a high, soft voice, she says, 'Grandfather, please give me some money. I'm going to the market.' She takes a bill from the altar and stuffs it into her coin purse. 'I'll be right back,' and she brings her hands together and nods her head in a quick bow.

Yongsu's Mother originally kept her gods in a narrow storage alcove off the porch and rented her spare room. She began to suspect that the gods disliked the alcove when she, her son, and her roomers' child were all sick at the same time in the middle of winter. One night her dead husband appeared in a dream. He boldly marched into the spare room while its occupants were in Seoul. Yongsu's Mother yelled at him, 'You can't go in there when people are away. They'll think you're going to take something.' Her husband answered, 'This is my room. I'll give you the rent money.' Yongsu's Mother continued to quarrel with her husband until she woke up.

The very next day, her roomers announced that they were moving to

Seoul. Someone else wanted to rent the room immediately, but Yongsu's Mother said that she would have to think about it. That night she dreamed that all of the grandmothers and grandfathers in her shrine left the alcove and followed Yongsu's Father into the spare room, calling as they passed, 'We'll give you the rent money, we'll give you the rent money.'

She told her dream to the Chatterbox Mansin who agreed that Yongsu's Mother must make the spare room into a shrine. Thereafter, she prospered as a *mansin*. Her grandmothers and grandfathers gave her the rent money.

This incident is typical of Yongsu's Mother's ongoing tug-of-war with her grandmothers and grandfathers. Her gods do well by her, but they are even more demanding than her clients' gods. She intended to give a *kut* every three years for their pleasure, but after a prosperous early spring, they made her ill to let her know that they wanted an annual *kut*. The next year, in the fall, she gave the grandmothers and grandfathers special feast food (*yŏt'am*) before her stepdaughter's wedding. The gods were angry because she hit the hourglass drum and roused them but did not give them a *kut*. Her luck was bad for several months. She purchased fabric to make new robes for the General and the Warrior, and gave another *kut* the following spring.

Like many children from Enduring Pine Village, her son Yongsu goes to the private Christian middle school in Righteous Town. The fees at the school are minimal and admissions relatively open, but pressure to convert is high. The gods in the shrine do not like Yongsu's daily brush with Christianity. They make his thoughts wander in school. He says he feels an urge to rush home. Yongsu's Mother told the principal that Yongsu's family had 'honored Buddha from long ago,' and asked him to understand that Yongsu cannot become a Christian. Then she went to her shrine, hit the cymbals, and implored her grandmothers and grandfathers: 'Please understand, please forgive. Yongsu has to get an education. Let him go to that place until he's gotten his education.'

The descent of the gods

A *mansin* engages in a battle of wills with the gods from the very beginning of her career. A woman is expected to resist her calling and struggle against the inevitable, but village women say that those who resist the will of the gods to the very end die raving lunatics. Strange, wild behavior marks a destined *mansin*. Yongsu's Mother describes the struggle:

> They don't know what they're doing. They yell, 'Let's go, let's go!' and go running out somewhere. They snatch food from the kitchen and run out into the

road with it. God-descended people swipe things and run away. They strike at people and shout insults.

    If I were a god-descended person and my husband were hitting me and calling me crazy woman, I'd shout back at him, 'You bastard! Don't you know who I am, you bastard?' That's what the Clear Spring Mansin did. Then she sat beside the road talking to the chickens. So funny!

The destined *mansin,* or god-descended person (*naerin saram*), can experience a variety of symptoms. According to Yongsu's Mother,

> It's very difficult for them. They're sick and they stay sick, even though they take medicine. And there are people who get better even without taking medicine. There are some who can't eat the least bit of food; they just go hungry. There are some who sleep with their eyes open, and some who can't sleep at all. They're very weak but they get well as soon as the gods descend in the initiation *kut.* For some people the gods descend gently, but for others the gods don't descend gently at all. So they run around like crazy women.

Although the destined *mansin* acts like a 'crazy woman,' Yongsu's Mother makes a distinction between the god-descended person (*naerin saram*) and someone struck temporarily insane (*mich'ida*) by angry household gods or ancestors. 'You just have to see them to tell the difference. Insane people look like they're in pain somewhere. The god-descended person wanders here and there singing out, "I'm this god, I'm that god."' The *mansin* exorcise insane people as swiftly as possible in a healing *kut* for fear that the possessing spirits will torment their victims to death. The *mansin* flourish knives and flaming torches, threatening, cajoling, and pleading with the offending spirits, urging them to depart (Kendall 1977). In the initiation *kut* for a god-descended person *(naerim kut),* the initiating *mansin* invites the gods to complete their descent and allow their chosen one to dance and sing as a *mansin.*

    A woman often endures considerable anguish before her initiation. The Chatterbox Mansin's story is typical. She was a young matron when the gods descended, a first son's wife living with her mother-in-law. She had already produced two healthy sons. Her husband was away in the air force when she began to exhibit bizarre behavior. She would wander about, talking in a distracted fashion. Worried, her mother-in-law sent for Chatterbox's sister, but when the sister arrived, Chatterbox was sitting in the main room, calmly sewing. She said that every night an old woman – a grandmother – came and asked her to go wandering about with her.

    Her sister thought that if Chatterbox was normal enough in the daytime and only behaved strangely at night, she would be all right soon enough. But a few days later, Chatterbox came back to her natal home, clapping her hands together and shrieking like a lunatic. She looked like a beggar woman in torn clothes. Her hair was a tangled mass down her back and her face was filthy. When her mother-in-law came to take her back home, she just sat on the porch and screamed. They tried to pull her up, but her legs stuck fast to the wooden boards of the porch. She asked for some water and poured it all over her body. That night she wandered away. She went into a house and stole a Buddha statue. When her family asked her why she did this, she said, 'I was told to do it.' For two weeks she went about clapping her hands and pilfering small objects. Then she disappeared completely.

Her family thought she was dead. Much later they heard that she had become the apprentice spirit daughter of the Boil-face Mansin, a great shaman (k'ŭn mudang) in the next county. The Boil-face Mansin had taken her in, initiated her, and was training her to perform kut. Over the years she learned chants, dances, and ritual lore.

During Chatterbox's distracted wanderings her mother-in-law began divorce proceedings. The woman never lived with her husband again and was forbidden to see her children. But when sorrow overwhelmed her, she would go to the school and, from a safe distance, watch her sons playing in the school yard. A quarrel with his stepmother prompted the oldest son to search out Chatterbox in the countryside. After the boy's flight her sons visited her every summer.

Chatterbox prospered as a mansin and built up her own clientele. She broke with her spirit mother after a bitter fight, claiming the shaman overworked and underpaid her. Today, some twenty years after the gods' initial descent, no trace of the haunted young matron remains. Well dressed in Western-style clothing, Chatterbox walks through the streets of the county seat where she has just purchased a new house. Today people in the area consider her a 'great shaman' and her own spirit daughter accuses her of stinginess.

By her own admission, Yongsu's Mother had an easy experience as a god-descended person. Widowed after only two years of marriage, she was left with two stepchildren and her own small son. She worked as a peddler, one of a limited number of occupations open to a woman who must support a family. At the end of the mourning period, she went to a kut at Chatterbox's shrine.

During an interlude in the kut, women danced the mugam in the Chatterbox Mansin's costumes to amuse their personal guardian gods and bring luck to their families. The Chatterbox Mansin told Yongsu's Mother to use the mugam and dance for success in her precarious business ventures. As Yongsu's Mother remembers it,

I said, 'What do you mean "use the *mugam?*"' It's shameful for me to dance like that.' But the Chatterbox Mansin kept saying, 'It'll give you luck. You'll be lucky if you dance.' So I put on the clothes and right away began to dance wildly. I ran into the shrine, still dancing, and grabbed the Spirit Warrior's flags. I started shouting, 'I'm the Spirit Warrior of the Five Directions,' and demanded money. All of the women gave me money. I ran all the way home. My heart was thumping wildly. I just wanted to die like a crazy woman. We talked about it this way and that way and decided there was no way out. So the next year I was initiated as a *mansin*.

Although Yongsu's Mother's possession was sudden and unique in its relative painlessness, there had been suggestions throughout her life that she would become a *mansin*.[1] In her early teens during the Korean War, she was fingered as a member of a right-wing youth organization and arrested by North Korean soldiers just before their retreat. Taken on the march north, she made a bold escape on the same night that the Mountain God appeared to her in a dream and said, 'It's already getting late.'

In late adolescence she had frightening hallucinations. The little Buddha statue a friend brought her from Japan burst into flames in the middle of the room. She watched her mother's face turn into a tiger's face. She wandered about at night, drawn to the stone Buddha near a neighborhood temple. Her mother held a healing *kut*. During the *kut* the girl fell asleep. A white-haired couple appeared and gave her a bowl of medicinal water to drink. When she woke up, she told her dream to the *mansin*, who was pleased. The *mansin* asked her to become her spirit daughter and be initiated as a *mansin*, but she and her mother refused.

Years later, on her wedding night, her sister-in-law dreamed that the new bride was sitting in the inner room hitting a drum. Overhead, on a rope line, hung all of the gods' clothes, as if a *kut* were in progress. Later, when her husband was fatally ill, Yongsu's Mother went to a *mansin*'s shrine for an exorcism. She set out her offerings and the *mansin* began to chant, but when Yongsu's Mother went to raise her arms over her head and bow to the ground, her arms stuck to her sides as if someone were holding them down. She could not budge them. It was destined that her husband would die and she would become a *mansin*. There was nothing she could do about it.

Yongsu's Mother was a young widow awash in economic difficulties when the gods descended. The Chatterbox Mansin was separated from her husband but living with her mother-in-law, the woman who would later insist on divorce. I am reluctant to speculate on the two initiates' sub-

---

[1] Pyŏngyang-mansin, one of Harvey's informants, reports a similar experience (Harvey 1979: 109).

conscious motivations, but Harvey (1979; 1980) suggests that severe role stress propels women like the Chatterbox Mansin and Yongsu's Mother into god-descended behavior. It is true that, as *mansin,* such women stand above the social and economic constraints imposed on a proper Korean wife, and as *mansin,* they wear the gods' costumes and speak with the gods' authority. But whatever personal and economic gratification she enjoys, the *mansin* and her family pay a price. Shamans were listed, under the occupational classification system of the Yi dynasty, among the despised 'mean people' (*ch'ŏnmin*) along with butchers, fortune-tellers, roving players, monks, and female entertainers. According to one early missionary, 'Sometimes the daughter of a genteel family may become a Mootang, though this is rare, as her people would rather kill her than have her madness take this form' (Allen 1896: 164).

Like the female entertainer, the *kisaeng,* the shaman engages in public display, singing and dancing. An element of ambiguous sexuality wafts about the *mansin*'s performance. In folklore and literature *mudang* are portrayed as 'lewd women,' and so they are often perceived (Wilson 1983). The *mansin* Cho Yŏng-ja told Ch'oe and Chang that the county chief had come to her home on the pretext of having his fortune told and had then insisted on sleeping with her. Disgusted, she contrived an escape. Thereafter all was coldness between the *mansin* and the county chief (Ch'oe and Chang 1967: 32-3).

The *mansin* play to their female audience, but when the supernatural Official sells 'lucky wine,' the costumed *mansin* roams through the house seeking male customers. The men have been drinking by themselves in a corner of the house, as far removed from the *kut* as possible. Now they emerge, red faced, and the bolder of their company dance a few steps on the porch. Men buy the Official's wine and tease the *mansin,* flourishing their bills in front of her face before securing the money in her chestband. An audacious man may try to tweak the *mansin*'s breast as he secures his bill.

The *mansin* is caught at cross purposes. By her coy, flirtatious performance, she encourages the men to spend more money on wine. But as a woman alone, she must defend herself from harassment and protect her reputation. Yongsu's Mother was resourceful.

It doesn't happen so much anymore, but when I first started going to *kut,* men would bother me. We were doing a *kut* at a house way out in the country, and I was going around selling the Official's wine. Some son-of-a-bitch grabbed my breast. I put out my hand so the drummer would go faster, then brought my arms up quick to start dancing. I knocked that guy against the wall. Afterwards, he asked me, 'What did you mean by that?' I said, 'Oh, that wasn't me, it was the honorable Official who did that.' Other times, I'd be drumming and some guy would say, 'Auntie, where is Uncle? What is Uncle doing now?' and go on like that. I'd reach out to beat the drum faster and slap the guy with the drumstick.

At the *kut* for the dead, performed outside the house gate, men gather off to the side. They gaze at the *mansin* garbed like a princess who sings the long ballad tale of Princess Pari, rapping the drum with elegant flicks of her wrist. My landlady told me of a famous *mansin*, now aged, who was once a beauty. 'When she did the *kut* for the dead, it would take forever. This one would carry her off on his back, and that one would embrace her.'

To the exemplar of Confucian virtue, the *mansin* offends simply because she dances in public. When an officer from the district police station tried to stop a *kut* in Enduring Pine Village, he threatened to arrest the *mansin* because 'they were dancing to drum music and students were watching.' The moral education of the young was thereby imperiled. An envelope of 'cigarette money' finally silenced this paragon.

It would be a distortion to paint the *mansin* I knew in northern Kyŏnggi Province as social pariahs. Since she has no husband, Yongsu's Mother's house is a favorite gathering place for village women. In their leisure moments they drop by to chat about the latest school fee, the inept village watch system, the new neighborhood loan association, or simply to gossip. Even the wife of the progressive village chief, though she disdains 'superstition', seeks out the company of the articulate, loquacious *mansin*. Yongsu's Mother is a favorite guest at birthday parties. She gets the singing started and makes people laugh. She can sometimes be persuaded to bring her drum so the women can dance.

But Yongsu's Mother lives under the shadow of potential insult. Village people say, 'Not so many years ago, even a child could use blunt speech [*panmal*] to a shaman.'[2] Although this is no longer true, when tempers flare Yongsu's Mother's occupation is still flung in her face. Yongsu's Mother and the widowed Mr. Yun were great friends. Village gossips expected them to marry. Mr. Yun's daughter-in-law rankled at the possibility. She finally exploded in a fit of rage, shrieking at Yongsu's Mother, 'Don't come into my house! I don't want a shaman to come into my house! It's bad luck if a shaman comes into your house.' Pride wounded to the quick, Yongsu's Mother avoided the Yun family and there was no more talk of marriage.

---

[2] Like the Japanese language, spoken Korean sentence endings are shorter or longer depending on the relative status of the speaker and the addressee. Adults use blunt endings, *panmal*, when addressing children, and children use them when addressing dogs.

After her stepdaughter's marriage Yongsu's Mother was anxious lest the groom discover her occupation. She did only one hasty New Year Rite for a client on the second day of the New Year since she expected a visit from the newlyweds on that day. She dreaded the thought of them walking in and catching her banging her cymbals in the shrine.

The Chatterbox Mansin's sister-in-law found her own children dancing in time to the drum rhythm during a *kut*. She slapped them soundly, then howled at her miserable fortune to have married into a shaman's house. Since this was all in the family, and the Chatterbox Mansin is never at a loss for words, whatever the circumstance, she snapped back, 'Well then, you knew this was a shaman's house. You didn't have to marry my brother and come to live here.'

The *mansin* shares in the ambiguous status of other glamorous but morally dubious female marginals, the actress, the female entertainer, and the prostitute. Like the others, she makes a living, often a comfortable living, by public performance in a society where so-called good women stay home. But the *mansin* is neither an actress nor a courtesan. She is the ritual specialist of housewives. The good women who stay home need her. She came from their midst, lives like them, and speaks to their anxieties and hopes.

The gods who have claimed a woman as a *mansin* leave her one lingering shred of respectability. It is well known that only by virtue of divine calling is she a shaman, and that is a compulsion fatal to resist.[3] Her neighbors assume that she did not want to become a *mansin*. She tells her story to clients, describes how she resisted the call with the last ounce of her strength and succumbed only after considerable suffering and in fear for her very life.

Like most respectable matrons, Yongsu's Mother had to be coaxed even to dance the *mugam* at a *kut*. She thought abandoned public dancing was shameful. Yet once she put on the *mansin*'s costume, instead of simply dancing to exhaustion like the other women, her gods descended. There was nothing to be done. After years of avoiding the warnings, Yongsu's Mother had to become a *mansin*.

The shaman also suffers the onus of charlatanry and greed. The *mansin* makes her living by interpreting the gods' will and manifesting their presence. Divine ultimatums fill her pockets with cash. Much of a *kut*'s comedy revolves around the tug-of-war between greedy, extortionate gods who demand more and more money and the housewife who stubbornly

---

[3] There are hereditary *mudang* families in the southernmost provinces. Whether by birth or divine will, the point is the same: the female religious practitioner does not voluntarily assume her role.

resists, argues, and then grudgingly capitulates. The gods peer into pockets and lift skirts, looking for cash. The women shout that they have spent everything. Then, giggling, they run and hide inside the house, only to reemerge, pockets bulging with more bills for another round with the greedy gods.

This is play and the rules are understood. In northern Kyŏnggi Province the *mansin* and her client settle the price of the *kut* far in advance, and the client brings the money in a bundle to the *mansin*'s shrine a few days before the *kut*. On the day of the *kut* the *mansin* retains a basic fee in a cloth bag tied to the drum. She returns the rest of the money to the housewife, who doles it out throughout the *kut*, paying off the eternally demanding gods and ancestors. When the housewife does not enter into the combative spirit of the event, the *mansin* say the *kut* 'tastes flat.' Yongsu's Mother told me with disgust, 'We did a *kut* in Tranquil Spring the other day, and the lady of the house didn't even know as much as you, Tallae. We'd ask her for money and she'd just hand the bill over with a blank expression on her face.'

Still, the *mansin*'s ceremonies cost money. A *kut* takes a significant lump of the family's budget, equivalent to a child's hundred-day party or a first-year birthday, occasions when the family provides an elaborate breakfast and wine for a vast array of neighbors and kin. By divine authority the *mansin* urges the family to spend money on exorcisms, shrine prayers, and *kut*. She advises them to dedicate robes, brass bells, knives, and musical instruments for demanding gods. There's the rub. The possibility of divine possession coexists with the potential for fakery, especially when the gods' demands enhance the shaman's income and prestige. The *mansin* must make a living, but she knows that she cannot push her clients too far. Her gods are demanding, but the *mansin* fears for her own image. Yongsu's Mother tries to disassociate herself from the greedy gods she serves. She gives back a portion of the fruits and candies her clients bring to the shrine. She stuffs money for a treat of wine into the pocket of a household patriarch to stifle potential grumbles over the cost of a *kut*. She complains,

Sometimes I hate all my grandfathers. They should cherish the unfortunate but instead they scorn them. When someone is poor, I tell them to come to the shrine for a ritual and bring only a small offering. I tell them it's all right. Then I go to the grandfathers' room. When the grandfathers speak they say, 'What's this? This person has set down so little,' and yell at them. It goes against my own feelings to talk like that, but I can't do anything about it. It's the grandfathers who make me say those things.

The false and greedy *mudang* is a common butt of satire in both folk literature and in contemporary Korean television dramas. Gale's translation of the seventeenth-century literati tale 'The Honest Witch' provides a unique twist. A reforming magistrate issues a ban, on pain of death, against the activities of all false *mudang* under his jurisdiction. One plucky *mudang* challenges him, claiming that his decree only applies to 'false *mudang*.' She demonstrates the veracity of her profession by summoning the magistrate's deceased friend who, speaking through the *mudang*, recalls intimate details of their past friendship. The magistrate, convinced, rewards the *mudang* and withdraws his decree (Gale [1913] 1963: 125-9). This magistrate is akin to some cosmopolitan Koreans who have confessed to me that although they had never before believed, they were confounded by a dead kinsman's appearance in a *kut*.

If the women of Enduring Pine Village accept that there are real shamans, they also assume that charlatans and sloppy performers gather where there is money to be made. The *mansin* level accusations among themselves and the village women make their own evaluations. The dramatic descent of the gods and the god-descended woman's tortuous resistance enhance the individual *mansin*'s legitimacy. Although shamanism is one of few potentially lucrative women's occupations, the woman who willingly or easily becomes a shaman would be suspect. Her extreme reluctance and suffering testify to those who will judge her that her calling is sincere and her gods are strong.

Initiation and training

When the *mansin* do an initiation *kut* (*naerim kut*), they dress the initiate in costumes for all of the gods of *kut*, segment by segment. A *mansin* stands beside the initiate and implores the gods to descend. The drum throbs. The initiate dances wildly, shouting out the gods' presence as they possess her. 'I'm the Mountain God Buddhist Sage, the Monk Buddhist Sage, I'm Buddhist Sage Maitreya,' or in the Spirit Warrior's garb, 'I'm the Spirit Warrior Who Rides the White Horse, the Spirit Warrior Archer, the Honorable Buddha Spirit Warrior ... ' *Mansin* scrawl long lists of deities as the initiate chants them. They hang the strips of paper on the walls to show the new *mansin* the myriad deities in her pantheon, the gods she can summon to *kut*.

The one initiation *kut* I observed was, in the *mansin*'s view, a fizzle. The gods never completed their descent into the initiate, they just 'came and went.' The *mansin* dressed the god-descended woman in the Buddhist Sage's costume and prayed. The initiate started to dance, grabbed the Spirit

Warrior's colored flags, and stood on the water jar. From the water jar she told Yongsu's Mother that she had a message for her; the gods said that Yongsu's Mother was heavy-hearted because she had gone up a sacred mountain with her querulous sister. After this half-hearted effort at divining, the god-descended woman gave up, removed the costume, and the *mansin* continued the *kut* themselves.

This was the Clear Spring Mansin's second attempt at initiating this same god-descended woman. A *kut* the year before had also failed. Yongsu's Mother thought the effort and expense were premature. The gods were not ready to descend. Yongsu's Mother contrasted this woman's failure to the performance of a properly god-descended initiate.

> She should have been dancing like crazy. Descended people wave their arms and dance whenever they hear the hourglass drum. They shout out, 'I'm this god, I'm that god.' She should have said things like, 'You're filthy with menstruation, why have you come here? Ugh, dirty person from a house of mourning!' but she didn't say anything like that. She might have said, 'Here's a woman who fights with her husband,' but she didn't. And she carried the Spirit Warrior's flags when she was the Buddhist Sage. She shouldn't do that. The Spirit Warrior Buddhist Sage comes later. She told me I went to the mountain with my sister. What's the big deal about that? She could have heard about that from the Clear Spring Mansin. It wasn't the Buddhist Sage descending. Some ancestral grand-mother [*chosang halmŏni*] in the house just rose up, that was all.

The ancestral grandmother rose up as a Body-governing God, a minor deity who might possess anyone. The initiate's behavior resembled an ordinary woman dancing *mugam* at *kut*, not a professional *mansin*.

After a successful initiation *kut* the *mansin* can invoke at will the visions the gods send her. She can now divine with coins and grains of rice. Three days after Yongsu's Mother's initiation *kut*, a woman came to her for a divination. Yongsu's Mother was so ill-prepared for her new role that she had to run to a kinswoman's house and borrow a tray for the divination rice and coins. Thereafter, clients kept appearing at her door. While her peddling business dribbled away to nothing, Yongsu's Mother began to derive a satisfactory income from divinations.

When women hear of a new *mansin*, they come to her shrine out of curiosity. Some, struck by the clarity of her diagnosis and the success of her ritual advice, remain her regular clients. Others, their curiosity satisfied, stay with their own regular *mansin* or continue to shop around. Yongsu's Mother described the hectic first New Year season after she became a *mansin*. 'The house was jammed with people. Everyone wanted to have their fortune told. I didn't eat. I couldn't even go outside to piss. I got weak, and that spring I was sick for a long time.'

The initiated *mansin* still has much to learn. She must master the long invocations, songs, and procedures of *kut*. The *mansin* who initiated her, her spirit mother (*sinŏmŏni*), brings her to *kut* where she hits the cymbals, sets up food offerings, and receives a few thousand won for her trouble. The new *mansin* invites more experienced *mansin* when her own clients hold a *kut,* but here she claims several measures of rice grain and more than a token share of the take.

A *mansin* begins manifesting the gods at *kut* by performing the Birth Grandmother and the Buddhist Sage. Okkyŏng's Mother, three years after her initiation, still has trouble with these relatively simple segments. She forgets to pick up a fan, misses whole portions of an invocation, or uses incomprehensible words from the dialect of her native Kyŏngsang Province.

After mastering the Buddhist-inspired spirits, a *mansin* manifests the Official and House Site Official, and gradually gains confidence, eventually summoning all of the gods of all the segments of *kut*. I have seen only the oldest and most experienced *mansin* – the Chatterbox Mansin, the Clear Spring Mansin, and the Bell Mansin – perform the long drum song to expel pollutions and invite the gods into the house. At the time I left the field, Yongsu's Mother was trying to learn the Death Messenger's 'Song of Lament' (Hoesimgok) from a paperbound book of shaman songs. If she could invoke and be possessed by the Death Messenger, she would be much in demand when *mansin* organize *kut* to send off dead souls.

A *mansin* develops her performing arts with practice, and she does homework. Her spirit mother instructs her and has her watch several *kut* before pressing her to do more than hit the cymbals. Yongsu's Mother likened this learning process to my own slowly expanding knowledge of *kut*. But the *mansin* consider their skilled performance a blend of talent, effort, and divine will. Yongsu's Mother told me, 'When I started going to *kut,* I thought "How can I do all that? Won't I be embarrassed to stand up in front of everyone?" But the grandfathers told me, "This is the right way, do this next."'

Ultimately a *mansin* masters a particular skill only through the will of her grandfathers. Yongsu's Mother sat at home practicing the *kut* drum rhythm over and over, and often threw down her drumstick in frustration. One night she heard the right rhythm in a dream. She was a strong drummer from then on. A *mansin* must not claim divine assistance prematurely. Okkyŏng's Mother installed an image of the Buddhist Sage in her shrine before she received any indication in her dreams that she should do so. Her luck was bad. Clients did not come to her home for divinations.

She quarreled with her parents-in-law, who went back to the country. Her husband had to look for a new job. On Yongsu's Mother's advice, Okkyŏng's Mother removed the image from her shrine and kept only a paper marker bearing the god's name.

Some *mansin* acquire additional gods and talents later in their careers. When Yongsu's Mother first became a *mansin,* the Clear Spring Mansin had been shamanizing for over ten years, but she was still poor and lived in a rented shack. Once when the Clear Spring Mansin was ill, she asked Yongsu's Mother to perform an exorcism. During the exorcism, Yongsu's Mother saw the Clear Spring Mansin's dead father as the Twelfth Spirit Warrior in her pantheon. In life the father had been a doctor of Chinese medicine, skilled in herbalogy and acupuncture. As the Twelfth Spirit Warrior, he is the special patron of acupuncture in his daughter's pantheon. After learning of her own father's divine influence, the Clear Spring Mansin kept a special image of the Twelfth Spirit Warrior in her shrine. Yongsu's Mother attributes the Clear Spring Mansin's current prosperity to the powerful Spirit Warrior. Through her physician father's divine influence, the Clear Spring Mansin can read pulses, although she has had no special training.

Because she originally divined his presence, the Twelfth Spirit Warrior 'plays well' when he possesses Yongsu's Mother in *kut* at the Clear Spring Mansin's shrine. She claims that he is fond of her, but he also makes demands. At the Clear Spring Mansin's *kut,* Yongsu's Mother drank some expensive wine and almost immediately felt severe stomach pains. Although she felt terrible, the other *mansin* insisted that she perform the sequence for the House Site Official. When she stood up to manifest the House Site Official, the Twelfth Spirit Warrior appeared out of sequence instead. He scolded her for not offering him wine before drinking some herself. Yongsu's Mother's pain was punishment but also an acknowledgement of a relationship, a public reminder of the Clear Spring Mansin's debt to her younger colleague. Yongsu's Mother's stomach pains stopped immediately after she purchased wine for the Spirit Warrior and asked his forgiveness.

Mansin teams at *kut*

As a *mansin* gains experience, her reputation for performing *kut* grows, and other *mansin* include her in their teams when they do *kut*. I have seen a minimum of three *mansin* perform cheap, quick *kut* in crowded rented rooms. Six *mansin* performed a *kut* to dispatch a dead bachelor's restless soul and cure his cousin's debilitating headaches. The family spared no expense, the house was full of guests, and the final send-off of dead souls lasted until the late afternoon of the second day.

A *mansin* makes from ten to fifteen thousand won per *kut*. The number of invitations she receives from other *mansin* depends on her known skill and her ability to work well with other *mansin*. Because the Officials and the Spirit Warrior 'play well' with Yongsu's Mother, other *mansin* invite her to perform these exhausting but highly entertaining and lucrative segments at *kut*. The Death Messenger plays well with the Mansin from Within the Wall, so well that her performance scared me. Yongsu's Mother invites the Mansin from Within the Wall when she does a *kut* to send off dead souls.

Kut teams form and reform following subtle rules of reciprocity. One *mansin* invites another, but if the favor is not returned, she invites someone else. If a *mansin* feels that she has not received fair recompence for her efforts at a *kut* organized by another *mansin,* she does not invite her to perform in her own *kut* and is reluctant to participate in future *kut*.

According to Yongsu's Mother, the Chatterbox Mansin is excessively greedy. When she performs the drum song at the start of a *kut,* she always claims the two thousand-won bills the housewife fastens to the drum strings at the start of the song. The money does not go into the common bag tied to the drum. When she does the final send-off, the Chatterbox Mansin also takes that money for herself. She is tight-fisted when she divides the common take among the *mansin* she has invited to a *kut*. Yongsu's Mother says that other *mansin* used to invite the Chatterbox Mansin far and wide to do *kut,* but they avoid her now. But the Chatterbox Mansin is successful in her own career and does not have to depend on the good graces of other *mansin*. She has collected numerous regular clients in her twenty years' practice and claims the grudging loyalty of Okkyŏng's Mother and Yongsu's Mother, the two *mansin* she initiated. Between *kut* for her own clients and *kut* for the other two *mansin*'s clients, she is sufficiently busy and prosperous. During the time I knew her, she moved from Willow Market to a new house she had purchased in Righteous Town.

Yongsu's Mother performed in thirty-five *kut* in the lunar year that began in February 1977. She organized eight of these *kut* herself for her own clients and invited other *mansin* to join her. In the spring she entertained her own shrine gods with a *kut* and asked three other *mansin* to help. She went to eleven of Okkyŏng's Mother's *kut*. The inexperienced *mansin* was enjoying a rush of business in a working-class neighborhood in Tranquil Spring, a new town on Seoul's periphery. The *mansin*'s sister lived in this neighborhood and sent for Okkyŏng's Mother when neighbors, mostly recent migrants, needed divinations.[4] Okkyŏng's Mother, Yongsu's Mother, and the Chatterbox Mansin did many *kut* in the tiny rooms of Tranquil Spring houses.

The Chatterbox Mansin and the Clear Spring Mansin each included Yongsu's Mother in five of their *kut*, and she went to six others organized by a variety of *mansin*. When Yongsu's Mother organizes her own *kut*, she invites the Chatterbox Mansin, the Clear Spring Mansin, and Okkyŏng's Mother. When she does a *kut* to send off dead souls, she invites the Mansin from Within the Wall. Early in the year she was disgusted with Okkyŏng's Mother's novice performance and excluded her from a few *kut*. Okkyŏng's Mother improved and the two women were drawn together by their mutual dissatisfaction with the Chatterbox Mansin. They also shared a lively sense of humor. Giggling like school girls, they would tease each other, 'Tallae, when you go back to America, find a nice widower with a big nose for Yongsu's Mother.' They asked each other for divinations when they were heavy-hearted, since a *mansin* cannot divine for herself.

In the same year Yongsu's Mother also drew closer to the older Clear Spring Mansin. The Clear Spring Mansin advised her to break with the Chatterbox Mansin and divined that Yongsu's Mother's gods would be happier if she did. Yongsu's Mother performed an exorcism for the Clear Spring Mansin's son when his injured leg would not heal. The Clear Spring Mansin read Yongsu's Mother's pulse when she was ill and recommended an herb doctor. In the same year the Clear Spring Mansin broke with her own spirit daughter in a bitter quarrel that arose when Yongsu's Mother caught the spirit daughter secreting away some of the money she had collected during a *kut*.

The *mansin* teams at *kut* are open and flexible. They form and reform from *kut* to *kut*, and a *mansin* works with a variety of other *mansin* during a year. Yet a *mansin* tends to favor certain of her colleagues out of long-time loyalty or to maintain reciprocity. *Mansin* who work often and well together develop close ties. They divine for each other and summon up each other's gods. But these are also potentially volatile professional relationships, formed around an arbitrary division of cash for services rendered. There is ample ground for jealousy and backbiting.

---

[4] Okkyŏng's Mother moved to Tranquil Spring after I left the field. One of her most enthusiastic clients had found her husband a job there. Many of the residents of Korea's fast-expanding towns are but a few years removed from the countryside. Networks of kinship and friendship still reach into the villages. Tranquil Spring shopkeepers and blue-collar wives called the village ritual specialist to deal with crises. She then settled in their midst.

Women who come to the *mansin*'s house

A shaman's divination (*mugŏri*) is the first step in any ritual therapy. Women like Grandmother Ch'an come to the *mansin*'s house when they suspect that malevolent forces lurk behind a sudden or persistent illness or domestic strife. In Yongsu's Mother's shrine I heard reports of inflamed lungs, an infected leg, fits of possession 'craziness', alcoholism, and dreamy, wandering states of mind. One woman, afflicted with this last complaint, feared that she was god-descended, but Yongsu's Mother laughed off her worries and divined more commonplace godly displeasure as the source of her problems. Other women who came to the shrine worried about their husbands' or sons' career prospects, or about sudden financial reverses. Should the husband switch jobs? Would the son receive his security clearance to work in Saudi Arabia? Thieves had broken into the family rice shop, what did that presage? Other women were anxious that adulterous husbands might abandon them. Some had only the vaguest suspicion that their spouses had 'smoked the wind', but one young woman was certain that her husband took the grain his mother sent up from the country and shared it with his mistress. One woman, caught in a compromising position by her enraged spouse, had fled to the *mansin* in fear of life and limb. And still other women asked about wayward children, stepchildren, or grandchildren whose transgressions ranged from mild rebelliousness to Christian zealotry, petty theft, and delinquency. A mother-in-law asked how she should deal with a runaway daughter-in-law. A daughter-in-law who had fled home asked if she should divorce her husband. An older woman wondered if she should join a married son's household.

The *mansin* chats with the women before fetching the divination tray. Sometimes the women begin to discuss their anxieties before the actual divination, but these are usually long-standing clients. Clients who come to the *mansin* for the first time tend to hold back and see how much the *mansin* can uncover in the divination.

The *mansin* brings in the divination tray, an ordinary low tray of the sort used for meals in any Korean home. The tray bears a mound of rice grains, a handful of brass coins (imitations of old Chinese money), and the brass bell rattle a *mansin* uses to summon up her visions.

'Well now, let's see,' says the *mansin*, settling down to a kneeling posture behind her tray. The client places a bill under the pile of grain on the tray. At Yongsu's Mother's shrine in 1977 and 1978, this fee was usually five-hundred or a thousand won. Now the *mansin* shakes the brass bells beside her own ear and chants, asking the gods to send 'the correct message.' She receives a message for each member of the client's family, beginning with the client's husband if he is alive. She announces each subject's name and age to the gods, tosses her coins on the tray, and spills handfuls of rice grains until the Great Spirit Grandmother speaks and sends visions.

Coin and rice configurations hint at the client's concerns. A broad spread of coins bespeaks quarrels between husband and wife or parent and child, or betrays financial loss. A long line of coins broken by one or two solitary coins at the end tells of someone leaving home, a change of employment, a death, or the inauspicious influence of an ancestor who died far from home. A few grains spilled on the floor caution financial prudence; the client should postpone switching jobs or buying a house.

The *mansin* describes a situation and asks for confirmation. 'Your husband has a cold or something, is that it?' 'Your thirteen-year-old daughter doesn't get along with her father, is that right?' The *mansin* develops the theme, weaving her visions together with her client's information. With more tosses of coins and grain, the Great Spirit Grandmother sends more specific visions. 'I see a steep embankment. Is there something like that near your house?' The woman and her neighbor nod affirmation. 'Be careful of that place.' To another woman, 'Your daughter has two suitors. One is quite handsome. The other is extremely clever but also very meticulous. Since your daughter isn't especially clever herself, she'll have a better life if she marries the second suitor, but she must watch her step and scrupulously manage her house.'

Sometimes she sights the discontented gods and ancestors of her clients' households. 'Is there a distant grandfather in your family who carried a sword and served inside the palace?' 'Did someone in your family die far from home and dripping blood?' She circles in on the supernatural source of her client's problems and suggests an appropriate ritual to mollify a greedy god's demands or send a miserable and consequently dangerous soul 'away to a good place.'

For a housewife to evaluate the skill of an individual *mansin* and trust her diagnosis, she must know the supernatural history of her husband's family and of her own kin. And if the *mansin* is convinced that there was 'a grandmother who worshiped Buddha,' or 'a bride who died in childbirth,' she tells her client, 'Go home and ask the old people, they know about these things.'

A foreigner, I was hopeless as a client. When Yongsu's Mother asked me if I had 'an aunt or uncle [*samch'on*] who died young,' I wrote home, half hoping to unravel a bit of family history. No such ghost, my mother wrote, 'unless one of your grandmothers had a secret life.' The *mansin* said, 'We don't know how you foreigners do things in America.' When I brought a Chinese-American friend for a divination, this same *mansin* acknowledged their affinity as East Sea People (Tongyang Saram), and would not let unclaimed ghosts slip by. Yongsu's Mother asked if there was someone in my friend's family who had died away from home or someone who died in childbirth, an ancestor who was an official perhaps. My friend explained that her father had been kidnapped as a boy in China and raised by foster parents, that he knew nothing at all about his own family. The *mansin* would not accept a dead end. 'When you're home for a visit, ask your mother. When the two of you are sitting around chatting, she'll tell you these things.' My friend again explained that her mother had already told her all she could about the family. Her father's origins were a mystery. Now the *mansin* grew concerned, appalled that a Chinese mother could send her married daughter off to set up housekeeping in a foreign land without telling her about the family ghosts and ancestors.

Seeing the year's luck

During the first two weeks of the lunar year, women crowd the *mansin*'s house to 'see the year's luck' (*illyŏn sinsurŭl poda*). The New Year marks a fresh, auspicious start for each household. A woman therefore gets a prognosis on each member of her family. If noxious influences threaten someone in her charge, she can 'make them clean' by performing simple rituals under the first full moon.

This is the peasants' winter slack season and the women are in a holiday mood when they come to the *mansin*'s house. Most arrive in groups. Waiting their turn, they bunch together in the hot-floor inner room. If the wait is long, they play cards, doze, or listen to other divinations. They sigh sympathetically for the woman whose divination reveals an adulterous husband, unruly child, or pitiable ghost. They coach the young matron who does not yet know the vocabulary of women's rituals. Not for them, the confidential atmosphere of the Western doctor's or analyst's office. The confessional's anonymity is missing here. The women enjoy each other's stories and accept each other's sympathy.

A woman, as a matter of course, receives divinations for her husband, herself, living parents-in-law, sons, unmarried daughters, sons' wives, and sons' children. Many women, however, pay an extra hundred or two hundred won for the fortunes of those whose ties stretch outside the woman's 'family', the family she enters at marriage and represents in the *mansin*'s shrine. Some women ask about a married daughter, her husband, and their children, or about other natal kin. During New Year divinations in 1978, one woman asked about her own mother, brother, and brother's wife, another about her own elder sister. Yongsu's Mother teased, 'What do you want to know about them for?' but provided the divinations. Women acknowledge their concern for mothers, married daughters, and siblings, but it costs more, an extra coin or two.

In the New Year divination the *mansin* predicts dangerous and advantageous months, warns against potentially dangerous activities, and suggests preventive ritual action. The following condensation of Yongsu's Mother's New Year divination for a seventy-year-old widow is an example.

My seventy-year-old lady, you shouldn't go on long trips; you must be careful now. Your children will receive succor; someone will come with aid in the seventh or eighth month. You will have some good news in the third or fourth month.

Your thirty-nine-year-old son should not visit anyone who is sick [since in this horoscope year, he is vulnerable to noxious influences]. His thirty-five-year-old wife should be heedful of things other people say about her. Their twelve-year-old son should be exorcised with five-grain rice left at the crossroads and by casting out a scarecrow stuffed with his name [because he has acquired an accretion of noxious influences and his year fate is bad]. The eight-year-old daughter will be lucky but you should burn a string of pine nuts, one for each year of her life, and address the moon on the night of the first full moon.

Your thirty-five-year-old son is troubled with sorrow and regret, but his luck is changing. There is no trouble between husband and wife, nothing to worry about there. Their seven-year-old child has a cold or something. This is a dangerous time for him so they must guard him carefully. Your unmarried thirty-year-old son doesn't even have a girl friend, but next year his prospects will improve. He should marry when he's thirty-two. He'll succeed in life when he's thirty-five or thirty-seven.

The scarecrow, five-grain rice left at the crossroads, and pine nuts burned under the moon are minor rituals performed on the fifteenth day of the lunar year. The first full moon marks the end of the New Year holidays, a time when women immunize a threatened family member, usually a child, against noxious influences lurking in the year's fortune. When the *mansin*'s visions reveal a swarm of noxious influences on the road, a growing splotch of red, she tells the child's mother or grandmother to leave five-grain rice at a crossroads, then wave it over the child's head and cast it out. A mother must warn her child to be especially mindful of traffic. When the *mansin* sees swimming fish, she tells the woman to write the child's name, age, and birthdate on a slip of paper and wrap the paper around a lump of breakfast rice on the morning of the fifteenth. The woman throws the packet into a well or stream saying, 'Take it, fish!' She substitutes the rice for a child with a drowning fate.

215

The *mansin* also cautions that children should not swim, go fishing, or climb mountains in certain months. Here the women sigh, 'How can I do that?' The *mansin* tells the housewife which family members, according to the particular vulnerability of their year horoscope, must disdain funerals, feasts, or visits to sick friends. She advises switching a sixty-first birthday celebration to a more auspicious month. She predicts the compatibility of a son's or daughter's lover or a matchmaker's candidate. She determines when 'the ancestors are hungry and the gods want to play,' and advises these families to hold *kut* early in the new year. The early spring is a busy season for the *mansin*.

In divination sessions a client receives a mingling of ritual information and common-sense advice. A soldier's wife, living in a rented room in Enduring Pine Village, worried about her husband's fidelity. A sympathetic neighbor brought her to Yongsu's Mother. The *mansin* suggested she dedicate a brass bell in the shrine for her husband's career success, then lectured her on prettying up and serving tasty food lest home life be as unappealing as 'rice cake that's already been chewed on.'

A melancholy young woman came to the shrine with her maternal grandmother. The woman had married for love, but now her husband was in America and had not written a letter for several months. In a nightmare the woman had seen her husband in a room full of women. Yongsu's Mother divined that a restless ghost, the husband's unmarried aunt, was disrupting the marriage out of jealousy. Yongsu's Mother exorcised the ghost, then suggested the woman go to her husband's parents in the country. She could cook and clean for them during the spring planting and establish herself as the distant son's acknowledged wife by building up a debt of gratitude in her favor. To the woman caught in adultery, she said bluntly, 'Burn incense and light candles in the shrine. Then go home and ask forgiveness. That's all you can do.'

A woman goes to the *mansin* with some ambivalence. She assumes the *mansin* will discern a supernatural problem and suggest ritual action. Rituals, be it an inexpensive exorcism or an elaborate *kut*, require cash. Hangil's Mother told me, 'I don't go to the *mansin*'s house anymore. They always tell you to do things that cost money, and I can't afford to do that. I'm just like a Christian now, only I don't believe in Jesus.' Though some women are cynical, Hangil's Mother is not. She advised me on the rituals I should perform for my own spirits and was almost invariably among the women watching a *kut* in Yongsu's Mother's shrine. A divination is the essential first step in a *mansin*'s treatment, but the whole process may stop here. Whenever Yongsu's Mother counseled a woman to dedicate a brass bell or sponsor a ritual, the client would almost always say, 'I'll have to talk it over with my husband,' or 'I'll have to see what the old people say.'

At home she weighs the potential benefits against the household budget. A woman told me, 'They say we ought to do a *kut* because a grandmother of this house was a great shaman, but it takes too much money.' Some women decide to wait and see if their problems will improve over time. There was, for example, the woman who said, 'Years ago, I went to a *mansin* in Righteous Town. Someone told me she was good, so I went to her by myself. My husband was losing money and I felt uneasy. The *mansin* said, "Do a *kut*," but I didn't.'

Others are satisfied with the *mansin*'s actions on their behalf:

> I was sick last year. I felt exhausted and my whole body ached. I went to the hospital for treatment and that took a lot of money ... After the exorcism I got better.

Or:

> We did a *kut* two years ago for my eldest son. He drank too much and had pains in his chest. He took Western medicine, but that didn't work. The Brass Mirror Mansin did a *kut* and he got better, so he didn't have to go to the hospital.

Some of the women were reluctant to attribute a successful cure directly and exclusively to the *mansin*'s efforts. 'The *mansin* did an exorcism and my daughter took medicine; she recovered.' There are also clients who claim total dissatisfaction with the *mansin*'s cure. Everyone in the Song family's immediate neighborhood knew that the entire household of the minor line became Christian when their healing *kut* did not cure the son's acute headaches. He recovered slowly over the next few months. Another woman said that she stopped believing when she learned that she had cancer of the womb. On the other side of the ledger was a young woman who, years ago, had prayed to the Christian god to spare her ailing parents. They died and she stopped believing. Now she was sponsoring a *kut*. Other women wonder if the *kut* the *mansin* advised might have saved an afflicted family member:

> Three years ago, I went to a *mansin* I'd heard was good. I went for my husband who was paralyzed. The *mansin* did an exorcism and told us to do a *kut*. We didn't do the *kut*, and my husband died.

or:

> My son died when he was sixteen years old. We should have gone to a *mansin*, but we didn't. There was something wrong with his thigh. It seemed fine from the outside. We couldn't see anything wrong and neither did the hospital. We went to the Western hospital and the hospital for Chinese medicine.

217

Some women who delay return later, and some do not. Some women visit other *mansin* who might confirm the diagnosis or provide a more impressive divination.[5] There are women who return the next day and hire Yongsu's Mother to take on their gods, ancestors, and ghosts. I found the *mansin*'s clients to be neither docile nor passive. They did not fit the pervasive Korean stereotype of naive country women cowed by a crafty shaman.

Of the forty-four divination sessions I recorded in my field notes during the lunar year 1977-1978, twenty women had no reason to return. They were women who lived far away and were only in the village for brief visits, women who went regularly to other *mansin* and wanted only a fresh perspective, and women who required only the year's luck or simple advice with no suggestion of supernatural malaise. Two were recent college graduates, friends of my assistant, who were curious about their marriage prospects. The mansin's visions indicated wrathful household gods or restless ancestors and ghosts in the households of twenty-four women. She told them to sponsor *kut* or minor rituals, make offerings in the shrine, or dedicate bells or costumes. How seriously did they take her advice? I can say with certainty that of the twenty-four clients only fourteen had Yongsu's Mother perform additional rituals. She went to exorcise the infant of a fifteenth client, but by the time she reached the house the baby was dying and the family decided it was no use. A few of the nine lost clients may have returned to Yongsu's Mother without my knowledge; the *mansin* may have performed a minor ritual that slipped by me. I suspect that most of these nine women decided against ritual expenses or went on to consult other *mansin*.

Six of the fourteen clients who followed Yongsu's Mother's advice had come to her house for the first time to receive divinations. I saw most of them at the shrine on several occasions thereafter. They appeared on Chilsŏng nal (lunar 7.7), made offerings in the shrine, and stayed to sing and dance in the late afternoon. They also came for New Year divinations and made New Year offerings in the shrine. When Yongsu's Mother held a *kut* for her own gods, these clients attended and bought divinations, drank lucky wine, and danced *mugam*. They have all become *tan'gol*, regular clients, at Yongsu's Mother's shrine.

---

[5] In her Sudong study, Soon-young Yoon found that, 'patients might change shamans as often as they did hospitals.' One woman, suffering from hypertension, went to eight shamans and four hospitals (S. Yoon 1977: 124). I discuss the issue of client's choice in more detail in [Kendall 1985] chapter 5.

The *tan'gol*

The term *tan'gol* means 'regular customer.' In Seoul people call themselves the *tan'gol* of a particular coffee shop, music parlor, restaurant, or tailor. The *tan'gol*'s face is known and the *tan'gol* receives special treatment. In return the *tan'gol* is loyal and brings in additional customers.

The Rice Shop Auntie was one of the women who became a *tan'gol* in the lunar year 1977-1978. When the Rice Shop Auntie first came to Yongsu's Mother for a divination, Yongsu's Mother threw down the coins with a show of frustration and disgust and scolded her, 'You've been going around all day, having your fortune told in seven different places. You've been wasting your money here and there when what you really need is a *kut*.' The Rice Shop Auntie confirmed that this was how she had spent the day, her rationale being, 'If all seven people say the same thing, then I'll do a *kut*. Otherwise, I won't.'[6]

Yongsu's Mother continued her divination. The Rice Shop Auntie claimed that Yongsu's Mother's analysis of her situation was the best she had heard all day. The Rice Shop Auntie had Yongsu's Mother organize a *kut* and thereafter became one of Yongsu's Mother's most enthusiastic clients. After the Rice Shop Auntie's *kut* three of her neighbors came to Yongsu's Mother for divinations. Within the next few months one sponsored a *kut* and two had Yongsu's Mother invoke their household gods (*kosa*). The Rice Shop Auntie and her friends visit the shrine in a laughing group. Whatever their expressed purpose, their visits always end in a round of wine. They invite Yongsu's Mother to their birthday parties since they are all of an age. The Rice Shop Auntie and her friends are Yongsu's Mother's best *tan'gol*.

The *mansin*'s *tan'gol* enjoys a special relationship not just with the *mansin* but with the grandmothers and grandfathers of her shrine. Yongsu's Mother counts twenty-four women as her *tan'gol*, and every year the number grows. They live in Enduring Pine Village, down the road in Willow Market, in Waterfall Valley, where she used to live, and in Righteous Town. Two of her Waterfall Valley *tan'gol* have moved to Seoul, but they come to her shrine every New Year. *Tan'gol* come to their *mansin*'s house to see the year's luck. They come during the year when they feel heavy-hearted. The *mansin* knows all of the ancestors, ghosts, and gods of her longtime clients' families. A powerful *mansin* dreams of her clients and anticipates their questions before they enter her house.

At the New Year *tan'gol* bathe, put on clean clothes, and carry rice, candles, fruit, and incense to the *mansin*'s shrine for the New Year ritual

---

[6] Harvey (1976: 192) reports a similar incident.

called Hongsu Megi.[7] The most powerful gods in their households and the most restless ancestors and ghosts appear when the *mansin* invokes them in her shrine. Endangered members of the family can be 'made clean' with an exorcism when ghosts and noxious influences are sent away at the end of Hongsu Megi. Finally, the *mansin* burns twists of thin paper, one for each member of the woman's household and one for each member of her married sons' households. The ashes waft high in the air, a good omen.

Tan'gol 'sell' children to the Seven Stars when the *mansin* divines that a son or grandson has a short life fate. The client dedicates a length of cloth (*myŏngdari*) with the child's name, birth date, and address. The *mansin* keeps the cloth in the shrine and jokingly calls the child 'my son.' If the child comes to her house with his mother during the New Year, he bows to the *mansin* as if she were an honored relative. She gives him fruit or candy and tells him to study hard. Women who have sold their children come to the shrine to worship the Seven Stars on the seventh day of the seventh lunar month in a ritual called Ch'ilsŏng Maji.

When a *mansin* holds a flower-greeting *kut* or a leaf-greeting *kut* – spring or autumn celebrations for her own shrine gods – she invites all her *tan'gol*. She uses all of the equipment the *tan'gol* have provided and wears the robes that bear their names. The *mansin* piles on several layers of robes so that all of the *tan'gol* gods can feast and dance at the *kut*. She displays all of the cloth *myŏngdari* that tie *tan'gol* children to the Seven Stars. When this god appears, the lengths of cloth are wafted through the air to bestow additional blessings on the children.

The *mansin* asks several *tan'gol* to provide some of the food consumed by the living and supernatural revelers at her annual *kut*. At Yongsu's Mother's last flower-greeting *kut* before I left Korea, I supplied several measures of grain for rice cake. I gave because I have an active Body-governing Official and, 'All the houses with [active] supernatural Officials are giving rice cake.' I also provided a pig's head. Another *tan'gol* contributed an impressive assortment of entrails to feast her own supernatural Official.

Household traditions and women's work

Women go to *mansin*'s shrines and to Buddhist temples as the ritual

---

7   *Megi* or *me*, contractions of *maji*, mean 'rice offered to Buddha.' Gary Ledyard (personal communication) suggests that since *maji* can also imply going out to greet the arrival of a notable; the term implies that women are going out to the *mansin*'s shrine to respectfully greet their own gods.

representatives of their families and households. They sponsor *kut* in the shrine and in their own homes, but never in other houses. Other houses have their own house gods. A bond like an electrical connection links the *mansin*'s house to the housewife's own dwelling. When clients leave after making offerings in the shrine or sponsoring a *kut* there, they give no farewell salutation. The *mansin* carefully reminds new clients of this necessary breach of etiquette, and tells the women to go straight home. A woman brings blessings from the shrine directly to her own house lest they be lost along the way. The woman leaves the shrine without a farewell and enters her own home without a greeting. Salutations mark boundaries and transitions; they are inappropriate here.

Any woman, old or young, married or single, can visit the *mansin*'s house and receive a divination, but the *tan'gol* who make seasonal offerings in the shrine and sponsor *kut* are female househeads, the senior women in their households. Commensurate with their temporal responsibilities, they come to the shrine on behalf of husbands, children, and retired parents-in-law. Some *tan'gol* are young matrons, but others are grandmothers whose concerns stretch beyond their own households to their married sons' households. They pray on behalf of sons, daughters-in-law, and grandchildren. Sometimes a worried mother brings her own daughter to the *mansin*. Occasionally mothers press their married daughters to hold a *kut* or perform a clandestine conception ritual, and mothers often pay an extra fee to include a married daughter's household in their divinations. A mother's concern for her own daughter might suggest pity for the suffering shared by all women, but it also suggests a mother's assumed ability to aid all of her children, even those who have left the ritual family she represents in the shrine.

My own relationship with Yongsu's Mother and her shrine was anomalous because, though as old as the younger *tan'gol*, I was a single woman. I therefore made offerings in the shrine for my natal family in America. Another anomaly was a young man who came to Yongsu's Mother's shrine for a divination and who subsequently dedicated his own brass bell. He was worried about his job, but his Christian wife refused to consult a *mansin* on his behalf. A neighbor woman and her husband brought him to Yongsu's Mother, everyone giggling a little at the incongruity of a man visiting a *mansin*'s house. It was as though he had cooked his family's evening rice or pickled their winter kimchee. Korean men are not inherently unqualified for these tasks, but it is the women who perform them, save in exceptional circumstances.

In the ideal flow of tradition, a daughter-in-law continues her mother-in-law's relationship with a particular *mansin*. The *mansin*'s spirit daughter inherits the shrine and the old *mansin*'s clients or her clients' daughters-in-

221

law. In practice, the relationship is far more flexible. The daughter-in-law sometimes favors a *mansin* close to her own age over the white-haired *mansin* her mother-in-law patronized. A spirit daughter may not enjoy the rapport her spirit mother had with clients. Some women switch *mansin* when they are dissatisfied with a diagnosis and cure. Other clients, like the Songs who converted to Christianity, stop visiting *mansin* altogether out of disappointment or because of diminishing returns. Other women said they stopped going to the *mansin*'s shrine because their present lives were 'free of anxiety' (*uhwani ŏptta*). Yongsu's Mother said, 'When things are fine, people don't do anything. When someone is sick, when they lose money, or when there's trouble with the police, then they do things like Hongsu Megi and *kut*.'

New clients come to the *mansin* from a variety of sources. During the New Year a group of neighbor women decide on impulse to have their fortunes told by the nearest *mansin*. Visiting their own families for the holiday, brides take their worries to their mother's *mansin*. Kinswomen and neighbors recommend a particular *mansin*. Neighbor women in a village hamlet or town alleyway know each other's worries. Older women take a maternal interest in young brides and sometimes bring a heavy-hearted woman to their own *mansin*. *Mansin* recommend kinswomen and neighbors to other *mansin* since they know these women's affairs too well to provide a convincing inspirational divination.[8] The East Town Mansin and the Clear Spring Mansin bring neighbors and kinswomen to Yongsu's Mother.

Apart from the gods' and ancestors' verbal presence, the rituals *tan'gol* perform in the *mansin*'s shrine parallel the offerings that women make in Buddhist temples. The officiant invokes and addresses divine beings with a flourishing of cymbals while the supplicant prostrates herself again and again before the altar. Some of the rice and delicacies she has placed on the altar are served again to the worshipers. At temple and shrine the women's prayers are the same: 'Make the children turn out well.' 'Make the house peaceful.' Women in temples and shrines advised me to 'ask for a good husband and a baby.'

The *mansin* calls her actions in the shrine Pulgong, a term usually glossed 'Buddhist mass.' The women of Enduring Pine Village themselves consider seasonal offerings at the *mansin*'s shrine and seasonal offerings at the Buddhist temple analogous practices. On Buddha's Birthday I went to the local temple with instructions from my landlady. 'It's just like going to a *mansin*'s house. You set your money down on the altar and you bow. You take two measures of rice, some fruit, and candles, just the same. They

---

[8] Harvey (1976: 191) also notes that shamans explicitly refuse to see neighbours or relatives.

do it on Buddha's Birthday [lunar 4.8] at the temple and on Seven Star Day [lunar 7.7] at the shrine.'

In Enduring Pine Village I found 'houses that visit the Buddhist temple,' and 'houses that visit the *mansin*'s house,' and a few 'houses that visit the Christian church.' The Christians stand outside the folk religious system, but shamanism and Buddhism blur. Yongsu's Mother and her clients called their shrine worship Pulgyo, 'Buddhism,' and the *mansin* often introduced me as 'a student of Buddhism.'

In houses that visit the Buddhist temple, women go up the mountain path once during the first two weeks of the new year and on lunar 7.7, when other women go to the *mansin*'s shrine. Women also go to Buddhist temples on Buddha's Birthday, and some women pray there on their own children's birthdays. And women visit the temple or the *mansin*'s shrine in adversity. According to my landlady, 'You go when someone is sick or when a son can't find work.' City families often visit temples before a child takes the university entrance examination.

Like women who visit the *mansin*'s shrine, women who make offerings at temples must bathe themselves and be free of menstrual pollution when they carry their offerings up the hillside. One woman recalls, 'We would bathe clean and wash our hair before we went to the temple. Then we'd put on clean clothing and wash all of the rice clean. When we got to the temple, we would pray for the whole family.' Okja's Mother says that she is too poor to make seasonal offerings at a temple, but she squeezes some of her limited resources to make a small offering when she is anxious. 'I couldn't afford to go this year on lunar 7.7, but I went on Buddha's Birthday because my husband was having so many difficulties at work. I didn't have any money to set on the altar, and I didn't bring any fruit, just a small measure of rice, some incense, and candles. They recited prayers and I bowed.'

From the perspective of women worshipers, shrine and temple do not represent discrete religions, but rather the different traditions of separate households. One household made seasonal offerings at both the shrine and the temple, but other women claim, 'It takes a lot of money to do both.' In her own shrine, Yongsu's Mother has enthroned gilt-plaster images of Pulsŏk Buddha (Pulsŏk Puch'ŏnim), Kwanyin Buddhist Sage (Kwanseŭm Pulsa), and Healing Buddha (Yaksa Puch'ŏnim), all borrowed from the Buddhist tradition. The Seven Stars and the Mountain God are honored in both shrine and temple. Some of the services *mansin* and monk perform are identical; a partial list includes performing masses (Pulgong), lettering paper charms (*pujŏk*), dedicating children (*myŏngdari*), and divining.

A daughter-in-law is expected to follow her mother-in-law in temple or shrine worship, but there are easy compromises and crossovers. Yonghui's

223

household is emphatically a house that visits the Buddhist temple. Yonghui's Mother pressed the backs of her hands together to impress upon me the incompatibility of Buddhist temples and *mansin*'s shrines. Yonghui's Grandmother warned me against spending so much time in a *mansin*'s house lest I be exploited. But other households are less rigid. When her husband was sick, my landlady prayed at the Buddhist temple; she also sponsored a *kut*. Yangja's Mother followed the traditions of her husband's family and bought a Buddhist talisman to protect her taxi driver husband. After her husband's second traffic accident, her mother brought her to the *mansin* and she became Yongsu's Mother's *tan'gol*. Other women told me that they used to go to the local temple but went to the *mansin* during a family crisis and thereafter transferred their allegiance. Some women, though they make seasonal offerings at temples, consult *mansin* for divinations. The daughter-in-law in a household of temple worshipers lowered her voice and told me that she periodically seeks out a *mansin*'s divinations for 'peace of mind.' She did not want her mother-in-law to hear this revelation. The women I interviewed who had broken with the traditions of their mothers-in-law happened also to be less accountable to the husband's house than women trained to succeed a mother-in-law. They were either the wives of secondary sons, living at a distance from the husband's kin, estranged from the husband's kin, or had never known a living mother-in-law.

Having outlined the basic structure of the housewife's and *mansin*'s working relationship, it remains for me to present the gods and ancestors that infuse these events with drama and personality. Restless spirits emerge from commonly held beliefs. The *mansin* uses her shamanic powers to conjure the particularly strong and dangerously discontented spirits of client households from assorted supernatural possibilities and to devise therapeutic rituals that bring past family history to bear on present anxieties.

References

Allen, H. N. 1896. 'Some Korean Customs: The Mootang', *Korean Repository* 3: 3-168.

Ch'oe, Kil-sŏng, and Chang, Chu-gun. 1967. *Kyŏnggido chiyŏk musok* (Shaman Practices of Kyŏnggi Province). Seoul: Ministry of Culture.

Gale, James S. 1963 (1913). *Korean Folk Tales: Imps, Ghosts, and Fairies*. Reprint. Tokyo: Charles E. Tuttle.

Harvey, Youngsook Kim. 1976. The 'Korean *Mudang* as a Household Therapist', in *Culture-Bound Syndromes, Ethnopsychiatry, and Alternate Therapies*, ed. W.

P. Lebra. Honolulu: University of Hawaii Press, pp. 189-98.

Harvey, Youngsook Kim. 1979. *Six Korean Women: The Socialization of Shamans*. St Paul: West.

Harvey, Youngsook Kim. 1980. 'Possession Sickness and Women Shamans in Korea', in N. Falk and R. Gross (eds), *Unspoken Worlds: Women's Religious Lives in Non-Western Cultures*. New York: Harper & Row, pp. 41-52.

Kendall, Laurel. 1977. 'Caught Between Ancestors and Spirits: A Korean *Mansin*'s Healing *Kut*', *Korea Journal* 17(8): 8-23.

Kendall, Laurel. 1985. *Shamans, Housewives and Other Restless Spirits: Women in Korean Ritual Life*. Honolulu: University of Hawaii Press.

Wilson, Brian. 1983. 'The Korean Shaman: Image and Reality', in L. Kendall and M. Peterson (eds), *Korean Women: View from the Inner Room*. New Haven: East Rock Press, pp. 113-28.

Yoon, Soon-young. 1977. 'Su-Dong Project Report'. Unpublished MS.

9. Understanding a (secular) primitive society

Berel Dov Lerner

Editor's introduction

Berel Lerner's article is framed by reference to Mary Douglas's essay 'Heathen Darkness' (1975) in which she challenges the 'myth of primitive piety'. He then contributes to the continuing reformation of academic disciplines by considering the secularity and/or religiosity of the Azande and Nuer. He does this by a 'broader and more careful reading of Evans-Pritchard's writings [than that of Peter Winch]'. He concludes that Evans-Pritchard's (E-P)

> studies of the Azande constitute a *critical analysis* of such a secular sensibility which happens to inform a traditional society. While Winch claims (but never in such harsh terms) that E-P was blind to Zande spirituality, it may be said that E-P explains why the Azande themselves are blind to the kind of spirituality embraced by Winch. Just as we are in danger of losing our ability to appreciate a religious perspective due to our 'conception of reality' which is 'deeply affected by the achievements and methods of the sciences', the Azande never developed such a perspective due to their own conception of reality which is deeply affected by the achievements and methods of magic.

That is, the worldviews of modernity and of the Azande in the early twentieth century (after which rapid changes took place) are comparable in their secularity.

It may seem perverse to include an argument about secularity in a work on religion. There are, however, important points to consider here. First, if 'religion' is to be useful as a critical term it cannot refer to every aspect of life, 'secularity' (apparently its opposite) may aid the refinement of its reference. Second, the religiosity and/or secularity of modernity remain contentious issues and it seems worthwhile to be alerted to the dangers of assuming secularity is unique to modernity. Third, framing this debate with reference to 'magic' encourages consideration of intellectualist, symbolist and other approaches to the study of religions and cultures (see Pals 2000). Fourth, Evans-Pritchard largely initiated consideration of the diversity of modes of rationality, e.g. demonstrating the central role played by magic in the construction of Zande society. Finally, perhaps, the similarities between magic and religion are clearly evident in their performative and experiential dimensions. Thus Lerner should be read not only alongside his chapter in *Indigenous Religions: A Companion*, but also in concert with those that surround it in this volume.

References

Douglas, Mary. 1975. 'Heathen Darkness', in *Implicit Meanings: Essays in Anthropology*. London: Routledge & Kegan Paul, pp. 73-82.

Pals, Daniel L. 2000. 'Intellect', in Willi Braun and Russell T. McCutcheon (eds), *Guide to the Study of Religion*. London: Cassell, pp. 155-67.

In her essay entitled 'Heathen Darkness',[1] the anthropologist Mary Douglas has exposed one of the most prevalent modern misunderstandings of 'primitive' societies, the myth of primitive piety:

> It seems to be an important premise of popular thinking about us, the civilised, and them, the primitives, that we are secular, sceptical and frankly tending more and more away from religious belief, and that they are religious. (p. 73)

Douglas goes on to discuss how the myth of primitive piety has served both religious and anti-religious ideologies, and more particularly, how it has thwarted the proper development of the anthropology of religion. There is always a risk involved in studying the religious life of traditional people; they may turn out to be thoroughly secular. In that case the ethnographer

---

[1] In her *Implicit Meanings: Essays in Anthropology* (London: Routledge & Kegan Paul, 1975), pp. 73-82.

is left to make an uncomfortable choice between publishing the heretical finding that 'My tribe hasn't got any religion' (p. 76) and blindly assuming that native secretiveness makes their faith impenetrable to outsiders. Most anthropologists avoid the problem altogether by attending to safer issues such as politics and economics. Furthermore, the assumption of a universal (and static) traditional piety makes a genuinely comparative study of religion impossible: *they* (the 'primitives') are religious, while *we* (the 'civilised') have become, after a long and twisted spiritual history, secular. Such a view hardly leaves room for any enlightening application of insights gained from the study of traditional societies to the analysis of the Western religious heritage or of our own contemporary spiritual situation. This predicament leads Douglas to proclaim the importance of the recognition of primitive secularity and heterodoxy for the understanding of religion: 'Unless we can think of tribes as secular, or given to mystery cults, dualist philosophies, or heterodoxies about the nature of grace and the godhead, the questions that have unleashed historic wars and mass executions, we have hardly begun the anthropology of religion' (p. 81). I would add that important work in the *philosophy* of religion has also been distorted by an inability to recognize primitive secularity.

Almost thirty years ago Peter Winch wrote an article entitled 'Understanding a Primitive Society' (UPS), in which he tried to defend and extend the argument made in his earlier book, *The Idea of a Social Science* (ISS).[2] Both works have become seminal texts for contemporary Anglo-American philosophy, and have together generated a whole literature of debate among philosophers, theologians and social scientists. In his article, Winch anchors a theoretical discussion of the intelligibility of religion and of cross-cultural understanding in examples taken from the mystical beliefs and practices of the Azande, a traditional people living on Africa's Nile–Congo divide. The source of these examples is the ethnographic classic, *Witchcraft, Oracles and Magic among the Azande*,[3] by the prominent British anthropologist, Sir E. E. Evans-Pritchard (hereafter: E-P). Since Winch's work is so well-known there is little point to my offering yet another summary of his philosophical arguments, especially as these have no direct bearing on the topic of the present essay. Instead, I shall concern myself with the spiritual attitudes Winch attributes to the Azande, and how a broader consideration of E-P's writings may lead to a different

---

[2] Peter Winch, 'Understanding a Primitive Society', *American Philosophical Quarterly*, 1 (1964): 307-24 and *The Idea of a Social Science and Its Relation to Philosophy* (second edition) (Atlantic Highlands: Humanities Press, 1992).

[3] E-P, *Witchcraft, Oracles and Magic among the Azande* (Oxford: Oxford University Press, 1937).

understanding of the spiritual condition of Zande society, an understanding which may be exemplary for Douglas's program of a reformed anthropology of religion.

Winch's reading of E-P is not entirely uncritical. A central aim of Winch's paper is to demonstrate that E-P is mistaken in pronouncing Zande magic ineffective and their belief in the existence of witches false. According to Winch, by judging magic ineffective, E-P applies a criterion appropriate to the evaluation of technologies to social practices which do not play a technological role in Zande society. Furthermore, says Winch, E-P's claim that Zande witches do not really exist involves the application of epistemological standards native to empirical science to the evaluation of beliefs which do not belong to a scientific theory.

Having rejected as misplaced the question of witchcraft's empirical reality, he suggests a different role for such notions and practices in Zande life:

> We have a drama of resentements, evil doing, revenge, expiation, in which there are ways of dealing (symbolically) with misfortunes and their disruptive effects on a man's relations with his fellows. (UPS, p. 321)

The idea of 'dealing with misfortunes' is fundamental for Winch's interpretation of Zande mysticism. Every human society is limited by the effectiveness of the technologies it has developed for the preservation and promotion of that which it holds dear, i.e. life, health, prosperity, security, and so on. When these are threatened by contingencies beyond the control of available technology, people must find ways to recognize their own limitations without being paralysed into inaction. While improved technology may remove a particular source of anxiety, it cannot offer a complete solution to the human predicament because something can always go wrong:

> He [the Zande man] may wish thereby, in a certain sense, to free himself from dependence on it [something important to his life yet over which he has imperfect control]. I do not mean by making sure that it does not let him down, because the point is that, whatever he does, he may still be let down. The important thing is that he should understand that and come to terms with it.
> (UPS, p. 320)

According to Winch, Zande magic, like Christian prayer, expresses such an attitude to the contingencies of life:

> I do not say that Zande magical rites are at all like Christian prayers of supplication in the positive attitude to contingencies which they express. What I do

suggest is that they are alike in that they do, or may, express an attitude to contingencies, rather than an attempt to control these.

(UPS, p. 321)

What would E-P say to all of this? Winch himself has always been aware that the relationship between his philosophy and E-P's ethnography is far from simple:

> The relationship between [Alasdair] MacIntyre, Evans-Pritchard and myself is a complicated one. MacIntyre takes Evans-Pritchard's later book, *Nuer Religion*, as an application of a point of view like mine in the *The Idea of a Social Science*; he regards it as an object lesson in the absurd results to which such a position leads, when applied in practice. My own criticisms of Evans-Pritchard, on the other hand, have come from precisely the opposite direction. I have tried to show that Evans-Pritchard did not at the time of writing *The Azande* agree with me *enough*; that he did not take seriously enough the idea that the concepts used by primitive peoples can only be interpreted in the context of the way of life of those peoples. Thus I have in effect argued that Evans-Pritchard's account of the Azande is unsatisfactory precisely to the extent that he agrees with MacIntyre and not me.

(UPS, p. 315)

While in the above paragraph, Winch is discussing meta-interpretive aspects of studying another culture, it might apply equally to the actual content of particular interpretations of traditional societies. Here again E-P's later work seems more congenial to Winch's views. While Winch implies that E-P of *The Azande* underestimates the religious depth of traditional mystical practices, *Nuer Religion* is a virtual panegyric to primitive spirituality. Thus E-P concludes his book on the Nuer with a statement which might as easily be applied to any of the great monotheistic religions:

> Though prayer and sacrifice are exterior actions, Nuer religion is ultimately an interior state. This state is externalized in rites which we can observe, but their meaning depends finally on an awareness of God and that men are dependent on him and must be resigned to his will. At this point the theologian takes over from the anthropologist.[4]

Now *that* is exactly the kind of spirituality which Winch wanted E-P to discover in Zande magic. Recognition of one's dependency on God and resignation to His will constitute the classic monotheistic solution to the problem of coming to terms with the contingencies of life.

---

[4] E-P, *Nuer Religion* (Oxford: Clarendon Press, 1956), p. 322.

230

Winch's reference to E-P 'at the time of writing *The Azande*' implies a process of change of heart. The old E-P was partially blind to the diversity of human experience; the new E-P is capable of appreciating Nuer society on its own terms. Similarly, one might think that the old E-P saw primitive ritual as false technology, while the new E-P recognizes its true spiritual depth. E-P himself had disavowed the errors of *The Azande* ten years before Winch's article was published!

I reject this interpretation of E-P's development. A more careful examination of E-P's writings reveals that rather than a change of heart, we have here a change of subject matter. According to E-P, the Azande and the Nuer are informed by fundamentally different attitudes towards life, as was immediately apparent to him upon encountering the latter:

> I had previously spent many months among the Azande people of the Nile–Uelle divide. From my earliest days among them I was constantly hearing the word *mangu*, witchcraft, and it was soon clear that if I could gain a full understanding of the meaning of this word I should have the key to Zande philosophy. When I started my study of the Nuer I had a similar experience. I constantly heard them speaking of *kwoth*, Spirit, and I realized that a full understanding of that word was the key to their – very different – Philosophy.
>
> (*Nuer Religion*, p. vi)

Another important difference between the two peoples involves their respective dependence on magic and medicine:

> Coming to the Nuer from Zandeland, where everyone is a magician and medicines are legion and in daily use, I was at once struck by their negligible quantity and importance in Nuerland, and further experience confirmed my first impression. I mention them chiefly for the reason that their rarity and unimportance are indicative of the orientation of Nuer thought, which is always towards spirit.
>
> (NR, p. 104)

Not only are the Azande more interested in witchcraft and magic than they are in Spirit, E-P believes that these concerns actually bar their way from approaching God:

> Witchcraft ideas play a very minor role [in Nuer religion], and magic a negligible one. Both are incompatible with a theocentric philosophy, for when both fortune and misfortune come from God they cannot also come from human powers, whether innate or learnt.
>
> (NR, pp. 316-17)

It is now possible to reappraise E-P's view of the Azande. E-P is completely aware of the importance for people to find a way to deal with the contingencies of life. Like Winch, he does not believe that it is possible to address the spiritual implications of the reality of human frailty by undertaking yet more practical measures. It is exactly for this reason that he refuses to attribute spiritual depth to Zande magic and witchcraft, for these notions teach that 'both fortune and misfortune ... come from human powers'. Azande magic does not point to human finitude, it is viewed 'as a tangible weapon of culture ... deriving its power from the knowledge of tradition and the abstinence of living men.'[5] Far from offering a way to 'express an attitude to contingencies, rather than an attempt to control these', E-P implies that Zande mysticism instills false confidence and blinds its practitioners to the real extent of their control over nature.

As we have seen, E-P argues that only theism, rather than magic, can foster a spiritually rich sensitivity to life's contingencies. Do the Azande, in addition to their magic, possess a theistic sensibility? In his essay 'Zande Theology'[6] (which could be less deceivingly titled 'Zande Atheology'), E-P completes his picture of Zande spirituality (or lack of it) by discussing the notion proposed by other writers that 'the idea of a Supreme Being is deeply anchored in Zande mentality' (p. 291). Not surprisingly, E-P finds that theistic concepts and practices play a very minor role in Zande life. They have little or no concern for God or gods, almost no mythology explaining the relationship between the divine and human realms, and spend practically none of their time in worship, prayer or sacrifice. For instance, he describes how the name of *Mbori*, a vague supernatural entity considered by some ethnographers to be the Zande Supreme Being, enters into day to day speech:

> As a fieldworker I must record that I have never heard a Zande pray and that I have seldom heard people utter his [Mbori's] name, and then only as an ejaculation of emotional intensity and with only the vaguest suggestion of doctrinal significance. I must confess also that I have found the greatest difficulty in obtaining either information about Mbori or arousing any interest in him ... (p. 299)

One could imagine that Mbori could somehow play the same role as the

---

[5] E-P, 'The Morphology and Function of Magic: A Comparative Study of Trobriand and Zande Ritual Spells', *American Anthropologist* 31 (1929): 619-41. Here cited as reprinted in John Middleton (ed.), *Magic, Witchcraft, and Curing* (New York: Natural History Press, 1967), pp. 1-22. Present quotation, p. 20.

[6] E-P, 'Zande Theology', in his *Social Anthropology and Other Essays* (New York: Free Press, 1962), pp. 288-329, here p. 300.

God of the great monotheistic religions, but in fact the Azande do not cultivate an attitude of dependence on Mbori similar to the notion of 'God's will' preached by Judaism, Christianity and Islam. Even at the hour of death, Mbori's providence is rarely mentioned:

> In sickness and death he [the Azande] thinks of witchcraft as their cause, and not of Mbori, who does not interfere in such matters, and he seeks to cure disease and avenge death through magical and oracular processes against witches and not by prayers to Mbori. Nevertheless, it appears that death is sometimes vaguely attributed to Mbori *when no other cause can be discovered*. [My emphasis – B.D.L.] (p. 300)

All-in-all, E-P paints a picture of a thoroughly secular Zande culture whose members take more-or-less effective practical measures to protect and promote their interests, but who are unwilling or unable to face up to the limitations of their powers. Their magic is not a proper medium for piety, their theistic faith almost non-existent. This description sounds startlingly familiar. A similar attitude has been central to the Western sensibility since the Enlightenment which promoted 'the view that the experiences of contingency and problems of meaning that were previously interpreted in religious terms and worked-off in cult practices can be radically defused' by technological solutions.[7] The Azande have their magic and we our technology; neither society is particularly comfortable with the idea that some contingencies will always remain beyond its control. Although our hubris may be better-founded than that of the Azande (our technology works better than their magic), both cultures (to the extent that the West is as thoroughly secular as the Azande!) share essentially the same spiritual condition.

On the opening pages of UPS, Winch suggests that the reason why anthropologists often depict magic as an irrational form of technology is that they accommodate their explanations to their own (Western) culture, 'a culture whose conception of reality is deeply affected by the achievements and methods of the sciences' (p. 307). What I am suggesting is that a broader and more careful reading of E-P's writings reveals that far from being the *product* of a narrowly Western, secular, and instrumental sensibility, E-P's studies of the Azande constitute a *critical analysis* of such a secular sensibility which happens to inform a traditional society. While Winch claims (but never in such harsh terms) that E-P was blind to Zande spirituality, it may be said that E-P explains why the Azande themselves are

---

[7] Jürgen Habermas, *The Theory of Communicative Action, Vol. 1: Reason and the Rationalization of Society*, trans. Thomas McCarthy (Boston: Beacon Press, 1984), p. 149.

blind to the kind of spirituality embraced by Winch. Just as we are in danger of losing our ability to appreciate a religious perspective due to our 'conception of reality' which is 'deeply affected by the achievements and methods of the sciences', the Azande never developed such a perspective due to their own conception of reality which is deeply affected by the achievements and methods of magic. That is exactly the kind of comparative hypothesis sought by Mary Douglas in her essay 'Heathen Darkness'. It would be fair to say that in the 1930s, Evans-Pritchard had already laid the cornerstone for Douglas's reformed anthropology of religion.

Ludwig Wittgenstein, in a set of remarks which inspired Winch's interpretation of the Azande, once wrote:

> What narrowness of spiritual life we find in [Sir James] Frazer! And as a result: how impossible for him to understand a different way of life from the English one of his time! Frazer cannot imagine a priest who is not basically an English Parson of our times with all his stupidity and feebleness.[8]

Sometimes it requires an even greater effort of the imagination to recognize that the weaknesses of our own culture may *reappear* in the most surprising places.[9]

[8]   Ludwig Wittgenstein, *Remarks on Frazer's Golden Bough*, trans. R. Rhees (Nottinghamshire: The Brynmill Press, 1979), p. 5e.
[9]   I wish to thank Professor Jacob Joshua Ross for discussing with me the issues within this paper.

Part III
Knowledge

10. Maori religion

T. P. Tawhai

Editor's introduction

Land, myth, ritual, gender, relationships, sovereignty are all potently presented in Paka Tawhai's chapter. The indigenous knowledge that it presents is concerned with the construction of persons, engagement in performance, and the importance of place. However, it is included here not only for these (very good) reasons, but also because it can be read as an exemplar of how the study of religions might be done. By theorizing about the nature of religion from a carefully enunciated situation in relation to the interests (ontology, performance, knowledge, and place) of a particular community, it contributes to debates about both researchers and those researched (see McCutcheon 1999; Smith 1999).

Tawhai's definition of religion is a powerful one that requires and rewards considerable reflection: 'The purpose of religious activity here is to seek to enter the domain of the superbeing and do violence with impunity.' This is to reiterate (once more) the engagement of religions with the messy realities of this-worldly life, integrating subsistence and relationships. How is one to honour the duties incumbent on hosts with ethical imperatives against the taking of life? If all life, not only human life, is of value, at some point everyone must do violence to thrive or survive. Religion, Tawhai claims, is a means of actively dealing with such conundrums.

Tawhai's point is deeply embedded in a discussion of traditional Maori knowledge. Although such knowledge is not traditionally used to explain Maori world-views and lifeways, it is variously elaborated in prestigious acts of speech-making and debate that remain central to Maori cultural life. In other words, such narra-

Reprinted from *The Study of Religion, Traditional and New Religion*, ed. Stewart Sutherland and Peter Clarke, Routledge, 1988. By permission of the Taylor & Francis Group.

tives are inappropriately considered to be codifications of 'mythology', let alone 'scriptures', but are summaries of knowledge whose implications are drawn out in relation to questions and needs in particular contexts. The point requires clarity of thought and expression because, as Tawhai indicates, there is danger in being misunderstood. It is all too simple for academics and others to imprison indigenous knowledges in a cage labelled 'myth' and apply alien hermeneutics. Russell McCutcheon's discussion of 'myth' serves as an invaluable hammer with which to knock this point home. He argues

> (1) that myths are not special (or 'sacred') but ordinary human means of fashioning and authorizing their lived-in and believed-in 'worlds,' (2) that myth as an ordinary rhetorical device in social construction and maintenance makes *this* rather than *that* social identity possible in the first place and (3) that a people's use of the *label* 'myth' reflects, expresses, explores and legitimizes their own self-image.
>
> (2000: 200)

Tawhai's chapter sets an excellent standard against which other writings about indigenous knowledges should be tested.

References

McCutcheon, Russell T. 1999. *The Insider/Outsider Problem in the Study of Religions*. London: Cassell.

McCutcheon, Russell T. 2000. 'Myth', in Willi Braun and Russell T. McCutcheon (eds), *Guide to the Study of Religions*. London: Cassell, pp. 190-208.

Smith, Linda T. 1999. *Decolonizing Methodologies: Research and Indigenous Peoples*. Otago: University of Otago Press; London: Zed Books.

ംഗ്

If you ask a Maori in, for example, a settlement such as Ruatoria where Maoris constitute a majority of the population, what he understands by religion, expect him to scratch his head in thought, before at length replying 'Whose religion?' Religion and Christianity may be synonymous words for him, but what they mean will vary between 'a human recognition of a superhuman controlling power', on the one hand, and 'the preaching of one thing and too often the doing of something else', on the other. It was religion in the latter sense that the Christians who 'brought Jesus to civilise the natives' in earlier days seemed to follow, showing up their God in an adverse light in the eyes of the ancestors, whose traditional gods acted swiftly and usually harshly. For all that, the ancestors were well able, soon after their contact with Christianity, to distinguish the Message from the messengers. The Maori of Ruatoria will accept that Christianity is an integral part of his fellow Maori's life, but that each will also have his own brand of religion, for historic and other reasons; for instance Maoris have the same religion as their forebears. While the Christian God provides Maoridom with its first Redeemer, he appears mostly to ignore needs at the temporal and profane level, leaving this domain to the ancestral gods who continue to cater for those needs. The *tohunga*, formally trained experts in various academic disciplines, say that in the 'long ago' the gods took an active interest in the affairs of humans, and interaction among them and the ancestors was the norm rather than the exception. Thus, in the long ago, marvellous events occurred, which would account, at least in part, for a past which today sounds more like fable than anything else.

Such issues as whether there was at some stage an entity that can be said to be the origin or architect of creation, and whether such an origin or architect had a single material form, if any, were and continue to be subjects of much speculation. Our typical Maori's tribal upbringing makes him familiar with the capacity of superhuman controlling powers to exist as they choose – in a single form, or transformed at will into numerous manifestations.

What immediately concerns him are such issues as the effectiveness of the relationship between a person and a superhuman controlling power in magnifying that person's capacity to work his will; or the constraints and obligations upon that person in order to sustain the relationship. The ability to accommodate these issues rests a great deal upon knowledge based in turn upon *korero tahito* (ancient explanations). These may be called 'myths', if that word refers to material the main purpose of which is to express the beliefs and values of people.

That the *korero tahito* persist in influencing the Maori's mind is evident during *hui* (large social gatherings). Whether it is the occasion of a *huritau* (birthday), or *tangi* (a gathering to deal with a bereavement), each elder present uses the forum. Gazing around in assessment of those present, he rises in his turn to his feet and with measured dignity expounds in solemn rhetoric. To make his points he invokes the imagery of the tribal myths, with apt gesture, and with references to the symbolism, for example of the art and carving of the meeting-house.

The following passage is transcribed and translated from a speech by a *tohunga* Arnold Reedy, recorded in 1966. It conveys something of the way in which biblical ideas and *korero tahito* continue to interact, in the Maori way of thinking.

Should I happen to meet with [the Apostle] Paul I would probably say to him, 'By Gosh, Paul, those thoughts conflict greatly in my mind.'

The reason is that Adam is the ancestor of the Hebrews and of the Israelites. Whereas ours is this other: Io the Parent. That's ours. From Him/Her are Papa and Rangi and then the Tamariki. Such is the Maori *whakapapa*, right from Tikitiki-o-rangi.

There, then is the difference between our God and the God of the Hebrews. The God of the Hebrews and Israelites they say has His residence in Heaven. Ours, and the God of our ancestors, resides there too. But they know that Tikitiki-o-rangi is the name of the residence of Io; it's there. Io has a house there, Matangireia by name. It has its own forecourt. All those sorts of things are there.

What er ... Paul is saying looks, to use an English term, very much confused, in my view.

Because, take Adam: Then said the God of the Hebrews, 'Let us create man after our image.' And so the God of the Hebrews created Adam. But when that Adam was born into this world, others resided there too, and he considered them: 'What an ineffectual state of affairs.' For sexual organs simply dangled there with nowhere to go, nowhere.

Let us observe the formalities in our discussion! [an elder's (female) voice] ...

People were born. What Paul is telling us here is that nobody was born. How did he manage it? He took hold of one of his ribs and yanked it out, and then said, 'This is Eve.' They had union and Cain and his younger brothers were born, the generations of whom Paul speaks; these are the Hebrews and the Israelites.

Look here, ours, not so; ours goes this other way. The *tamariki* of Papa and Rangi resided, but that God continued to reside above, the beginning and the ending. The visaged one, the faceless one. Io, Io the Parent, he is the beginning, he is the ending.

But the *tamariki* of this couple [Papa and Rangi] resided between them. Gradually, eventually, a stifled sense overwhelmed them; they of course being all male, there were no female ones. Some began to say, 'Let us kick our parents into separating, so that we may emerge into the ordinary world of light.' Others spoke. Tu Matauenga began to say, 'Let us slay our *matua*, slay them.' And others were saying, 'No, that is too shameful.' From that time hence, Tu Matauenga is god of war, of bloodshed.

Some began to say, 'How shall we proceed?' Tane lay down and raised his feet. Hmm! He began to kick, causing gradual separation, and hence was called by that name of his, Tane-toko-Rangi [Tane sunderer of the sky] – and so, there is separation, there is separation.

But at the separation of Papa, I of course do not agree with what Paul says; there is strong conflict in my mind, the matter is this other way. They were separated and the *tamariki* emerged.

Rongomaraeroa was guardian of fern; that's the Minister of Agriculture. Is it not so? Tu Matauenga, Minister of War – War Department. Er ... , Tane-nui-a-rangi: that was god of the forests.

Minister of Forests ...

Tangaroa, Tangaroa of the Marine Department. They now have these posts, they have. (Money had not been invented at that time.)

But here is the problem. These people were all male; there was no female. These people considered their situation: 'By golly, comrades, this is a distressing state! Just us, wherever you look it's the same.' Each one with his (male) sexual appendages. Gradually they became highly distressed by their own company. They began to ponder, 'What shall we do, what shall we do?'

'It is well!', Tane-nui-a-rangi informs them, 'it is well. I have the prescription for our disorder.' He, Tane-nui-a-rangi, proceeded to the beach at Kurawaka and arrived. He began to heap up sand, more sand. He pondered his appearance, and began to mould (the heap) into shape similar to his own. But he added length to the hair ... etc.

'O Ropi [the female elder, Mrs Ngaropi White], these are the words of Wi-o-te-rangi, O Ropi.'

The Maori on the street of Ruatoria, nowadays at least, is content with the knowledge that he has access to the expertise of *tohunga* like Arnold Reedy. To outsiders he is inclined to present a front of learning, as a defence against anything that might question the worth of his tribal culture; the treasures transmitted to him by his ancestors.

Before turning to the main task I will note something about myself. The aim is to indicate some of the traditional constraints under which I write, and also to provide some data concerning the reliability of individual sources. I am of Ngati Uepohatu, a tribe whose unextinguished fires, lit by our explorer ancestor Maui, burn in the Waiapu valley near East Cape. The continuously burning fires refer to the State of being unconquered, and in turn refer to the tribe's unsullied prestige; that is the purity, *inter alia*, of its *korero tahito*. Maui is the legendary Maui Tikitiki a Taranga (Maui of the topknot of Taranga, his mother) who as our *korero tahito* explains discovered and settled Aotearoa (New Zealand). The name Aotearoa means 'long twilight', unlike the brief equatorial ones Maui and his crew were used to. Maui had voyaged out and Mount Hikurangi of Aotearoa had seemed to thrust up out of the sea as he sailed toward shore. Noah on the other hand had waited patiently and it was the waters which subsided thereby exposing Mount Ararat. (I think this reflects something of the philosophies of the two peoples. The Maori view is that things come to those with the courage to get them. The Judaic view is that things come to those who can wait.)

My understanding is that each tribe has its own system of ancient explanations. The apparently permanent migration of some Maori into the tribal territories of other Maori has complicated the picture in some ways.

241

And in relation to that and other matters, I recall an often quoted precept of the ancestors which goes: if you must speak, speak of your own. I speak of *korero tahito* and accordingly speak of Ngati Uepohatu ones. Our *korero tahito* have in the telling more or less depended in the past upon such factors as the appropriateness of the emotional climate in which it is told, the messages stated by the surroundings on the occasion, the body language of the narrator and the attributes that the human voice lends to words. Written presentation takes these things away. More than that, it tends to rigidify what has and should remain pliant. Flexibility in our *korero tahito* enables them to accommodate the capacity of the narrator to render them more relevant to the issues of the day. It is therefore with misgivings and a sense of danger that I must explain that this telling is only for this time, and that tomorrow I would tell it another way.

Te Po

> *Te Kore* evolved through aeons into *Te Po*. *Te Po* also evolved through generations countless to man to the stage of *Te Ata* (the Dawn). From *Te Ata* evolved *Te Aoturoa* (familiar daytime) out of which in turn evolved *Te Aomarama* (comprehended creation). The state of *Whaitua* emerges (the present tense is used to animate the narrative) with the recognition of space. There are several entities present. Among these are Rangi potiki and Papa who proceed to have offspring namely: Tane, Tu Matauenga (Tu for short), Rongomatane (Rongo for short) and Haumie tiketike (Haumie for short). The *korero tahito* ends.

In the Maori conception the creation is a great kin unit, and thus is thought of as having a genealogical structure. The genealogy begins with Te Kore. In the dialect of the Maori on the street of Ruatoria, the article *te* has both negative and positive meaning, rendering Te Kore as an ambiguous name or title. Te Kore can mean either 'The Nothing' or 'Not The Nothing', and in the Maori's thinking ambiguity is a trait of the super-being and superior things. For reasons I have been unable to ascertain, Te Kore is hardly mentioned, and the common reference is instead to Te Po. The *tohunga* Arnold Reedy when asked what Te Po was, replied: 'The never-ending beginning.'

Te Po is not thought of as object, or as context. It is said that Te Po is oneness, meaning among other things that Te Po is both object and context.

The employment of the genealogical framework means that to reach Te Po would take a journey in mind, and a return in spirit to former times. During such former times the awareness of our pre-human ancestors operated at the intuitive level only. The situation is sometimes likened to that of a person who is in the grip of sleep, and in that unconsciousness nevertheless senses that although it is night now, dawn is at hand.

Reproduction occurs at the intuitive level. Te Po logically would be the forebear of the Maori on the street in Ruatoria. However, the Maori has a strong impression that Te Po is not subject to logic, that Te Po is remote not only on account of the lapse of time but probably more importantly on account of magnitude. It is such as to appear to him to render it fanciful and perhaps even dangerous for him to contemplate Te Po as one of his pre-human ancestors. (The danger is not from Te Po whose magnitude and remoteness put in doubt an interest by Te Po in earthly activities and their performers. An assertion as to genealogical connection has the effect of boosting one spiritually, the boost being dependent on the spiritual level of the one being connected to genealogically. The danger is that at higher spiritual levels, different laws of nature operate and may not necessarily contribute to human survival.)

While Te Po is recognised as a superhuman controlling power, Te Po is not invoked as are some younger superhuman controlling powers. As far as the Maori is concerned the controlling power of Te Po is indirect, controlling those superpowers to whom we can relate directly.

The tamariki of Rangi and of Papa

The *tamariki* [*Tamariki* translates as 'children'. The word in fact refers to persons of the group who belong in the generational category to which one's natural children do or would have belonged. The group can be as large a one as the tribe] named are Tane, Tu, Rongo, Haumie and Tawhiri matea (Tawhiri for short). Tawhiri, son of Rangi, is half-brother to the others and is eldest. The *tamariki* perceive it is dark, their world consisting as it does of the valleys and hollows between the bodies of Rangi and Papa who are in close embrace. The feeling of cramp and a longing for light is general. There does not seem to be any prospect of change. Except for Tawhiri, the *tamiriki* agree to a proposal to separate Rangi and Papa, the former to be removed afar off and the latter to be retained as nurturing parent. [Rangi potiki and Papa, supported by Tawhiri, resist separation. This is the first time in the *korero tahito* that there is opposition to differentiation or expansion, and the intervening factor is *aroha* (love, sympathy). The separation is physical only. Rangi sends his *aroha* down in the rains which are his tears to Papa who responds by sending up her greetings at dawn in the rising mists. Although physically apart they are united in spirit, their *aroha* binding them as one. The saying that 'aroha is the one great thing' may have originated here, and it is tempting to suppose that some ancestors appreciated the process of condensation without which life on this planet as we know

243

it would not exist.] The retention of one parent is the idea of Tane, as is also the advice that force only adequate to accomplish separation and no more should be applied. All four brothers in turn attempt to bring about separation but it is Tane's effort alone that brings success and in that role he gains the title of Tane-toko-Rangi (Tane who sets Rangi asunder). [Tane, Tane mahuta, Tane-toko-Rangi and so on is similar to Dad, Mr Chairman at the Rugby Club meeting, Major in the army and so on: the same individual wearing different hats.] With the change in role the name of Rangi becomes Rangi nui (the sky) and that of Papa becomes Papa tuanuku (the earth).

Tawhiri brooding over the maltreatment of Rangi and of Papa projects thoughts that assume material form as the clouds, rains, sleet, storms. In the spirit of revenge Tawhiri unleashes these upon his brothers. They wreak havoc with all except Tu who withstands their assault. Tu, who had urged the others to present a united front against the assault, and who had been ignored, now turns upon his brothers and uses them for food and for his other needs. The *korero tahito* ends.

The addition to intuitive perception of sensory perception proves expansive and the plot of complex interrelationships is seen to thicken. Expression of experiences now requires physical terms such as cramp, but also emotional terms such as *aroha* (sympathy, love) and the feelings that make for the spirit of revenge. Possession by the *tamariki* of human attributes provides a basis for assuming that, exalted as they are, they are sufficiently human as to be approachable by the Maori. Sometimes as themselves, but more often in their forms as manifestations, the *tamariki* are recognised superhuman controlling powers. Thus Tane manifest as Tane mahuta (trees and birds) is invoked by those who have business in the forest. Rongo manifest as Rongomaraeroa (sweet potato) is invoked during the cropping season.

The purpose of religious activity here is to seek to enter the domain of the superbeing and do violence with impunity: to enter the forest and do some milling for building purposes, to husband the plant and then to dig up the tubers to feed one's guests. Thus that activity neither reaches for redemption and salvation, nor conveys messages of praise and thanksgiving, but seeks permission and offers placation.

From this *korero tahito* together with the Te Po one we see that humans consist of a tangible and an intangible part. Implicitly both originate in Te Po. The intangible part is *wairua* (soul). There is also the *mauri* (essence or potential) but how it relates to *wairua* is unclear. The word 'essence' is appropriate in that it conveys the idea of that which cannot be analysed further. The word 'potential' is appropriate in so far as it refers to the unrealised. *Mauri* construed very briefly in terms of power is *mana*. The privileges and constraints that accompany the possession of *mana* is the *tapu*. And the dread or awe that surrounds the possession of *mana* is *wehi*. A chief is often greeted with the words: *haere mai te mana te tapu me te wehi*, 'Welcome to the powerful, the privileged and the awesome.' The Maori on the street of Ruatoria speaks of the *mauri* of carving, the *mauri* of oratory and so on. And by that he means the spiritual climate that surrounds the carver and his carving, especially during the creative process, the spiritual climate that surrounds the orator and his words, especially during the moments of delivery.

Tane and Hine-aha-one (Earth Maiden)

Tane observed that the *tamariki* without exception were male and so set about redressing the imbalance. Using the female substance, the earth, Tane formed the first anthropomorphic female and mediated the spirit into her through his breath. He called this manageable female Hine-ahu-one and begat from her a daughter called Hine-titama. Tane took her to wife. One day she asked him who her father was, and his reply was that she might ask the walls of the house. [The walls of the house were of timber and Tane was referring to his many roles: the father, husband, giver of shelter and so on.] When she learned the answer she fled in shame and eventually arrived at Rarohenga, the underworld. [The shame did not, as is sometimes supposed, spring from the incest but from a violation by Tane of a fundamental principle of social relations, namely sharing. So long as there was only one woman Tane was entitled to her exclusively. As soon as there were more than one under his jurisdiction he was bound to share. This he failed to do.] Tane followed and implored her to return with him to the world of light. She declined, saying that she would remain to welcome their descendants into her bosom after the completion of their lives in the world of light and that he should return there and welcome them into it. Tane tearfully agreed. In her new role Hine-titama is called Hinenui-i-te-po (Great lady of te po). The *korero tahito* ends.

The *tamariki* lack the generative power and on this account there is some sense of failure. The Maori on the street of Ruatoria has only vague notions about the whole thing. The power that the *tamariki* lack is possessed by Hine-ahu-one who transmits it to her daughter Hine-titama. Hine-titama bears children for whom it is clear for the first time that this life has an end. Henceforth it may be said that people are born only to die and because of this the womb has sometimes been referred to as *te whare o te mate* (the house of death). The Maori on the street of Ruatoria is disinclined to subscribe to this piece of inverted logic. As descendant of Maui he knows the myth that tells how his ancestor met his end: strangled while attempting to enter the womb of the slumbering Hine-titama in her role as

Hine-nui-i-te-po. In his view it is an ignominious end. Some say Maui wished to return to the pre-born state and others that he wanted to obtain immortality. But the *korero tahito* about Ruaumoko tells us of man's innate wish to be born, and as for immortality, the *wairua* (soul) lives forever.

At the end of this life the physical part of the dead return, rather than proceed, to the bosom of the ancestress Hine-nui-i-te-po. The *po* in her name has made for an interpretation such as the 'grand lady of the night'. I wonder whether the reference is not Te Po – the 'grand lady of Te Po'? If this is so then the boundaries of Te Po lie on the other side of conception and through the doorway that is death. This interpretation of that part of her name seems to be borne out in the addresses made to the dead in the form of farewells and travelling directions: *haere atu ki ou tipuna te hanga tamoko kei Te Po* ('precede us to your ancestors, the tattooed ones at Te Po').

Tane and Tu

These two had contrasting personalities. Tane was peaceable and philosophic while his younger brother was aggressive and a man of action. The brothers clashed. For his part in that affair Tane was given the lordship of Tikitiki-nui-a-rangi – the fourth heaven – and with the role the title Tane-nui-a-rangi. [The creation includes many heavens and also basement levels. The numbers are in question; mention is made of twelve heavens and at least four basement levels. The higher the level the more spiritual the environment.] Tu for his part lost the power to travel to the different heavens. The *korero tahito* ends.

In retrospect we can trace the growth of expansion and can say that it is a propensity in the creation. It was present at the level of awareness or consciousness and then extended into the physical level; more specifically into the realm of bodily experience and of geographic realms.

In the Tane and Tu *korero tahito* the field of expansion is *mana*. The *mana* of Tu is in the temporal field; that of Tane-nui-a-rangi is in the divine field, with one foot nevertheless in the temporal field. This situation has not, however, been taken to mean that the flow of *mana* from the realm of Tane into that of Tu is more fluid than vice versa. This expansion is not expressed as a feeling or reaching toward a God or origin at this stage or for a long time to come. Emphasis is sometimes placed upon the element of confrontation, the situation that appears to have developed when the two *mana* came into contact. However, this *korero tahito* is not mentioned among explanations of the rites invoked when different *mana* are brought together; as for example, the rites invoked when visitor and host come together on the occasion of a *hui*.

Tane-nui-a-rangi

An information release from Naherangi – the eleventh heaven – reached Tane-nui-a-rangi; that three baskets of knowledge had been made available at Naherangi for the taking. Competition would be intense. The chances that Tane-nui-a-rangi would win the baskets appeared slight indeed, but of those closely associated with man's genealogical tree he was the one with the greatest chances of success in that venture. It transpired that Tane-nui-a-rangi was successful notwithstanding fierce harassment by Whiro, lord of one of the infernal regions. Tane-nui-a-rangi has the three baskets with him at the moment in his fourth heaven. The ancient explanation ends.

The source of much knowledge, the difficulties that were faced in order to obtain it, the willingness of no less than Tane-nui-a-rangi to face those difficulties, the high motivations required of students before they are considered fit persons to come in contact with knowledge of a superior kind, all these are indications that knowledge should be prized.

(I had thought that the significance of the number three – the number of baskets –would have struck people not in a numerical sense but as representing a balance of knowledge to enable one to live a balanced life. Like the three-fingered hands on many carvings, the three represents a useful, because balanced, piece of anatomy.)

Maui Tikitiki a Taranga

Taranga has a miscarriage and miscarriages are normally born dead. There was a social role for the dead foetus, and that was to provide the focal point for the rites to appease the soul thought to have been angered by this denial of the opportunity to live life. But this miscarriage has been born alive, and of course society has no role and therefore no place for the person whose time of arrival is not yet.

Taranga cut off her tikitiki – topknot – wrapped the foetus in it and flung the bundle into the sea. This is washed ashore in due course and morning finds the bundle entangled in kelp upon the beach. Sunshine causes the placenta encasing the foetus to shrink and strangulation is averted when a seagull pecks away the placenta. More dead than alive the foetus is espied by Tane-nui-a-rangi who removes it to Tikitiki-nui-a-rangi. The foetus survives as the child Maui-tikitiki-a-Taranga – Maui of the topknot of Taranga. Among other activities Maui delves into the three baskets of knowledge. When Maui is capable of deciding whether to remain in Tikitiki-nui-a-rangi or to return to the world of men he opts for the latter. The ancient explanation ends.

The abnormal circumstances in which Maui first sees light singles him out as unusual. The apparent withholding of his mother's personality to prop up his own during the first hours of life precludes him from being a social being. He is then denied a place on the breast of Papa tuanuku – a right of every human. Thus the gates opened to humans into this life have been shut in his face.

Physically too, the chances of enjoying life are waning. Nature itself seems to have reversed its function. The protecting placenta is threatening to strangle him, and the energy-giving rays of Tama-nui-te-ra (the sun) are threatening to deprive him of what scarce energy remains to him. Starved as well, it appears he is being discouraged from this life and forced to turn his face to the next. The reference to him as *my mokopuna*, by Tanenui-a-rangi, confirms that Maui is indeed more of the next world than of this. One with such a disposition is ready to delve into the baskets of knowledge.

Conclusion

Sir Apirana Ngata, considering in 1930 doing a doctorate in Maori social organisation, left as the introductory part of rough notes the following:

> The thesis is that after 140 years contact with the kind of civilisation the English brought to these islands there are indications that the Maori is settling down to a regime under which he finds he can exist side by side with the Pakeha [European] or at some distance from the Pakeha, not merely physically but rather socially, economically, morally and religiously so as to make the Maori communal life possible in the same country.

This chapter bears out Ngata's thesis, in respect at least of the Ngati Uepohatus during the 1980s.

Further reading

Alpers, A. 1964. *Maori Myths and Tribal Legends*. London: John Murray.
Best, E. 1982 [1924]. *Maori Religion and Mythology*, 2 parts. Wellington: Government Printer.
Binney, J., Chaplin, G. and Wallace, C. 1979. *Mihaia: The Prophet Rua Kenana and His Community at Maungapohatu*. Wellington: Oxford University Press.
Metge, J. 1976. *The Maoris of New Zealand*, rev. edn. London: Routledge &

Kegan Paul.

Reed, A.W. 1972. *Maori Myth and Legend*. Wellington: Reed.

Salmond, A. 1975. *Hui – A Study of Maori Ceremonial Gatherings*. Wellington: Reed.

Schimmer, E. 1996. *The World of the Maori*. Wellington: Reed.

Simmons, D. 1976. *The Great New Zealand Myth: A Study of the Discovery and Origin Traditions of the Maori*. Wellington: Reed.

11. He Taonga Tuku Iho, Hei Ara: A gift handed down as a pathway

Emma Webber-Dreadon

Editor's introduction

In addition to reinforcing the discussion of indigenous knowledges and their application, Emma Webber-Dreadon invaluably demonstrates the integration between contemporary spirituality and contemporary culture. Colonialism, modernity, industrialisation, and urbanisation have all generated problems to which one response has been the evolution of social work institutions, procedures, and methods. If modernity is permeated with dichotomous oppositions, social workers have to deal with far more messy realities. This has led to some of the theory and protocols of their activities being amenable to alternatives that might encourage the embrace of indigenous structures and practices. In that light, Webber-Dreadon provides

> a definitive description of an iwi ['tribal'] based community, a framework that has been developed which embraces traditional concepts of well-being and practice principles from the framework that could prove useful for social workers and supervisors when working with whanau, hapu and iwi.

A diagram powerfully encapsulates a series of dynamics, relationships, processes, influences, environments, and so on. It combines a spiral which 'embraces all and implies reflection' with a set of steps that 'implies connection and action'.

Reprinted from *Te Komako: Social Work Review*, New Zealand Association of Social Workers, 1997. By permission of Aotearoa New Zealand Association of Social Workers. The article was originally misprinted with the title 'Matua whakapai tou Marae, ka whakapai ai I te marae o tangata: First set in order your own marae before you clean another'.

Webber-Dreadon concludes:

Cultural frameworks of social work are diverse. All knowledge is culturally derived. Techniques and methods used in social work practice are diverse owing to the many cultures that exist. It is how a social worker practices those techniques and methods to promote positive change for tangata whenua [indigenous/local people] and other cultures. It is particularly important for social workers to know and accept the structures and practices of the tangata whenua, so that they can work in partnership towards more positive changes.

This is a profoundly positive and anti-colonial approach to the multicultural realities of contemporary New Zealand and to the bi-cultural lifeways of most Maori and, indeed, most indigenous people elsewhere. Some may dwell in a Fourth World suppressed by Old, New and/or Third World states and cultures. But many are integrated in other ways into late-/post-modernity. Thus, in a short article, Webber-Dreadon manages to convey a rich sense of the problems and the possibilities for indigenous peoples. In doing so she also provides an insight into the relevance of Maori traditional knowledges. Finally, she ends by citing a popular statement that resists the mystification of religion and the postponement of its rewards to an afterlife – religion is not (or at least not always) an opiate but (can be) an engagement and a provocation of further engagement with people:

Mau e ki mai, he aha te mea nui?
Maku e ki atu,
He tangata, he tangata, he tangata.

If you ask what is the greatest thing
I will tell you
It is people, people, people.
         (Taitokerau Whakatauki)

∾

What is offered in this article is some insights for when working with whanau, hapu and iwi, gained over time. What will be provided is a definitive description of an iwi-based community, a framework that has been developed which embraces traditional concepts of well-being and practice principles from the framework that could prove useful for social workers and supervisors when working with whanau, hapu, and iwi. My interpretation will be from a Ngati Kahungunu and Ngati Pahauwera

251

perspective and as such will discuss whanau, hapu, iwi in relation to community. The processes and procedures in the framework are based on a range of insights concerning positive change ideals. I will explain how the framework may assist a social worker promote positive change when working with whanau, hapu and iwi. Special acknowledgment to Paraiere Huata and Turoa Haronga, for the 'gifts' which have helped me form and shape this model.

Background

The continued lack of knowledge and misunderstanding of whanau, hapu and iwi concepts is an historic issue for Maori. Concern among Maori about the failure of social workers to develop their knowledge of Maori has gained momentum since the beginning of the nineteen eighties and more especially since the implementation of the Children, Young Persons and Their Families Act (1989). The institutional and community welfare dependency that varying governments and society in general have created over the years along with their continued lack of understanding and ignorance of Maori society, has economically, socially and spiritually alienated Tangata Whenua. As Ian Shirley points out: 'Welfare agencies ... had no understanding of Maori society, its values or its aspirations, and little appreciation of its support networks' (Shirley 1979: 101).

There are a number of definitions of community. For whanau, hapu, iwi, the concept of community is nothing new. A personal definition of a community is that it is a 'collective of people who share a common interest, language, rules, concerns, values and culture, and that in order to protect or preserve that interest or humanity, they work towards solving issues collectively.' The community has distinctive structure, culture, territorial boundaries and whakapapa (lineage). In other words the social organisation and structure of Maori society are based on kinship and the collective way in which they co-operate. Pearson recognises these basic concepts when stating, 'Maori settlement in New Zealand still represents the closest approximations to traditional concepts of community' (Pearson et al. 1990: 34).

Another writer accurately depicts the concept of a traditional hapu-based society when stating, 'Community stems from the Maori tradition of a decentralised, co-operative society' (Davey and Dwyer 1984: 6).

Awhiowhio Poutama: describing the framework

In the beginning, Io dealt in the realm of Te Korekore. Io spoke to his inner self and issued the command to create. Io laid the foundations for the universe, hence Papatuanuku (Mother earth) and Ranginui (Sky father) were created. Papatuanuku and Ranginui laid close together and they had many children. This was the beginning and they were seen as 'whaanau' (family). It was this mythical beginning, on which tangata whenua established their right to use the natural resources of the earth mother.

This right was further reinforced within the belief that tangata whenua were an integral part of nature and that it was their responsibility to take care of the whenua (land), and tangata (people). Tangata whenua see themselves as part of a whole universe and living in harmony and balance with their physical, spiritual and natural world (Department of Health 1984: 21). For this reason, I have used a conceptual view incorporating 'whakawhanaungatanga' (birth, the collective, collective birth) to create a framework '*Awhiowhio Poutama*', within an '*ecological contextual approach*' as described by Vygotsky (1978).

This is based on a 'Kopene' gifted to me by the people of Wairau. 'The spiral represents an eel on the bow of a canoe meaning "strength". The bird's head represents moving forward – going from strength to strength.' The Poutama embraced by Awhiowhio depicts the stairway to the twelve heavens, which contains the sacred gifts of knowledge and spirituality. This stairway represents empowerment and portrays action.

The Awhiowhio-Poutama is built on the foundations of Papatuanuku reaching up toward Ranginui, connected by the Mauri (the life force). The connection of Ranginui and Papatuanuku on which the foundations are built embraces the spiritual aspects and all that is on this earth. It is surrounded by wairua (inner spirit), hinengaro (emotions), tinana (the self), ihi (fierceness), wehi (alertness), and mana (self respect/self esteem).

Chief Judge Durie explains the spiral as a line that reaches out to turn back in on itself, spiralling inwards eventually reaching a consensus point at the centre. He goes on to liken it to decision making by Maori.

When we use the old way we sit around the hall looking to an empty space in at the centre and confronting one another. We emulate the circle. When we discuss the topic ... we talk around it ... It is rude to come too quickly to the point ... slowly, gradually ... taking on board everyone's thoughts en route, but circling inwards until eventually a consensus point is reached ... the koro says ... that the authority is in ourselves to make our own decisions affecting our own affairs, our own future and our own children ... the decisions we make must be made in a way that upholds group harmony. (Durie, 1986)

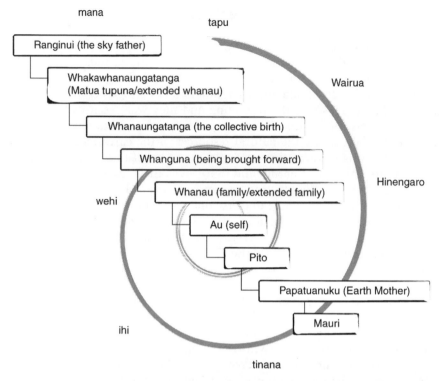

Figure 1: This Kopene is a representation of a taonga gifted to me by the people of Wairau. The spiral represents an eel on the bow of a canoe, meaning 'strength'. The bird's head represents 'To move forward'. 'To go from strength to strength'.

A similar structure is reflected in the Awhiowhio-Poutama. It espouses base principles of trust and collective decision making between the people and the social worker as giver/s and the receiver/s. Its primary philosophy is 'to link, strengthen and empower whanau, hapu, iwi, and to connect them by reciprocity and relationship'. All of these inter-relate, and connect the 'grass roots practice' and a 'place of learning'. Together, they portray knowledge (Past), reality (Present), and hope (Future). Using the framework enables one to maintain the connection between 'practice and theory'. The three main principles Awhiowhio is based upon are:

1. It embraces the 'au', the whanau and whakawhanaungatanga relationship, as well as connecting the past, present and future on its journey. Reflecting as it goes 'to look back is to look forward';

2. It is a method of gathering information to place into the kete in the

centre, so that it may assist with decision-making; and

3. The centre is where the issues are brought forward so that whanau, hapu, and iwi can make their own decisions.

When dealing with issues, the awhiowhio has a structure that comprises relatively formal rules. However, there are no hard and fast boundaries, so it can be adapted to suit the occasion.

The Poutama depicts the stairway to knowledge and spirituality and is embraced by the Awhiowhio. It represents empowerment and portrays action. Its value platforms are:

• practice what you preach

• climb or descend slowly and surely

• be honest in your endeavours

• remember those who have passed by, those who are here now and those to come.

With each step, the beginning at the pito (navel), the 'au' (I/me) changes as do the dimensions and relationships as they pertain to well-being.

This framework is not aimed at the individual, but at a collection of individuals both past and present, to which members have a responsibility to protect, collectively and individually. Hence *Respect* and *Responsibility* are the underpinning values. It is holistic in its application and includes a spiritual dimension. This allows autonomy for tangata whenua in decision making. If the Awhiowhio-Poutama fragments, it loses the 'mauri' that connects Ranginui and Papatuanuku. If this occurs, then we are no more.

Social work principles

A Social Worker has many roles within the realms of this 'framework' but the first and foremost principle is to take responsibility and allow the self empowerment (tino rangatiratanga) of whanau, hapu, iwi by whanau, hapu and iwi. It includes community participation realising that for some it is a journey recognising and acknowledging their being Maori. For some, the journey of self discovery is a path of reflection and absorption, believing in our tipuna and their processes and that they are valuable and valid. It is a social worker's role to promote 'collective action', so that whanau, hapu, and iwi can take part in making decisions and changes for themselves. This is illustrated by Paulo Freire:

> Go to the people, live with them learn from them, love them. Start with what
> they know. Build with what they have but with the best leaders. When the work
> is done, the task accomplished, the people will say we have done this for our-
> selves. (Hope 1984)

A social worker is merely the agent for change and in order to action that
responsibility one must know who they are, where they come from and
where they are going. They must know the issue of concern and the nature
of their relationship with the clients and whanau involved. Decisions by
whanau and social workers should not be made in isolation or without
support. It should include the participant/s and their whanau. The pro-
ceeding action will require respect and trust, so that the social worker may
be able to assist the people to reflect and action their decisions, so that they
may know it is their decision. As Freire states: 'A real humanist can be
identified more by his trust in the people, which engages him in their
struggle than by a thousand actions in their favour, without that trust'
(Freire 1970: 41).

Secondly, it is important for a social worker to recognise the process a
debate takes within a Maori setting. It is important to acknowledge that
decisions are made by consensus and in general agreement, after much
discussion and debate. As Walker states:

> In a whanau situation, each adult person is able to express a view. At hapu level
> designated persons presented the views of the hapu. At Iwi, the Hapu repre-
> sentatives drawn from the whanau groups are able to express the views of their
> Iwi. (Walker 1982: 69)

In a similar vein a Social Worker's contribution to a situation is evaluated
through those same members of whanau, hapu, iwi, based on the work
done, and how it is done. Self evaluation or an evaluation done by an
individual is inappropriate:

> Ehara taku toa I te toa takitahi engari he toa takitini taku toa.

> (My valour is not that of the individual but that of the multitude.)

Role of supervisors

Supervisors and managers in my experience have been unable to provide
good quality supervision from a bicultural or Maori holistic approach, due
to their lack of objectivity and colonial bias. It is suggested that when using
the Awhiowhio-Poutama framework, it is necessary that a dual or multi-

process of supervision be utilised. It would include three or more persons. The first being the supervisor involved, secondly tangata whenua knowledgeable in the area of social work, thirdly a kuia or kaumatua to enhance and add to the process. Any additional persons would be from a whanau concept and it is envisaged that all members would work together as a team.

The concept of whanau, hapu and iwi has became a powerful symbol of tangata whenua and as such individuals cannot be seen in isolation. The base 'solving' principle of individualist, or 'I' centred, statements needs to be re-aligned into the more communal or collective use of 'we' statements as illustrated by the Awhiowhio cultural framework. This whanau, hapu, iwi process is an everyday action for Maori Social Workers and is a further gift that enhances skills required for social work practice.

Other knowledge and skills requiring a cultural paradigm shift might include basic communication and interpersonal skills; facilitation, mediation, planning and organisational skills; time management, writing, assessment and negotiation skills; better knowledge of networks, the court system and interpretation of required legislation; human development and behaviour as it relates to Maori, and last but not least, knowledge of The Treaty of Waitangi and Puao Te-Ata-Tu.

Maori Social Workers may also need some of the above. Is your agency or organisation able to provide you, your supervisors and social workers with adequate training to enskill them toward practice excellence? Are they able to provide for the need to understand the concepts of whanau, whanaungatanga and whakawhanaungatanga, Io, Te Po, Nga kete o te matau-ranga Maori e toru, mauri, wehi, ihi, mana whare tangata, whakapapa, karakia, inoi, poutama, matakite, tohunga, kaumatua, kuia, kawa and so on?

Conclusion

Working for the common good and understanding of tangata whenua is the pathway to well-being. These tasks and skills inter-weave themselves around the values and attitudes, where they complement and create reliable and consistent work practices for social workers.

There are many challenges and opportunities that exist for community and social workers' delivery providing a service to whanau, hapu, iwi. Social work is an investment to our people at the 'knife-edge' of iwi development. Effective social work can only be practiced in circumstances of organisational integrity, where it will play an important part in the transformation of whanau, hapu, and iwi development. The reality being that if this is not achieved tangata whenua will effectively remain dependent upon government controlled bodies such as the Children, Young Persons and Their Families Service receiving a service from largely ineffective social workers.

Cultural frameworks of social work are diverse. All knowledge is culturally derived. Techniques and methods used in social work practice are diverse owing to the many cultures that exist. It is how a social worker practices those techniques and methods to promote positive change for tangata whenua and other cultures. It is particularly important for social workers to know and accept the structures and practices of the tangata whenua, so that they can work in partnership towards more positive changes.

Mau e ki mai, he aha te mea nui?
Maku e ki atu,
He tangata, he tangata, he tangata.

If you ask what is the greatest thing
I will tell you
It is people, people, people.
(Taitokerau Whakatauki)

References

Campbell, P. 1978. *History of Child Welfare in New Zealand*. Christchurch: Canterbury University.

Davey, J. and P. Dwyer. 1984. *Meeting Needs in the Community*. Wellington: New Zealand Planning Council.

Department of Health. 1984. *Hui Whakaoranga*. Waititi Marae, 19-22 March.

Department of Social Welfare. 1988. *Pua-Te-Ata-Tu*. Wellington: Department of Social Welfare.

Durie, E. T. 1986. 'Ancestral Law, Civil Law and the Law of Gifts' A speech given by Chief Judge Durie (at the return home of the) Te Maori Exhibition, Dominion Museum, Wellington, New Zealand. (SOWK811/511A Social Work Practice Workbook, Victoria University, Wellington.)

Freire, P. 1970. *Pedagogy of the Oppressed*. New York: Seabury Press.

Gilray, B. 1995. 'Challenges and Opportunities'. Paper prepared for an assignment at Massey University, Palmerston North.

Hope, A. 1984–. *Training for Transformation: A Handout for Community Workers*. Gweru: Mambo Press.

Pearson, D., P. Spoonley, and I. Shirley. 1990. *NZ Society: A Sociological Introduction*. Wellington: Victoria University. (SOWK831/521 Workbook.)

Shirley, I. 1979. *Planning for Community*. Palmerston North: Dunmore Press.

Vygotsky, L. S. 1978. *Mind in Society*. Cambridge, MA: Harvard University Press.

Walker, R. 1982. *Developmental Tracks: The Theory and Practice of Community Development*, Palmerston North: Dunmore Press.

12. 'Sun's Marbles' and 'Roimata'

Patricia Grace

Editor's introduction

Academic writing, flirting with authority and obsessed with footnotes, is rarely the best way to convey the flavour and passion of life or religion. The following extracts exemplify the wealth of recent creative writing by indigenous authors. They are included here in an attempt to encourage a more sensual response and understanding. In particular, the work of Patricia Grace enables a richer, more emotionally satisfying and intellectually stimulating, experience of Maori expertise with language and life.

'Sun's Marbles' opens *Sky People*, a collection of stories that form a tapestry resonating with the oratory of the *marae* and illuminating the present with the light of traditional knowledge. Risking a dangerous oversimplification, all such knowledge arises from primordial events in which potential is provided with increasing possibilities in which to unfold. The essence of everything, and the essences of each thing, find – or struggle to create – a place in which they can achieve for themselves and also pass on potential to others of their kind. The central characters in Grace's book, all 'sky people', are those precocious, sometimes capricious, troublesome, but engaging people who yearn for light, love, excellence and notoriety. Sometimes this results in terrible danger and appalling loss, but frequently generates further possibilities. Such risks are enfolded in the original act of intimate violence: the separation of FatherSky and MotherEarth. The concomitant opening of space for the couple's children is further made habitable by a much later generation (of humans this time, and indeed Maori) by the actions of Maui and his brothers in slowing Sun's journey across Sky. (This event is also portrayed/replicated on the cover of *Indigenous Religions: A Companion*.) Just like Cyrano de Bergerac in Rostand's (1996) 'heroic comedy', whose life (as performed on stage and film) is framed and encapsulated by the word 'panache', the lives of 'sky people' are replete with beauty, majesty, pain. Equally, the writing of their lives requires comedy and heroism in large measures.

If 'Sun's Marbles' might be considered to draw on what might be labelled 'myth', 'Roimata' powerfully conveys an experience-near sense of a typical Maori 'ritual'. Neither of these words ('myth' and 'ritual') should be assumed to be straight-forward or entirely adequate. They are both part of the vocabulary of academia seeking understanding and, clearly, not always succeeding. It is especially important in dealing with such terms that they are read as critical terms, tools of a discipline (i.e. a continuous contest and refinement of approaches) rather than 'native' or everyday words. To translate the terms into the latter would require a full con-sideration of the history and polemics of European histories and cultures – and a further contestation about the imposition of its discourse both 'at home' and 'abroad'. At any rate, in 'Roimata' Patricia Grace explores one woman's encounter with death and mourning. It might be usefully read alongside other material regarding Maori spirituality in this and its *Companion* volume (e.g. the latter explains some of the Maori language used here). It also expands material on ritual, especially those rituals that deal with mortality.

Reference

Rostand, Edmond. 1996 (1897). *Cyrano de Bergerac: A Heroic Comedy in Five Acts,* trans. Christopher Fry. Oxford: Oxford University Press.

കൈ

'Sun's Marbles'

When Maui booby-trapped Sun then clobbered him over the head with a hunk of bone shaped like two parts of a bootmaker's last, he won, for all time, high praise as the pioneer of daylight saving.

It was a surprise attack.

It was a violent act.

During the beating, which was resolute and prolonged, Sun lost some of his marbles, most of which went skittering out to stardom. Some, however, dropped to Earth, who caught them tidily, although she didn't really want them because she understood that these pretty things could be dangerous. But she was stuck with them. She couldn't send them back because Gravity was so lopsided, so she hid them deep in her pockets.

Earth had an instinct for hiding things. In the early days when she and Sky were close together, hiddenness had been a way of life. Everything had been hidden between these two. Light could not penetrate and there was no room to swing a cat's ancestor.

There was no 'above' and 'below' in those days. No direction was different from any other – no 'vertical', 'horizontal' or 'diagonal' as Earth and Sky rolled together in each other's arms. Or alternatively, every position was above or below, every direction was north, south, east and west, every angle was vertical, horizontal or diagonal. But there was no superiority and Challenge had not been born, even though there was an inkling of it in the minds of some of Earth and Sky's children. There was the potential.

Parents speak to each other in double language, spell out secrets so that children will not understand what they are talking about. But children get an inkling, if not of the content of the secret, then at least of the idea that there is a secret, something to be discovered, to be gleaned from whisperings if they keep on listening in the dark, keep adding one little piece of nothingness to another.

Earth and Sky were born out of Darkness and therefore knew about Light, and this was the secret they wanted to keep to themselves so that their children would remain children, keep their innocence and stay with them forever.

But the children were patient listeners, and blind, innocent and squashed between their ever-embracing parents as they were, they got to talking. The listeners and decoders of secret language among them had worked out that there was something else. There was something being kept from them by their parents and they would not be satisfied until they found out what it was. It was to do with otherness, other realms, the other side. It was when the children first talked to each other about these matters that Dissatisfaction was first expressed, but not clearly expressed and not clearly understood.

What came out of the discussion was that there was a desire by most of the children to have greater understanding. If they were to have greater understanding, then their known world had to be changed.

They had to get outside of it somehow, but they were bound on all sides by the locked bodies of their parents. They were squashed and breathless and realised they would have to separate their parents if they were to become free. How were they to do this from their position of powerlessness?

261

There were Plants, but none of them were upright and were only as vines creeping about in the dark. There was Water but it was stagnated and lifeless. There was Wind, but it was only as stale breath. Conflict, being a metaphor for People, was only the beginnings of an idea.

So the offspring of Sky and Earth began trying to move the parents away from each other, pushing, pulling, prising, but were not successful until Plant Life stopped creeping about, tried standing, then just kept on doing what it normally did – that is, grow – but from a different perspective. That's when Perspective and Direction began to be understood. After some eras Sky was lifted off Earth by upwardly mobile Plant Life and the children found out about Light.

Wind had been the dissenter from all this, and after the big event became angry with all those who had had anything to do with separating his mother and father. So he called up northerlies, southerlies, easterlies, westerlies, nor'westers, sou'easters, storms, hurricanes and tornadoes – and stirred up chaos amongst Plants and Waters and the Creatures who, now that there was Light and Space, had been released among them.

It was while Wind was having his tantrums that Earth realised that some of her kids needed protection against others, and she did her best to hide some of the less protected ones until it was safe for them to come out again. She had fought long and hard against being separated from Sky, but now that it was done she was determined to make the best of the situation.

Well, all this Light. All this Space. It was almost too much of a good thing. Plants and Creatures spread everywhere. Water became seas, lakes and rivers, and became inhabited by Swimmers. Eventually People made an appearance, but this didn't happen without a great deal of trauma, which included incest, personality change, family break-up and solo parenthood.

In spite of all this Earth and Sky did the best they could to be good providers. They tried to take an interest in what was happening.

When the latest addition came along, these People, Earth and Sky were fascinated, and pleased and thought that living apart and allowing Light and Space had some compensations after all. In fact they indulged these latest offspring, gave them free rein, but soon found that the more they were given the more they wanted.

These Johnny-come-latelies reckoned life would be better if they had a bit more daytime, even though they were told they should be grateful for what they had. In the olden days their ancestors had had no daylight at all. This kind of talk fell on deaf ears.

Anyhow Maui was the one who took up the cause on People's behalf. Maui was a foundling, who in his formative years hadn't known his true parentage; and he was born ugly, which didn't help matters. But to offset these seeming disadvantages he was of impeccable stock and had a mother who saw opportunities and was prepared to give him up at birth in order that his gifts be allowed to develop. Also, he was part human – a combination of Worldly and Other Worldly – so it was appropriate that he should be the one to act as a go-between for People.

In taking up the challenge to lengthen daylight he beat up Sun so badly that Sun hobbled about like an old koroua and from then on took many hours to travel across the face of Sky.

And that was when Earth, seeing the beating handed out to Sun, hid Sun's marbles away because she knew instinctively that they would be dangerous in the wrong hands. She knew that these latest, very demanding offspring were not mature enough to take responsibility for them.

Later on, this same Maui, who must have learned Irresponsibility from the human side of his genealogy, went to get Fire for his earthly cousins. Because of the immature way he handled the situation, Fire had to be sent to hide in the bodies of trees so that Maui and these earthlings wouldn't play fast and loose with it.

Anyway, these Teina, younger sisters and brothers of Winds, Waters, Plants, Animals, Birds, Insects, Reptiles and Fish, were really too big for their boots. Upstarts. In many ways they took after Maui, being Potiki, last born. Like Maui they had outsized attitude problems and didn't care what happened or who got hurt as long as they got their own way.

These ones had no idea of how to look after their own best interests either, and without the approval of those more mature and knowledgeable than themselves, began to change the order of things.

They began to kill their Tuakana – that is, their older brothers and sisters – without good reason, and to destroy their living places. The more powerful ones among them stole food and took over the living places of the less powerful ones of their own tribe too.

And they weren't satisfied with that. They'd heard about Sun's marbles and that Earth had hidden them somewhere. They knew they'd never be happy until they found them, and they began to search. They made great holes all over Earth, shifting or destroying Plants and Animals as well as the powerless members of their own tribe.

At last they found Sun's marbles in Earth's deepest pockets and with these they made objects in their own likeness – that is, they made objects capable of enormous destruction that were not able to be properly controlled. During the making of these objects there was so much waste that many of their own tribe had to be shifted away from their homes to make room for it, many had to run in fear of it. Many had nowhere to go and had to live with it. They became ill and maimed, gave birth to sick children, died painfully.

Sun could do nothing on the day when he rose, unaware, and was straightjacketed by Maui's snare. And when that bone came cracking down on him, chipping off bits, he could only hold tight and hope his days weren't ended.

Sky is no butterfingers and was deft in gathering in Sun's marbles, and though it was no accident that he allowed a few to go Earthward, he later came to regret this.

It was instinct that caused Earth to tuck these bright things away. Neither she nor Sky realised at the time that their children could become their enemies, or that they themselves could be enslaved. They were indulgent parents inclined to put unacceptable behaviour down to teething problems, hyperactivity, high intelligence, or precocity.

But later they began to ask themselves where they'd gone wrong. Was it because of their separation that these children had become so grasping, so out of control? Had Sky been too distant? Had Earth been too over-compensating? What could they have done about it anyway? Was it all a question of Light?

'Roimata'

Morning came slowly giving outline to the sea and hills, patterning the squares of houses, moulding the rocks, the power poles and the low scrub. At the far end of the beach around the wharekai, shadows were already moving.

The tide was low again and the birds were shifting, rising, calling, circling under the solid cloud, eyeing the water, dropping, turning, then rising again.

I took a towel from my bag and went down to the sea to wash. The night's cold was still on the water as I waded in. It was a salt cleansing that washed not only the road dust away. It was a discarding, or a renewal, like the washing of hands that takes leave of death and turns one toward the living.

I dressed and spread my towel on the ground to dry. There was more waiting to be done yet so I sat down where I could not be seen, or not recognised. I did not wish to enter the house of death alone so I waited for

Reprinted from *Potiki* by Patricia Grace, published in Great Britain by The Women's Press Ltd, 1995, 34 Great Sutton Street, London EC1V 0LQ. By permission of The Women's Press Ltd and Penguin Books (N.Z.) Limited.

other visitors that I knew would come.

At mid-morning I heard a bus approaching. It stopped up on the road behind me, and people in it began to stir. I knew that they would have been travelling for most of the night and would now be putting on warm clothing and folding their rugs, and that the women would be tucking greenery in under their headscarves.

The bus started up again and began to move slowly along past the houses to the end of the road where the people would get out, assemble, and wait to be called on to the marae.

I picked up my bag and followed the bus to the assembling place, where I greeted each person and was greeted by each in turn. They put the bag in the bus for me where I would leave it until the formalities were over. The sky had come closer to the earth and white sea was driving onto the shore. I was aware of hunger and glad of the awareness. At the wharenui the people had gathered under the verandah to call us to them.

The first call came and we were treading slowly across the marae. Call and countercall filled the space across the sacred ground, sky shrouded the hills, the sea gashed its forehead on the rocks as the rain began.

At the stomach of the marae we stopped to tangi for death, for the deaths from many ages and the deaths from all the many places, for all the many dead that gathered there with us. We wept for a particular death but I did not yet know whose death, in particular, we wept for. A glance had told me that it was one of Hemi's immediate family that had died as none of them was present on the verandah. They waited for us I knew, inside the house with their deceased.

Then we were called forward again, called in out of the rain. We stepped onto the verandah to remove our shoes, then into the house where we moved to the seating that had been arranged for us. In front of us were the people in dark clothing seated about the finely draped casket. There were the flowers and the photographs.

At one side of the casket were Granny Tamihana and Mary with their heads bowed, and on the other was Mary's older sister Rina, her aunts, and a woman and some children whom I did not know. Adjacent to us where I had not yet looked would be Hemi and his brother Stan with other members of the family.

Absent from among the mourners was Hemi's and Mary's mother, but she was present in the photographs against the wall, and what I knew by then was that she was present amongst us in death.

'Tihei maurimate ... '

And twelve years had never been.

'Come forward, come forward. Beach the great canoe of that place. Bring with you the many deceased from there, from that mountain and

265

that river, being the deceased of the many ages of the past and present and the many parts of this land. Many are the dead, as many as the myriads of stars. Assemble the many deceased from there, with the many deceased of the place where we now stand. Assemble them together with the singing bird who sleeps here now, so that they may all be wept for together ... '

The paua-shell eyes are many-coloured and vigilant. They encircle the world of day and the world of dreaming, and they encircle the assembled from all the places and from all ages. Twelve years had never been.

'Then go on your way, great ones, loved ones, from the many parts of the land. Return to the Homeland, following in the footsteps of those who have gone ahead, following in the footsteps marked out in the beginning. ...

'And now let there be joining – the dead to the dead, the living to the living. Let the strands fall together. We greet you the living. This hill calls to that mountain, this sea calls to that river, hear the calling. Let the strands fall together entwining so that we are one ... '

Behind the eyes the seas drummed, white birds lifted into the storm.

'You have gone
As the song bird
Flown,
But my foot is caught
In the root
Of the flower tree.

You have gone
And here I am
Alone,
The flowers fall
Like rain.'

Rain plunged against the roof and wind harried the doorway as one speaker followed another. Bodies moved and eyes glared in the known way, as the legacies of words were spoken and the chants were sung.

'We greet you, ground that we traversed. We greet you house of people, house of people from here ...

'And now
Lie here sister
In this ancestral house,
Listen to the sea sounds
And the crying of the hills,
Wrap death's fine cloak about you
And wrap about you also
Our words and tears,

Leave us then and go
Carried by the sounds of waters
The speakings of words
Go to the night everlasting
Where the many gather ...

'And living family we hear your call. We greet you and divide sorrow amongst all of us so that it may be lessened.

'We are split and empty
As the shell of the kihikihi
Which clings to the bole of a tree
But hear the cry
Tatarakihi tatarakihi.
We give you our greetings. Greetings to all of us.'

We stood and moved to greet the people, to hongi, to embrace, to tangi for this particular loss and for the fact of death. I moved gradually to greet and to tangi with old Granny Tamihana who had stood to carry out the arduous task of sorrowing, and then I moved to Mary who had not forgotten me. We pressed our noses, we kissed and embraced. 'Look at Mummy. She's so pretty. She's so nice. Is she, Roimata?'

I looked into the casket at the thin quiet face and dark hair. They had dressed her in a blouse of white chenille and lace, and pinned to it was a Mary of Sorrows medallion that I remembered she always wore. But that seemed so long ago. At her throat was a locket that she wore on special occasions, open now, and showing the tiny photographs of the son and daughter who had died as children. Covering her to the waist was the finely woven cloak with its feather border, and on top of that the mere pounamu. 'Pretty,' I said. Twelve years, but I had not forgotten how to talk to Mary. 'Pretty, and nice.'

The Sister and the aunts held me to them and we wept for all sorrow that had occurred since last we had met, but especially for this one. Then I greeted the woman and children that I did not know – but knowing that the woman could have been Hemi's wife, and that the children could be his. Hemi and I greeted each other formally, then held each other closely as we wept for the death of his mother, and for all death. Then I moved to greet his brother and cousins in a similar way.

As we went out to wash there was another group assembling at the edge of the marae.

13. A Declaration of the Independence of New Zealand and the Treaty of Waitangi

Editor's introduction

Self-expression, sovereignty, proactive engagement with modernity and colonization, and other manifestations of pride and/or assertions of prestige, are common
themes in contemporary indigenous discourse. However, they are often considered recent, non-traditional – and therefore 'inauthentic' – and even reactionary
changes in indigenous cultures. The following texts challenge such responses.

It is well known that relationships between the modern, colonizing nation states
and indigenous peoples are generally founded on treaties or other legal statements.
(That is, even the African/Atlantic slave trade was codified by legislation as if that
and force were the only kind of legitimation required.) It is equally well known that
such treaties and legalities have often been imposed by those states following some
degree of military conquest. And few people can be ignorant of the duplicity of
States and legislatures in ignoring, rescinding, or otherwise making a nonsense of
even those documents established on, and enshrining the sovereignty of both
parties. Perhaps the only question is whether people are aware of the continuing
dynamic by which indigenous sovereignty is diminished in confrontation with the
nations that envelope them now.

The following texts demonstrate that none of this is new. Firstly, in 1835 a
council of Maori leaders declared the Independence of New Zealand. In the presence of James Busby ('His Britannic Majesty's Resident'), two members of the
Church Missionary Society, and two British merchants, the Declaration was signed
by thirty-four chiefs. Busby signed a statement that reads:

> I certify that the above is a correct copy of the Declaration of the Chiefs, according to the
> translation of Missionaries who have resided ten years and upwards in the country; and it

is transmitted to His Most Gracious Majesty the King of England, at the unanimous request of the chiefs.

Further Rangatira, chiefs, added their signatures – a total of fifty-two by 22 July 1839. However, in 1840 a treaty was signed at Waitangi which has become the foundation not only of the nation state of New Zealand but also of the State's relationship with Maori, and also of Maori rights within the nation. For further discussion of the Treaty and its contemporary relevance, see Orange 1987.

What does this have to do with religion and the study of religion? Firstly, religion plays various interesting roles in the production and fate of these two documents. Both Maori and British signatories approached one another as spiritual as well as political and trading people. New Zealanders will, of course, be familiar with the difficulties that have ensued from differences between Maori and English versions of the Treaty. Much of the debate is around the intention of the signatories with regard to *mana* and its meanings. Again, this demonstrates the integral importance of religious worldviews and socio-economic and political relationships. Note that this point is made with reference to both British and Maori in the case of these documents. Even when 'religion' was being constructed as personal belief by elite ideologues, their actions demonstrated its inseparability from performance beyond the 'inner' and 'spiritual' realms they hypothesized. Almost any other treaty between European or Euro-colonial powers and indigenous peoples might have served a similar function.

Reference

Orange, Claudia 1987. *The Treaty of Waitangi*. Wellington: Bridget Williams Books.

෬ඁ෬

He Wakaputanga o te Rangatiratanga o Nu Tireni

A Declaration of the Independence of New Zealand

Text in Te Reo Maori

1. Ko matou, ko nga Tino Rangatira o nga iwi o Nu Tireni i raro mai o Hauraki kua oti nei te huihui i Waitangi i Tokerau i te ra 28 o Oketopa

1835, ka wakaputa i te Rangatiratanga o to matou wenua a ka meatia ka wakaputaia e matou he Wenua Rangatira, kia huaina, Ko te Wakaminenga o nga Hapu o Nu Tireni.

2. Ko te Kingitanga ko te mana i te wenua o te wakaminenga o Nu Tireni ka meatia nei kei nga Tino Rangatira anake i to matou huihuinga, a ka mea hoki e kore e tukua e matou te wakarite ture ki te tahi hunga ke atu, me te tahi Kawanatanga hoki kia meatia i te wenua o te wakaminenga o Nu Tireni, ko nga tangata anake e meatia nei e matou e wakarite ana ki te ritenga o o matou ture e meatia nei matou i to matou huihuinga.

3. Ko matou ko nga tino Rangatira ka mea nei kia huihui ki te runanga ki Waitangi a te Ngahuru i tenei tau i tenei tau ki te wakarite ture kia tika ai te wakawakanga, kia mau pu te rongo kia mutu te he kia tika te hoko-hoko, a ka mea hoki ki nga tauiwi o runga, kia wakarerea te wawai, kia mahara ai ki te wakaoranga o to matou wenua, a kia uru ratou ki te wakaminenga o Nu Tireni.

4. Ka mea matou kia tuhituhia he pukapuka ki te ritenga o tenei o to matou wakaputanga nei ki te Kingi o Ingarani hei kawe atu i to matou aroha nana hoki i wakaae ki te Kara mo matou. A no te mea ka atawai matou, ka tiaki i nga pakeha e noho nei i uta, e rere mai ana ki te hoko-hoko, koia ka mea ai matou kite Kingi kia waiho hei matua ki a matou i to matou Tamarikitanga kei wakakahoretia to matou Rangatiratanga.

Kua wakaaetia katoatia e matou i tenei ra i te 28 Oketopa, 1835, ki te aroaro o te Reireneti o te Kingi o Ingarani.

[The text is followed by the signatures or marks of 34 chiefs, dated 28 October 1835, followed by others until 52 had signed by 22 July 1839. These leaders represented Maori from North Cape to the River Thames.]

Text in English

1. We, the hereditary chiefs and heads of the tribes of the Northern parts of New Zealand, being assembled at Waitangi, in the Bay of Islands, on this 28th day of October, 1835, declare the Independence of our country, which is hereby constituted and declared to be an Independent State, under the designation of The United Tribes of New Zealand.

2. All sovereign power and authority within the territories of the United

Tribes of New Zealand is hereby declared to reside entirely and exclusively in the hereditary chiefs and heads of tribes in their collective capacity, who also declare that they will not permit any legislative authority separate from themselves in their collective capacity to exist, nor any function of government to be exercised within the said territories, unless by persons appointed by them, and acting under the authority of laws regularly enacted by them in Congress assembled.

3. The hereditary chiefs and heads of tribes agree to meet in Congress at Waitangi in the autumn of each year, for the purpose of framing laws for the dispensation of justice, the preservation of peace and good order, and the regulation of trade; and they cordially invite the Southern tribes to lay aside their private animosities and to consult the safety and welfare of our common country, by joining the Confederation of the United Tribes.

4. They also agree to send a copy of this Declaration to His Majesty the King of England, to thank him for his acknowledgement of their flag; and in return for the friendship and protection they have shown, and are prepared to show, to such of his subjects as have settled in their country, or resorted to its shores for the purposes of trade, they entreat that he will continue to be the parent of their infant State, and that he will become its Protector from all attempts upon its independence.

Agreed to unanimously on this 28th day of October, 1835, in the presence of His Britannic Majesty's Resident.

English witnesses –
(Signed) Henry Williams, Missionary, C.M.S.
        George Clarke, C.M.S.
        James C. Clendon, Merchant.
        Gilbert Mair, Merchant.

I certify that the above is a correct copy of the Declaration of the Chiefs, according to the translation of Missionaries who have resided ten years and upwards in the country; and it is transmitted to His Most Gracious Majesty the King of England, at the unanimous request of the chiefs.

(Signed)   JAMES BUSBY,
British Resident at New Zealand.

Te Tiriti o Waitangi

The Treaty of Waitangi

Text in Te Reo Maori

Ko Wikitoria te Kuini o Ingarani i tana mahara atawai ki nga Rangatira me nga Hapu o Nu Tirani i tana hiahia hoki kia tohungia ki a ratou o ratou rangatiratanga me to ratou wenua, a kia mau tonu hoki te Rongo ki a ratou me te Atanoho hoki kua wakaaro ia he mea tika kia tukua mai tetahi Rangatira – hei kai wakarite ki nga Tangata maori o Nu Tirani – kia wakaaetia e nga Rangatira maori te Kawanatanga o te Kuini ki nga wahikatoa o te wenua nei me nga motu – na te mea hoki he tokomaha ke nga tangata o tona Iwi Kua noho ki tenei wenua, a e haere mai nei.

Na ko te Kuini e hiahia ana kia wakaritea te Kawanatanga kia kaua ai nga kino e puta mai ki te tangata maori ki te Pakeha e noho ture kore ana.

Na kua pai te Kuini kia tukua a hau a Wiremu Hopihona he Kapitana te Roiara Nawi hei Kawana mo nga wahi katoa o Nu Tirani e tukua aianei amua atu ki te Kuini, e mea atu ana ia ki nga Rangatira o te wakaminenga o nga hapu o Nu Tirani me era Rangatira atu enei ture ka korerotia nei.

Ko te tuatahi

Ko nga Rangatira o te wakaminenga me nga Rangatira katoa hoki ki hai i uru ki taua wakaminenga ka tuku rawa atu ki te Kuini o Ingarani ake tonu atu – te Kawanatanga katoa o o ratou wenua.

Ko te tuarua

Ko te Kuini o Ingarani ka wakarite ka wakaae ki nga Rangatira ki nga hapu – ki nga tangata katoa o Nu Tirani te tino rangatiratanga o o ratou wenua o ratou kainga me o ratou taonga katoa. Otiia ko nga Rangatira o te wakaminenga me nga Rangatira katoa atu ka tuku ki te Kuini te hokonga o era wahi wenua e pai ai te tangata nona te wenua – ki te ritenga o te utu e wakaritea ai e ratou ko te kai hoko e meatia nei e te Kuini hei kai hoko mona.

Ko te tuatoru

Hei wakaritenga mai hoki tenei mo te wakaaetanga ki te Kawanatanga o te Kuini – Ka tiakina e te Kuini o Ingarani nga tangata maori katoa o Nu Tirani ka tukua ki a ratou nga tikanga katoa rite tahi ki ana mea ki nga tangata o Ingarani.

[signed] W. Hobson Consul & Lieutenant Governor

Na ko matou ko nga Rangatira o te Wakaminenga o nga hapu o Nu Tirani ka huihui nei ki Waitangi ko matou hoki ko nga Rangatira o Nu Tirani ka kite nei i te ritenga o enei kupu. Ka tangohia ka wakaaetia katoatia e matou, koia ka tohungia ai o matou ingoa o matou tohu.

Ka meatia tenei ki Waitangi i te ono o nga ra o Pepueri i te tau kotahi mano, e waru rau e wa te kau o to tatou Ariki.

[Signed at Waitangi on 6 February 1840, and subsequently further north and in Auckland. Over 200 signatures are appended but there is considerable debate about them.]

Text in English

Her Majesty Victoria Queen of the United Kingdom of Great Britain and Ireland regarding with Her Royal Favour the Native Chiefs and Tribes of New Zealand and anxious to protect their just Rights and Property and to secure to them the enjoyment of Peace and Good Order has deemed it necessary in consequence of the great number of Her Majesty's Subjects who have already settled in New Zealand and the rapid extension of Emigration both from Europe and Australia which is still in progress to constitute and appoint a functionary properly authorized to treat with the Aborigines of New Zealand for the recognition of Her Majesty's sovereign authority over the whole or any part of those islands – Her Majesty therefore being desirous to establish a settled form of Civil Government with a view to avert the evil consequences which must result from the absence of the necessary Laws and Institutions alike to the native population and to Her subjects has been graciously pleased to empower and to authorize me William Hobson a Captain in Her Majesty's Royal Navy Consul and Lieutenant Governor of such parts of New Zealand as may be or hereafter shall be ceded to Her Majesty to invite the confederated and independent Chiefs of New Zealand to concur in the following Articles and Conditions.

Article the first
The Chiefs of the Confederation of the United Tribes of New Zealand and the separate and independent Chiefs who have not become members of the Confederation cede to Her Majesty the Queen of England absolutely and without reservation all the rights and powers of Sovereignty which the said Confederation or Individual Chiefs respectively exercise or possess, or may be supposed to exercise or to possess over their respective Territories as the sole sovereigns thereof.

273

Article the second

Her Majesty the Queen of England confirms and guarantees to the Chiefs and Tribes of New Zealand and to the respective families and individuals thereof the full exclusive and undisturbed possession of their Lands and Estates Forests Fisheries and other properties which they may collectively or individually possess so long as it is their wish and desire to retain the same in their possession; but the Chiefs of the United Tribes and the individual Chiefs yield to Her Majesty the exclusive right of Preemption over such lands as the proprietors thereof may be disposed to alienate at such prices as may be agreed upon between the respective Proprietors and persons appointed by Her Majesty to treat with them in that behalf.

Article the third

In consideration thereof Her Majesty the Queen of England extends to the Natives of New Zealand Her royal protection and imparts to them all the Rights and Privileges of British Subjects.

[Signed] W. Hobson Lieutenant Governor

Now therefore We the Chiefs of the Confederation of the United Tribes of New Zealand being assembled in Congress at Victoria in Waitangi and We the Separate and Independent Chiefs of New Zealand claiming authority over the Tribes and Territories which are specified after our respective names, having been made fully to understand the Provisions of the foregoing Treaty, accept and enter into the same – in the full spirit and meaning thereof in witness of which we have attached our signatures or marks at the places and the dates respectively specified.

Done at Waitangi this Sixth day of February in the year of Our Lord one thousand eight hundred and forty.

[The English text was signed at Waikato Heads in March or April 1840 and at Manukau on 26 April 1840. Only thirty-nine chiefs signed. However, it became the official version.]

14. I am indigenist: Notes on the ideology of the Fourth World

Ward Churchill

Editor's introduction

Ward Churchill's own evaluation of this article says:

> What has been presented here has been only the barest outline, a glimpse of what might be called an 'indigenist vision.' I hope that it provides enough shape and clarity to allow anyone who wishes to pursue the thinking further to fill in at least some of the gaps I have not had the time to address, and to arrive at insights and conclusions of their own. Once the main tenets have been advanced, and I think to some extent that has been accomplished here, the perspective of indigenism is neither mystical nor mysterious.

According to Robert Allen Warrior, 'Though Churchill retains some concern in "I am Indigenist" with a unitary indigenous experience, he focuses much more on a definition of his ideology that relies on political practices rather than on consciousness' (Warrior 1995: 128).

That is, in previous writings (e.g. Churchill 1982), Churchill allegedly synthesizes indigenous consciousness and experience into a singular message (also see Ortiz 1982). Clearly there are commonalities in all experiences of being subject to colonialism and its various expressions of terror. The resonances with any other writing arising from resisting or confronting colonial power/terror are evident throughout this piece. Thus, although there are obvious differences between Churchill and Gerald Vizenor (e.g. Vizenor 1994) – as there are between Churchill

Reprinted from *The Z Papers*, Vol. 1, No. 3. By permission of the author.

and other indigenous writers confronting colonialism (e.g. see the diverse responses of Maori writers, Ihimaera 1998 and Smith 1999) – there is also common ground.

Churchill's vision is of a robust indigenous challenge to the image constructed and presented by modernity. This entails an insistence on the continuity of sovereignty held by indigenous nations alongside a call to enact that sovereignty in particular sociopolitical, cultural, and economic engagements. Churchill expands and expounds his message in other works that will repay reading (e.g. Churchill 1992 and 1994).

In the study of indigenous religions this essay has particular value in confronting stereotypes and insisting on the right to self-determination and self-expression. Churchill also names a variety of other significant 'indigenist' writers in a variety of genres. This expansion of voices and styles promises to enrich the study of religions which sometimes engages only with more 'mythological' tales. Irwin (1998) provides a similar incitement to expand our interaction with 'Native Voices in the Study of Native American Religions'. Activist and imaginative writings are complemented by autobiographies and biographies. These should lead to a more nuanced understanding of indigenous religions, especially if consulted alongside presentations in other media (e.g. 'ritual' and 'art').

References

Churchill, Ward. 1982. 'White Studies: The Intellectual Imperialism of Contemporary U.S. Education', *Integrateducation* 19(1-2): 51-7.

Churchill, Ward. 1992. *Fantasies of the Master Race: Literature, Cinema, and the Colonization of American Indians*, ed. M. Annette Jaimes. Monroe: Common Courage.

Churchill, Ward. 1994. *Indians Are Us? Culture and Genocide in Native North America*. Monroe: Common Courage.

Ihimaera, Witi (ed.). 1998. *Growing Up Maori*. Auckland: Tandem Press.

Irwin, Lee. 1998. 'Native Voices in the Study of Native American Religions', in *Critical Review of Books in Religion 1998*. Atlanta: Scholars Press, pp. 97-147.

Ortiz, Roxanne Dunbar. 1982. 'The Fourth World and Indigenism: Politics of Isolation and Alternatives', *Journal of Ethnic Studies* 12(1): 79-105.

Smith, Linda T. 1999. *Decolonizing Methodologies: Research and Indigenous Peoples*. Dunedin: University of Otago Press.

Vizenor, Gerald. 1994. *Manifest Manners: Postindian Warriors of Survivance*. Hanover: Wesleyan University Press.

Warrior, Robert Allen. 1995. *Tribal Secrets: Recovering American Indian Intellectual Traditions*. Minneapolis: University of Minnesota Press.

❧

The growth of ethnic consciousness and the consequent mobilization of Indian communities in the Western hemisphere since the early 1960s have been welcomed neither by government forces nor by opposition parties and revolutionary movements. The 'Indian Question' has been an almost forbidden subject of debate throughout the entire political spectrum, although racism, discrimination and exploitation are roundly denounced on all sides. (Roxanne Dunbar Ortiz)

Indians of the Americas

Very often in my writings and lectures, I have identified myself as being 'indigenist' in outlook. By this, I mean that I am one who not only takes the rights of indigenous peoples as the highest priority of my political life, but who draws upon the traditions – the bodies of knowledge and corresponding codes of value – evolved over many thousands of years by native peoples the world over. This is the basis upon which I not only advance critiques of, but conceptualize alternatives to the present social, political, economic, and philosophical status quo. In turn, this gives shape not only to the sorts of goals and objectives I pursue, but the kinds of strategy and tactics I advocate, the variety of struggles I tend to support, the nature of the alliances I am inclined to enter into, and so on.

Let me say, before I go any further, that I am hardly unique or alone in adopting this perspective. It is a complex of ideas, sentiments, and understandings which motivates the whole of the American Indian Movement, broadly defined, here in North America. This is true whether you call it AIM, or Indians of All Tribes (as was done during the 1969 occupation of Alcatraz), the Warriors Society (as was the case with the Mohawk rebellion at Oka in 1990), Women of All Red Nations, or whatever.[1] It is the spirit of resistance that shapes the struggles of traditional Indian people on the land, whether the struggle is down at Big Mountain, in the Black Hills, or up at James Bay, in the Nevada desert or out along the Columbia River in what is now called Washington State.[2] In the sense that I use the term, indigenism is also, I think, the outlook that

---

[1] For what is probably the best available account of AIM, IAT, and WARN, see Peter Matthiessen's *In the Spirit of Crazy Horse* (New York: Viking, (2nd ed.) 1991). On Oka, see Linda Pertusati, *In Defense of Mohawk Land: Ethnopolitical Conflict in Native North America* (Albany: State University of New York Press, 1997).

[2] On James Bay, see Boyce Richardson's *Strangers Devour the Land* (Post Mills, VT: Chelsea Green, (2nd ed.) 1991).

guided our great leaders of the past: King Philip and Pontiac, Tecumseh and Creek Mary and Osceola, Black Hawk, Nancy Ward and Satanta, Lone Wolf and Red Cloud, Satank and Quannah Parker, Left Hand and Crazy Horse, Dull Knife and Chief Joseph, Sitting Bull, Roman Nose and Captain Jack, Louis Ríel and Poundmaker and Geronimo, Cochise and Mangus, Victorio, Chief Seattle, and on and on.[3]

In my view, those, Indian and non-Indian alike, who do not recognize these names and what they represent have no sense of the true history – the reality – of North America. They have no sense of where they've come from or where they are and thus can have no genuine sense of who or what they are. By not looking at where they've come from, they cannot know where they are going or where it is they should go. It follows that they cannot understand what it is they are to do, how to do it, or why. In their confusion, they identify with the wrong people, the wrong things, the wrong tradition. They therefore inevitably pursue the wrong goals and objectives, putting last things first and often forgetting the first things altogether, perpetuating the very structures of oppression and degradation they think they oppose. Obviously, if things are to be changed for the better in this world, then this particular problem must itself be changed as a matter of first priority.

In any event, all of this is not to say that I think I am one of the significant people I have named, or the host of others, equally worthy, who've gone unnamed. I have no 'New Age' conception of myself as the reincarnation of someone who has come before. But it is to say that I take these ancestors as my inspiration, as the only historical examples of proper attitude and comportment on this continent, this place, this land on which I live and of which I am a part. I embrace them as my heritage, my role models, the standard by which I must measure myself. I try always to be worthy of the battles they fought, the sacrifices they made. For the record, I have always found myself wanting in this regard, but I subscribe to the notion that one is obligated to speak the truth, even if one cannot live up to or fully practice it. As Chief Dan George once put it, I 'endeavor to persevere,' and I suppose this is a circumstance which is shared more-or-less equally by everyone presently involved in what I refer to as 'indigenism.'

Others whose writings and speeches and actions may be familiar, and who fit the definition of indigenist – or 'Fourth Worlder,' as we are sometimes called – include Winona LaDuke and John Trudell, Simon Ortiz, Russell Means and Leonard Peltier, Glenn Morris and Leslie Silko, Jimmie Durham, John Mohawk and Oren Lyons, Bob Robideau and Dino

---

[3] While it is hardly complete, a good point of departure for learning about many of the individuals named would be Alvin M. Josephy's *The Patriot Chiefs* (New York: Viking, 1961).

278

Butler, Ingrid Washinawatok and Dagmar Thorpe. There are scholars and attorneys like Vine Deloria, Don Grinde, Pam Colorado, Sharon Venne, George Tinker, Bob Thomas, Jack Forbes, Rob Williams and Hank Adams. There are poets like Wendy Rose, Adrian Louis, Dian Million, Chrystos, Elizabeth Woody and Barnie Bush.

There are also many grassroots warriors in the contemporary world, people like the Dann sisters, Bernard Ominayak, Art Montour and Buddy Lamont, Madonna Thunderhawk, Anna Mae Aquash, Kenny Kane and Joe Stuntz, Minnie Garrow and Bobby Garcia, Dallas Thundershield, Phyllis Young, Andrea Smith and Richard Oaks, Margo Thunderbird, Tina Trudell and Roque Duenas. And, of course, there are the elders, those who have given, and continue to give, continuity and direction to indigenist expression; I am referring to people like Chief Fools Crow and Matthew King, Henry Crow Dog and Grampa David Sohappy, David Monongye and Janet McCloud and Thomas Banyacya, Roberta Blackgoat and Katherine Smith and Pauline Whitesinger, Marie Leggo and Phillip Deer and Ellen Moves Camp, Raymond Yowell and Nellie Red Owl.[4]

Like the historical figures I mentioned earlier, these are names representing positions, struggles, and aspirations which should be well-known to every socially-conscious person in North America. They embody the absolute antithesis of the order represented by the 'Four Georges' – George Washington, George Custer, George Patton and George Bush – emblemizing the sweep of 'American' history as it is conventionally taught in that system of indoctrination the United States passes off as 'education.' They also stand as the negation of that long stream of 'Vichy Indians'[5] spawned and deemed 'respectable' by the process of predation, colonialism, and genocide the Four Georges signify.

The names I have listed cannot be associated with the legacy of the 'Hang Around the Fort' Indians, broken, disempowered, and intimidated by their conquerors, or with the sellouts who undermined the integrity of their own cultures, appointed by the United States to sign away their peoples' homelands in exchange for trinkets, sugar, and alcohol. They are not the figurative descendants of those who participated in the assassination of people like Crazy Horse and Sitting Bull, and who filled the ranks of the colonial police to enforce an illegitimate and alien order against their own. They are not among those who have queued up to roster the régimes installed by the U.S. to administer Indian Country from the 1930s onward,

---

[4] The bulk of those mentioned, and a number of others as well, appear in *The Indigenous Voice: Visions and Realities*, 2 vols (London: Zed Books, 1988).

[5] The term 'Vichy Indians' comes from Russell Means. See his 'The Same Old Song,' in my *Marxism and Native Americans* (Boston: South End Press, (2nd ed.) 1989), pp. 19-33.

the craven puppets who to this day cling to and promote the 'lawful authority' of federal force as a means of protecting their positions of petty privilege, imagined prestige, and often their very identities as native people. No, indigenists and indigenism have nothing to do with the sorts of Quisling impulses driving the Ross Swimmers, Dickie Wilsons, Webster Two Hawks, Peter McDonalds, Vernon Bellecourts and David Bradleys of this world.[6]

Instead, indigenism offers an antidote, a vision of how things might be that is based in how things have been since time immemorial, and how things must be once again if the human species, and perhaps the planet itself, is to survive much longer. Predicated on a synthesis of the wisdom attained over thousands of years by indigenous, landbased peoples around the globe – the Fourth World or, as Winona LaDuke puts it, 'The Host World upon which the first, second and third worlds all sit at the present time' – indigenism stands in diametrical opposition to the totality of what might be termed 'Eurocentric business as usual.'[7]

Indigenism

The manifestation of indigenism in North America has much in common with the articulation of what in Latin America is called *indigenismo*. One of the major proponents of this, the Mexican anthropologist/activist Guillermo Bonfil Batalla, has framed its precepts this way: '[I]n America

---

[6] Ross Swimmer is an alleged Cherokee and former Philips Petroleum executive who served as head of the U.S. Bureau of Indian Affairs under Ronald Reagan and argued for suspension of federal obligations to Indians as a means of teaching native people 'self-reliance.' Dickie Wilson was head of the federal puppet government on Pine Ridge Reservation during the early 1970s, and while in this position, he formed an entity, called the GOONs, to physically assault and frequently kill members and supporters of AIM. Webster Two Hawks was head of the National Tribal Chairman's Association funded by the Nixon administration. He used his federally-sponsored position to denounce Indian liberation struggles. Peter McDonald – often referred to as 'McDollar' in Indian Country – utilized his position as head of the puppet government at Navajo to sell his people's interests to various mining corporations during the 1970s and '80s, greatly enriching himself in the process. Vernon Bellecourt is a former Denver wig stylist who moved to Minneapolis and became CEO of a state-chartered corporation funded by federal authorities to impersonate the American Indian Movement. David Bradley is a no-talent painter living in Santa Fe whose main claim to fame is in having made a successful bid to have the federal government enforce 'identification standards' against other Indian artists; he has subsequently set himself up as a self-anointed 'Identity Police,' a matter which, thankfully, leaves him little time to produce his typical graphic schlock. To hear them tell it, of course, each of these individuals acted in the service of 'Indian sovereignty.'

[7] See Winona LaDuke's 'Natural to Synthetic and Back Again,' the preface to Churchill, *Marxism and Native Americans*, pp. i–viii.

280

there exists only one unitary Indian civilization. All the Indian peoples participate in this civilization. The diversity of cultures and languages is not an obstacle to affirmation of the unity of this civilization. It is a fact that all civilizations, including Western civilization, have these sorts of internal differences. But the level of unity – the civilization – is more profound than the level of specificity (the cultures, the languages, the communities). The civilizing dimension transcends the concrete diversity.'[8]

The differences between the diverse peoples (or ethnic groups) have been accentuated by the colonizers as part of the strategy of domination. There have been attempts by some to fragment the Indian peoples ... by establishing frontiers, deepening differences and provoking rivalries. This strategy follows a principal objective: domination, to which end it is attempted ideologically to demonstrate that in America, Western civilization is confronted by a magnitude of atomized peoples, differing from one another (every day more and more languages are 'discovered'). Thus, in consequence, such peoples are believed incapable of forging a future of their own. In contrast to this, the Indian thinking affirms the existence of one – a unique and different – Indian civilization, from which extend as particular expressions the cultures of diverse peoples. Thus, the identification and solidarity among Indians. Their 'Indianness' is not a simple tactic postulated, but rather the necessary expression of an historical unity, based in common civilization, which the colonizer has wanted to hide. Their Indianness, furthermore, is reinforced by the common experience of almost five centuries of [Eurocentric] domination.[9]

'The past is also unifying,' Bonfil Batalla continues. 'The achievements of the classic Mayas, for instance, can be reclaimed as part of the Quechua foundation [in present-day Guatemala], much the same as the French affirm their Greek past. And even beyond the remote past which is shared, and beyond the colonial experience that makes all Indians similar, Indian peoples also have a common historic project for the future. The legitimacy of that project rests precisely in the existence of an Indian civilization, within which framework it could be realized, once the "chapter of colonialism ends." One's own civilization signifies the right and the possibility to create one's own future, a different future, not Western.'[10]

As has been noted elsewhere, the 'new' indigenist movement Bonfil Batalla describes equates 'colonialism/imperialism with the West; in

---

[8]   Guillermo Bonfil Batalla, *Utopía y Revolución: El Pensamiento Político Contemporáneo de los Indios en América Latina* (Mexico City: Editorial Nueva Imagen, 1981), p. 37; translation by Roxanne Dunbar Ortiz.

[9]   Ibid., pp. 37-8.

[10] Ibid., p. 38.

opposing the West ... [adherents] view themselves as anti-imperialist. Socialism, or Marxism, is viewed as just another Western manifestation.'[11] A query is thus posed: What, then, distinguishes Indian from Western civilization? Fundamentally, the difference can be summed up in terms of [humanity's] relationship with the natural world. For the West ... the concept of nature is that of an enemy to be overcome, with man as boss on a cosmic scale. Man in the West believes he must dominate everything, including other [individuals]. The converse is true in Indian civilization, where [humans are] part of an indivisible cosmos and fully aware of [their] harmonious relationship with the universal order of nature. [S]he neither dominates nor tries to dominate. On the contrary, she exists within nature as a moment of it ... Traditionalism thus constitutes a potent weapon in the [indigenous] civilization's struggle for survival against colonial domination.[12]

Bonfil Batalla contends that the nature of the indigenist impulse is essentially socialist, insofar as socialism, or what Karl Marx described as 'primitive communism,' was and remains the primary mode of indigenous social organization in the Americas.[13] Within this framework, he remarks that there are 'six fundamental demands identified with the Indian movement,' all of them associated with sociopolitical, cultural, and economic autonomy (or sovereignty) and self-determination:

First there is land. There are demands for occupied ancestral territories ... demands for control of the use of the land and subsoil; and struggles against the invasion of ... commercial interests. Defense of land held and recuperation of land lost are the central demands. Second, the demand for recognition of the ethnic and cultural specificity of the Indian is identified. All [indigenist] organizations reaffirm the right to be distinct in culture, language and institutions, and to increase the value of their own technological, social and ideological practices. Third is the demand for [parity] of political rights in relation to the state ... Fourth, there is a call for the end of repression and violence, particularly that against the leaders, activists and followers of the Indians' new political organizations. Fifth, Indians demand the end of family planning programmes which have brought widespread sterilization of Indian women and men. Finally, tourism and folklore are rejected, and there is a demand for true Indian cultural

---

[11] Roxanne Dunbar Ortiz, *Indians of the Americas: Human Rights and Self-Determination* (London: Zed Books, 1984) p. 83.

[12] Ibid. p. 84.

[13] For an excellent overview on the implications of Marx's thinking in this regard, see the first couple of chapters in Walker Connor's *The National Question in Marxist-Leninist Theory and Strategy* (Princeton, NJ: Princeton University Press, 1984).

expression to be respected. The commercialization of Indian music and dance are often mentioned ... and there is a particular dislike for the exploitation of those that have sacred content and purpose for Indians. An end to the exploitation of Indian culture in general is [demanded].[14]

In North America, these indigenista demands have been adopted virtually intact and have been conceived as encompassing basic needs of native peoples wherever they have been subsumed by the sweep of Western expansionism. This is the idea of the Fourth World explained by Cree author George Manuel, founding president of the World Council of Indigenous Peoples:

> The 4th World is the name given to indigenous peoples descended from a country's aboriginal population and who today are completely or partly deprived of their own territory and its riches. The peoples of the 4th World have only limited influence or none at all in the nation state [in which they are now encapsulated]. The peoples to whom we refer are the Indians of North and South America, the Inuit (Eskimos), the Sami people [of northern Scandinavia], the Australian aborigines, as well as the various indigenous populations of Africa, Asia and Oceana.[15]

Manuel might well have included segments of the European population itself, as is evidenced by the ongoing struggles of the Irish, Welsh, Basques and others to free themselves from the yoke of settler-state oppression imposed upon them as long as 800 years ago.[16] In such areas of Europe, as well as in 'the Americas and [large portions of] Africa, the goal is not the creation of a state, but the expulsion of alien rule and the reconstruction of societies.'[17]

That such efforts are entirely serious is readily evidenced in the fact that, in a global survey conducted by University of California cultural geographer Bernard Neitschmann from 1985 to 1987, it was discovered that of the more than 100 armed conflicts then underway, some 85 percent were being waged by indigenous peoples against the state or states which had laid claim to and occupied their territories.[18] As Theo van Boven, former director of the United Nations Division (now Center) for Human

---

[14] Dunbar Ortiz, *Indians of the Americas*, p. 85.

[15] George Manuel and Michael Posluns, *The Fourth World: An Indian Reality* (New York: Free Press, 1974).

[16] On the Irish and Welsh struggles, see Peter Berresford Ellis, *The Celtic Revolution: A Study in Anti-Imperialism* (Talybont, Wales: Y Lolfa, 1985). On the Basques, see Kenneth Medhurst, *The Basques and Catalans* (London: Minority Rights Group Report No. 9, Sept 1977).

[17] Dunbar Ortiz, *Indians of the Americas*, p. 89.

[18] Bernard Neitschmann, 'The Third World War,' *Cultural Survival Quarterly*, 11(3) (1987).

Rights, put it in 1981, the circumstances precipitating armed struggle 'may be seen with particular poignancy in relation to the indigenous peoples of the world, who have been described somewhat imaginatively – and perhaps not without justification – as representing the fourth world: the world on the margin, on the periphery.'[19]

The issue of land in North America

What must be understood about the context of the Americas north of the Río Grande is that neither of the nation-states, the United States and Canada, which claim sovereignty over the territory involved has any legitimate basis at all in which to anchor its absorption of huge portions of that territory. I am going to restrict my remarks in this connection mostly to the United States, mainly because that is what I know best, but also because both the United States and Canada have evolved on the basis of the Anglo-Saxon common law tradition.[20] So, I think much of what can be said about the United States bears a certain utility in terms of understanding the situation in Canada. Certain of the principles, of course, also extend to the situation in Latin America, but there you have an evolution of nation-states based on the Iberian legal tradition, so a greater transposition in terms is required.[21] The shape of things down south was summarized eloquently enough by the Peruvian freedom fighter Hugo Blanco with his slogan, 'Land or Death!'[22]

The United States, during the first ninety-odd years of its existence, entered into and ratified more than 370 separate treaties with the peoples indigenous to the area now known as the 48 contiguous states.[23] There are a number of important dimensions to this, but two aspects will do for our purposes here. First, by customary international law and provision of the

[19] Geneva Offices of the United Nations, Press Release, Aug. 17, 1981 (Hr/1080).

[20] For an excellent analysis of this tradition from an indigenist perspective, see Robert A. Williams, Jr., *The American Indian in Western Legal Thought: The Discourses of Conquest* (New York: Oxford University Press, 1990).

[21] On the Iberian legal tradition, see James Brown Scott, *The Spanish Origin of International Law* (Oxford: Clarendon Press, 1934).

[22] Hugo Blanco, *Land or Death: The Peasant Struggle in Peru* (New York: Pathfinder, 1972). Blanco was a marxist, and thus sought to pervert indigenous issues through rigid class analysis – defining Indians as 'peasants' rather than by nationality – but his identification of land as the central issue was and is nonetheless valid.

[23] The complete texts of 371 of these ratified treaties can be found in Charles J. Kappler (ed.), *American Indian Treaties, 1778-1883* (New York: Interland, 1973). The Lakota scholar Vine Deloria, Jr., has also collected the texts of several more ratified treaties which do not appear in Kappler, but which will be published in a forthcoming collection.

284

U.S. Constitution itself, each treaty ratification represented a formal recognition by the federal government that the other parties to the treaties – the native peoples involved – were fully sovereign nations in their ownright.[24] Second, the purpose of the treaties, from the U.S. point of view, was to serve as real estate documents through which the United States acquired legal title to specified portions of North America from the indigenous nations it was thereby acknowledging already owned it.

From the viewpoint of the indigenous nations, of course, these treaties served other purposes: the securing of permanently guaranteed borders to what remained of their national territories, assurance of the continuation of their ongoing self-governance, trade and military alliances, and so forth. The treaty relationships were invariably reciprocal in nature: Indians ceded certain portions of their land to the United States, and the United States incurred certain obligations in exchange.[25] Even at that, there were seldom any outright sales of land by Indian nations to the United States. Rather, the federal obligations incurred were usually couched in terms of perpetuity. The arrangements were set up by the Indians so that, as long as the United States honored its end of the bargains, it would have the right to occupy and use defined portions of Indian land. In this sense, the treaties more nearly resemble rental or leasing instruments than actual deeds. And what happens under Anglo-Saxon common law when a tenant violates the provisions of a rental agreement?

The point here is that the United States has long since defaulted on its responsibilities under every single treaty obligation it ever incurred with regard to Indians. There is really no dispute about this. In fact, there is even a Supreme Court opinion, the 1903 Lonewolf case, in which the good 'Justices' held that the United States enjoyed a 'right' to disregard any treaty obligation to Indians it found inconvenient, but that the remaining treaty provisions continued to be binding upon the Indians. This was, the high court said, because the United States was the stronger of the nations involved and thus wielded 'plenary' power – this simply means full power – over the affairs of the weaker indigenous nations. Therefore, the court felt itself free to unilaterally 'interpret' each treaty as a bill of sale rather than a rental agreement.[26]

---

[24] The constitutional provision comes at Article I, Section 10. Codification of customary international law in this connection is explained in Sir Ian Sinclair, *The Vienna Convention on the Law of Treaties* (Manchester: Manchester University Press, (2nd ed.) 1984).

[25] See generally, Vine Deloria, Jr., and Clifford E. Lytle, *American Indians, American Justice* (Austin: University of Texas Press, 1983).

[26] Lonewolf v. Hitchcock, 187 U.S. 553 (1903). For analysis, see Ann Laquer Estin, 'Lonewolf v. Hitchcock: The Long Shadow,' in Sandra L. Cawallader and Vine Deloria, Jr. (eds), *The Aggressions of Civilization: Federal Indian Policy Since the 1880s* (Philadelphia: Temple University Press, 1984), pp. 215-45.

Stripped of its fancy legal language, the Supreme Court's position was (and remains) astonishingly crude. There is an old adage that 'possession is nine-tenths of the law.' Well, in this case the court went a bit further, arguing that possession was all of the law. Further, the highest court in the land went on record boldly arguing that, where Indian property rights are concerned, might, and might alone, makes right. The United States held the power to simply take Indian land, they said, and therefore it had the 'right' to do so. This is precisely what the nazis argued only thirty years later, and the United States had the unmitigated audacity to profess outrage and shock that Germany was so blatantly transgressing against elementary standards of international law and the most basic requirements of human decency.[27]

For that matter, this is all that Sadam Hussein stood for when he took Kuwait – indeed, Iraq had a far stronger claim to rights over Kuwait than the United States has ever had with regard to Indian Country – with the result that George Bush began to babble about fighting a 'Just War' to 'roll back naked aggression,' 'free occupied territory,' and 'reinstate a legitimate government.' If he were in any way serious about that proposition, he would have had to call air strikes in on himself instead of ordering the bombing of Baghdad.[28]

Be that as it may, there are a couple of other significant problems with the treaty constructions by which the United States allegedly assumed title over its landbase. On the one hand, a number of the ratified treaties can be shown to be fraudulent or coerced, and thus invalid. The nature of the coercion is fairly well known; perhaps a third of the ratified treaties involved direct coercion. Now comes the matter of fraud, which assumes the form of everything from the deliberate misinterpretation of proposed treaty provisions to the Senate's alteration of treaty language after the fact and without the knowledge of the Indian signatories.

On a number of occasions, the United States appointed its own preferred Indian 'leaders' to represent their nations in treaty negotiations.[29] In at least one instance, the 1861 Treaty of Fort Wise, U.S. negotiators appear to

---

27 Probably the best exposition of the legal principles articulated by the U.S. as being violated by the nazis may be found in Bradley F. Smith, *The Road to Nuremberg* (New York: Basic Books, 1981).

28 A fuller enunciation of this thesis may be found in my 'On Gaining "Moral High Ground": An Ode to George Bush and the "New World Order",' in Cynthia Peters (ed.), *Collateral Damage: The 'New World Order' at Home and Abroad* (Boston: South End Press, 1992), pp. 359-72.

29 For the origins of such practices, see Dorothy V. Jones, *License for Empire: Colonialism by Treaty in Early America* (Chicago: University of Chicago Press, 1982). A good survey of U.S. adaptations will be found in Donald Worcester (ed.), *Forked Tongues and Broken Treaties* (Caldwell, ID: Caxton, 1975).

have forged the signatures of various Cheyenne and Arapaho leaders.[30] Additionally, there are about 400 treaties which were never ratified by the senate and were therefore never legally binding, but upon which the United States now asserts its claims concerning lawful use and occupancy rights to, and jurisdiction over, appreciable portions of North America.[31]

When all is said and done, however, even these extremely dubious bases for U.S. title are insufficient to cover the gross territoriality at issue. The federal government itself tacitly admitted as much during the 1970s in the findings of the so-called Indian Claims Commission, an entity created in 1946 to make 'quiet' title to all illegally taken Indian land within the lower 48 states.[32] What the commission did over the ensuing thirty-five years was in significant part to research the ostensible documentary basis for U.S. title to literally every square foot of its claimed territory. It found, among other things, that the United States had no legal basis whatsoever – no treaty, no agreement, not even an arbitrary act of Congress – to fully one-third of the area within its boundaries.[33]

At the same time, the data revealed that the reserved areas still nominally possessed by Indians had been reduced to about 2.5 percent of the same area.[34] What this means in plain English is that the United States cannot pretend to have even a shred of legitimacy in its occupancy and control of upwards of thirty percent of its 'home' territory. And, lest such matters be totally lost in the shuffle, I should note that it has even less legal basis for its claims to the land in Alaska and Hawai'i.[35] Beyond that, its 'right' to assert dominion over Puerto Rico, the 'U.S.' Virgin Islands, 'American' Samoa, Guam, and the Marshall Islands tends to speak for itself.

---

[30] The travesty at Fort Wise is adequately covered in Stan Hoig's *The Sand Creek Massacre* (Norman: University of Oklahoma Press, 1961), pp. 13-17.

[31] Deloria compilation, forthcoming.

[32] On the purpose of the commission, see Harvey D. Rosenthal, 'Indian Claims and the American Conscience: A Brief History of the Indian Claims Commission,' in Imre Sutton (ed.), *Irredeemable America: The Indians' Estate and Land* (Albuquerque: University of New Mexico Press, 1985, pp. 35-86). One must read between the lines a bit.

[33] Russel Barsh, 'Indian Land Claims Policy in the United States,' *North Dakota Law Review*, 58 (1982), pp. 1-82.

[34] The percentage is arrived at by juxtaposing the approximately fifty million acres within the current reservation landbase to the more than two billion acres of the lower 48 states. According to the Indian Claims Commission findings, Indians actually retain unfettered legal title to about 750 million acres of the continental U.S.

[35] Concerning Alaska, see M. C. Berry, *The Alaska Pipeline: The Politics of Oil and Native Land Claims* (Bloomington: Indiana University Press, 1975). On Hawai'i, see the Haunani-Kay Trask, *From a Native Daughter: Colonialism and Sovereignty in Hawai'i* (Monroe, ME: Common Courage Press, 1993).

Indian land recovery in the United States?

Leaving aside questions concerning the validity of various treaties, the beginning point for any indigenist endeavor in the United States centers, logically enough, in efforts to restore direct Indian control over the huge portion of the continental United States that was plainly never ceded by native nations. Upon the bedrock of this foundation, a number of other problems integral to the present configuration of power and privilege in North American society can be resolved, not just for Indians, but for everyone else as well. It is probably impossible to solve, or even to begin meaningfully addressing, certain of these problems in any other way. But still, it is, as they say, 'no easy sell' to convince anyone outside the more conscious sectors of the American Indian population itself of the truth of this very simple fact.

In part, uncomfortable as it may be to admit, this is because even the most progressive elements of the North American immigrant population share a perceived commonality of interest with the more reactionary segments. This takes the form of a mutual insistence upon an imagined 'right' to possess native property, merely because they are here, and because they desire it. The Great Fear is, within any settler-state, that if indigenous land rights are ever openly acknowledged, and native people therefore begin to recover some significant portion of their land, the immigrants will correspondingly be dispossessed of that which they have come to consider 'theirs' (most notably, individual homes, small farms, ranches and the like).

Tellingly, every major Indian land recovery initiative in the United States during the second half of the twentieth century – the Western Shoshone, those in Maine, the Black Hills, the Oneida claims in New York State are prime examples – has been met by a propaganda barrage from right-wing organizations ranging from the Ku Klux Klan to the John Birch Society to the Republican Party warning individual non-Indian property holders of exactly this 'peril.'[36]

I will debunk some of this nonsense in a moment, but first I want to take up the posture of self-proclaimed leftist radicals in the same connection. And I will do so on the basis of principle, because justice is supposed to matter more to progressives than to rightist hacks. Let me say that the pervasive and near-total silence of the left in this connection has been quite

---

[36] A good exposition on this phenomenon may be found in Paul Brodeur, *Restitution: The Land Claims of the Mashpee, Passamaquoddy, and Penobscot Indians of New England* (Boston: Northeastern University Press, 1985).

illuminating. Non-Indian activists, with only a handful of exceptions, persistently plead that they cannot really take a coherent position on the matter of Indian land rights because, 'unfortunately,' they are 'not really conversant with the issues' (as if these are tremendously complex).

Meanwhile, they do virtually nothing, generation after generation, to inform themselves on the topic of who actually owns the ground they are standing on. The record can be played only so many times before it wears out and becomes just another variation of 'hear no evil, see no evil.' At this point, it does not take Einstein to figure out that the left does not know much about such things because it has never wanted to know, or that this is so because it has always had its own plans for utilizing land it has no more right to than does the status quo it claims to oppose.

The usual technique for explaining this away has always been a sort of pro forma acknowledgment that Indian land rights are of course 'really important stuff' (yawn), but that one 'really does not have a lot of time' to get into it (I'll buy your book, though, and keep it on my shelf even if I never read it). Reason? Well, one is just 'overwhelmingly preoccupied' with working on 'other important issues' (meaning, what they consider to be more important things). Typically enumerated are sexism, racism, homophobia, class inequities, militarism, the environment, or some combination. It is a pretty good evasion, all in all. Certainly, there is no denying any of these issues their due; they are all important, obviously so. But more important than the question of land rights? There are some serious problems of primacy and priority imbedded in the orthodox script.

To frame things clearly in this regard, let us hypothesize for a moment that all of the various non-Indian movements concentrating on each of these issues were suddenly successful in accomplishing their objectives. Let us imagine that the United States as a whole were somehow transformed into an entity defined by the parity of its race, class and gender relations, its embrace of unrestricted sexual preference, its rejection of militarism in all forms and its abiding concern with environmental protection (I know, I know, this is a sheer impossibility, but that is my point).

When all is said and done, the society resulting from this scenario is still, first and foremost, a colonialist society, an imperialist society in the most fundamental sense and with all that this implies. This is true because the scenario does nothing at all to address the fact that whatever happens is on someone else's land, not only without their consent, but with an adamant disregard for their rights to the land. Hence, all it means is that the immigrant or invading population has rearranged its affairs in such a way as to make itself more comfortable at the continuing expense of indigenous people. The colonial equation remains intact and may even be reinforced by a greater degree of participation and vested interest in maintenance of the colonial order among the settler population at large.[37]

The dynamic here is not very different from that evident in the American Revolution of the late eighteenth century, is it? And we all know very well where that led. Should we therefore begin to refer to socialist imperialism, feminist imperialism, gay and lesbian imperialism, environmentalist imperialism, Afroamerican and la Raza imperialism? I would hope not.[38] I would hope this is all just a matter of confusion, of muddled priorities among people who really do mean well and who would like to do better. If so, then all that is necessary to correct the situation is a basic rethinking of what it is that must be done, and in what order. Here, I would advance the straightforward premise that the land rights of 'First Americans' should be a priority for anyone seriously committed to accomplishing positive change in North America.

But before I suggest everyone jump up and adopt this priority, I suppose it is only fair that I investigate the converse of the proposition: If making things like class inequity and sexism the preeminent focus of progressive action in North America inevitably perpetuates the internal colonial structure of the United States, does the reverse hold true? I will state unequivocally that it does not.

There is no indication whatsoever that a restoration of indigenous sovereignty in Indian Country would foster class stratification anywhere, least of all in Indian Country. In fact, all indications are that when left to their own devices, indigenous peoples have consistently organized their societies in the most class-free manner. Look to the Haudenosaunee (Six Nations Iroquois Confederacy) for an example. Look to the Muscogee (Creek) Confederacy. Look to the confederations of the Yaqui and the Lakota, and those pursued and nearly perfected by Pontiac and Tecumseh. They represent the very essence of enlightened egalitarianism and democracy. Every imagined example to the contrary brought forth by even the most arcane anthropologist can be readily offset by a couple of dozen other illustrations along the lines of those I just mentioned.[39]

Would sexism be perpetuated? Ask the Haudenosaunee clan mothers, who continue to assert political leadership in their societies through the present day. Ask Wilma Mankiller, recent head of the Cherokee Nation, a people who were traditionally led by what were called 'Beloved Women.'

---

[37] The problem is partially but insightfully examined in Ronald Weitzer, *Transforming Settler States: Communal Conflict and Internal Security in Zimbabwe and Northern Ireland* (Berkeley: University of California Press, 1992).

[38] It is entirely possible to extend a logical analysis in this direction. See, for instance, J. Sakai, *Settlers: The Mythology of the White Proletariat* (Chicago: Morningstar Press, 1983).

[39] Sharon O'Brien, *American Indian Tribal Governments* (Norman: University of Oklahoma Press, 1989).

Ask a Lakota woman – or man, for that matter – about who owned all real property in traditional society, and what that meant in terms of parity in gender relations. Ask a traditional Navajo grandmother about her social and political role among her people. Women in most traditional native societies not only enjoyed political, social, and economic parity with men, but they also often held a preponderance of power in one or more of these spheres.

Homophobia? Homosexuals of both genders were, and in many settings still are, deeply revered as special or extraordinary, and therefore spiritually significant, within most indigenous North American cultures. The extent to which these realities do not now pertain in native societies is exactly the extent to which Indians have been subordinated to the mores of the invading, dominating culture. Insofar as restoration of Indian land rights is tied directly to the reconstitution of traditional indigenous social, political, and economic modes, one can see where this leads; the Indian arrangements of sex and sexuality accord rather well with the aspirations of feminism and gay rights activism.[40]

How about a restoration of native land rights precipitating some sort of 'environmental holocaust?' Let us get at least a little bit realistic here. If one is not addicted to the fabrications of Smithsonian anthropologists about how Indians lived,[41] or George Weurthner's eurosupremicist Earth First! fantasies about how we beat all the woolly mammoths and mastodons and sabertoothed cats to death with sticks,[42] then this question is not even on the board. I know it has become fashionable among *Washington Post* editorialists to make snide references to native people 'strewing refuse in their wake' as they 'wandered nomadically' about the 'prehistoric' North American landscape.[43] What is this supposed to imply? That we, who were mostly 'sedentary agriculturalists' in any event, were dropping plastic and aluminum cans as we went?

As I said, let us get real. Read the accounts of early European invaders

---

[40] These matters are covered quite well in Janet Silman (ed.), *Enough Is Enough: Aboriginal Women Speak Out* (Toronto: Women's Press, 1987).

[41] The Smithsonian view of Indians has been adopted even by some of the more self-consciously 'revolutionary' organizations in the United States. For a classic example, see Revolutionary Communist Party, USA, 'Searching for the Second Harvest,' in Churchill, *Marxism and Native Americans*, pp. 35-58.

[42] The thesis is, no kidding, that Indians were the first 'environmental pillagers,' and it took the invasion of enlightened Europeans like the author of the piece to save the American ecosphere from total destruction by its indigenous inhabitants; George Weurthner, 'An Ecological View of the Indian,' *Earth First!* 7(7), Aug. 1987.

[43] Paul W. Valentine, 'Dances with Myths,' *Arizona Republic*, Apr. 7, 1991 (Valentine is syndicated, but is on staff at the *Washington Post*).

about what they encountered: North America was invariably described as being a 'pristine wilderness' at the point of European arrival, despite the fact that it had been occupied by fifteen or twenty million people enjoying a remarkably high standard of living for nobody knows how long. 40,000 years? 50,000 years?[44] Longer? Now contrast that reality to what has been done to this continent over the past couple of hundred years by the culture Weurthner, the Smithsonian and the *Post* represent, and you tell me about environmental devastation.[45]

That leaves militarism and racism. Taking the last first, there really is no indication of racism in traditional indigenous societies. To the contrary, the record reveals that Indians habitually intermarried between groups and frequently adopted both children and adults from other groups. This occurred in precontact times between Indians, and the practice was broadened to include those of both African and European origin, and ultimately Asian origin as well, once contact occurred. Those who were naturalized by marriage or adoption were considered members of the group, pure and simple. This was always the native view.[46]

The Europeans and subsequent Euroamerican settlers viewed things rather differently, however, and foisted off the notion that Indian identity should be determined primarily by 'blood quantum,' an outright eugenics code similar to those developed in places like Nazi Germany and apartheid South Africa. Now, that is a racist construction if there ever was one. Unfortunately, a lot of Indians have been conned into buying into this anti-Indian absurdity, and that is something to be overcome. But there is also solid indication that quite a number of native people continue to strongly resist such things as the quantum system.[47]

As to militarism, no one will deny that Indians fought wars among themselves both before and after the European invasion began. Probably

[44] A fine selection of such early colonialist impressions can be found in the first few chapters of Richard Drinnon's *Facing West: The Metaphysics of Indian Hating and Empire Building* (New York: Schocken, 1980). On the length of indigenous occupancy in the Americas, see George F. Carter, *Earlier Than You Think: A Personal View of Man in America* (College Station: Texas A&M University Press, 1980). On precontact population, see Henry F. Dobyns, *Their Number Become Thinned: Native American Population Dynamics in Eastern North America* (Knoxville: University of Tennessee Press, 1983).

[45] For a succinct but reasonably comprehensive survey of actual precontact indigenous material and intellectual realities, see Jack Weatherford, *Indian Givers: How the Indians of the Americas Transformed the World* (New York: Fawcett Columbine, 1988).

[46] Jack D. Forbes, *Black Africans and Native Americans: Race, Color and Caste in the Evolution of Red-Black Peoples* (New York: Oxford University Press, 1988).

[47] On federal quantum policy, see my essay, 'The Crucible of American Indian Identity: Native Tradition versus Colonial Imposition in Postconquest North America,' *American Indian Culture and Research Journal*, 22(2) 1998.

half of all indigenous peoples in North America maintained permanent warrior societies. This could perhaps be reasonably construed as 'militarism.' But not, I think, with the sense the term conveys within the European/ Euroamerican tradition. There were never, so far as anyone can demonstrate, wars of annihilation fought in this hemisphere prior to the Columbian arrival. None. In fact, it seems that it was a more-or-less firm principle of indigenous warfare not to kill, the object being to demonstrate personal bravery, something that could be done only against a live opponent. There is no honor to be had in killing another person, because a dead person cannot hurt you. There is no risk.

This is not to say that nobody ever died or was seriously injured in the fighting. They were, just as they are in full-contact contemporary sports like football and boxing. Actually, these kinds of Euroamerican games are what I would take to be the closest modern parallels to traditional Indian warfare. For us, it was a way of burning excess testosterone out of young males and not much more. So, militarism in the way the term is used today is as alien to native tradition as smallpox and atomic bombs.[48]

Not only is it perfectly reasonable to assert that a restoration of native control over unceded lands within the United States would do nothing to perpetuate such problems as sexism and classism, but the reconstitution of indigenous social standards that this would entail stands to free the affected portions of North America from such maladies altogether. Moreover, it can be said that the process should have a tangible impact in terms of diminishing such things elsewhere. The principle is this: Sexism, racism, and all the rest arose here as a concomitant to the emergence and consolidation of the eurocentric nation-state form of sociopolitical and economic organization. Everything the state does, everything it can do, is entirely contingent upon its maintaining internal cohesion, a cohesion signified above all by its pretended territorial integrity, its ongoing domination of Indian Country.

Given this, it seems obvious that the literal dismemberment of the nation-state necessary for Indian land recovery correspondingly reduces the ability of the state to sustain the imposition of objectionable policies within itself. It follows that realization of indigenous land rights serves to undermine or destroy the ability of the status quo to continue imposing a racist, sexist, classist, homophobic, militaristic order upon non-Indians.

A brief aside: Anyone with doubts as to whether it is possible to bring

---

[48] Probably the best examination of Indian warfare and 'militaristic' tradition is Tom Holm's 'Patriots and Pawns: State Use of American Indians in the Military and the Process of Nativization in the United States,' in M. Annette Jaimes (ed.), *The State of Native America: Genocide, Colonization and Resistance* (Boston: South End Press, 1992), pp. 345-70.

about the dismemberment from within of a superpower state in this day and age, ought to sit down and have a long talk with a guy named Mikhail Gorbachev. It would be better yet if one could chew the fat with Leonid Breznev, a man who we can be sure would have replied in all sincerity, only twenty years ago, that this was the most outlandish idea he'd ever heard. Well, look on a map today, and see if you can find the Union of Soviet Socialist Republics. It ain't there, folks. Instead, you are seeing – and you will see it more and more – the reemergence of the very nations Léon Trotsky and his colleagues consigned to the 'dustbin of history' clear back at the beginning of the century. These megastates are not immutable. They can be taken apart. They can be destroyed. But first we have to decide that we can do it and that we will do it.

So, all things considered, when indigenist movements like AIM advance slogans like 'U.S. Out of North America,' non-Indian radicals should not react defensively. They should cheer. They should see what they might do to help. When they respond defensively to sentiments like those expressed by AIM, what they are ultimately defending is the very government, the very order they claim to oppose so resolutely. And if they manifest this contradiction often enough, consistently enough, pathologically enough, then we have no alternative but to take them at their word: that they really are at some deep level or another aligned, all protestations to the contrary notwithstanding, with the mentality that endorses our permanent dispossession and disenfranchisement, our continuing oppression, our ultimate genocidal obliteration as self-defining and self-determining peoples. In other words, they make themselves part of the problem rather than becoming part of the solution.

Toward a North American union of indigenous nations

There are certain implications to Indian control over Indian land that need to be clarified, beginning with a debunking of the 'Great Fear,' the reactionary myth that any substantive native land recovery would automatically lead to the mass dispossession and eviction of individual non-Indian home owners. Maybe in the process I can reassure a couple of radicals that it is okay to be on the right side of this issue, that they will not have to give something up in order to part company with Pat Buchanan on this. It is hard, frankly, to take this up without giggling, because of some of the images it inspires. I mean, what are people worried about here? Do all of you really foresee Indians standing out on the piers of Boston and New York City, issuing sets of waterwings to long lines of non-Indians so they can all swim back to the Old World? Gimme a break.

294

Seriously, one can search high and low, and never find an instance in which Indians have advocated that small property owners be pushed off the land in order to satisfy land claims. The thrust in every single case has been to recover land within national and state parks and forests, grasslands, military reservations and the like. In some instances, major corporate holdings have also been targeted. A couple of times, as in the Black Hills, a sort of joint jurisdiction between Indians and the existing non-Indian government has been discussed with regard to an entire treaty area.[49] But even in the most hardline of the indigenous positions concerning the Black Hills – that advanced by Russell Means in his TREATY Program, where resumption of exclusively Lakota jurisdiction is demanded – there is no mention of dispossessing or evicting non-Indians.[50] Instead, other alternatives, which I will take up later, were carefully spelled out.

In the meantime, though, I would like to share with you something the right-wing propagandists never mention when they are busily whipping up non-Indian sentiment against Indian rights. Recall that I said that the quantity of unceded land within the continental United States makes up about one-third of the landmass? Let's just round this off to thirty percent, because there is the matter of 2.5 percent of the overall landbase still set aside as Indian reservations. Now juxtapose that thirty percent to the approximately 35 percent of the same landmass the federal government presently holds in various kinds of trust status. Add the ten or twelve percent of the land the individual states hold in trust. That adds up to a thirty-percent Indian claim against a 45 to 47 percent governmental holding.[51] Never mind the percentage of the land held by major corporations. Conclusion? It is, and always has been, quite possible to accomplish the return of every square inch of unceded Indian Country in the United States without tossing a single non-Indian homeowner off the land on which they live.

Critics – that is the amazingly charitable self-description employed by those who ultimately oppose the assertion of indigenous rights in any form and as a matter of principle – are always quick to point out that the problem with this arithmetic is that the boundaries of the government trust areas do not necessarily conform in all cases to the boundaries of unceded areas. That is true enough, although I would just as quickly point out that

---

[49] Referred to here is the so-called 'Bradley Bill' (S.1453), introduced before the Senate by Bill Bradley in 1987. For analysis, see the special issue of *Wicazo Sa Review* 14(1) (Spring 1988) devoted to the topic. Also see 'The Black Hills Are Not For Sale'.

[50] Russell Means and Ward Churchill, *TREATY: A Platform for Nationhood* (Porcupine, SD: TREATY Campaign, 1982).

[51] Barsh, 'Indian Land Claims'.

more often than not they do correspond. This 'problem' is nowhere near as big as it is made out to be. And there is nothing intrinsic to the boundary question which could not be negotiated once non-Indian America acknowledges that Indians have an absolute moral and legal right to the quantity of territory which was never ceded. Boundaries can be adjusted, often in ways which can be beneficial to both sides involved in the negotiation.[52]

Let me give you an example. Along about 1980, two Rutgers University professors, Frank and Deborah Popper, undertook a comprehensive study of land-use patterns and economy in the Great Plains region. What they discovered is that 110 counties – one quarter of all the counties in the entire Plains region falling within the western portions of the states of North and South Dakota, Nebraska, Kansas, Oklahoma, and Texas, as well as eastern Montana, Wyoming, Colorado, and New Mexico – have been fiscally insolvent since the moment they were taken from native people a century or more ago.

This is an area of about 140,000 square miles, inhabited by a widely dispersed non-Indian population of only around 400,000 attempting to maintain school districts, police and fire departments, road beds and all the other basic accoutrements of 'modern life' on the negligible incomes which can be eked from cattle grazing and wheat farming on land which is patently unsuited for both enterprises. The Poppers found that without considerable federal subsidy each and every year none of these counties would ever have been 'viable.' Nor, on the face of it, will any of them ever be. Bluntly put, the pretense of bringing Euroamerican 'civilization' to the Plains represents nothing more than a massive economic burden on the rest of the United States.

What the Poppers proposed on the basis of these findings is that the government cut its perpetual losses by buying out the individual land-holdings within the target counties and converting them into open space wildlife sanctuaries known as 'Buffalo Commons.' The whole area would in effect be turned back to the bison which were very nearly exterminated by Phil Sheridan's buffalo hunters back in the nineteenth century as a means of starving 'recalcitrant' Indians into submission. The result would, they argue, be both environmentally and economically beneficial to the nation as a whole.

It is instructive that such thinking has gained increasing credibility and support from Indians and non-Indians alike, beginning in the second half

---

[52] A number of examples may be found in Mark Frank Lindley's *The Acquisition and Government of Backward Country in International Law: A Treatise on the Law and Practice Relating to Colonial Expansion* (London: Longmans Green, 1926).

of the 1980s. Another chuckle here: Indians have been trying to tell non-Indians that this would be the outcome of fencing in the Plains ever since 1850 or so, but some folks have a real hard time catching on. Anyway, it is entirely possible that we will see some actual motion in this direction over the next few years.[53]

So, let us take the Poppers' idea to its next logical step. There are another hundred or so economically marginal counties adjoining the 'perpetual red ink' counties already identified. These do not represent an actual drain on the U.S. economy, but they do not contribute much either. They could be 'written off' and lumped into the Buffalo Commons with no one feeling any ill effects whatsoever. Now add in adjacent areas like the national grasslands in Wyoming, the national forest and parklands in the Black Hills, extraneous military reservations like Ellsworth Air Force Base, and existing Indian reservations. This would be a huge territory lying east of Denver, west of Lawrence, Kansas, and extending from the Canadian border to southern Texas, all of it 'outside the loop' of U.S. business as usual. The bulk of this area is unceded territory owned by the Lakota, Pawnee, Arikara, Hidatsa, Crow, Shoshone, Assiniboine, Cheyenne, Arapaho, Kiowa, Comanche, Jicarilla and Mescalero Apache nations. There would be little cost to the United States, and virtually no arbitrary dispossession or dislocation of non-Indians if the entire Commons were restored to these peoples. Further, it would establish a concrete basis from which genuine expressions of indigenous self-determination could begin to reemerge on this continent, allowing the indigenous nations involved to begin the process of reconstituting themselves socially and politically and to recreate their traditional economies in ways that make contemporary sense. This would provide alternative socioeconomic models for possible adaptation by non-Indians and alleviate a range of considerable costs to the public treasury incurred by keeping the Indians in question in a state of abject and permanent dependency.

Critics will undoubtedly pounce upon the fact that an appreciable portion of the Buffalo Commons area I have sketched out – perhaps a million acres or so – lies outside the boundaries of unceded territory. That is the basis for the sorts of multilateral negotiations between the United States and indigenous nations I mentioned earlier. This land will need to be 'charged off' in some fashion against unceded land elsewhere and in such a way as to bring other native peoples into the mix. The Poncas, Omahas, and Osages, whose traditional territories fall within the area in question,

[53] Probably the only accessible material to date on the Buffalo Commons idea is unfortunately a rather frothy little volume. Anne Matthews, *Where the Buffalo Roam: The Storm Over the Revolutionary Plan to Restore America's Great Plains* (New York: Grove Weidenfeld, 1992).

come immediately to mind, but this would extend as well to all native peoples willing to exchange land claims somewhere else for actual acreage in this locale. The idea is to consolidate a distinct indigenous territory while providing a definable landbase to as many different Indian nations as possible in the process.

From there, the principle of the Buffalo Commons cum Indian Territory could be extended westward into areas that adjoin or are at least immediately proximate to the Commons area itself. The fact is that vast areas of the Great Basin and Sonoran Desert regions of the United States are even more sparsely populated and economically insolvent than the Plains. A great deal of the area is also held in federal trust. Hence, it is reasonable, in my view at least, to expand the Commons territory to include most of Utah and Nevada, northern Montana and Idaho, quite a lot of eastern Washington and Oregon, most of the rest of New Mexico, and the lion's share of Arizona. This would encompass the unceded lands of the Blackfeet and Gros Ventre, Salish, Kutenai, Nez Percé, Yakima, Western Shoshone, Goshutes and Utes, Paiutes, Navajo, Hopi and other Pueblos, Mescalero and Chiricahua Apache, Havasupi, Yavapai and O'odam. It would also set the stage for further exchange negotiations to consolidate this additional territory in order to establish a landbase for a number of other indigenous nations.

At this point, we have arrived at an area comprising roughly one-third of the continental United States, a territory that, regardless of the internal political and geographical subdivisions effected by the array of native peoples within it, could be defined as a sort of 'North American Union of Indigenous Nations.' Such an entity would be in a position to assist other indigenous nations outside its borders but still within the remaining territorial corpus of the United States to resolve land claim issues accruing from fraudulent or coerced treaties of cession (another fifteen or twenty percent of the present 48 states).

It would also be in a position to facilitate an accommodation of the needs of untreatied peoples within the United States, the Abenaki of Vermont, for example, and the Hawaiian and Alaskan natives. Similarly, it would be able to help secure the self-determination of U.S. colonies like Puerto Rico. One can see the direction the dominoes would begin to fall.

Nor does this end with the United States. Any sort of indigenous union of the kind I have described would be as eligible for admission as a fully participating member of the United Nations as, say, Croatia and the Ukraine have recently shown themselves to be. This would set a very important precedent, insofar as there has never been an American Indian entity of any sort accorded such political status on the world stage.

The precedent could serve to pave the way for comparable recognition

298

and attainments by other Native American nations, notably the confederation of Incan peoples of the Andean highlands and the Mayans of
present-day Guatemala and southern Mexico (Indians are the majority
population, decisively so, in both locales), and from there, other indigenous nations elsewhere around the world. Again, one can see the direction
the dominoes would fall. If we are going to have a 'New World Order,' let
us make it something just a bit different from what George Bush and his
friends had in mind. Right?

Sharing the land

There are several closely related matters that should be touched upon
before wrapping this up. One has to do with the idea of self-determination
or what is meant when indigenists demand the unrestricted right for native
peoples. Most non-Indians, and even a lot of Indians, seem confused by
this and want to know whether it is not the same as complete separation
from the United States, Canada, or whatever the colonizing power may be.
The answer is 'not necessarily.'

The unqualified acknowledgment of the right of the colonized to total
separation ('secession') from the colonizer is the necessary point of
departure before any exercise of self-determination can occur. Decolonization means the colonized can then exercise the right to total separation in
whole or in part, as they see fit, in accordance with their own customs and
traditions, and their own appreciation of their needs. They decide for
themselves what degree of autonomy they wish to enjoy and thus the
nature of their political and economic relationship(s), not only with their
former colonizers, but with all other nations as well.[54]

My own inclination, which is in some ways an emotional preference,
tends to run toward complete sovereign independence, but this is not the
point. I have no more right to impose my preferences on indigenous
nations than do the colonizing powers; each indigenous nation will choose
for itself the exact manner and extent to which it expresses its autonomy,
its sovereignty. To be honest, I suspect very few would be inclined to adopt
my sort of 'go it alone' approach (and, actually, I must also admit that part
of my own insistence upon it often has more to do with forcing concession
of the right from those who seek to deny it than it does with putting it into
practice). In any event, I expect there would be the hammering out of a

---

[54] For one of the best elaborations of these principles, see Zed Nanda, 'Self-Determination in
International Law: Validity of Claims to Secede,' *Case Western Reserve Journal of International Law* 13 (1981).

number of sets of international relations in the 'free association' vein, a welter of variations of commonwealth and home rule governance.[55]

The intent here is not, no matter how much it may be deserved in an abstract sense, to visit some sort of retribution, real or symbolic, upon the colonizing or former colonizing powers. It is to arrive at new sets of relationships between peoples that effectively put an end to the era of international domination. The need is to gradually replace the existing world order with one that is predicated in collaboration and cooperation between nations. The only way to ever really accomplish this is to physically disassemble the gigantic state structures – structures that are literally grounded on systematic intergroup domination; they cannot in any sense exist without it – which are still evolving in this neoimperialist era. A concomitant of this disassembly is the inculcation of voluntary, consensual interdependence between formerly dominated and dominating nations and a redefinition of the word 'nation' itself to conform to its original meaning: bodies of people bound together by their bioregional and other natural cultural affinities.[56]

This last point is, it seems to me, crucially important. Partly, this is because of the persistent question of who gets to remain in Indian Country once land restoration and consolidation have occurred. The answer, I think, is, up to a point, anyone who wants to. By 'anyone who wants to' I mean anyone who wishes to apply for formal citizenship within an indigenous nation, thereby accepting the idea that s/he is placing him/herself under unrestricted Indian jurisdiction and will thus be required to abide by native law.[57]

Funny thing – I hear a lot of non-Indians asserting that they reject nearly every aspect of U.S. law, but the idea of placing themselves under anyone else's jurisdiction still leaves them pretty queasy. I have no idea how many non-Indians might actually opt for citizenship in an indigenous nation, but I expect there will be some. And I suspect some native people have been so indoctrinated by the dominant society that they will elect to remain within it rather than availing themselves of their own citizenship. So there will be a bit of a trade-off in this respect.

Now, there is the matter of the process working only 'up to a point.' This point is very real. It is defined not by political or racial considerations

---

[55] A prototype for this sort of arrangement exists between Greenland (populated mainly by Inuits) and Denmark; Gudmundur Alfredsson, 'Greenland and the Law of Political Decolonization,' *German Yearbook on International Law*, 25 (1982).

[56] Although my argument comes at it from a very different angle, the conclusion here is essentially the same as that reached by Richard Falk in his *The End of World Order: Essays in Normative International Relations* (New York: Holmes & Meier, 1983).

[57] This is the basic idea set forth in *TREATY*.

300

but by the carrying capacity of the land. The population of indigenous nations everywhere has always been determined by the number of people that could be sustained in a given environment or bioregion without overpowering and thereby destroying it.[58] A very carefully calculated balance, one that was calibrated to the fact that in order to enjoy certain sorts of material comfort human population must be kept at some level below saturation, was always maintained between the number of humans and the rest of the habitat. In order to accomplish this, native peoples have always incorporated into the very core of our spiritual traditions the concept that all life forms and the earth itself possess rights equal to those enjoyed by humans.

Rephrased, this means it would be a fundamental violation of traditional native law to supplant or eradicate another species, whether animal or plant, in order to make way for some greater number of humans or to increase the level of material comfort available to those who already exist. Conversely, it is a fundamental requirement of traditional law that each human accept his or her primary responsibility of maintaining the balance and harmony of the natural order as it is encountered.[59]

One is essentially free to do anything one wants in an indigenous society so long as this cardinal rule is adhered to. The bottom line with regard to the maximum population limit of Indian Country as it has been sketched in this presentation is some very finite number. My best guess is that a couple of million people would be pushing things right through the roof. Whatever. Citizens can be admitted until that point has been reached, and no more. And the population cannot increase beyond that number over time, no matter at what rate. Carrying capacity is a fairly constant reality; it tends to take thousands of years to change, if it changes at all.

Population and environment

What I am going to say next will probably startle a few people (as if what has been said already has not). I think this principle of population restraint is the single most important example Native North America can set for the rest of humanity. It is the thing that is most crucial for others to emulate.

[58] The concepts at issue here are brought out very well in William R. Catton, Jr., *Overshoot: The Ecological Basis of Revolutionary Change* (Urbana: University of Illinois Press, 1982).

[59] For further elaboration, see Vine Deloria, Jr., *God Is Red* (New York: Delta, 1973). The ideas have even caught on, at least as questions, among some Euroamerican legal practitioners; see Christopher D. Stone, *Should Trees Have Standing? Towards Legal Rights for Natural Objects* (Los Altos, CA: William Kaufman, 1972).

Check it out. I just read that Japan, a small island nation that has so many people they are literally tumbling into the sea, and that has exported about half again as many people as live on the home islands, is expressing 'official concern' that its birth rate has declined very slightly over the last few years. The worry is that in thirty years there will be fewer workers available to 'produce' and then to 'consume' whatever is produced.[60]

Ever ask yourself what is used in 'producing' something? Or what is being 'consumed'? Yeah. You got it. Nature is being consumed and with it the ingredients that allow ongoing human existence. While it is true that nature can replenish some of what is consumed, this can only be done at a certain rate. This rate has been vastly exceeded, and the excess is intensifying by the moment. An overburgeoning humanity is killing the natural world, and thus itself. It is no more complicated than that.[61] Here we are in the midst of a rapidly worsening environmental crisis of truly global proportions, every last bit of it attributable to a wildly accelerating human consumption of the planetary habitat, and we have one of the world's major offenders expressing grave concern that the rate at which it is able to consume might actually drop a notch or two. Think about it. I suggest that this attitude signifies nothing so much as stark, staring madness. It is insane, suicidally, homicidally, and ecocidally insane. And, no, I am not being rhetorical. I mean these terms in a clinically precise fashion. But I do not want to convey the impression that I am singling out the Japanese. I only used them as an illustration of a far broader pathology called 'industrialism' – or, more lately, 'postindustrialism' – a sickness centered in an utterly obsessive drive to dominate and destroy the natural order (words like 'production,' 'consumption,' 'development,' and 'progress' are no more than code words masking this reality).[62]

It is not only the industrialized countries that are afflicted with this disease. One by-product of the past five centuries of European expansionism and the resulting hegemony of eurocentric ideology is that the latter has been drummed into the consciousness of most peoples to the point where it is now subconsciously internalized. Everywhere, you find people thinking it 'natural' to view themselves as the incarnation of god on earth ('created in the image of God') and thus duty-bound to 'exercise dominion over nature' in order to 'multiply, grow plentiful, and populate the land' in ever

---

[60] CNN 'Dollars and Cents' reportage, May 27, 1992.

[61] The idea is developed in detail in Jeremy Rifkin's *Entropy: A New World View* (New York: Viking, 1980). It should be noted, however, that the world view in question is hardly new; indigenous peoples have held it all along.

[62] One good summary of this, utilizing extensive native sources – albeit many of them go unattributed – is Jerry Mander's *In the Absence of the Sacred: The Failure of Technology and the Survival of Indian Nations* (San Francisco: Sierra Club Books, 1991).

increasing 'abundance.'[63] The legacy of the forced labor of the latifundia and inculcation of Catholicism in Latin America is a tremendous over-burden of population who devoutly believe that 'wealth' can be achieved (or is defined) by having ever more children.[64] The legacy of Mao's implementation of a 'reverse technology' policy – the official encourage-ment of breakneck childbearing rates in his already overpopulated country, solely as a means to deploy massive labor power to offset capitalism's 'technological advantage' in production – resulted in a tripling of China's population in only two generations.[65] And then there is India ...

Make absolutely no mistake about it. The planet was never designed to accommodate six billion human beings, much less the ten billion predicted to be here a mere forty years hence.[66] If we are to turn power relations around between people and between groups of people, we must also turn around the relationship between people and the rest of the natural order. If we do not, we will die out as a species, just like any other species that irrevocably overshoots its habitat. The sheer number of humans on this planet needs to come down to about one quarter of what it is today, or maybe less, and the plain fact is that the bulk of these numbers are in the Third World.[67] So, I will say this clearly: not only must the birth rate in the Third World come down, but the population levels of Asia, Latin America, and Africa must be reduced over the next few generations, beginning right now.

Of course, there is another dimension to the population issue, one that is in some ways even more important, and I want to get into it in a minute. But first I have to say something else. This is that I do not want a bunch of Third Worlders jumping up in my face screaming that I am advocating 'genocide.' Bullshit. It is genocide when some centralized state or some colonizing power imposes sterilization or abortion on target groups. It is not genocide at all to recognize that we have a problem and take the logical steps ourselves to solve it. Voluntary sterilization is not a part of genocide.

[63] If this sounds a bit scriptural, it is meant to. A number of us see a direct line of continuity from the core imperatives of Judeo-Christian theology, through the capitalist secularization of church doctrine and its alleged marxian antithesis, right on through to the burgeoning tech-notopianism of today. This is a major conceptual cornerstone of what indigenists view as eurocentrism (a virulently anthropocentric outlook in its essence).

[64] The information is in André Gunder Frank's book, but the conclusion is avoided; André Gunder Frank, *Capitalism and Underdevelopment in Latin America: Historical Studies of Chile and Brazil* (New York: Monthly Review, 1967).

[65] See Jerome Ch'en, *Mao and the Chinese Revolution* (New York: Oxford University Press, 1967).

[66] Paul R. Ehrlich and Anne H. Ehrlich, *The Population Explosion* (New York: Simon and Schuster, 1990).

[67] Extrapolating from the calculations of Catton in *Overshoot*.

Voluntary abortion is not a part of genocide. And, most importantly, educating ourselves and our respective peoples to bring our birth rates under control through conscious resort to birth control measures is not a part of genocide.[68]

What it is is taking responsibility for ourselves again; it is taking responsibility for our destiny and our children's destiny. It is about rooting the ghost of the Vatican out of our collective psyches, along with the ghosts of Adam Smith and Karl Marx. It is about getting back in touch with our own ways, our own traditions, our own knowledge, and it is long past time that we got out of our own way in this respect. We have an awful lot to unlearn and an awful lot to relearn, and not much time in which we can afford the luxury of avoidance. We need to get on with it.

The other aspect of population I want to take up is that there is another way of counting. One way, the way I just did it, and the one that is conventionally done, is to simply point to the number of bodies or 'people units.' That is valid enough as far as it goes, but it does not really go far enough. This brings up the second method, which is to count by relative rate of resource consumption per body – the relative degree of environmental impact per individual – and to extrapolate this into people units.

Using this method, which is actually more accurate in ecological terms, we arrive at conclusions that are a little different than the usual notion that the most overpopulated regions on earth are in the Third World. The average resident of the United States, for example, consumes about thirty times the resources of the average Ugandan or Laotian. Since a lot of poor folk reside in the United States, this translates into the average yuppie consuming about seventy times the resources of an average Third Worlder.[69] Every yuppie born counts as much as another seventy Chinese.

Lay that one on the next soccer mom who approaches you with a baby stroller and an outraged look, demanding that you put your cigarette out, eh? It is plainly absurd for any American to complain about smoking when you consider the context of the damage done by overall U.S. consumption patterns. Tell 'em you'll put the butt out when they snuff the kid and not a moment before. Better yet, tell 'em they should snuff themselves, as well as the kid, and do the planet a real favor. Just 'kidding' (heh-heh).

Returning to the topic at hand: multiply the U.S. population by a factor of thirty – a noticeably higher ratio than either western Europe or Japan – in order to figure out how many Third Worlders it would take to have the

---

68 Sound arguments to this effect are advanced in Paul R. Ehrlich and Anne H. Ehrlich, *Population/Resources/Environment* (San Francisco: W. H. Freeman, 1970).

69 Paul R. Ehrlich and Anne H. Ehrlich, from their book *Healing the Earth*, quoted in CNN series *The Population Bomb*, May 1992.

same environmental impact. I make that to be 7.5 billion U.S. people units. I think I can thus safely say the most overpopulated portion of the globe is the United States.

Either the consumption rates really have to be cut in this country, especially in the more privileged social sectors, or the number of people must be drastically reduced, or both. I advocate both. How much? That is a bit subjective, but I will tentatively accept the calculations of William Catton, a respected ecologist and demographer. He estimated that North America was thoroughly saturated with humans by 1840.[70] So we need to get both population and consumption levels down to what they were in that year or preferably a little earlier. Alternatively, we need to bring population down to an even lower level in order to sustain a correspondingly higher level of consumption.

Here is where I think the reconstitution of indigenous territoriality and sovereignty in the West can be useful with regard to population. You see, land is not just land; it is also the resources within the land, things like coal, oil, natural gas, uranium, and maybe most important, water. How does that bear on U.S. overpopulation? Simple. Much of the population expansion in this country over the past quarter-century has been into the southwestern desert region. How many people have they got living in the valley down there at Phoenix, a place that might be reasonably expected to support 500?

Look at LA: twenty million people where there ought to be maybe a few thousand. How do they accomplish this? Well, for one thing, they have diverted the entire Colorado River from its natural purposes. They are siphoning off the Columbia River and piping it south. They have even got a project underway to divert the Yukon River all the way down from Alaska to support southwestern urban growth and to irrigate a proposed U.S. agribusiness penetration of northern Sonora and Chihuahua. Whole regions of our ecosphere are being destabilized in the process.

Okay, in the scenario I have described, the entire Colorado watershed would be in Indian Country, under Indian control. So would the source of the Columbia. And diversion of the Yukon would have to go right through Indian Country. Now, here's the deal. No more use of water to fill swimming pools and sprinkle golf courses in Phoenix and LA. No more watering Kentucky bluegrass lawns out on the yucca flats. No more drive-thru car washes in Tucumcari. No more 'Big Surf' amusement parks in the

---

[70] This would be about fifty million, or less than one-fifth the present U.S. population; Catton, *Overshoot*, p. 53.

middle of the desert. Drinking water and such for the whole population, yes.

Indians should deliver that. But water for this other insanity? No way. I guarantee that will stop the inflow of population cold. Hell, I will guarantee it will start a pretty substantial outflow. Most of these folks never wanted to live in the desert anyway. That's why they keep trying to make it look like Florida (another delicate ecosystem which is buckling under the weight of population increases).[71]

And we can help move things along in other ways as well. Virtually all the electrical power for the southwestern urban sprawls comes from a combination of hydroelectric and coal-fired generation in the Four Corners area. This is smack dab in the middle of Indian Country, along with all the uranium with which a 'friendly atom' alternative might be attempted and most of the low sulfur coal. Goodbye to the neon glitter of Las Vegas and San Diego. Adios to air conditioners in every room. Sorry about your hundred-mile expanses of formerly streetlit expressway. Basic needs will be met, and that's it.

This means we can also start saying goodbye to western rivers being backed up like so many sewage lagoons behind massive dams. The Glen Canyon and Hoover dams are coming down, boys and girls. And we can begin to experience things like a reduction in the acidity of southwestern rain water as facilities like the Four Corners Power Plant are cut back in generating time and eventually eliminated altogether. What I'm saying probably sounds extraordinarily cruel to a lot of people, particularly those imbued with the belief that they have a 'God-given right' to play a round of golf on the well-watered green beneath the imported palm trees outside an air-conditioned casino at the base of the Superstition Mountains. Tough. Those days can be ended without hesitation or apology.

A much more legitimate concern rests in the fact that a lot of people who have drifted into the southwest have no place to go to. The places they came from are crammed. In many cases, that's why they left. To them, I say there's no need to panic; no one will abruptly pull the plug on you or leave you to die of thirst. Nothing like that. But quantities of both water and power will be set at minimal levels. In order to have a surplus, you will have to bring your number down to a certain level over a certain period. At that point, the levels will again be reduced, necessitating another

---

[71] This is essentially the same argument, without ever quite arriving at the obvious conclusion, advanced by Marc Reisner in his *Cadillac Desert* (New York: Penguin, 1986).

population reduction. Things can be phased in over an extended period – several generations, if need be.[72]

Provision of key items such as western water and coal should probably be negotiated on the basis of reductions in population and consumption by the United States as a whole rather than simply the region served. This would prevent population shifts being substituted for actual reductions.[73] Any such negotiated arrangement should also include an agreement to alter the U.S. distribution of food surpluses and the like, so as to ease the transition to a lower population and a correspondingly greater self-sufficiency in hard-pressed Third World areas.

The objective inherent in every aspect of this process should be, and can be, to let everyone down as gently as possible from the long and intoxicating high that has beset so much of the human species in its hallucination that it, and it alone, is the only thing of value and importance in the universe. In doing so, and I believe only in doing so, can we fulfill our obligation to bequeath our grandchildren, and our grandchildren's grandchildren, a world that is fit (or even possible) to live in.[74]

I am indigenist

There are any number of other matters that should be discussed, but they will of necessity have to await another occasion. What has been presented here has been only the barest outline, a glimpse of what might be called an 'indigenist vision.' I hope that it provides enough shape and clarity to allow anyone who wishes to pursue the thinking further to fill in at least some of the gaps I have not had the time to address, and to arrive at insights and conclusions of their own. Once the main tenets have been advanced, and I think to some extent that has been accomplished here, the perspective of indigenism is neither mystical nor mysterious.

[72] A good deal of the impact could also be offset by implementing the ideas contained in John Todd and George Tukel, *Reinhabiting Cities and Towns: Designing for Sustainability* (San Francisco: Planet Drum Foundation, 1981).

[73] For purposes of comparison, see *Funding Ecological and Social Destruction: The World Bank and International Monetary Fund* (Washington, D.C.: Bank Information Center, 1990). By contrast, the concept described in the text might be dubbed 'Struggling for Ecological and Social Preservation.'

[74] Many indigenous peoples take the position that all social policies should be entered into only after consideration of their likely implications, both environmentally and culturally, for descendants seven generations in the future. Consequently, a number of seemingly good ideas for solving short-run problems are never entered into because no one can reasonably predict their longer-term effects. See Sylvester M. Morey (ed.), *Can the Red Man Help the White Man? A Denver Conference with Indian Elders* (New York: Myrin Institute, 1970).

In closing, I would like to turn again to the critics, the skeptics, those who will decry what has been said here as being 'unrealistic' or even 'crazy.' On the former score, my reply is that as long as we define realism, or reality itself, in conventional terms – the terms imposed by the order of understanding in which we now live – we will be doomed to remain locked forever into the present trajectory. We will never break free, because any order, any structure, defines reality only in terms of itself. Consequently, allow me to echo a sentiment expressed during the French student revolt of 1968: 'Be realistic; demand the impossible!'[75] If you read through a volume of American Indian oratory, and there are several available, you will find that native people have been saying the same thing all along.[76]

As to my being crazy, I would like to say thanks for the compliment. Again, I follow my elders and my ancestors – and R. D. Laing, for that matter – in believing that when confronted with a society as obviously insane as this one, the only sane posture one can adopt is what that society would automatically designate as crazy.[77]

I mean, Indians were not the ones who turned birthing into a religious fetish while butchering off a couple hundred million people with weapons of mass destruction and systematically starving another billion or so to death. Indians never had a Grand Inquisition, and we never came up with a plumbing plan to reroute the water flow on the entire continent. Nor did we ever produce 'leaders' of the caliber of Ronald Reagan, Jean Kirkpatrick and Ross Perot. Hell, we never even figured out that turning prison construction into a major growth industry was an indication of social progress and enlightenment. Maybe we were never so much crazy as we were congenitally retarded.

Whatever the reason – and please excuse me for suspecting it might be something other than craziness or retardation – I am indescribably thankful that our cultures turned out to be so different, no matter how much abuse and sacrifice it entailed. I am proud to stand inside the heritage of native struggle. I am proud to say I am an unreconstructable indigenist. For me, there is no other reasonable or realistic way to look at the world. And I invite anyone who shares that viewpoint to come aboard, regardless of your race, creed, or national origin.

Maybe Chief Seattle said it best back in 1854: 'Tribe follows tribe, and nation follows nation, like the waves of the sea. Your time of decay may be

[75] Allan Priaulx and Sanford J. Ungar, *The Almost Revolution: France, 1968* (New York: Dell, 1969).

[76] See, for example, Virginia Irving Armstrong (ed.), *I Have Spoken: American History Through the Voices of the Indians* (Chicago: Swallow Press, 1971).

[77] R. D. Laing, *The Politics of Experience* (New York: Ballantine, 1967).

distant, but it will surely come, for even the white man whose god walked with him and talked with him as friend with friend, cannot be exempt from the common destiny. We may be brothers after all. We will see.'[78]

---

[78] Armstrong, *I Have Spoken*, p. 79.

15. Australian icons: Notes on perception

Gordon Bennett

Editor's introduction

Problems of perception, portrayal, representation, reproducibility, visuality, and the sensuality and embodiedness of life and knowledge – and much more! – are the domain of artists. Certainly we need critical interventions and provocations such as those provided by Benjamin (1968), but someone who combines critical self-reflection with artistic creativity can be exceptionally illuminating. Gordon Bennett's essay is from an important, engaging, and stimulating book that announces a new project: 're-imagining art and colonialism in the Pacific'. It certainly provides more than a beginning to the project, offering a standard that others will find hard to follow. But in doing so it also calls for the re-imagination and re-consideration of art and colonialism (together and separately, and not alone) everywhere else.

    Gordon Bennett's art, itself, is significant (search the Internet and copious evidence of exhibitions and citations will be returned). His discussion of several significant works from a series is contextualized by consideration of his upbringing and conditioning, and that of other Australians – white and Aboriginal, or both at once, and others. It engages with the internationally recognized forms of European-Australian colonial art and of contemporary Central Desert Aboriginal art. It playfully combines reproduction (utilizing images of ships and stereotypical 'noble-savage' Aboriginal) from various media and cultural contexts (e.g. 'high' and 'popular'), and confronts the viewer with an implicit call for widespread re-construction.

Reprinted from *Double Vision: Art Histories and Colonial Histories in the Pacific*, ed. Nicholas Thomas and Diane Losche, Cambridge University Press, 1999. By permission of Cambridge University Press and the author.

The chapter is included here because it challenges notions of tradition, syncretism, authenticity, reproduction, representation, and a host of other themes that necessarily situate academic discourse in relationship(s) with colonialism. (Remember that opposition is as much a relationship as acquiescence or complicity.) For example, Bennett links the topographical art of Western Desert Aboriginal people ('they depict the landscape and events that happened within it') with his own 'psycho-topographical' work ('maps' of 'major icons of my cultural conditioning').

At the same time, but at a more basic level, perhaps, Bennett's chapter not only rewards reading alongside discussion of art in *Indigenous Religions: A Companion*, but also alongside discussion of place and 'the Dreaming' both there and in other chapters among these *Readings*. Interesting intersections also occur between this chapter and Pia Altieri's (2000) discussion of intellectual property rights, reproduction, and meaning in relation to Native American 'art'. It would also be of inestimable value to meditate on Bennett's chapter in concert with Diane Losche's 'The Importance of Birds' (1999) and other chapters in the volume both come from. Beyond any mere information or ethnography, these demonstrate the ubiquity of processes that academia has tended to attribute either solely to itself or solely to its indigenous alterities.

In short, these are chapters not only about art but also about the art of living and the arts of academia.

References

Altieri, Pia. 2000. 'Knowledge, Negotiation and NAGPRA: Reconceptualizing Repatriation Discourse(s)', in Peter Edge and Graham Harvey (eds), *Law and Religion in Contemporary Society: Communities, Individualism and the State*. Aldershot: Ashgate, pp. 129-49.

Benjamin, Walter. 1968. 'The Work of Art in the Age of Mechanical Reproduction', in *Illuminations: Essays and Reflections*. London: Pimlico, pp. 211-44.

Losche, Diane. 1999. 'The Importance of Birds: Or the Relationship between Art and Anthropology', in Nicholas Thomas and Diane Losche, *Double Vision: Art Histories and Colonial Histories in the Pacific*. Cambridge: Cambridge University Press, pp. 210-28.

In 1988 I began to paint the series *Notes on Perception* (see illustrations pages 313 and 314) after seeing a reproduction of a painting by Yala Yala

Gibbs Tjungurrayi. I was fascinated by the shimmering quality of the untitled work which was achieved with just black, white and red ochres. I decided that I would do a work on paper using a similarly restricted palette of red oxide, white and Paynes grey.

The paintings of the Western Desert Aboriginal people are topographical in that they depict the landscape and events that happened within it. Most paintings contain information about the relationships between people, land and Dreamtime beings and events. Traditionally ceremonial paintings contain information concerning the beliefs and laws by which order and continuity of Aboriginal societies are maintained. In other words, they are vehicles for a socialization and cultural conditioning process. A sense of one's identity and place in the world is thus constructed and maintained.

In thinking about my own cultural conditioning, in the so-called 'mainstream' of Australian culture, and how it was given continuity and reinforced by similar means – such as images, myths, stories in books, on television and at school – I reflected on how much my mind seemed to me like a landscape with the stream of my conscious, rational self traversing it and passing by the various sites of knowledge, images and memories that informed my sense of identity and my 'place' in the world I live in; a kind of 'psycho-topographical' map.

Since I had a strictly Euro-Australian upbringing and education I came to learn about Australian history and Aborigines with a Eurocentric bias and perspective. This Eurocentric perspective was particularly evident in the 1988 bicentennial celebrations. Throughout these celebrations specific events that were deemed important were re-enacted by people in period costume and broadcast on television, reproduced in magazines, comme-morated in books, and so on. The tall ships event is a case in point. The images of ships became important because they recalled the 'romance' of adventure and danger faced by the First Fleet, and the opening up of the 'New World' of unexplored territories for 'settlement' and exploitation.

Thus images of ships were being widely reproduced and contributing to the effect of reinforcing this nation's colonial identity; but what about the full story? The images being reproduced were a form of very selective memory that served to reinforce an even more selective history which I, and most 'mainstream' Australians, were taught in school and which was an unchallenged part of the mindset of popular culture. Thus during the bicentennial celebrations people wondered why the Aborigines were not celebrating, but protesting. Holes in one's education often lead to a lack of understanding.

I began the series *Notes on Perception* by selecting a detail, or reduced section, of a reproduced historical image; specifically, a painting of Captain Cook. I photocopied the selected part, enlarged it and then projected it

Australian Icon (Notes on Perception No. 1), 1989, Gordon Bennett, oil and acrylic on paper, 76 × 57 cm. Private collection. Photograph: Gordon Bennett.

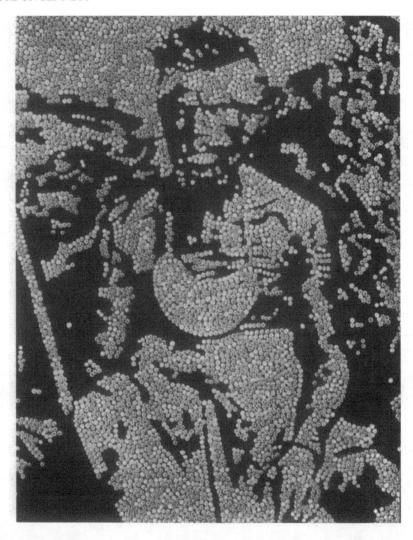

Australian Aborigines (Notes on Perception No. 4), 1989, Gordon Bennett, acrylic on paper, 66.5 × 52 cm. Private collection. Photograph: Gordon Bennett.

onto a piece of paper. I saw this as a kind of ritual practice that in a sense replicated, or even parodied, the selective process of a teleological historical perspective. I painted the image in the quick gestural brushstrokes of what may be termed a western art tradition. Then, in the spaces between the brushstrokes, I inserted dots (some of which were created by the photocopy enlargement process) in what many people refer to as an

Aboriginal art tradition. I combined Cook with an image of an Aborigine's head in classical 'noble savage' pose with face uplifted (from a beer coaster), and enclosed it in a box-like structure created by perspective lines that converged to a vanishing point in the centre of Cook's eye.

The resultant image I related to as a kind of psycho-topographical 'map' of two of the major icons of my cultural conditioning. I called the work *Australian Icon (Notes on Perception No. 1)*. I continued the series with images and details of nineteenth century photographic postcards that staged Aboriginal people in supposedly 'natural environments'. By re-contextualizing these images I gave them new meaning, placing them in another time and place and in new relationships to the present with its different sense of world view and the benefit of a critical distance to the time in which they were produced. I called these works *Australian Aborigines (Notes on Perception No. 2; 3; 4, and so on)*.

These works relate to the evolution of an Aboriginal stereotype – that is, what a 'real' Aborigine looks like. Everyone could, and still can, 'picture' an Aborigine in their mind's eye, and this picture has become the internalized icon against which contemporary Aborigines are measured. This is an ongoing problem for many people whose skin is never quite dark enough, or hair never quite curly enough, to satisfy some observers who feel that their stereotype overrides another person's self-definition.

The method of gestural brushstrokes and dots in the works on paper combine at close range to obscure the image. The image is dissolved in brushstrokes and dots until one steps back a short distance from the surface to find the image 'reveals' itself. This is important in that it is essentially one's mind that constructs the image out of the mass of data, which is paint on a surface perceived by the means of sight. What the mind constructs is based on the past learnt experience of cultural conditioning and culturally relative knowledge.

Australian Icon (Notes on Perception No. 6) is a detail from a larger work depicting a ship in a storm. Which particular ship is unimportant. It is its 'shipness' that is important. Up close to the image it is difficult to determine anything except paint on a surface. At a distance the ship will appear as the mind recognizes and constructs it. The observer sees a sailing ship because of the mind's perception of 'shipness' - the image resembles what a sailing ship is supposed to look like based on previous experience of sailing ships, or images of them. What the image of a ship means to the observer is relative to that person's cultural associations as to their purpose, historical context, and so on.

When viewed by an observer familiar with Australian history, a ship is very likely to be interpreted in relation to the First Fleet, or even Captain Cook's *Endeavour*, especially when the image was produced in the year after the bicentenary, as was *Notes on Perception No. 6*. From the *Notes on Perception* series of works on paper, or 'drawings' as they may be referred to, I selected particular images for larger works on canvas. The ship image in *Australian Icon,* the same as in *Notes on Perception No. 6,* was chosen specifically to evoke the romantic notions of adventure, danger, exploration and discovery that forms a major part of the mythology informing an Australian 'mainstream' identity. This series is part of an overall body of work that is dealing with the deconstruction of my 'mainstream' Australian identity, as it was constructed through the culture in which I was born and raised, and its relationship to my 'Aboriginality', which was an inheritance through my mother's lineage – but also an identity constructed solely within the parameters of a Eurocentric perspective.

I believe this process I have undertaken to be relative to the greater Australian context of black and white relationships, insofar as I am a measure of 'mainstream' Australia, given the shared environment of Anglo-Celtic cultural conditioning, and the socialization process of my upbringing and my experience of, and even participation in, the racially biased beliefs of popular Australian culture.

Part IV
Land

16. Sacred site, ancestral clearing, and environmental ethics

Deborah Bird Rose

Editor's introduction

Environmentalism has generated a vast and often passionate literature. Much of this explicitly focuses on the degree to which indigenous peoples have, or have not, been environmentally friendly (or 'green') – a concern often motivated by a quest for resources for ecological motivation and mobilization. Whether this is just must be questioned, given the pervasive link between genocide and ecocide in colonialism, and given the systemic disenfranchisement of indigenous peoples globally. It is also linked to a perennial interest of academia in (other) people's cosmology or understanding of their place in the scheme of things. A third position, both mediating between and also entwined with some cosmologies and environmentalisms, is what Hong-key Yoon calls 'geomentality', explaining that he uses it to refer to

> an established manner (mentality) or taken-for-granted way of cognising the environment which conditions humanity–nature relationships: namely, the mentality regarding geographical environment which is held by a group of people or an individual. Geomentality is

Reprinted from *Emplaced Myth: Space, Narrative, and Knowledge in Aboriginal Australia and Papua New Guinea*, ed. Alan Rumsey and James F. Weiner, University of Hawai'i Press. By permission of the author. The 'Myths to Minerals' conference was a stimulating event; I am grateful to Alan Rumsey and Jimmy Weiner for organizing it, and for their subsequent comments on my presentation, as well as for the discussion that took place throughout the conference. Peter Dwyer read a draft of this chapter and offered detailed and constructive comments. It will be clear that my thinking has been strongly influenced by my friend and professor Jane Goodale. It was a privilege to work comparatively with her Melanesian ethnography. Errors and oddities are all mine.

expressed in human behaviour through the manner which the geographic information is organised and classified, e.g., in making maps, naming places, and conceptualising landscapes.

(Yoon 1986)

George Tinker further demonstrates the interrelation between environmentalism, cosmology, and geomentality, as well as academia and activism, by arguing that

> we need communal stories that can generate 'functional' theologies, or, better yet, functional mythologies, that will undergird the life of the community (the lives of communities) in new and vibrant ways. The contemporary crisis calls for imagining new stories that can generate life and not conquest – whether cultural, military, economic, or intellectual! (Tinker 1997: 173)

His point that 'sometimes a single truth is not enough to explain the balance of the world around us' is eloquent not only in relation to environmentalism and to dialogue between neighbouring communities about respected or sacred places, but also to all attempts to relate respectfully.

In the following chapter, Deborah Bird Rose provides a 'story' that focuses on what she calls 'the work of the world: the work that generates and regenerates living things'. With reference to two 'case studies' – 'sacred sites' and country in the Victoria River District of the Northern Territory of Australia, and the clearing and forest among the Kaulong people of New Britain – she again provides both a narrow focus (see Connors 2000: 15) and examples 'indicative of a systemic problem that is pervasively political and intellectual' (Tinker 1997: 154). This creative tension might be enhanced by consideration of the permeability of borders, boundaries, and categories (see Douglas 1992, and Thompson 2001).

Rose discusses particular geomentalities, modes of subsistence, and environmentalisms, but also argues about globalized issues of 'development' and politics that affect everyone. She concludes:

> the politics of sacred sites is not separable from the politics of environmental ethics, and both are undergoing a tortured refinement in the globalizing activities known as development. The deep issue is not about protecting sites, species, or geographical/ecological zones in isolation but about enabling ephemeral life (including our own) to flourish. Political, social, and spiritual life thus converges on contested lands, and on questions of which soils will sustain life, which rivers will flow, which species will live or die, which forests will grow, and which peoples will exercise responsibility.

Persons, subsistence, communication, politics, art, location, and other seemingly discrete aspects of human life are all 'grown' (as Ruel (1997) says of some rites of passage) in complex and messy interrelationships.

In addition to powerfully making visible the pervasive contestation over land engendered by colonialism, Rose also demonstrates the essentially collaborative nature of academic discourse. Again, one story – or storyteller – is not enough. Her references situate her work in the context of ongoing conversations that attempt to exercise responsibility with knowledge. The politics of academic research and its dissemination are visible and implicated in the stories we tell and the lives we lead. Such integration (which happens whatever some may claim about distance and objectivity) is a central motif of the worldviews and lifeways of interest in this chapter.

Among other things, this makes Rose's discussion (and the book from which it is drawn) an invaluable addition to dialogue about Aboriginal Law, or the 'Dreaming' (also see Rose 1992; Mowaljarlai and Malnic 1993; Turner 2001).

References

Connors, Sean. 2000. 'Ecology and Religion in Karuk Orientations toward the Land', in Graham Harvey (ed.), *Indigenous Religions: A Companion*. London: Cassell, pp. 139-51.

Douglas, M. 1992. *Purity and Danger: An Analysis of Concepts of Pollution and Taboo*. London: Routledge.

Mowaljarlai, David, and Jutta Malnic. 1993. *Yorro Yorro: Aboriginal Creation and the Renewal of Nature*. Rochester: Inner Traditions.

Rose, Deborah Bird. 1992. *Dingo Makes Us Human: Life and Land in an Aboriginal Australian Culture*. Cambridge: Cambridge University Press.

Ruel, M. 1997. 'Growing the Girl', in *Belief, Ritual and the Securing of Life: Reflexive Essays on a Bantu Religion*. Leiden: Brill, pp. 76-99.

Thompson, Charles D. 2001. *Maya Identities and the Violence of Place: Borders Bleed*. Aldershot: Ashgate.

Tinker, G. 1997. 'An American Indian Theological Response to Ecojustice', in Jace Weaver (ed.), *Defending Mother Earth*. Mary Knoll: Orbis, pp. 153-76.

Turner, David. 2001. 'From Here into Eternity: Power and Transcendence in Australian Aboriginal Music', in Karen Ralls MacLeod and Graham Harvey (eds), *Indigenous Religious Musics*. Aldershot: Ashgate, pp. 35-55.

Yoon, Hong-key. 1986. *Maori Mind, Maori Land*, Berne: Peter Lang.

This chapter moves toward issues of environmental ethics through an examination of geographies of generative space. My focus is on what I call the work of the world: the work that generates and regenerates living things. I look first to an Australian case study: 'sacred sites' and country in the Victoria River District of the Northern Territory. I then look at the clearing and forest among the Kaulong people of New Britain as represented by Jane Goodale (1995) in her recent ethnography *To Sing with Pigs Is Human*. In contrast to the work of scholars of religious studies, who see the sacred as the product of ritual work, my analysis is in confluence with that of scholars such as Povinelli (1993) in Australia and Goodale (1995) in Papua New Guinea in showing how relationships between enduring sources and ephemeral life are sustained through the everyday work of the world. I conclude by examining some comparative issues between hunter-gatherer and shifting horticultural modes of subsistence in the context of global development.

I am using the term 'environmental ethics' in a loose sense rather than in a technical sense, taking it to refer to a system of responsibilities that humans hold in relation to nonhumans. In the past few decades discussions of the environmental ethics of non-Western people have increased exponentially. As in so many other discussions that contrast the West and its chosen others, while any given author usually refers to specific peoples, there is a generalized lumping together of indigenous peoples in contrast to people of the West (see Fajans 1998 and Jorgensen 1998 for deconstructions of homogenizing views of 'others'). And yet, the ways in which people conceptualize the generative structure of their world and their own place in that structure are fundamental to any analysis of how they construe human responsibility and accountability. Different understandings implicate humans in different relationships of responsibility toward their world, and the quality of difference has a great bearing on how they define and target human responsibilities toward nonhumans.

Peter Dwyer's (1996) brilliant essay 'The Invention of Nature' is a recent link in the distinguished lineage of anthropological studies in Papua New Guinea that engage with and destabilize Western concepts of 'nature' and 'culture' (for example, Strathern 1980 and Wagner 1981). Dwyer examines the relationships between people and landscapes in three Papua New Guinea societies: Kubo, Etolo, and Siane. He finds degrees of separation such that at one end of his transect Kubo people engage in small amounts of gardening and large amounts of hunting/gathering. Human activity permeates the whole landscape, and the whole landscape is humanized (p. 168). At the other end of the transect, Siane people expend most of their energy and time in gardening. Their actions generate a distinction between a humanized area and its periphery. Dwyer contends that this 'created periphery of the visible world, increasingly divorced from human contact and understanding, emerges as "nature" (p. 178). In contrast, among the

Kubo the world is all 'cultural'; there is 'no 'nature' (p. 178). Dwyer suggests that hunter-gatherer peoples (and in an evolutionary sense, primal peoples whoever they may have been) like the Kubo inhabit a world that is all culture rather than all nature.

My work with Aboriginal Australians indicates this to be the case (see Rose 1996). Like Dwyer, I am concerned with 'the ways people live within' their landscape, and 'with the impress of them upon it and of it upon them' (Dwyer 1996: 162). An impress is a set of traces of productive activity. How, then, is production understood? What are the sources of life, and how are human actions toward those sources evaluated and enjoined? These questions take us to environmental ethics via a path through generative sources and the responsible actions of living things.

Hunter-gatherer land management

The analysis I pursue here depends on a body of very recent knowledge that is in the process of reconfiguring most of what once stood as conventional wisdom concerning Aboriginal hunter-gatherers. I can present my case study most coherently if I first summarize this new knowledge.

Western thought pervasively and profoundly has contrasted those who cultivate the soil with those who do not. Many of the differences between cultivation and hunter-gatherer modes of subsistence have been conceptualized in Western thought by reference to human intentional action in the world. According to Ingold (1996: 148), 'the producer is seen to intervene in natural processes, from a position at least partially outside them; the forager is supposed never to have extricated him- or herself from nature in the first place.' The nature–culture dichotomy, although now destabilized in many contexts, continues to situate hunter-gatherer people ambiguously. Ingold (1996: 147), for example, notes that contemporary usage that replaces the term 'hunter-gatherer' with the term 'forager' perpetuates both the dichotomy and the slippage: like animals, foragers graze across a landscape.

Contemporaneously, a revolution in anthropological thought is quietly taking place in Australia concerning the relationships between Indigenous people and their country. In recent years, issues of indigenous land management have come to be understood as questions for research. In Australia the long-term lack of research, like the lack of general public awareness of these issues, is connected with the settler view that Aboriginal people were parasites on nature. Elkin (1954: 15) gave the mark of scientific authority to this view in a book first published in 1938: 'The food-gathering life is parasitical; the Aborigines are absolutely dependent on what nature produces without any practical assistance on their part.' This view of parasitism was intricately connected to the view of *terra nullius*: the idea that the land was untransformed underpinned the idea that the land was unowned. By this logic, Aboriginal 'parasites' were excluded from forms of ownership by reason of their own nature (lack of culture).

An important corollary was that hunter-gatherers did not shape the landscape, or, that the landscape was shaped by them only as a byproduct of their foraging actions. Williams and Hunn's (1982) publication *Resource Managers* marks a key moment in shifting the accepted conventions surrounding these issues (see also Williams and Baines 1993). The start of the demolition of the parasite view, however, dates to Rhys Jones' (1969) work on the use of fire in a system of land management. He called this system fire-stick farming, and his use of the term 'farming' was deliberate (Jones 1995). Inaccurate as it is in attributing the culture of cultivation to Aboriginal people, it provocatively struck an intellectual and political nerve. Since Jones' original work, numerous studies have shown Aboriginal people's proactive care of Australian fauna, flora, and ecosystems. It is becoming increasingly evident that both the distribution and the diversity of Australian biota across the continent are artifacts of Aboriginal people's intentional actions. This is not to say that Aboriginal people have always and only managed ecosystems well; knowledge and practice are not always in synchrony for Aboriginal people any more than for others (Lewis 1993: 10). This new knowledge indicates that when Europeans arrived here the continent was an artifact of Aboriginal people's active and intentional management (Jones 1969; 1985).

The implications of this new knowledge are enormous. Research is in a very early stage; it is interdisciplinary and has yet to be fully accepted within any mainstream discipline. It has been assimilated unevenly, and often crudely. A little more than a decade ago there was debate about whether Aboriginal people actually did engage in fire-stick farming (Horton 1982); today it is almost universally accepted that they consciously managed large portions of the continent through the use of fire, and contemporary Anglo-Australian land managers now seek to use fire to manage landscapes in North Australia. In addition, there are studies that deal with the aesthetics of burnt country (Head 1994) and the spiritual and emotional meanings of fire (Bradley 1995).

Looking at the continent as a whole, it is now evident that the actions of Indigenous people are clearly responsible for maintaining the open grasslands that covered much of the continent (Jones 1969), for the preservation of specific stands of fire-sensitive vegetation such as acacia (Kimber 1983), cypress (Bowman 1995; Bowman and Panton 1993), and remnant rain forests (Russell-Smith and Bowman 1992), for the protection of refugia including breeding sanctuaries (Newsome 1980), and the preservation of sources of permanent water in arid environments (Latz 1995; a brief summary of many of these issues is found in Rose 1996). In addition, their actions are directly responsible for the distribution of many plants (Hynes and Chase 1982; Kimber 1976; Kimber and Smith 1987), and probably for the distribution of some fauna, such as freshwater crayfish (Horwitz and Knott 1995). If research continues to produce new knowledge at the current rate, it is probable that I am discussing only the tip of the iceberg. As conquerors we are able to understand Aboriginal organization of country only retrospectively, and undoubtedly much of the evidence we would want to examine has been obliterated. Yet, while there are many open questions, there is no doubt that indigeneous people's care of country has shaped and sustained the biota of this continent.[1]

This new knowledge has yet to make a significant impact upon anthropological thought. I believe that when it does it will require major rethinking about how we understand the history of our species, how we understand differences between modes of subsistence, how we understand philosophical issues of being and becoming in the world. I believe that there are major implications for how we Westerners understand our own dichotomized thinking and for how we impose our knowledge systems on others (see Dwyer 1996).

Sacred sites: law and responsibility

My analysis is alert to both the poetics and the politics of the sacred (Chidester and Linenthal 1995: 1-42), but I emphasize the architectonics of sacred space. Nancy Munn's (1996) essay 'Excluded Spaces' detours around conventions that reproduce static separations of space and time, and thus is able to provide the outline of a theory that links space and time through human action; my work here continues this project. I use the term 'sacred' in this Australian Aboriginal context with the intention of encompassing both the substantival concept of world creative powers and the situational practices through which people bring that power forth into the world in the form of living things.

---

[1] At its most basic, this fact has been known for a long time. The Australian explorer Major Mitchell described the interrelationship between Aboriginal people, their fires, kangaroos, and grass: 'Fire, grass, kangaroos, and human inhabitants, seem all dependent on each other for existence in Australia, for any one of these being wanting, the others could no longer continue ... But for this simple process, the Australian woods had probably contained as thick a jungle as those of New Zealand or America, instead of the open forests in which the white men now find grass for their cattle ... ' (quoted in Rolls 1981: 249).

In Aboriginal Australia, the living world is a created world, brought into being as a world of form, difference, and connection by creative beings called Dreamings (see Morphy 1996 for a discussion of the term). The Australian continent is crisscrossed with the tracks of the Dreamings: walking, slithering, crawling, flying, chasing, hunting, weeping, dying, birthing. They were performing rituals, distributing the plants, making the landforms and water, establishing things in their own places, making the relationships between one place and another. They left parts of themselves, looked back and looked ahead, and still traveled, changing languages, changing songs, changing skin.[2] They were changing shape from animal to human and back to animal and human again, becoming ancestral to particular animals and humans. Through their creative actions they demarcated a world of difference and of relationships that crosscut difference. Victoria River people articulate the view that in their part of the world everything came into being by Dreaming, and every ephemeral thing exists because of and through relationships established by Dreaming.

The places where Dreamings traveled, where they stopped, and where they lived the events of their lives and deaths, these tracks and sites make up the sacred geography of Australia. Sacred geography defines the structures of embeddedness that are the sources of ephemeral life, human and nonhuman. These structures are characterized by intersections, overlap, and crosscuttings; there is thus a web of relatedness in which everything is connected to something that is connected to something, and so forth. It is not the case that everything is connected to every other thing, but rather that nothing is without connection, and 'there is no alien world of mere things' or of things with no meaning (Sutton 1988: 13).

Sites and tracks, origins and connections – Dreaming creation is the source and template for a 'dynamic jurisprudence of duty' (Jacobson 1992) that is called Law in Aboriginal English. The dynamism in this system derives from the fact that sentience and agency are located all through the system: in human and nonhuman persons, in trees, rocks, stones, and hills; wherever Dreamings are, there sentience is. Wherever the dead people are, there sentience is. Rainbows, wild women, and all manner of extraordinary beings along with the more 'ordinary' beings pervade the world, imbuing it with sentience. Crucially, the conditions for being are exactly that – conditions. Life in all its transience is a continuous bringing forth. This process, the coming forth of it all, happens through intentional action on the part of sentient beings. Daily life is lived on the 'threshold of

---

[2] Minimally this term 'skin' refers to social categories the English technical terms for which are 'section,' 'subsection,' 'semimoiety,' and the like (depending on the precise organization of the skins).

unfolding events,' to borrow Scott's (1996: 73) eloquent phrase; it happens because sentient beings discharge the responsibilities that are theirs by law.

In this created world, life is embedded within sites and relationships. The bringing forth of life and law is what life is – an unfolding of relationships, a bringing forth of life in its embedded complexity. The process can be examined through several lenses: country, totems, and individuals. The life and law that are contained in sites unfold out into the world in a dynamic system of interdependent units, each of which is called 'country' in Aboriginal English. Country is an organizing unit of life, sustained in mutual interdependence with other equivalent units; clusters of mutually interdependent countries constitute systems that are roughly congruent with ecological zones (Peterson 1976).

Life and law also, and equally, unfold out into the world in a dynamic system of totemic consubstantialities. Most totems are both living species and Dreaming figures. Like the structure of tracks and sites, the structure of totemic categories is built on intersections and overlaps. Totemic consubstantiality is exclusive, but it is also massively crosscut. Matrilineal totems cut across patrilineal ones, for example, and subsection totems cut across both. Different categories intersect each other, and the people who are related in one context are differentiated in another context. Every difference is crosscut by some other difference, and intersubjectivity is embedded in multicentered systems.

Dreaming action unfolds out into the world in the bodies of specific human beings through processes of conception, birth, and growth. With conception, Dreaming propels itself into a child-to-be. Characteristically, 'spirit' enters a food resource that is killed by the father of the child-to-be, is eaten by the mother, and is born into the world as a new person (Povinelli 1993: 137-9; Rose 1992: 59). Throughout childhood, people are nourished by the food of the country. Victoria River people say that country gives them body, and having the body of the country generates responsibilities toward the nurturing country (Rose 1992: 61, 107-10).

In sum, relatedness is the meat of life, situating people's bodily presence in shared projects that link human and nonhuman interests around intersecting and crosscutting contexts of tracks, countries, totems, and sites. Every discrete category is linked to other discrete categories through kinship, and is crosscut by other discrete categories; thus the concept of exclusivity is both sustained (because categories are discrete) and demolished (because they are crosscut). This system links species, places, and regions, and leaves no region, place, species, or individual standing outside creation, life processes, and responsibilities.

The action that brings life forth from its source is the work of the world. Dreamings changed over into living things that grow, mature, and die. In the monsoonal tropics of the Victoria River District, the transience of this kind of everyday life is expressed by reference to seasons and growth. The rain annually washes the marks of the actions of people, plants, and animals away from the face of the earth; human and animal tracks are washed out, plants die. The kind of life that ends in death is spoken of in these kinds of ways, and it is understood that people quite literally will be washed away, although current mortuary practices are disabling this system.

Dreaming bodies endure as sites; their life continues to happen in the world precisely through the ephemeral. Through actions of knowledgeable living things (a category that is not exclusively human) the enduring life of the source is brought into ephemeral existence. It is not just that the power of a site is located at a center 'from which a space with uncertain or ambiguously defined limits stretches out' (Munn 1996: 453). Rather, it is also the case that the site is unfolded out into the country in the lives of the living things who belong there, and through the actions of the living things who are responsible there. Dreaming is thus actualized transiently in the present, and the perduring life of the world is carried by ephemeral life-forms. All living things are held to have an interest in the life of the living things with whom they are connected because their own life is dependent upon them. Care requires presence, not absence, and a fundamental proposition of contemporary Victoria River people is that those who destroy their country destroy themselves.

Organizing the country

To be connected is thus to be in a relation of mutual care. My friend and teacher Hobbles Danayarra offered a succinct explanation of his people's responsibilities toward land, stating that 'before white people, Aboriginal people were just walking around organizing the country.' As I have indicated, research into how Aboriginal people organize the country is still very new. My interest here is with the connections of embeddedness entailed in this created world. A major context for care is country, as I have indicated. Country is a nourishing terrain (Rose 1996); it is the place where ephemeral bodies, time, and sentience come into being and carry on the work of the world that makes further unfolding possible. We have a good literature to help us understand ritual practice (Strehlow 1970 is excellent), but bringing forth is equally a product of everyday life. As Povinelli (1993: 139 states, 'All hunting trips interact with the sentient landscape, and the sentient landscape most commonly encounters humans engaged in economic, not ritual, activity.' It is a matter of presence: you put your body in the country to do the work of the country, and the country gives you body.

The main technology for the organization of country is and was knowledge. Knowledge is country-specific, and virtually the whole body of knowledge for any given country is related to the generation of life in and around that country. Countries are interdependent, so not the case that one person's knowledge is restricted only to one country, or that countries are self-sufficient in their knowledge, but the case that each country has its own specificities, the knowledge of which belongs to some people and not to others: where resources are located, where permanent water is to be found, which ecological events signal other ecological events, weather signs and patterns, where the sacred and dangerous places are and what restrictions apply to them, how to address the sentient land, water, trees, and stones, and what kinds of fires to light in particular land-forms at particular times of day and year. The most publicly secret knowledge is linked to sacred sites, but all knowledge – of land-forms, resource locations, water sources, seasonal markers, environmental history, medicinal plant animal behavior, floristics, plant phenology, and much more – belongs to the people of the country and is shared among people who have a range of responsibilities there.

Human beings are not the only sentient beings who organize the country. I know less about the responsibilities of nonhuman animals but some points are formally articulated. Flying foxes, for example, are linked to the Rainbow Snake, and in the Victoria River District they go to the riverside during the late dry season, and they tell the Rainbow Snake to bring rain. Through the system of totemic consubstantialities, some human beings are also flying foxes, and some human beings are linked to rain (light and dark rain) in various ways. The knowledge of the organization of these connections between different segments of the living world is held to be powerful, and a lifetime of learning promotes ever greater understandings of connections.

Responsibilities of care are organized along connections. They thus overlap and crosscut. Nothing is responsible for every other thing, and every thing has responsibilities of care and is the subject of care from others. For humans this means knowing where your responsibilities lie and respecting the limits of your responsibilities. Practices of care cluster around three main projects: practices of memory and education that enable the knowledge gained in one generation to be coded and transmitted to new generations; practices that ensure that resources are not overused; and care of habitats. The first goes beyond my purposes here, other than to note that stories, songs, and other forms of site-based knowledge are major vehicles for ecological memory. The second includes practices such as replanting portions of yams for next year, localized and temporary hunting

329

prohibitions, temporary food taboos, prohibitions on hunting in breeding season, and prohibitions against waste (see, for example, Baker 1993: 139). The third project includes practices such as burning firebreaks around the rain forests where the yams grow. The use of fire is well documented compared to other practices,[3] but the most important consideration, and the most urgent area for further research at this time, is the convergence of practices. Thus, to take one example, Latz, a botanist who has carried out extensive work in Central Australia, notes that the most sacred/protected places are likely to be places where a number of Dreamings meet up or cross over. He describes them this way: 'There's a lot of dreaming trails which cross over, these are really important places. They are so sacred you can't kill animals or even pick plants. And of course you don't burn them. You might burn around them in order to look after them' (Latz 1995: 70).

It is urgent to keep at the fore a key aspect of this paradigm: you cannot bring forth yourself. Humans are embedded in the habitats or ecosystems that nurture them. In the Victoria River District, people say that their country gives them body. The relationship is reciprocal: you take care of the country, the country takes care of you. You come into being only through relationships. Not only your origin but your ability to keep on living from day to day is embedded within the relations that nurture you. The generation of life is the process by which life is unfolded by the actions of transient living things in interaction with Dreaming presence. The process rests on subject–subject reciprocity: an intersubjectivity of bringing forth. Persons are immanent in those portions of the world that are theirs, and those portions of their world are immanent in them (see also Ingold 1986: 139). Ephemeral persons are embedded in the world, and by the work of their lives as they 'walk around organising the country,' they bring forth the life of the world.

The conventional Western division between pragmatic action and mythico-religious action breaks down completely in practices of care, as Ingold (1996) recently argued, and as Huber (1980) demonstrated in a Melanesian case study. All practices are understood to affect the life of the

---

[3] The logic of care is based in long-term interests that include humans and nonhumans, regions as well as countries. The actual enforcement of practices of care is social and is based on immediate interest. To harm the country, or to harm a particular species, is to harm the people of that country or that species (see Rose 1992 for an example of the social consequences of harm) and is treated as an act of aggression. For example, starting a fire that burns out of control and goes into someone else's country is an act of aggression for which the punishment, in the Victoria River district, is asserted to have been death. Law surrounding the use and misuse of fire is in decline all over Australia, as the contexts of practice decline. Bradley (1995) discusses this issue; see also Bright (1995) for a brief discussion of misuse of fire.

country, and thus to engage in care is to engage in bringing forth the life of the country while making oneself available also to be brought forth. An 'increase' ritual is just as pertinent as a well-organized fire; indeed, these dimensions are simply not separate. For example, Nanikiya Munungurritj, an Aboriginal traditional owner of eastern Arnhem Land, and a ranger with the Dhimurru Land Management organization, spoke about burning his country, saying that you sing the country before you burn it. In your mind you see the fire, you know where it is going, and you know where it will stop. Only then do you light the fire (personal communication).[4]

Is this production? Ingold argues (1996: 148) that the term 'production' invokes a Western view: 'planned intervention in nature launched from the separate platform of society.' He endorses Bird-David's (1992: 40) suggestion of the appropriateness of the term 'procurement' in its connotative range of 'management, contrivance, acquisition, getting, gaining.' In my view, neither 'production' nor 'procurement' does justice to the mutuality of Aboriginal Australian ecological interactions. The practices I have discussed here involve knowledgeable care based on mutual engagement among mutual embedded living things. I use the term 'generation of life' to refer to this matrix of connection and mutual care.

It is probable that the current environmental devastations that many Victoria River people see and have experienced have heightened their awareness of the fragile contingency of the living world, but the relationship of mutual unfolding that exists between the enduring and the ephemeral speaks to a world that is ever emergent and ever contingent. The concept of congealed action, it seems to me, must be balanced by an analysis that links the daily and ephemeral with current and ancestral labor. Ingold's (1996: 139) examination of Myers' (1986) Pintupi ethnography, for example, follows a train of logic that holds human action within landscape rather than positioning it as external, and reaches the conclusion that 'the landscape ... is ... life's enduring monument.' The landscape of linked sites and tracks is well understood in this way. But if we regard landscape in the more proactive and living sense of country – the webs of ephemeral life – then we see a continuously coming into being, process. It is not held fixed by cultural reproduction but is nurtured and sustained through cultural procreation. Flourishing life is evidence of current and ancestral labor, but it is not a monument in any enduring sense, for it all comes undone when the organization fails.[5]

Life is thus an ever emergent becoming, carried by the ephemeral beings

---

[4] Talk presented to the Bushfire '97 conference, Darwin, July 8-10, 1997.
[5] I will have to leave for another publication the important question of how Aboriginal people conceptualize and evaluate loss, especially extinctions.

whose work is to keep life happening. The sacred is actualized through the everyday work of the world, and Dreaming continues to happen for as long as ephemeral beings do the work of the world. I believe that the structure of relationships of responsible care can be glossed as a system of environmental ethics for purposes of comparison and dialogue. In brief, the system I have been describing is one of multi-centered subjectivities embedded in overlapping and crosscutting relationships of care that encompass, or are believed to involve, whole ecosystems. The system of connection is sustained through actions of mutual bringing forth exercised by the living things whose ephemeral lives actualize the perduring possibilities and conditions of life.

Ancestral clearing

In this section I draw most particularly on Jane Goodale's (1995) study of the Kaulong people of New Britain. I will suggest that for Kaulong people the work of the world consists in sustaining a managed system of continuity that is parallel to and differentiated from the self-sustaining system of the forest. In comparison with the system of embedded connections and mutual bringing forth that characterizes the Aboriginal case, the Kaulong case indicates a gradient of disembedding.

Goodale's analysis focuses on the work of differentiation:

- to differentiate the clearing from the forest, and thus to demarcate a specifically human space

- to differentiate humans from forest animals, through the production of gardens

- to differentiate one human from another through competive knowledge and exchange.

Kaulong people are gardeners as well as hunter-gatherers. The taro they grow in their shifting agricultural plots is regarded as the foundational food for humans, but forest resources constitute 40 percent to 60 percent of the people's food consumption (p. 69). Gardens are cut out of the forest. They last for a bit more than a year before being left to revert to forest, and they are constantly at risk from pigs (p. 81).

Sacred space is modeled as sites of origin: the hole in the ground from which came taro (p. 78), the site (hole or tree) from which came the ancestor of a contemporary descent group, and the clearing or hamlet (*bi*) that is the unambiguously human place (p. 117). Human origin myths relate how the founding ancestor(s), a man or a brother and sister, emerged from their source in the forest. The brother worked to make a clearing, planted a ficus (fig) tree in the center and fruit trees around the periphery, and built a main house. Brother and sister, or father and daughter, are the generative ancestors; the woman got a husband elsewhere, and the man and woman of the clearing founded a group of cognates who are consubstantial not only with each other but also with the foundational place and its resources (p. 113).

Within the clearing are located the ficus tree of the ancestor; the fruit trees, which are consistently cared for and replaced as they die; the main house, beneath which members of the group for the place were buried in times past; and the sites of former main houses, which were abandoned when there was no more room for burials (p. 117). The open ground of the clearing is '*the* unambiguous human place' (p. 117). It is where all the activities of intergroup sociality, exchange, singing, and pig killing take place. The blood of pigs is in the soil of the clearing along with the bones of ancestors (p. 117).

Cognatic groups of people who link themselves to a foundational place are not exclusive groups but rather overlapping kindreds. A given person maintains links to three or four ancestral places. These places 'are far more than mere points of reference. They symbolize the core meaning of kinship and of being. Coming from the same place is the essence of sharing an identity not only with other people, but also with all the non-human resources of the place as well' (p. 115).

Goodale's work on concepts of replacement is well known. In her view, the generation of human lives through time is managed by the Kaulong according to a cultural model of replacement that links humanity to domesticated plants. Taro is the key model of human replacement. Like humans, taro has its origins in the ground; it is brought out of its source and into the gardens of human beings with physical labor and magical words (pp. 78-80). Taro stalks are kept and replanted from one period of growth to the next, and thus from one garden to the next. The corms are the key food for humans, and managed properly they are not destroyed in the eating. Rather, stalks are saved and replanted, so that a single taro ancestor has a continuous life of growth, replanting, growth and replanting. The plant grows and is consumed, and grows again, while the substance remains identical. This taro life cycle serves as an ideal for humans. Children are understood to be replacements for their parents, and human life is devoted to the twin projects of personal growth and replacement for the future.

Goodale proposes that forest and clearing are complementary and opposing kinds of space:

In the Kaulong world, the forest and the garden are two contrasting spaces in which to live and work and become human. The forest is quite clearly the preferred place of the two, but it is equally clear that it is a place where humans are just another creature, occupying the same space as animals, insects, birds and spirits. But while both men and women spoke of the forest with an emotional attachment quite unlike the way they spoke of a garden, it was in the gardens that they worked to become differentiated and human. (Goodale 1995: 85)

Kaulong ephemera

According to Goodale, the cycle of life begins and ends in the forest (1995: 234), and the forest is self-sustaining. Differentiation is a process of disembedding; it seems to be accomplished by human intentional action on three scales. The clearing is brought out of an enduring forest, is maintained for generations as the major site for public human achievement, and subsequently returns to forest. Gardens are on another scale: they, too, are carved out of the forest, but they are worked for only a year or two before being left to recede back into the forest. Human life constitutes a third scale; it is brought out of the forest and into the garden and clearing, where it is sustained through human action, until at death it moves back into the forest (p. 235). Personal labor in making gardens, maintaining clearings, and achieving personal renown and replacement thus establishes a human figure differentiated from the forest ground. Taro gardens are human-generated space. Past and future for garden space is the forest, while the taro itself is managed continuously from one garden to the next. The Kaulong are explicit: they walk the taro from place to place, and the histories of their travels constitute tracks through the forest. A human, like a garden, is brought out of the forest and reverts to forest at death (p. 245). Transgenerational lines of humans are like taro: substance is carried from garden to garden, and from adult to child across generations.

Using Weiner's (1988: 9) theoretical framework, we could say that the forest is the given cosmic flow that human moral action halts and channels into distinctions for socially important purposes. What is 'precipitated' out of human labor as it diverts the forest flow is a kind of space and a kind of production for replacement, both of which are differentiated from the space and reproduction of the forest.

Kaulong people know themselves to be animals, and thus 'of the forest,' according to Goodale, yet they strive to differentiate themselves and to become humans 'of the clearing.' The work of differentiating humans from other animals, and of differentiating the gardens and clearings from the forest, is captured and expressed in the endings of the songs to commemorate the dead (p. 243). Song endings speak to that margin where the forest meets the clearing, and to the cold fires of abandoned clearings. The work of the Kaulong world is to ensure the continuity of clearing, taro, and generations, so that while the ephemeral comes from and returns to the forest, human labor channels certain forms of life into a parallel and disembedded system of continuous and identical substance and discontinuous space.

Thus, Kaulong people have not separated culture from nature so much as they have generated a geographical and cultural divide that runs through the domains that Westerners generally refer to as culture and nature. The Kaulong divide turns on humanized and nonhumanized worlds. Aspects of humanity, and types of nonhuman life, are included within each 'world.' Thus, within the nonhuman world there is the self-sustaining forest and those aspects of human beings that are most properly thought of as 'of the forest.' Within the humanized world there are taro humans, pig humans, and human humans. This distinction is similar to, and finds ethnographic parallels with, that made by Biersack (1996) in relation to Paiela gardens. In her understanding of Paiela metaphysics, 'animals are inherently social and political, not natural' (p. 4). The fence marks a 'boundary between a receding and largely irrelevant mere nature ... and a worked-on or worked-up crafted nature' (p. 4). Kaulong and Paiela devote cultural attention to a threshold site (edge of clearing, fence) that marks the achievement of differentiation, and labor becomes visible within the clearing.

The action of differentiation is a disembedding of the unambiguously human world from the ambiguous world of the forest. For the Kaulong, the generation of life reproduces differentiation by sustaining discontinuity. The Kaulong distinction between different kinds of processes for the generation of life is a corollary to the division between forest and garden. The forest is self-sustaining, while only humans can and do manage lines of continuity (human and taro) across discontinuous sites of differentiation. The site of a garden is cleared from the forest, but the source is not of the forest: the source of gardens is other gardens. Differentiation thus interrupts the pervasive mutuality that characterizes the Aboriginal system and introduces gradients of connection.

Site and clearing: environmental ethics

The Kaulong division of ecosystems into those that are understood to be self-sustaining and those that are sustained by humans makes a separation into ground and figure and thus articulates human action as an interruption of the given ground. The organization of human responsibility toward the world is thus diminished in comparison with the Aboriginal Australian system I have described. In respect of taro, human responsibility remains essential, but the greater part of the landscape has become an environment for which humans are not responsible. Thus, responsibility for a few demarcated 'human' species is accompanied by diminished responsibility for a large number of 'nonhuman' species. Greater responsibility for the small-scale ecologies of the garden and the clearing are accompanied by greatly diminished responsibility for the large-scale ecology of the forest. The contrast between humans and pigs can be thought to say something about responsibility: if pigs are what humans would be if they were not human, then the implication is that if humans were to revert to the forest they would revert to a world of no responsibility. It would be a world of all ground and no figure.

The shrinking of responsibilities suggests a shift not only in focus but also in reciprocities and connectedness. Victoria River Aboriginal people assert that humans are just one of the species with law for country; others share responsibilities in ritual and in everyday practice. In asserting that other species take responsibilities, they do not seek to devalue or evade their own human obligations; rather such assertions stress co-action in a world of connection. Consubstantialities overlap and crosscut each other so that most of the living world is brought into relationships of shared substance and mutual responsibility. By contrast, it does not appear that the Kaulong expect that anyone, or any living things, have a responsibility for them. Goodale's analysis of the Kaulong people's passionate pursuit of individuation and differentiation seems to point to a worldview in which nonhuman living things neither share responsibilities nor reciprocate them. If responsibilities are taken as the figure, then the world of Victoria River people's responsibilities is all figure; there is no given ground.

This line of thought leads me back to the issue of human culture being progressively extracted from nature (Ingold 1994: 3). According to the logic I have developed here, it appears that human 'culture' may indeed loosen its embeddedness in the world. The Kaulong case suggests, and Biersack's and Dwyer's analyses lend credence to the idea, that a disengagement of human activity from the world happens as an outcome of conceptual divisions that separate the world into domains for which humans bear a responsibility and domains for which they do not. Kaulong people, of course, are surrounded by forest, are knowledgeable in respect to the forest, and clearly hold it to be a valuable zone not only for resource use but for restfulness. To the extent, however, that they see themselves as part of the forest, they hold that to be a condition to be overcome. The result is a diminution of human responsibility in the living world, a cline in the organization of responsibilities toward other living things across a gradient of cultural/ecological zones, and a loss of complexity. As Dwyer (1996) argues so lucidly, the practice of cultivation is not the causal factor in the 'invention of nature.' And yet, the intensification of labor toward processes of differentiation detaches human responsibilities from portions of the world and turns cultural attention toward sites of differentiation and processes of disembedding. There is thus a major contrast with the Aboriginal case, where cultural attention is turned toward sustaining relationships of mutual embeddedness.

Environmental politics

When Aldo Leopold (1976) kicked off the current round of interest in environmental ethics in his 1949 book *A Sand County Almanac*, he contended that a new domain of ethics must evolve. His argument was that human ethics have evolved in a sequence, and that the direction of change is toward ever widening circles of responsibility: 'The land ethic simply enlarges the boundaries of the community to include soils, waters, plants and animals' (pp. 202-3). While I agree completely with the view that our current global culture of exploitation is in urgent need of an expanded ethic of responsibility, it is clear that Aboriginal 'caring for country' embodies both an ethic and a structure of responsibility that answers Leopold's call in many important respects.[6]

From an evolutionary perspective it would seem that intensification of labor and production entails a diminution of connection and responsibility, and it follows from that proposition that the diminution works both ways. That is, as humans define themselves as ever less responsible to and for the world, they find themselves ever less cared for by other living things. My ethnographic endeavor does not lie in the field of evolution, however, and for me the most interesting possibilities in this analysis center on the inescapably brutal facts of our contemporaneous lives.

Wagner has written that 'the dangers of working out our own problems on the soils and in the hearts and minds of other peoples should not be overlooked' (quoted in Dwyer 1996: 182). It is not possible to talk about 'sacred sites' in Australia today without acknowledging the concerted effort on the part of many politicians and developers to contest concepts of the sacred, and especially to marginalize or eliminate Aboriginal people's

---

[6] 'Caring for country' also answers many of the criticisms that are directed toward an ethic of care in relation to environmental ethics, and in other contexts. In several recent papers I discuss this and the ethics of dialogue around environmental issues (for example, Rose 1999).

participation in the ongoing management and development of the continent. The shadow of these issues has hovered around my analysis. When Hobbles spoke of organizing the country, his further implication, of course, was that colonization was disorganizing the country in the most destructive fashion.

I address these issues directly, albeit briefly, in order to link the ephemeral and the sacred to current politics. Near the Aboriginal community of Pigeon Hole on Victoria River Downs station there is a Dreaming site for lilies. There is a stone at the site, which is the source for water lilies (Nymphae spp). The lilies at this billabong are believed to have been placed here by the Nanganarri Dreaming Women, and the stone contains the life and law of lilies. When I accompanied Anzac Munnganyi there in 1989 he struck the stone with green leaves; this is his country, and it is his work to perform this ritual. In this case, however, his action was simply a demonstration with the purpose of proofing of evidence for a claim to land under the *Aboriginal Land Rights (NT) Act* of 1976. At the site there was by then only a murky billabong surrounded by trampled mud, with not a single lily to be seen. This is country that has been grazed by cattle for more than one hundred years. The lilies disappeared in the 1930s, as near as I can determine. There are two closely related billabongs, and Hobbles Danayarra explained that the traditional owners had been able to bring the lilies back to the other billabong, but not to this one. Rituals for lilies for this billabong are no longer performed, as it is believed to be a hopeless case under current land use patterns.

Europeans label this type of land use 'developing the North.' It was the driving ideology even before Anglo-Australians got here. Responsibilities toward living things are organized so differently in systems driven by conquest and its development counterpart, and the destruction of species and systems is so massive, that Indigenous people like Hobbles end up saying that white people must be mad.

In 1986 I pulled up at the side of the road to film some of the most spectacular erosion in the Victoria River District. I asked another teacher/ friend, Daly Pulkara, what he called this country. He looked at it long and heavily before he said: 'It's the wild. Just the wild.' He then went on to speak of quiet country – the country in which all the care of generations of his people is evident to those who know how to see it. Quiet country stands in contrast to the wild: we were looking at a wilderness, man-made and cattle-made. This wild was a place where the life of the country was falling down into the gullies and washing away with the rains (see also Rose 1988).

Life was washing away, and so was the possibility of life. I have suggested that in this indigenous system labor is made visible in the ephemeral.

In quiet country Daly could see the action of his forebears as they had worked to bring forth life; he could see this because he knew the difference between organized country and entropic country. His history, and the ancestral labor, accrued not only in the enduring geomorphology but in ephemeral living systems. And, as he said, the damage was killing both life and time: 'We'll run out of history,' he said, 'because *kartiya* [Europeans] fuck the Law up and [they're] knocking all the power out of this country' (Rose 1992: 234).

In sum, the politics of sacred sites is not separable from the politics of environmental ethics, and both are undergoing a tortured refinement in the globalizing activities known as development. The deep issue is not about protecting sites, species, or geographical/ecological zones in isolation but about enabling ephemeral life (including our own) to flourish. Political, social, and spiritual life thus converges on contested lands, and on questions of which soils will sustain life, which rivers will flow, which species will live or die, which forests will grow, and which peoples will exercise responsibility.

References

Baker, R. 1993. 'Traditional Aboriginal Land Use in the Borroloola Region', in N. Williams and G. Baines (eds), *Traditional Ecological Knowledge*. Canberra: Centre for Resource and Environmental Studies, Australian National University, pp. 126-43.

Biersack, A. 1996. 'The Human Condition and its Transformations: Nature and Society in the Paiela World', paper presented at the annual meeting of the American Anthropological Association.

Bird-David, N. 1992. 'Beyond "The Hunting and Gathering Mode of Subsistence": Culture-Sensitive Observations of the Nayaka and Other Modern Hunter-Gatherers', *Man* 27:19-42.

Bowman, D. 1995. 'Why the Skillful Use of Fire Is Critical for the Management of Biodiversity in Northern Australia', in D. Rose (ed.), *Country in Flames: Proceedings of the 1994 Symposium on Biodiversity and Fire in North Australia*. Canberra and Darwin: Biodiversity Unit, Department of the Environment, Sport, and Territories, and North Australia Research Unit, pp. 105-12.

Bowman, D., and W. Panton. 1993. 'Decline of *Callitris intratropica* in the Northern Territory: Implications for Pre- and Post-colonisation Fire Regimes', *Journal of Biogeography* 20: 373-81.

Bradley, J. 1995. 'Fire, Emotion and Politics: A Yanyuwa Case Study', in D. Rose (ed.), *Country in Flames: Proceedings of the 1994 Symposium on Biodiversity and Fire in North Australia*. Canberra and Darwin: Biodiversity Unit, Department of the Environment, Sport, and Territories, and North Australia Research

Unit.

Bright, A. 1995. 'Burn Grass', in D. Rose (ed.), *Country in Flames: Proceedings of the 1994 Symposium on Biodiversity and Fire in North Australia.* Canberra and Darwin: Biodiversity Unit, Department of the Environment, Sport, and Territories, and North Australia Research Unit.

Chidester, D. and E. Linenthal (eds). 1995. *American Sacred Space.* Bloomington: Indiana University Press.

Dwyer, P. 1996. 'The Invention of Nature', in R. Ellen and K. Fukui (eds), *Redefining Nature: Ecology, Culture, and Domestication.* Oxford: Berg, pp. 157-86.

Elkin, A. P. 1954 (1938). *The Australian Aborigines: How to Understand Them.* Sydney: Angus & Robertson.

Fajans, J. 1998. 'Transforming Nature, Making Culture: Why the Baining Are Not Environmentalists', *Social Analysis* 42: 12-27.

Goodale, J. C. 1995. *To Sing with Pigs Is Human: The Concept of Person in Papua New Guinea.* Seattle and Washington: University of Washington Press.

Head, L. 1994. 'Landscapes Socialised by Fire: Post-contact Changes in Aboriginal Fire Use in Northern Australia, and Implications for Prehistory', *Archaeology in Oceania* 29: 172-81.

Horton, D. 1982. 'The Burning Question: Aborigines, Fire and Australian Ecosystems', *Mankind* 13: 237-51.

Horwitz, P. and B. Knott. 1995. 'The Distribution and Spread of the Yabby Cherax Destructor Complex in Australia: Speculations, Hypotheses and the Need for Research', *Freshwater Crayfish* 10: 81-91.

Huber, P. 1980. 'The Anggor Bowman: Ritual and Society in Melanesia', *American Ethnologist* 7: 43-57.

Hynes, R. and A. Chase. 1982. 'Plants, Sites, and Domiculture: Aboriginal Influence upon Plant Communities in Cape York Peninsula', *Archaeology in Oceania* 17: 38-50.

Ingold, T. 1986. 'Territoriality and Tenure: The Appropriation of Space in Hunting and Gathering Societies', in T. Ingold, *The Appropriation of Nature: Essays on Human Ecology and Social Relations.* Manchester: Manchester University Press, pp. 130-64.

Ingold, T. 1994. 'From Trust to Domination: An Alternative History of Human-Animal Relations', in A. Manning and J. Serpell (eds), *Animals and Human Society: Changing Perspectives.* London: Routledge, pp. 1-22.

Ingold, T. 1996. 'Hunting and Gathering as Ways of Perceiving the Environment', in R. Ellen and K. Fukui (eds), *Redefining Nature: Ecology, Culture, and Domestication.* Oxford: Berg, pp. 117-55.

Jacobson, A. 1992. 'The Idolatry of Rules', in D. Cornell, M. Rosenfeld, and D. Carlson (eds), *Deconstruction and the Possibility of Justice.* London: Routledge, pp. 95-151.

Jones, R. 1969. 'Fire-Stick Farming', *Australian Natural History* 16: 224-8.

Jones, R. 1985. 'Ordering the Landscape', in I. Donaldson and T. Donaldson (eds), *Seeing the First Australians.* Sydney: George Allen & Unwin, pp. 181-209.

Jones, R. 1995. 'The Legacy of the Fire-Stick' in D. Rose (ed.), *Country in Flames: Proceedings of the 1994 Symposium on Biodiversity and Fire in North Australia*. Canberra and Darwin: Biodiversity Unit, Department of the Environment, Sport, and Territories, and North Australia Research Unit.

Jorgensen, D. 1998. 'Whose Nature? Invading Bush Spirits, Travelling Ancestors, and Mining in Terefolmin', *Social Analysis* 42: 100-16.

Kimber, R. 1976. 'Beginnings of Farming? Some Man–Plant–Animal Relationships in Central Australia', *Mankind* 10(3): 142-51.

Kimber, R. 1983. 'Black Lightning: Aborigines and Fire in Central Australia and the Western Desert', *Archaeology in Oceania* 18: 38-45.

Kimber, R. and M. Smith. 1987. 'An Aranda Ceremony', in E. Mulvaney and J. White (eds), *Australians to 1788*. Sydney: Fairfax, Syme, and Weldon Associates, pp. 220-37.

Latz, P. 1995. 'Fire in the Desert: Increasing Biodiversity in the Short Term, Decreasing It in the Long Term', in D. Rose (ed.), *Country in Flames: Proceedings of the 1994 Symposium on Biodiversity and Fire in North Australia*. Canberra and Darwin: Biodiversity Unit, Department of the Environment, Sport, and Territories, and North Australia Research Unit, pp. 77-86.

Leopold, A. 1976 (1949). *A Sand County Almanac, and Sketches Here and There*. London: Oxford University Press.

Lewis, H. 1993. 'Traditional Ecological Knowledge – Some Definitions', in N. Williams and G. Baines (eds) *Traditional Ecological Knowledge*. Canberra: National Centre for Resource and Environmental Studies, Australian National University.

Morphy, H. 1996. 'Empiricism to Metaphysics: In Defence of the Concept of the Dreamtime', in T. Bonyhady and T. Griffiths (eds), *Prehistory to Politics: John Mulvaney, the Humanities, and the Public Intellectual*. Melbourne: Melbourne University Press, pp. 163-89.

Munn, N. 1996. 'Excluded Spaces: The Figure in the Australian Aboriginal Landscape', *Critical Inquiry* 22: 446-65.

Myers, F. 1986. *Pintupi Country, Pintupi Self: Sentiment, Place, and Politics among Western Desert Aborigines*. Washington, D.C.: Smithsonian Institution Press.

Newsome, A. 1980. 'The Eco-Mythology of the Red Kangaroo in Central Australia', *Mankind* 12(4): 327-34.

Peterson, N. 1976. 'The Natural and Cultural Areas of Aboriginal Australia: A Preliminary Analysis of Population Groupings with Adaptive Significance', in N. Peterson (ed.), *Tribes and Boundaries in Australia*. Canberra: Australian Institute of Aboriginal Studies, pp. 50-71.

Povinelli, E. 1993. *Labor's Lot: The Power, History, and Culture of Aboriginal Action*. Chicago: University of Chicago Press.

Rolls, E. 1981. *A Million Wild Acres*. Ringwood: Penguin.

Rose, D. 1988. 'Exploring an Aboriginal Land Ethic', *Meanjin* 47(3): 378-87.

Rose, D. 1992. *Dingo Makes Us Human: Life and Land in an Aboriginal Australian Culture*. Cambridge: Cambridge University Press.

Rose, D. 1996. *Nourishing Terrains: Australian Aboriginal Views of Landscape and Wilderness*. Canberra: Australian Heritage Commission.

Rose, D. 1999. 'Indigenous Ecologies and the Ethic of Connection', in N. Low (ed.), *Global Ethics for the Twenty-first Century*. London: Routledge, pp. 175-86.

Russell-Smith, J. and D. Bowman. 1992. 'Conversion of Monsoon Rainforest Isolates in the Northern Territory, Australia', *Biological Conservation* 59: 51-63.

Scott, C. 1996. 'Science for the West, Myth for the Rest? The case of James Bay Cree Knowledge Construction', in L. Nader (ed.), *Naked Science: Anthropological Inquiry into Boundaries, Power, and Knowledge*. New York: Routledge, pp. 69-86.

Strathern, M. 1980. 'No Nature, No Conflict: The Hagen Case', in C. MacCormack and M. Strathern (eds), *Nature, Culture and Gender*. Cambridge: Cambridge University Press, pp. 174-222.

Strehlow, T. G. H. 1970. 'Geography and the Totemic Landscape in Central Australia: A Functional Study', in R. Berndt (ed.), *Australian Aboriginal Anthropology*. Nedlands: University of Western Australia Press, pp. 91-129.

Sutton, P. 1988. 'Dreamings', in *Dreamings: The Art of Aboriginal Australia*. Ringwood: Viking Penguin, pp. 13-32.

Wagner, R. 1981. *The Invention of Culture*. Chicago: University of Chicago Press.

Weiner, J. F. 1988. *The Heart of the Pearl Shell: The Mythological Dimension of Foi Sociality*. Berkeley: University of California Press.

Williams, N. and G. Baines. 1993. *Traditional Ecological Knowledge*. Canberra: Centre for Resource and Environmental Studies, Australian National University.

Williams, N. and E. Hunn. 1982. *Resource Managers: North American and Australian Hunter-Gatherers*. Washington, D.C.: American Association for the Advancement of Science.

17. The watchful world

Richard K. Nelson

Editor's introduction

Richard Nelson's book powerfully explores the author's relationships with Koyu-kon people and the living and lived-in land that they share. In brief, 'Traditional Koyukon people live in a world that watches.' But it is not only that the forest has eyes:

> The surroundings are aware, sensate, personified. They feel. They can be offended. And they must, at every moment, be treated with proper respect. All things in nature have a special kind of life, something unknown to contemporary Euro-Americans, something powerful.

In this chapter, Nelson 'describes the nature of nature, as it is understood by the Koyukon people'. It is, he says, 'a general account of principles underlying Koyukon belief, a background for the more specific chapters to follow'. Because it underlies the rest of his book, it serves here to ground the previous discussions of cosmology, geomentality, environmentalism, and so on, in the everyday lived-realities of one specific indigenous community. It should not be taken as definitive of all indigenous understandings of, or relationships with, the 'nature of nature', but as a discussion of a specific example. However, Nelson notes that 'Native American ideologies sharing a similar view are widely described in the literature and may be read for comparison'. Similarities (and differences too) may be found in the worldviews and lifeways of other peoples. Taking Hallowell's work as a clue, of course, we might care to notice that since 'people' might be a more inclusive term than 'human', then Nelson's discussion might require an equally detailed discussion

Reprinted from *Make Prayers to the Raven*, 1983. By permission of the University of Chicago Press.

of how other forest-dwelling persons (e.g. ravens) understand the 'nature of nature'. Certainly, their wilful, deliberate engagement, participation, communication and agency are significant to those Nelson discusses.

All of this is important, and sufficient reason for including Nelson in this collection. However, there is one further important reason for considering Nelson's work: his relationships and engagement with the land and those who live in it. For example, Nelson writes, 'I cannot be certain I comprehend these principles as a Koyukon person would; and so the discussion should be read as my interpretation of what I saw and was told.'

Whether his use of words like 'nature' and 'supernatural' reflect understanding or misunderstanding is debatable. It is, therefore, important that Nelson situates himself in his research and writing as someone attempting to understand the intellectual baggage of his own culture, and those experiences shared with hosts who encounter the world in ways that challenge the inward-looking individuality of modernity.

The literature interested in indigenous understandings and constructions of the world (and possibly of 'nature' if there is such a place distinct from others) has grown tremendously in the last decade. Among the best of this writing – but focusing only on particular or diverse Native North American contexts – see Kelley and Francis 1994; Basso 1996; McNeley 1997; Weaver 1997; Champagne 1999. Grim (2001) offers an important collection of some of the best writing on ecology among a wide diversity of indigenous peoples.

References

Basso, Keith H. 1996. *Wisdom Sits in Places: Landscape and Language among the Western Apache*. Albuquerque: University of New Mexico Press.

Champagne, Duane. 1999. *Contemporary Native American Cultural Issues*. Walnut Creek: Altamira.

Grim, John. 2001. *Indigenous Traditions and Ecology*, Cambridge, MA: Harvard University Press.

Kelley, Klara B. and Harris Francis. 1994. *Navajo Sacred Places*. Bloomington: Indiana University Press.

McNeley, James K. 1997. *Holy Wind in Navajo Philosophy*. Tucson: University of Arizona Press.

Weaver, Jace (ed.). 1997. 'An American Indian Theological Response to Ecojustice', in *Defending Mother Earth*. Maryknoll: Orbis.

ஒஒ

There's always things in the air that watch us.

A way of seeing

This chapter describes the nature of nature, as it is understood by the Koyukon people. It is a general account of principles underlying Koyukon belief, a background for the more specific chapters to follow. As I said in the Introduction, I cannot be certain I comprehend these principles as a Koyukon person would; and so the discussion should be read as my interpretation of what I saw and was told. In spite of these shortcomings, I believe that the perspective it offers on the Koyukon view of nature is basically correct. Native American ideologies sharing a similar view are widely described in the literature and may be read for comparison.

Traditional Koyukon people live in a world that watches, in a forest of eyes. A person moving through nature – however wild, remote, even desolate the place may be – is never truly alone. The surroundings are aware, sensate, personified. They feel. They can be offended. And they must, at every moment, be treated with proper respect. All things in nature have a special kind of life, something unknown to contemporary Euro-Americans, something powerful.

> I remember, when I was a boy, walking alone into a huge, beautiful, darkened cathedral. My entire body was alive with a sensation of being watched – by the walls and windows, the pews and pulpit, by the air itself. Now I have felt that again, but this time when I was traveling alone in the forest.
>
> Perhaps many of us have felt what the Koyukon people describe from their experiences in nature. The surroundings are different, but the sensations may be alike. The ultimate source of these feelings is less important than the fact that they exist, for what each of us learns to be real is completely real, regardless.
>
> (Huslia journal, February 1977)

Over a span of millennia, the Koyukon people and their ancestors have sustained themselves directly from their surroundings. The intimacy of their relationship to nature is far beyond our experience – the physical dependence and the intense emotional interplay with a world that cannot be directly altered to serve the needs of humanity. This close daily inter-action and dependence upon an omnipotent natural universe have pro-found importance to the Koyukon people and provide a theme upon which their cultural lives converge.

Koyukon perceptions of nature are aligned on two interconnected levels. The first of these is empirical knowledge. The practical challenges of survival by hunting, fishing, and gathering require a deep objective understanding of the environment and the methods for utilizing its resources. In short, the Koyukon people are sophisticated natural historians, especially well versed in animal behavior and ecology.

But their perception of the natural environment extends beyond what Westerners define as the empirical level, into the realm of the spiritual. The Koyukon inherit an elaborate system of supernatural concepts for explaining and manipulating the environment. From this perspective the natural and supernatural worlds are inseparable, and environmental events are often caused or influenced by spiritual forces. Detailed explanations are provided for the origin of natural entities and for the causation of natural events (which seldom, if ever, take place purely by chance). Furthermore, behavior toward nature is governed by an array of supernaturally based rules that ensure the well-being of both humans and the environment.

It is important to understand that Koyukon beliefs about nature are as logical and consistent as they are powerful, but that they differ substantially from those prevailing in modern Western societies. Our own tradition envisions the universe as a system whose functioning can be explained through rationalistic and scientific means. The natural and supernatural worlds are clearly separated. Environmental events are caused by ongoing evolutionary and ecological processes, or else they happen purely by chance. Finally, modern Western cultures regulate human behavior toward nature and its resources primarily on the basis of practical rather than religious considerations.

For the traditional Koyukon Athapaskans, ideology is a fundamental element of subsistence, as important as the more tangible practicalities of harvesting and utilizing natural resources. Most interactions with natural entities are governed in some way by a moral code that maintains a proper spiritual balance between the human and nonhuman worlds. This is not an esoteric abstraction, but a matter of direct, daily concern to the Koyukon people. Failure to behave according to the dictates of this code can have an immediate impact on the violator's health or success. And so, when Koyukon people carry out their subsistence activities they make many decisions on the basis of supernatural concerns. The world is ever aware.

From the distant time

As the Koyukon reckon it, all things human and natural go back to a time called *Kk'adonts'idnee*, which is so remote that no one can explain or understand how long ago it really was. But however ancient this time may be, its events are recounted accurately and in great detail through a prodigious number of stories. *Kk'adonts'idnee* (literally, 'in Distant Time it is said') is the Koyukon word for these stories, but following from its conversational use I will translate it simply as Distant Time.

The stories constitute an oral history of the Koyukon people and their environment, beginning in an age before the present order of existence was established. During this age 'the animals were human' – that is, they had human form, they lived in a human society, and they spoke human (Koyukon) language. At some point in the Distant Time certain humans died and were transformed into animal or plant beings, the species that inhabit Koyukon country today. These dreamlike metamorphoses left a residue of human qualities and personality traits in the north-woods creatures.

Taken together, the Distant Time stories describe a primordial world and its transfiguration into modern form. Some are so long that a single narration may require many evenings, even several weeks of evenings, for a complete telling. Stories of this kind – widely known as legends, myths, or folklore – are found throughout North America and elsewhere. It is common practice, however, to vastly underrate their significance in the lives of people like the Koyukon. They are not regarded as simple entertainment (though they are appreciated as such), and they are certainly not considered fictional. Stories of the Distant Time are, first of all, an accounting of origins. They are a Koyukon version of Genesis, or perhaps of Darwin. Woven into the plots of many stories are innumerable subplots or asides, which often describe the origins of natural entities.

The scope of Distant Time stories ranges from the minute to the cosmological. They explain the beginnings of entities that inhabit the sky – the sun, moon, and aurora. They account for certain weather phenomena, such as thunderstorms, which are the transformed embodiment of a formerly human spirit. For this reason thunderstorms have consciousness and can be turned away by people who know how to influence them. Features of the earth, such as prominent hills or mountains, are also given some accounting in these stories. For example, a hill near Huslia is called 'Giant's Fire-makers' (*Yiłkuh tł'aala'*), because it was formed when a giant man lost his flints there.

A central figure in this ancient world was the Raven (it is unclear, perhaps irrelevant, whether there was one Raven or many), who was its creator and who engineered many of its metamorphoses. Raven, the contradiction – omnipotent clown, benevolent mischief-maker, buffoon, and deity. It was he, transformed into a spruce needle, who was swallowed by a woman so she would give birth to him as a boy. When the boy was old enough to play, he took from beneath a blanket in her house the missing sun and rolled it to the door. Once outside, he became Raven again and flew up to return the sun to the sky, making the earth light again.

And it was he who manipulated the natural design to suit his whim or fancy. When he first created the earth, for example, the rivers ran both ways, upstream on one side and downstream on the other. But this made life too easy for humans, he decided, because their boats could drift along in either direction without paddling. So Raven altered his creation and made the rivers flow only one way, which is how they remain today.

There are hundreds of stories explaining the behavior and appearance of living things. Most of these are about animals and a few are about plants. No species is too insignificant to be mentioned, but importance in the Koyukon economy does not assure a prominent place in the stories. Many of the stories about animal origins are like this one:

> When the burbot [ling cod] was human, he decided to leave the land and become a water animal. So he started down the bank, taking a piece of bear fat with him. But the other animal people wanted him to stay and tried to hold him back, stretching him all out of shape in the process. This is why the burbot has such a long, stretched-out body, and why its liver is rich and oily like the bear fat its ancestor carried to the water long ago.

At the end of Distant Time there was a great catastrophe. The entire earth was covered by a flood, and under the Raven's supervision a pair of each species went aboard a raft. These plants and animals survived, but when the flood ended they could no longer behave like people. All the Distant Time humans had been killed, and so Raven recreated people in their present form. My Koyukon teachers were well aware of the biblical parallel in this story, and they took it as added evidence of the story's accuracy. None suggested that it might be a reinterpretation of Christian teaching.

Distant Time stories were usually told by older people who had memorized the lengthy epics and could best interpret them. But children were also taught stories, simpler ones that they were encouraged to tell, especially as they began to catch game. Doing this after setting out their traps or snares would please the animals and make them willing to be caught.

Today's elders can recall the long evenings of their youth, when Distant Time stories made the hours of darkness pass easily. In those days houses were lit by burning bear grease in a shallow bowl with a wick, or by burning long wands of split wood, one after another. Bear grease was scarce, and the hand-held wands were inconvenient, so in midwinter the dwellings were often dark after twilight faded. Faced with long wakeful

348

hours in the blackness, people crawled into their warm beds and listened to the recounting of stories.

The narratives were reserved for late fall and the first half of winter, because they were tabooed after the days began lengthening. Not surprisingly, the teller finished each story by commenting that he or she had shortened the winter: 'I thought that winter had just begun, but now I have chewed off part of it.' Or, more optimistically, 'When I woke up in the morning, my cabin was just dripping with water!' In this case the narrator implies that the spring thaw has suddenly begun.

Distant Time stories also provide the Koyukon with a foundation for understanding the natural world and humanity's proper relationship to it. When people discuss the plants, animals, or physical environment they often refer to the stories. Here they find explanations for the full range of natural phenomena, down to the smallest details. In one story a snowshoe hare was attacked by the hawk owl, which was so small that it only managed to make a little wound in its victim's shoulder. Koyukon people point out a tiny notch in the hare's scapula as evidence that the Distant Time events really took place.

The narratives also provide an extensive code of proper behavior toward the environment and its resources. They contain many episodes showing that certain kinds of actions toward nature can have bad consequences, and these are taken as guidelines to follow today. Stories therefore serve as a medium for instructing young people in the traditional code and as an infallible standard of conduct for everyone.

Nobody made it up, these things we're supposed to do. It came from the stories; it's just like our Bible. My grandfather said he told the stories because they would bring the people good luck, keep them healthy, and make a good life. When he came to songs in the stories, he sang them like they were hymns.

The most important parts of the code are taboos (*hutlaanee*), prohibitions against acting in certain ways toward nature. For example, in one story a salmon-woman was scraping skins at night with her upper jaw, and while doing this she was killed. This is why it is taboo for women to scrape hides during the night. Hundreds of such taboos exist, and a person who violates them (or someone in the immediate family) may suffer bad luck in subsistence activities, clumsiness, illness, accident, or early death. In Koyukuk River villages it is a rare day when someone is not heard saying, '*Hutlaanee!*' ('It's taboo!').

Personalities in nature

Stories of the Distant Time often portray the animal-people as having distinctive personalities, and this affects the way a species is regarded today. Often these personalities can be known only through the stories, because the animals do not visibly express them any longer. People sometimes have strong positive or negative feelings about particular species because of the way they are portrayed in the stories.

The sucker fish, for example, was a great thief in the Distant Time and so it is not well thought of. One man told me he could never bring himself to eat this fish, knowing what it had been and fearing that it would make a thief of him:

> Even in springtime, sometimes we run short of food. But if we catch a sucker in the net, I just can't eat him.

People will sometimes characterize someone by referring to an animal's personality. In fact, Jetté (n.d.*a*) writes that Yukon River Koyukon may inquire about a person by asking, 'What animal is he?' Someone known as a thief may be described as 'just like a sucker fish.' When a person talks big, promises a lot but accomplishes little, or gets ahead by trickery, he or she is said to be 'just like a raven.' Although Raven is the creator, he is portrayed in the stories as a lazy trickster who usually finds a way to get ahead by the efforts of others. The Koyukon have a kind of jocular respect for ravens, mocking their personality but still awed by their spirit power.

When I asked about relatedness among animals, people usually answered with reference to their social behavior and personality. For example, a Distant Time story reveals that bears and porcupines are cousins, and people cite as proof their occasional sharing of a den. When relatedness is not mentioned in a story it may be revealed by a tendency to 'get along.' Muskrats and beavers often live close together and they eat the same kinds of plants, so they are considered relatives. Wolves may kill a loose dog, which shows that the two are not related.

Animal relationships are also shown by shared characteristics, but usually not those chosen by Western taxonomists. One story of the Distant Time says that all the smaller animals were related as sisters who lived together in an underground house. These included red squirrel, mink, fox, several owl species, short-tailed weasel, ptarmigan, and others. Another related group includes the four water mammals: otter, mink, beaver, and muskrat. Stories also reveal that the raven is mink's uncle. And in obviously paired species, the larger is considered the older brother to the smaller – brown bear to the black bear, for example, and flicker to the woodpecker.

The Koyukon people conceptualize a natural order, but its structure and foundation are quite different from our own. No one described to me a system of phylogeny or biological interrelatedness, but I did not probe this matter exhaustively and may have failed to ask the right questions. Such a system might exist, or perhaps the world's makeup is sufficiently explained in the stories.

The place of humans in a natural order

> When Raven created humans, he first used rock for the raw materials, and people never died. But this was too easy so he recreated them, using dust instead. In this way humans became mortal, as they remain today.

How does humanity fit into the world of nature and the scheme of living things? For the Koyukon, humans and animals are clearly and qualitatively separated. Only the human possesses a soul (*nukk'ubidza*, 'eye flutterer'), which people say is different from the animals' spirits. I never understood the differences, except that the human soul seems less vengeful and it alone enjoys immortality in a special place after death. The distinction between animals and people is less sharply drawn than in Western thought – the human organism, after all, was created by an animal's power.

The Koyukon seem to conceptualize humans and animals as very similar beings. This derives not so much from the animal nature of humans as from the human nature of animals. I noted earlier, for example, that today's animals once belonged to an essentially human society, and that transmutations between human and animal form were common. One of my Koyukon teachers said, however, that after the Distant Time people and animals became completely separate and unrelated.

Animals still possess qualities that Westerners consider exclusively human, though – they have a range of emotions, they have distinct personalities, they communicate among themselves, and they understand human behavior and language. They are constantly aware of what people say and do, and their presiding spirits are easily offended by disrespectful behavior. The interaction here is very intense, and the two orders of being coexist far more closely than in our own tradition. But animals do not use human language among themselves. They communicate with sounds which are considered their own form of language.

The closeness of animals to humans is reinforced by the fact that some animals are given funeral rituals following the basic form of those held for people, only on a smaller scale. Wolverines have a fairly elaborate rite, and bears are given a potlatch-like feast. In these cases, at least, animal spirits

351

are placated much as human souls are after death.

Most interesting of all is animal behavior interpreted to be religious. 'Even animals have their taboos,' a woman once told me. From her grandfather, she learned that gestating female beavers will not eat bark from the fork of a branch, because it is apparently tabooed for them. The late Chief Henry had told her of seeing a brown bear kill a ground squirrel, then tear out its heart, lungs, and windpipe and leave them on a rock. Again, the organs must have been taboo (*hutłaanee*).

Once, on a fall hunt afoot in the *Kk'oonootna* (Kanuti on maps) headwaters, the late Chief Henry shot and wounded a young caribou. It fell and the rest of the herd ran away. But a short while later its mother returned:

> She came back to it. And she started circling it the way the sun goes around ... At the end of that she put her muzzle where the blood was leaking down. She kept her muzzle down there for a while. I don't know what she was doing, maybe drinking its blood. And then she circled it the same direction again. And she put her muzzle on the other side where the blood was leaking down. And she kept her muzzle there for awhile. At the end she took her muzzle away. And all that time the calf was holding up its head. And it pushed out its muzzle and shook itself like this. And then it took off and it looked like it was flying up river. And the late Linus said, 'Look at that – she made medicine to her child.'
> I guess that she made medicine to it and there was nothing wrong with it.
> (Jones n.d.: 4-5)

The distinction between humans and animals is further blurred by recognition of a human creature that occupies the wildlands and remains almost totally alien from society. This is *nik'inla'eena*, 'the sneaker,' called 'woodsman' in English. Woodsmen are as real as any other inhabitant of the Koyukon environment, but they are extremely shy and quick to vanish when people come near. They are said to be humans who became wild either after committing murder or engaging in cannibalism. Occasionally they harass people or steal from them, but they are not a great danger. People tell countless stories about encounters with woodsmen (see [Nelson 1983] chap. 10) and regard them as regular inhabitants of the environment. They are especially interesting as a bridge across the narrow gap between humans and animals, or between the worlds of humanity and nature.

Nature spirits and their treatment

From the Distant Time stories, Koyukon people learn rules for proper conduct toward nature. But punishment for offenses against these rules is given by powerful spirits that are part of the living, present-day world. All animals, some plants, and some inanimate things have spirits, vaguely conceptualized essences that protect the welfare of their material counterparts. They are especially watchful for irreverent, insulting, or wasteful behavior toward living things. The spirits are not offended when people kill animals and use them, but they insist that these beings (or their remains) be treated with the deference owed to the sources of human life.

Not all spirits are possessed of equal power. Some animal species have very potent spirits called *biyeega hoolaanh*, which are easily provoked and highly vindictive. These dangerous spirits can bring serious harm to anyone who offends them, taking away luck in hunting or trapping and sometimes causing illness, disability, or even death. Animals possessed of such spirits include the brown bear, black bear, wolverine, lynx, wolf, and otter. The beaver and marmot have similarly powerful spirits but are not so vengeful.

The remaining mammals, birds, fish, and some plants and inanimate things have less powerful spirits. Although these are very real and can inflict punishment (usually bad luck in taking the species), all my instructors agreed that no Koyukon word exists for this kind of spirit. In response to my perplexed questioning, one person explained:

> The animal and its spirit are one in the same thing. When you name the animal you're also naming its spirit. That's why some animal names are *hutlaanee* – like the ones women shouldn't say –because calling the animal's name is like calling its spirit. Just like we don't say a person's name after they die … it would be calling their spirit and could be dangerous for whoever did it.

While most Koyukon adults seem to concur on the basic premises of their ideology, they vary widely in their opinions about the specifics and apparently do not feel inclined toward a rigid, systematized theology. This often left me confused, no doubt because of my Judeo-Christian background; and if my account of certain concepts is amorphous or inconsistent it properly reflects my learning experience. Koyukon people must find us painfully compulsive and conformist about our systems of belief.

Perhaps this helps to explain some differences between my learning and that of Jetté (1911: 101, 604, 605) and Loyens (1966: 90). They found, for example, that whereas each human has a spirit of its own, animals have a collective spirit for each species. As the quotation shows, my teachers envisioned no such 'keeper spirits' overseeing whole species. Individual animals, like individual humans, have their own spirits. Again, perhaps only an outsider would be troubled by this apparent inconsistency.

When an animal is mistreated, I was told, its individual spirit is

353

affronted, but all members of its species may become aloof from the offender. In former times, shamans could manipulate spirits for the opposite effect. They made dream visits to 'animal houses' that were filled with spirits of a particular animal, then attracted them to certain parts of the country to enrich the harvest there.

Many other supernatural beings inhabit the traditional Koyukon world (see Jetté 1911 for a full accounting), but these seem to have little importance today. Perhaps Christian teachings displaced or undermined these beliefs, unlike those concerned with spirits of natural entities. Devices used to catch and kill animals – such as nets, snares, and deadfalls – also have powerful spirits (*biyeega hoolaanh*) with many associated taboos. Like the spirits of natural entities, these are still considered important today. For example, if a person borrows someone else's snare, he or she may take sick or die from its spirit power. Similarly, stealing a snared animal exposes the thief to grave danger from the spirits of both the snare and its catch.

Proper treatment of natural spirits involves hundreds of rules or taboos (*hutlaanee*), some applying to just one species and others having much more general effects. The rules fall into three main categories – first, treatment of living organisms; second, treatment of organisms (or parts of organisms) that are no longer alive; and third, treatment of nonliving entities or objects. I will briefly summarize these rules, leaving the specific details for later chapters [Nelson 1983].

Treatment of living organisms

Koyukon people follow some general rules in their behavior toward living animals. They avoid pointing at them, for example, because it shows disrespect, 'like pointing or staring at a stranger.' They also speak carefully about animals, especially avoiding boastful talk about hunting or trapping exploits.

A man who said he would trap many beavers was suddenly unable to catch any; and someone who bragged about bear hunting was later attacked and seriously hurt. In fact, bears are so powerful that every word spoken about them is carefully chosen. Trapped animals are also treated respectfully, and powerful ones like the wolf or wolverine may be addressed in special ways before they are killed. One man said that he always asks trapped animals for luck: 'My animal, I hope that more of you will come my way.'

Keeping wild animals as pets is also prohibited, except for species whose personality traits are valued in humans. A child who keeps a red fox will become mischievous, but if a boy raises a hawk owl he will acquire its hunting skill and cleanliness. People seldom keep pets, because they are likely to suffer, offending their spirits and causing illness or bad luck for those involved in their captivity. A woman told me of losing her small child about a year after the death of a baby hawk owl her family had kept. The tragic connection was clear.

Taking individual animals away to zoos, even catching and releasing them alive as part of studies, is a spiritual affront that can cause a species to shun the area. For this reason Koyukon people are opposed to wildlife research in their country if it involves live capture of animals.

> We have respect for the animals. We don't keep them in cages or torture them, because we know the background of animals from the Distant Time. We know that the animal has a spirit – it used to be human – and we know all the things it did. It's not just an animal; it's lots more than that.

Following from this, Koyukon people believe that animals must be treated humanely. The spirits are not offended because humans live by hunting, but people must try to kill without causing suffering and to avoid losing wounded animals. A starving moose, mired in deep snow near Huslia, was fed daily until it regained strength and could walk away. Once a man found a black bear with cubs, driven from their den by groundwater, hopelessly starving in the deep snow. He ended their suffering, then dismembered and covered their unusable carcasses, lest he offend their spirits by killing without at least symbolic utilization. 'We'll come back for this later,' he told his companion, a placating remark that he knew he would not abide by.

Treatment of killed game

The rules for showing respect to killed animals and harvested plants are myriad. I will give some general principles and a few illustrations here, leaving fuller details for the discussion of each species. There must be hundreds of taboos I never heard about, however, so this book contains only a sampling.

> Today I was told about a man who had once jokingly stuffed debris into the opened jaws of a dried pike head nailed on a cabin door to ward off bad spirits. His companions were horrified that he would open himself to retaliation from the animal's spirit.
> 'When you do something like that – when you don't show respect for animals

355

– it's just like making fun of the Bible.'

(Huslia journal, March 1977)

The remains of animals and plants are treated with the deference owed to something sacred. For example, when fur animals (such as mink, beaver, or wolf) are brought inside the house for skinning, their names should not be mentioned, nothing should be burned lest the smell offend their spirits, metallic noises should be avoided, and even if it is unfrozen and skinned the carcass should be kept indoors overnight. One way to prevent difficulties is to plug the nostrils of smell-sensitive animals like mink by smearing lard on them. Cloth may also be wrapped around an animal's head to protect it from offensive noises.

> I had bad luck with fox this year. Come to think of it, I was using noisy power tools while I had a fox in the house. Guess that's why . . . it's got really sensitive ears. When you get bad luck like this you just have to let it wear off. There's nothing else you can do.

There are also rules for proper butchering of game – for example, certain cuts that should be made or avoided for a particular species. There are rules for proper care of meat, such as keeping all meat covered when it is outside, protecting it from scavengers or from any insinuation that it is not respected. And a multitude of rules govern who eats an animal or parts of it. Young adults and especially women of childbearing age are subject to a wide array of these. Rules for each species will be detailed in the forthcoming chapters.

Finally, there are regulations to ensure that unusable parts of animals are respectfully disposed of. For example, bones of water animals such as beaver, muskrat, and mink should be cast into a lake or river. Bones of large land animals should be put in a dry place away from the village or completely burned in a remote spot. And the remains of small animals ought to be hung in bushes or burned (cf. Clark 1970: 86). Adherence has declined today, but many people scrupulously avoid leaving animal remains to rot on the ground (especially where someone might walk over them) or mixing them with household trash.

Punishment for ignoring or violating these regulations depends on the power of the living thing and the gravity of the offense. Spirit vengeance can be as severe as death or decades of bad luck in catching a species. Disregarding the prohibitions against eating certain foods usually causes clumsiness or other physical problems. Only old people who no longer hunt can eat red-necked grebe, for instance, because this bird is awkward on land. A young person who ate it would become slow and clumsy or would have children with these shortcomings. I never understood whether animal spirits cause such 'contagious' reactions, but the innumerable food taboos are generally respected as an important way of protecting health and well-being.

Many of the rules apply to everyone, regardless of age or sex. But a large number of special restrictions apply to women between puberty and menopause. Koyukon women are skilled and active providers – they hunt, fish, trap, and gather on their own or along with men. Although they are competent and productive, they are somewhat limited by their possession of special power that can easily alienate or offend natural spirits.

The menses (hutłaa) has its own spirit that contains the essence of femininity, and it can bring bad luck with animals, feminize men and alienate animals from them, or even cause sickness or death. To avoid these dangers, Koyukon women were traditionally secluded during menstruation (some pubescent girls are still briefly sequestered at the first menstruation), and they continue to follow a multitude of special taboos regulating their use of animals and their behavior toward them.

Spirits of the physical world

Elements of the earth and sky are imbued with spirits and consciousness, much in the way of living things, and there are codes of proper behavior toward them. Certain landforms have special powers that must be placated or shown deference, for example. Even the weather is aware: if a man brags that storms or cold cannot stop him from doing something, 'the weather will take care of him good!' It will humble him with its power, 'because it knows.'

> In falltime you'll hear the lakes make loud cracking noises after they freeze. It means they're asking for snow to cover them up, to protect them from the cold. When my father told me this, he said *everything* has life in it. He always used to tell us that.

The earth itself is the source of a preeminent spiritual power called *sinh taala'* in Koyukon. This is the foundation of medicine power once used by shamans, and because of it the earth must be shown utmost respect. One person who was cured by medicine power years ago, for example, still abides by the shaman's instructions to avoid digging in the earth. Berry plants have special power because they are nurtured directly from the earth. 'People are careful about things that grow close to the ground,' I was told, 'because the earth is so great.'

RICHARD K. NELSON

The manifestations of luck

Luck is the powerful force that binds humanity to the nature spirits and their moral imperatives. For the Koyukon people, luck is a nearly tangible essence, an aura or condition that is 'with' someone in certain circumstances or for particular purposes. Luck can be held permanently or it can be fleeting and elusive. It is an essential qualification for success – regardless of a person's skill, in the absence of luck there is no destiny except failure.

The source of luck is not clearly explained, but most people are apparently born with a certain measure of it. The difficulty is not so much in getting it as in keeping it. Luck is sustained by strictly following the rules of conduct toward natural things. People who lose their luck have clearly been punished by an offended spirit; people who possess luck are the beneficiaries of some force that creates it. Koyukon people express luck in the hunt by saying *bik'uhnaatltonh* – literally, 'he had been taken care of.'

> If a person has good luck, catches game, it is because something created the world, and that is helping him to get what he needs.

Luck, or the absence of it, is specific to particular animals or even certain activities. A woman who violates tanning taboos may fail in preparing hides. Each person is possessed (or dispossessed) of luck for all the entities he or she interacts with. Thus a man told me that he had always been lucky hunting bears until he inadvertently treated one the wrong way. For many years afterward his luck was gone – he never took a single bear. Finally the effect wore off and since regaining his luck he has killed at least one bear each season.

Luck can be passed along to others, but it is a lot like money. The one who gives it up may be left with nothing. To illustrate, when beaver snaring was made legal years ago, it was very hard for young people to learn how to do it. The older men knew but were reluctant to reveal their ways, because telling someone how to make a trapping set also gives him your luck. Eventually people reach an age of inactivity, when their measure of luck becomes superfluous. Then they can confer their luck on others by simply wishing it so. This is why children often present their first-killed game to elders, and why young hunters give liberal shares of their catch to old men who no longer go out onto the land.

Possessions like sleds, fishnets, rifles, or snowshoes are also infused with luck. A man lamented to me that one of his high-caliber rifles had failed to kill a bear coming out of its den although it was at close range. He had to use another gun to finish the animal. This gun was 'out of luck,' he explained, and he suspected that a young woman had rendered it useless by stepping over it.

Putting on another person's mittens can either take away his luck or give him yours. Once I was traveling with a man whose hands became painfully cold, so I offered him my extra mittens. He finally took them, explaining that since I was leaving Huslia I could get along without luck in things like trapping. But a short while later he decided to take them off and endure the cold instead.

Luck is a finite entity, specific to each natural thing or even to certain activities. It can be lost, transferred, and recovered. Luck binds people to the code of proper behavior toward the natural world. And so success in living on the land involves far more than a mastery of technical skills. It requires that a sensitive balance be maintained between each person and the conscious forces of the environment.

Gifts from the spirits of nature

The Koyukon people live in a world full of signs, directed toward them by the omniscient spirits. The extraordinary power of nature spirits allows them to reveal or determine future events that will affect humans. This understanding is sometimes divulged to watchful human eyes through the behavior of animals or other natural entities.

Rare or unusual events in nature are generally interpreted as signs, often foretelling bad fortune. People say that events like this are taboo (*hutłaanee*), and they encounter them with fear. For example, a Huslia woman said that it is ominous to hear a raven calling in the night. She had heard it only once in her life, and two weeks later her brother-in-law suddenly died. It is also a bad sign to find an animal that has died in strange or bizarre circumstances. A woman found an owl dead in the entangling meshes of her fishnet, and later that year her daughter died. Another woman discovered a ptarmigan hanging dead by a single toe from a willow branch. Her grandfather, a shaman, warned that it was powerfully ominous; and death came to her newborn child the following spring.

Occurrences like these are both fascinating and frightening, and sometimes people talk as if they not only foretell but also cause the events that follow. Not all signs indicate bad luck, and not all come in strange ways. Some animals, like owls and ravens, give signs in their calls and flight patterns. These might lead a hunter to game, forecast the weather, or tell of good or bad hunting luck. And a few signs also come from the physical world, such as heavy hoarfrost, a powerful evil omen. These and others are described in later chapters.

359

Very rarely, a beluga [a small arctic whale] swims far up the Yukon, and it is a sign of death. Years ago one was seen near a Koyukon village, whose people chased and shot it. The animal was lost, and later some people saw its remains downstream. After that the village began to decline and some of its people died badly – from freezing and drowning. (Huslia journal, December 1977)

Not all signs come directly from nature. Dreams are sometimes taken as forecasts of good or bad luck in hunting, although I was told little about it. In the Koyukon village of Nulato, Sullivan (1942: 122-3) learned that people can receive dream signs about hunting or trapping from the spirits of animals. Bloody or murderous dreams reveal that an animal will be killed. Other foreshadowing events are more mundane – for example, if loops in the tie of a sled rope form the shape of ears, it is a sign of hunting luck. If such loops form when one lashes a pair of snowshoes, they will bring good luck to someone who uses them.

Although Koyukon people are helpless to change signs given them through natural spirits, they can sometimes use these powers to influence the course of events. Spirits can be propitiated, asked to benefit people or to contravene an evil sign. One way of doing this is to make 'prayers' to certain animals, entreating them for good health or good luck. Such prayers are given especially to ravens, because their powerful spirits often show benevolence toward people. Appeals may be specific or general. For example, when people see certain birds migrating southward in the fall, they may speak to them: 'I hope you will return again and that we will be here to see you.' It is a request that birds and people may survive the uncertainties of winter.

Living things, or parts of them, can also be used as religious objects, again to tap the power of their abiding spirits. Hunters and travelers camp beneath large trees as much for spiritual as physical protection. Skins of certain animals (salmon, least weasel, flicker) are used as amulets, treasured possessions that bring good luck or avert the sudden malevolence of a harmful power.

There are also a few ways of using plant or animal spirits to affect physical things. For example, a fishnet can become 'full of bad luck,' especially if it is used by a woman who violates a taboo against eating freshly caught fish (which are not considered completely dead) while she is menstruating. This malevolence may be counteracted with an unidentified plant, possibly bluebell, which is called łookk'a lodaaldloya ('something that lies in the fish's mouth'). The net is hung up and this plant is burned under it so the smoke drifts up throught the meshes.

By understanding the manifestations of spirit powers in nature, Koyukon people are able to foresee and sometimes change the course of events.

They can help to create good fortune, they can avoid hardship or shortage, they can prepare themselves for preordained happenings that lie ahead, and they can sometimes directly influence the environment to their own benefit.

Harnessing the powers of nature

Modern Koyukon views of nature are strongly influenced by a cultural tradition that is probably not practiced today or that exists only as a remnant at best. This is the tradition of shamanism, the use of medicine power to control nature spirits directly. Although shamanism apparently is seldom, if ever, practiced today, most adult Koyukon have seen and experienced it many times in their lives. Medicine power has been used to cure many people of illnesses that they believe would otherwise have killed them. Today the old medicine people seem to have vanished without passing their skills along, but the concepts and beliefs surrounding them remain intact.

Koyukon shamans (*diyinyoo*; singular *diyininh*) did not have power themselves, but they knew how to use the spirit forces that surrounded them in nature. With this they could do good or evil, according to their personal inclinations. Each shaman – who might be either a man or a woman – had special associations with a number of familiar spirits. For example, one man 'called for' Wood Frog, Birch Woman, Raven, Northern Lights, and others when he made medicine. Some spirit associations were begun in dreams (Sullivan 1942: 120), but this man inherited his animal helpers from an uncle. Often he used the raven spirit to 'scare away the sickness in someone,' mimicking a raven's melodious cawing, spreading his arms like wings, and bouncing on both feet as a raven would. One of my Koyukon instructors who was sickly in his youth said that this man had cured him many times.

Aside from curing (or causing) sickness, shamans used spirit power to manipulate the environment for their own or someone else's benefit. Before caribou hunting, for example, they made medicine to bring animals to the hunters, to foretell their chances of success, or to show them where to find game. Spirit helpers assisted them by communicating with a protective spirit of the caribou (Sullivan 1942: 79-80). As I mentioned earlier, shamans could also attract animal spirits to a given area of land, creating abundance there.

When shamans were active, they sometimes sent their spirit animals to the villages or dwellings of persons they wanted to harm. Unusual appearances of wild animals in settlements were presumed to be shaman's

361

work. These animals were never killed because it would cause grave danger to the one who did it. It was always a bad sign to see a creature of the wildlands in a settlement, because it indicated danger from medicine power.

An old shaman, now dead, once said that 'all of the medicine people in Alaska' worked their power together in the First World War, trying to help the United States toward victory. In so doing they shifted their source of power – the *sinh taala'* from the earth itself – far away from their homeland and onto the battlefields. But they lacked the power to bring it all back and it became somewhat diffused. After that the shamans' medicine powers began to wane.

Older people of the Koyukuk villages, who are ever watchful of their surroundings, say the loss of medicine people has disrupted the balance of natural things. Animals have nearly always avoided people, because since the end of the Distant Time they have lived apart from human society. Only as dangerous emissaries of the shamans did they lurk among village dwellings.

But today the older order is changing and animals have begun penetrating the human sector of the world. Moose wander near the villages, occasionally into them; fox tracks encroach on the limits of settlements; and mink sometimes come around houses in the night. Most distressing of all ravens have begun scavenging within villages. Huslia people say that ravens stayed away from their town until a few years ago, even though no one bothered or shot them. They just preferred to find their food out in the surrounding country.

A man once told me that a raven had walked fearlessly near him as he tended his dogs, looking for any scraps of food he might have dropped. He watched it and said, 'Go ahead, eat by the dogs. But then please make them pull well.' The bird flew away and did not come back again. He said it made him anxious and fearful, though he did not explain why.

A woman expressed her troubled thoughts about this as she described the ravens perching in low trees hear her house and searching for food among her dogs. They are like orphans, she said, living as helpless tramps in a place where they do not belong, seeming to care little about their self-respect. This is happening, she believes, because the shamans have gone and they no longer use the ravens' power. So now their spirits are adrift – helpless waifs without a purpose – somehow no longer able to watch over the well-being of their animal representations.

People should be using this power, she surmised, to keep the world in its ageless balance. The strange behavior of ravens, the most powerful among animals, surely indicates that this balance has gone awry. Medicine people were essential links in the pattern of nature – they helped keep the world in

362

proper order. If ravens came near a settlement in times past, shamans told them to fly away and live out on the land where they belonged. But today no one has the power to maintain and reinforce this proper arrangement among living things.

When I went to Fairbanks I saw a raven sitting on a streetlight pole. It looked all oily and messed up, just like it didn't take care of itself at all. I was upset about it, so I looked around to see if anybody could hear me. Then I just talked to it like my grandfather did. I said I wished it would go out where it could live off scraps from hunted animals; then it wouldn't be so poor and helpless.

The Koyukon view of nature

For traditional Koyukon people, the environment is both a natural and a supernatural realm. All that exists in nature is imbued with awareness and power; all events in nature are potentially manifestations of this power; all actions toward nature are mediated by consideration of its consciousness and sensitivity. The interchange between humans and environment is based on an elaborate code of respect and morality, without which survival would be jeopardized. The Koyukon, while they are bound by the strictures of this system, can also manipulate its powers for their own benefit. Nature is a second society in which people live, a watchful and possessive one whose bounty is wrested as much by placation as by cleverness and craft.

Moving across the sprawl of wildland, through the forest and open muskeg, Koyukon people are ever conscious that they are among spirits. Each animal is far more than what can be seen; it is a personage and a personality, known from its legacy in stories of the Distant Time. It is a figure in the community of beings, once at least partially human, and even now possessed of attributes beyond outsiders' perception.

Not only the animals, but also the plants, the earth and landforms, the air, weather, and sky are spiritually invested. For each, the hunter knows an array of respectful gestures and deferential taboos that demand obedience. Violations against them will offend and alienate their spirits, bringing bad luck or illness, or worse if a powerful and vindictive being is treated irreverently.

Aware of these invisible forces and their manifestations, the Koyukon can protect and enhance their good fortune, can understand signs or warnings given them through natural events, and can sometimes influence the complexion of the environment to suit their desires. Everything in the

363

Koyukon world lies partly in the realm beyond the senses, in the realm we would call supernatural.

References

Clark, Annette McF. 1970. 'Koyukon Athapaskan Ceremonialism', *Western Canadian Journal of Anthropology* 2(1): 80-8.

Jetté, Julius. 1911. 'On the Superstitions of the Ten'a Indians', *Anthropos* 6: 95-108, 241-59, 602-15, 699-723.

Jetté, Julius. n.d. 'Koyukon dictionary (untitled)'. Unpublished manuscript provided by Gonzaga University.

Jones, E. n.d. (draft of 1979). *The Stories Chief Henry Told*. Fairbanks: Alaska Native Language Center, University of Alaska.

Loyens, William J. 1966. 'The Changing Culture of the Nulato Koyukon Indians'. Unpublished PhD dissertation., University of Wisconsin. Ann Arbor: University Microfilms.

Nelson, R. K. 1983. *Make Prayers to the Raven*. Chicago: University of Chicago Press.

Sullivan, Robert J. 1942. *The Ten'a Food Quest*. Washington, DC: Catholic University of America Press.

Index of Subjects

365

Index of Authors

INDEX OF AUTHORS

Index of Nations, Peoples and Groups

371